D1552875

This edition brings together for the first time key texts representing the writings of the medieval English mystics. The texts are newly edited from the manuscripts, and are supplemented with textual and explanatory notes and a glossary. The book focusses on five major authors, Richard Rolle, Walter Hilton, the anonymous author of *The Cloud of Unknowing*, Dame Julian of Norwich, and Margery Kempe. Shorter works are presented whole, where possible, and accompanied by extracts from the mystics' longer works; extracts from contemporary translations into English are also included to illustrate the reception of European mystical texts in later medieval England. Overall, this volume makes accessible some of the best work by English contemplatives and visionaries of the Middle Ages.

English Mystics of the Middle Ages

English Mystics
of the
Middle Ages

Edited by

BARRY WINDEATT

Fellow of Emmanuel College, Cambridge, and
University Lecturer in English

CAMBRIDGE
UNIVERSITY PRESS

BV
5077
.E54
E54
1994

Published by the Press Syndicate of the University of Cambridge
The Pitt Building, Trumpington Street, Cambridge CB2 1RP
40 West 20th Street, New York, NY10011–4211, USA
10 Stamford Road, Oakleigh, Melbourne 3166, Australia

© Cambridge University Press 1994

First published 1994

Printed in Great Britain at the University Press, Cambridge

A catalogue record for this book is available from the British Library

Library of Congress cataloguing in publication data

English mystics of the Middle Ages / edited by Barry Windeatt.
    p. cm.
  Includes bibliographical references.
  ISBN 0 521 32740 7 (hardback)
   1. Mysticism – England. 2. Mysticism – History – Middle Ages,
600–1500 – Sources. I. Windeatt, B. A. (Barry A.)
BV5077.E54E54   1993   248.2′2′09420902 0 dc20   93–36180 CIP

ISBN 0 521 32740 7 hardback

VN

CONTENTS

vii

ACKNOWLEDGEMENTS

For permission to publish from manuscripts I am most grateful to the following: His Grace the Archbishop of Canterbury and the Trustees of Lambeth Palace Library; the Marquess of Bath; the British Library; the Public Record Office; the Bibliothèque Nationale, Paris; Lincoln Cathedral Chapter Library; at Oxford: the President and Fellows of St John's College, and the Bodleian Library; and at Cambridge: the Master and Fellows of Emmanuel College, the Master and Fellows of Gonville and Caius College, the Master and Fellows of Pembroke College, the Master and Fellows of St John's College, the Master and Fellows of Trinity College, the Syndics of the Fitzwilliam Museum, and the Syndics of the Cambridge University Library.

ABBREVIATIONS

AC	*Analecta Cartusiana*
Allen, *Writings*	H. E. Allen, *Writings Ascribed to Richard Rolle Hermit of Hampole and Materials for his Biography* (New York, 1927)
BL	British Library
CUL	Cambridge University Library
DownR	*Downside Review*
EC	*Essays in Criticism*
EETS, o. s.	Early English Text Society, original series
ELH	*English Literary History*
E&S	*Essays and Studies*
ES	*English Studies*
Horstman	*Yorkshire Writers*, ed. C. Horstman, 2 vols. (London, 1895)
LV	Julian of Norwich, *Revelations* (longer version)
MAE	*Medium Ævum*
MLR	*Modern Language Review*
MMTE	*The Medieval Mystical Tradition in England*, ed. M. Glasscoe, 5 vols. (Exeter, 1980, 1982; Woodbridge, 1984, 1987, 1992)
MS	*Mediaeval Studies*
NM	*Neuphilologische Mitteilungen*
PBA	*Proceedings of the British Academy*
PL	*Patrologia Latina*, ed. J. P. Migne, 217 vols. (Paris, 1844–)
RES	*Review of English Studies*
SB	*Studies in Bibliography*
SV	Julian of Norwich, *Revelations* (shorter version)

EDITORIAL NOTE

All the texts in this volume have been newly edited from manuscript sources, but the space available makes full critical editions inappropriate. One manuscript is selected to serve as a base text in each case and is emended where necessary, in the light of readings from one or two other manuscripts (or conjecturally in the case of a unique manuscript). Significant departures from the manuscript used as the basis of a text are signalled in the edited text by square brackets. Emendations are recorded in footnotes to the text, according to the following conventions: the reading adopted in the text is followed, after the square bracket, by the sigil of the manuscript from which the emendation has been adopted, then by the reading of the base manuscript (and then, in some cases, by the readings of other manuscripts consulted).

The texts edited for this volume have not been modernized except in the following details. Obsolete letter forms have been replaced by modern equivalents: *thorn* is represented as *th*; *yogh* is represented as *gh* or *y* (occasionally as final *z*). *I/J, i/j, U/V* and *u/v* have been normalized according to modern practice. Initial *ff* appears as *F* or *f*. All abbreviations and contractions have been silently expanded. Capitalization, word division, punctuation and paragraphing are editorial. Quotations in the notes from Middle English works in modern editions and from manuscripts follow the forms found there. 'Alle maner of pinchers' are referred to on p. 70 below.

Quotation from the works of the *Cloud*-author is from P. Hodgson (ed.), *'The Cloud of Unknowing' and 'The Book of Privy Counselling'*, EETS, o.s. 218 (London, 1944) and *'Deonise Hid Divinite' and Other Treatises on Contemplative Prayer*, EETS, o.s. 231 (London, 1955). Quotation from the longer version of Julian of Norwich is from M. Glasscoe (ed.), *Julian of Norwich: A Revelation of Love* (Exeter, 1976).

INTRODUCTORY ESSAY

For sith in the first biginnyng of holy chirche in the tyme of persecucion, dyverse soules and many weren so merveylously touchid in sodeynte of grace that sodenly, withoutyn menes of other werkes comyng before, thei kasten here instrumentes, men of craftes, of here hondes, children here tables in the scole, and ronnen withoutyn ransakyng of reson to the martirdom with seintes: whi schul men not trowe now, in the tyme of pees, that God may, kan and wile and doth – ye! touche diverse soules as sodenly with the grace of contemplacion?

(The Book of Privy Counselling, p. 90[1])

The later Middle Ages in England were indeed to prove such an age of contemplative saints, and 'the medieval English mystics' are often now grouped together. Viewed with one kind of hindsight, something new stirs with the writings of Richard Rolle (d. 1349), broadens and gathers in the later fourteenth century – with Walter Hilton, Julian of Norwich, and the anonymous author of *The Cloud of Unknowing* – and also includes a corpus of translations into English of other mystical writings that point to contemporary interest in contemplation. Like most retrospects on 'movements' or 'schools' of writers, such a view simplifies both the continuities with earlier traditions and between the writers themselves. Hindsight differently focussed might emphasize the substantial earlier literature on contemplation available in England, or the tradition of meditations in the vernacular.[2] Independent and original in their time the English mystics of the Middle Ages nonetheless remain. On the most demanding of subjects they write in their own tongue at a new level of intensity and complexity in English prose, while the surviving translations of continental mystics show no significant influence on the most creative English mystical writers.[3] Their subject must be demanding, for it is nothing less than the way to God through love, and their aim is to give their reader direction, charting and signposting a schematic, progressive ascent. Mere

knowledge or learning for its own sake is of no avail, and they dismiss
it. The way to perfection described by the English mystics stands open
– although the demandingness of contemplation will preclude all but
the committed – and witnesses to the appeal of the inner life to a
growing section of contemporary men and women readers, whether in
solitary, monastic or secular life.[4]

It is towards the cultivation and extension of that inward life that
the English mystics seek to express their own understanding of the art
of mystical loving. Rolle or Hilton achieved a much wider readership
than the *Cloud*-author or Julian, and their approaches are as
distinctive as their styles. A text that advises 'First gnawe on the nakid
blinde felyng of thin owne being' (*The Book of Privy Counselling*, p.
94) is working with different aims and assumptions from one that
declares 'In this felynge myne undyrstandynge was lyftyd uppe into
heven, and thare I sawe thre hevens . . .' (*Revelations of Divine Love*, p.
196). Yet there are signs of interchange between mystics, of reading
and commenting on the experiences and writings of others. Most vivid
of interactions between the English mystics is Margery Kempe's
memory of her visit to consult Julian of Norwich, and she reports the
anchoress as having a contemporary reputation as an expert in
discerning truth and deception in revelations, locutions, 'sweetness
and devotion' (p. 231). Margery has evidently been affected by Rolle's
work, and it is his unforgettable example and pervasive influence on
subsequent perceptions of contemplative experience in medieval
England that prompt some of the intertextuality between the English
mystics. Coming in his wake, such later English advisers on contemplation
as Hilton or the *Cloud*-author are often writing, albeit implicitly,
'against' Rolle, at least in the sense that for them some of Rolle's work
prompted reservations and qualifications (although probably not such
late work as *The Form of Living*). One surviving 'Defence' of Rolle by
Thomas Bassett, against the now-lost criticisms of a Carthusian
detractor, insists that God does reveal his secrets to the humble and
simple of heart, and seeks to counter the charges that Rolle made men
judges of themselves and that more have been led astray than have
profited by his writings.[5]

Neither the *Cloud*-author nor Hilton refers directly to Rolle, or
denies the experiences to which he lays claim. Yet both are recurrently
concerned to offset any spiritually undesirable influence of their
predecessor. As Rolle memorably described it – especially in *Incendium*

Amoris – his own experience might seem too easily accessible: its sensory qualities could encourage the impressionable to mistake merely physical sensations for mystical experience. The *Cloud*-author apparently has Rolle's followers in mind when advising caution about 'couȵfortes, sounes, & gladnes, & swetnes' (ch. 48), or when characterizing would-be contemplatives who feel a physical sensation of heat in their breasts '& ȝit, parauenture, þei wene it be þe fiir of loue', concluding sharply: 'For I telle þee trewly þat þe deuil haþ his contemplatyues, as God haþ his' (ch. 45). Hilton gives a similarly strong warning on the fire of love misconceived bodily rather than spiritually (*The Scale of Perfection*, I, 26); he also warns against 'felyng in þe bodily wittes', whether 'in sownyng of þe ere, or saueryng in þe mouth, or smellyng at þe nese, or elles any felable hete as it wer fyr, glouand and warmand þe brest', because such is not true contemplation (I, 10; CUL MS Add. 6686, p. 284), and a comparable warning occurs in his *Epistle on the Mixed Life* (p. 122). In *The Scale* (I, 44) Hilton also seeks to allay the recipient's disquiet, caused by what sounds like a reading of Rolle on devotion to the Holy Name (p. 151), and *Of Angels' Song* sets Rolle's teachings on the hearing of heavenly melody in a proper context for Hilton's correspondent.

Near the close of *Angels' Song* Hilton's warning against the 'naked mynde' (p. 136) might be read as a comment on the *Cloud*-author's teachings, and the works of these two contemporary Midlands writers on contemplation do point to some interchange and mutual criticism, some learning from each other.[6] At three points *The Cloud* acknowledges and refers its reader to 'another man's work', in each case possibly referring to Book I of *The Scale*. In recommending 'Redyng, Þinkyng & Preiing', *The Cloud* declares: 'Of þeese þre þou schalt fynde wretyn in anoþer book of anoþer mans werk moche betyr þen I can telle þee' (ch. 35), perhaps referring to Hilton's account in *The Scale* (I, 15). On the vexed question of whether 'counfortes and sounes and swetnes' be good or evil, *The Cloud* comments: 'þou mayst fynde it wretyn in anoþer place of anoþer mans werk a þousandfolde betir þan I kan sey or write' (ch. 48),[7] which could well refer to Hilton's discussion in *Scale*, I, 10. When the *Cloud*-author expresses reservation about 'wher anoþer man wolde bid þee gader þi miȝtes & þi wittes holiche wiþ-inne þi-self, & worschip God þere' (ch. 68) – although he pays tribute to this other teacher: 'þof al he sey ful wel & ful trewly, ȝe! and no man trewlier & he be wel conseiuid' – he may be criticizing such contexts as Hilton's advice to 'drawe in þi thoʒtes' (I, 25; p.298) or 'Geder þen þi hert togeder' (I, 87; p. 357). Indeed, it may be that while the *Cloud*-author responds to Book I of *The Scale*, Hilton in Book II sometimes writes with the *Cloud*-author in mind. His warning against the misunderstanding of spiritual language in material and spatial terms (pp. 161–2) may reflect Hilton's absorption of *The Cloud*'s insistent teachings on this point. Yet Hilton's very different application of the idea of the 'lighty mirknes' (p. 163) shows his distinctive independence, while the Christocentric emphases of Book II of *The Scale* may express implicitly Hilton's critique of the *via negativa* in *The Cloud* and his concern to redress the balance. In his *Privy Counselling* the *Cloud*-author may himself be seeking to respond to such a criticism, to offset his earlier work's emphasis on leaving behind meditation on the manhood and Passion of Christ (p. 96), although in *The Cloud* he could not have been more succinct (pp. 76–7). In the preface to *The Mirrour of the Blessed Lyf of Jesu Christ*, his early fifteenth-century translation of the pseudo-Bonaventuran *Meditationes vitae Christi*, Nicholas Love, prior of the Mount Grace Charterhouse, notes that to 'symple soules . . . contemplacion of þe monhede of cryste is more likyng, more spedefull & more sykere þan is hyʒe contemplacion of þe godhed',[8] and the English mystics make such a distinction in pursuing their own way to 'hyʒe contemplacion' (e.g. *Cloud*, ch. 12; *Scale*, I, 35).

When early in *Privy Counselling* the author dismisses the criticisms that 'I here sum men sey' – that 'my writyng to thee and to other is so harde and so heigh . . .' (p. 80) – he brings together the English mystics' alertness to their works' reception and a mode of intimate address, apparently directed in the first instance to a personally known recipient, which is characteristic of many of their writings. In *Mixed Life* Hilton is moved in part to write to his addressee 'for tendre affeccioun of love whiche thou haste to me' (p. 112). *The Cloud* was initially written (as is made clear, p. 73) for the direction of a particular twenty-four year old disciple, although the manner of address in the prologue ('whatsoever thou be that this book schalt have in possession', p. 69) shows an awareness that what was written for one known individual will come to be seen and used by a wider unknown readership. The opening of *Privy Counselling* confronts this matter directly: the author prefers to write what he thinks 'moste speedful' to his particular 'goostly frende' rather than to write generally for a general audience, trusting that among others who may read his work those similarly disposed may find something rewarding to them (p. 78). Even in the epistles that Rolle writes as if to known women recipients ('Til the I write specialy', p. 25; 'Loo, Margarete', p. 66) there is provision for 'thou, or another that redes this' (p. 30), as in the mention of alternatives ('or if thou be na mayden', p. 28). In the longer, presumably later version of her *Revelations* Julian addresses herself more emphatically and confidently in the first person plural to her 'even-Cristen'; in Book II of *The Scale* Hilton apparently envisages a wider audience than the anchoress to whom Book I is ostensibly written, although even here Hilton comments: 'Thou schalt be saufe as anker incluse, and noght only thou bot all Cristen soules' (p. 150). The mystics' counselling directed to particular cases becomes more widely available without losing the immediacy of its address. *Mixed Life* sets out Hilton's interpretation of such a 'mixed' life for the benefit of a known individual in specific circumstances, yet the appeal of his theme is such that the epistle is copied unchanged in itself but with an emended opening address to a more general audience (p. 280, n. 5).

In one manuscript of *The Scale of Perfection* is written the message: 'My hert is ful heuy to send ȝow þis boke for I supposid þat ȝe suld hafe comen home þat we myght hafe comend togedir þer of' (Trinity College, Dublin, MS 122 A 5 7). The English mystics' writings are often composed as if to inscribe such an intimate interchange, in the manner of a personal letter that stands in for a confidential conversation, and so represents part of a larger implied dialogue between author and recipient.[9] 'A thousand mile woldest thou renne to comoun mouthly with one that thou wist that verrely felt it' (p. 101), and as an opening device to chapters, sections or whole works the mystics recurrently write as if responding to a request for guidance and direction. *Of Angels' Song* begins in this way (p. 131), as does the 'Pilgrimage to Jerusalem' chapter of *The Scale* (p. 157), while another chapter opens as if Hilton is reacting to his recipient's request to moderate the difficulty and adjust the level of his writing (p. 150). That both the interpolation in this same chapter on the Holy Name (1, 44) and the later interpolation on charity (1, 70) begin with the similar 'But now, seist thou . . . ' (p. 151) and 'But now seist þou . . . ?'[10] may indicate that such passages – evidently authentic, although absent from some manuscripts – represent Hilton's later responses to questions posed by some readers of his work. Such anticipations of a reader's possible questions, doubts and uncertainties are a characteristic feature of the implied dialogue that structures many of the mystics' writings. Hilton makes adroit use of the device (pp. 123, 170), and it occurs in Rolle's epistles (pp. 39, 58). Boldest use of such imagined questions from a reader is made by the author of *The Cloud*, not least when a question is forestalled only for the speaker to admit that it is unanswerable: 'But now thou askest me and seiest: "How schal I think on himself, and what is hee?" And to this I cannot answere thee bot thus: "I wote never!"' (p. 75). It is the *Cloud*-author whose mode of address to his contemplative pupil may recall that of a seasoned coach, coaxing a pace from an athlete under training: 'Lette not therfore, bot travayle therin tyl thou fele lyst' (p. 70). It is also the *Cloud*-author who in *Privy Counselling* shrewdly confronts the issue of authorial control implicit in such one-sided 'dialogues': 'Lo! here maist thou see that I coveite sovereinte of thee. And trewly so I do, and I wol have it!' (p. 92).[11]

   Why does a mystic *write*? To praise God? To make a record of experience, as a witness? To instruct others, as a guide? It is the impetus to offer direction, to share knowledge, that constitutes one unifying feature in theme and form among the English medieval mystics. To read them is to be in the presence of an experienced guide to a process that implies a progression or an ascent ('I wyll that thou be ay clymbande tyll Jhesu-warde', p. 50). No wonder that in *De Utilitate*, his Latin letter to Adam Horsley, Hilton exclaims: 'If not even the least of the arts can be learned without some teacher and instructor, how much more difficult it is to acquire the Art of Arts, the perfect service of God in the spiritual life, without a guide?' and he criticizes those so overconfident as 'to set out on the way of the spiritual life without a director or capable guide, whether it be a man or a book. . . .'[12] A book in place of a man: the medieval mystics aim to be that guide to the Art of Arts, although the limits of books are acknowledged ('For a soule þat is clene sterid bi grace to vse of þis werkynge may see more in an hour of swilk gostly mater þan myȝt be writen in a grete book', *Scale*, II, 46; BL MS Harley 6579, fol. 140r). The mystics offer guidebooks, maps and manuals, and readers are urged to read them over not once but repeatedly (pp. 69, 240, 247). They represent instructions for use, for an art of loving to be put into practice beyond the process of reading and not to be confused with it. Indeed, *The Cloud* specifically warns against possibly mistaking the pleasures of the text for contemplative vocation: 'Alle þoo þat redyn or heren þe mater of þis book be red or spokin, & in þis redyng or hering þink it good & likyng þing, ben neu*er* þe raþer clepid of God to worche in þis werk, only for þis likyng steryng þat þei fele in þe tyme of þis redyng' (ch. 75). Any frisson of interest quickened by the literary effectiveness of the writing as art is not to be confounded with the soul's movement towards contemplation. Attainment lies over the horizon: it can rarely be more than adumbrated within the text and – always excepting Rolle – the English mystics are not generally concerned to strain after descriptive effects. Dame Julian, whose career begins in vision, leaves a text in which description is framed and transmuted by contemplation, while both Hilton (p. 158) and the author of *The Cloud* (ch. 33) cast themselves as still travelling towards a goal, and so having limited personal experience from which to describe what they nonetheless assist their readers towards.

'If thou aske what contemplacioun is, it is hard for to telle or utterly diffine', as one English version of Rolle admits (p. 19), although such definition is the concern of almost every piece in this book. All description falls short – 'For al that is spokyn of it is not it, bot of it', as *Privy Counselling* notes (p. 92) – but the higher contemplation is defined in *The Scale* as illumination:

> for to se by vnderstondyng sothfastnes whilk is God and also gostly thynges with a soft swete bre*n*nand loue in hym, so p*er*fitely þat by rauyschyng of þis loue þe soule is oned for þe tyme and conformed to þe ymage of þe Trinite. Þe biginnyng of þis contemplacio*u*n may be feled in þis lyfe, bot þe fulhed of it is keped in þe blis of heuen. (I, 8; CUL MS Add. 6686, p. 282)

Nor is contemplative accomplishment to be won by study or booklearning, and may be hindered (pp. 17, 101, 250). In short, 'oure soule, bi vertewe of this reformyng grace, is mad sufficient at the fulle to comprehende al him by love, the whiche is incomprehensible to alle create knowable might' (*Cloud*, p. 71). One other thing is clear: fulfilment may only be yearningly awaited and prepared for, never claimed: 'The swetnesse of contemplacioun . . . cometh not thoruh merite ne diserte of man, but oonly of the free yifte of God' (*Mendynge*, p. 21).

To communicate something of that sweetness, that love, mystics can only fall back on the language of human relationships and of sense perception. Yet to do so, they know, is to risk falsification and confusion. It is precisely the overlap between spiritual and fleshly

understandings of love that can be variously exploited in two
intriguing discussions: the account of 'extatik' love made vivid to the
reader by analogy with the symptoms of lovesickness in *The Doctrine
of the Hert* (pp. 253–8), and the shrewd analysis of the gradations
between spiritual and physical love in the eighth of the *Eight Chapters
on Perfection* (pp. 146–8). As in *The Doctrine*, the impetus of mystical
love may often be conveyed by associating it with the urgency of desire
and courtship. The soul's languishing love for God may be linked with
allusions to the Song of Songs, or 'Book of Love' as the mystics term it
(pp. 54, 257), and both Rolle's prose and his inset lyrics convey such a
longing love (pp. 32, 57). Even *The Cloud of Unknowing* can remark of
God 'He is a gelous louer' (ch. 2), and metaphors of erotic and nuptial
love are everywhere in mystical writing: 'A swete Ihesu . . . Bi-twene
þin armes ley I me, bi-twene myn armes cluppe I þe . . . ' as the
fourteenth-century prose poem *A Talking of the Love of God*
ecstatically concludes.[13] In opening *Ego Dormio* Rolle casts himself as
a proxy to woo the recipient not for himself but for his Lord, and so to
bring her to Christ's bed (p. 24–5), while Margery Kempe hears God
spelling out to her – most literal-minded of visionaries – the conjugal
intimacies that will follow her mystical marriage to the Godhead (p. 235).

Not for nothing did the *Eight Chapters* end with a warning on the
perilous interchange by which spiritual love might become physical. By
extension it was a warning that applied to the problems for some
readers in understanding metaphorical uses of the language of love and
sense perception that so helped mystics to express their longing love
('Hym verily seand and fu[l]sumly feland, hym gostly heryng, and hym
delectably smellyng and hym swetely swelowyng', *Revelations of Divine
Love*, LV, ch. 43). It is to metaphors of sight ('For contemplacion es a
syght', p. 66) that mystics naturally return ('Thanne thou schalt biholde
with thin ighen – what? – sothli, God!', p. 174). But they draw too on the
other senses ('Fonde for to touche bi desire good gracious God as he is',
p. 81; 'Contemplacion is a risyng of hert into God that tastith sumdele
of heuenly swettnesse & savourith', p. 248). Through the language of
the senses the mystics strive to convey the fullness of contemplative
experience, but they must also advise on inevitable fluctuations, on
feelings of absence and desolation ('This is the game on love. His
absence schal make thee for to morene aftir him and lyve in longyng,
and his presence schal fille thee with pyment of his swetnesse and make
thee liik drunken', p. 177). Metaphors of drunkenness are often used to

express a rapturous sense of escape from normal consciousness (pp. 250, 258), drunk with the love of Jesus ('For with that precious licour only mai thi soule be fulfillid', p. 159). It is the opening to fulfilment that Hilton explores through his teaching on reforming the image of God in man's soul, and the mystics draw on various metaphors to convey the developing processes of contemplative life. There is the journey, which Hilton uses in *Scale*, II, 21 (pp. 157–60), and there are ladders (pp. 249, 282), on the way to a destination that may be likened to a deliquescence ('al molten in God', p. 246), a drowning (pp. 89, 238, 262) or a death, as in the death of Rachel (pp. 31, 90).[14]

In heaping up a list of metaphors and setting them alongside each other in *Scale*, II, 40 (p. 163), Hilton points to the limits of all metaphorical language about contemplation. Among the English mystics, both Hilton and the *Cloud*-author consistently alert their reader to the spiritual pitfalls in construing 'bodily' a language meant 'goostly': in being confused by all the sensory, material and spatial implications in metaphorical language. Hilton's own powerful imagination is applied precisely in warning against too literal an understanding of lifting up one's sight to God ('He schal not renne out with his thoght as he wolde clymbe aboven the sunne and persen the firmament and ymagynen the majeste as it were a light of an hundred sunnes. Bot he schal rather drawe downe the sunne and al the firmament, and forgeten it and kesten it bineth him . . .' p. 161). The *Cloud*-author also counsels repeatedly against misunderstanding metaphorical language, and he distrusts metaphors of progression or movement in contemplation: 'the werke of this booke' should 'rather be clepid a sodeyn chaunging then any steedly steryng' (*Cloud*, ch. 59). Instead, 'it suffiseth inough a naked entent directe unto God' (p. 77), or indeed 'a nakid entent strechinge into God' (p. 79). Taken to its limits by so skilled a writer, his own kind of 'negative capability' allows that alongside incitements to suppress the imagination utterly the *Cloud*-author can also urge the most striking spiritual stratagems – surrender, subterfuge, concealment – in the most imaginative terms (e.g. chs. 32, 47). 'Haue no wonder whi þat I speke þus childly, & as it were folily & lackyng kyndly discrecion', he remarks after a playful passage in which he distills his wisdom and discretion for one of a circle of like-minded friends who will understand: 'I haue ben sterid many day boþe to fele þus & þink þus & sey þus, as weel to som oþer of my specyal freendes in God, as I am now vnto þee' (ch. 47).

Daunting as much of the mystics' advice may sound, the range of 'friends in God' to whom Hilton addresses works of spiritual guidance in the course of his career (pp. 108–9) is a pointer – along with ownership of manuscripts[15] – to the appeal of writings about contemplation in late medieval England, both to lay and religious readers.[16] The diversity of addressees and of spiritual needs reflects Hilton's breadth of understanding and suggests his developing sympathy for a greater accessibility of contemplative experience beyond the strictly contemplative life. Definitions and descriptions of the active and contemplative lives – of Martha and Mary (Luke 10. 38–42) – are a staple of the literature (pp. 64, 112–13, 153), but for all its wise caution Hilton's *Mixed Life* works out a distinctive understanding in practical terms of the possibilities for such a 'mixed' life, where room is made for contemplation amid the everyday cares of 'real' life. The recipient of Hilton's epistle is advised to achieve a balance between his responsibilities as parent and landowner and the impetus to contemplation. Interruptions and distractions are frustrating, yet must be accepted charitably as part of his unchangeable circumstances by the would-be contemplative, and there may be limits to what can be achieved by those still in active life (pp. 129–30). In his *Emendatio Vitae* Rolle had declared contemplatives who also preach to be more meritorious than solitaries (p. 22), and there is recurrent concern for possible interchange between action and contemplation in the lives of individuals. *The Abbey of the Holy Ghost* is directed to those who for whatever reason may not be in religion but who nonetheless wish to pursue an inner life.[17] *The Prickynge of Love*, while not reproaching those given over to contemplative life, declares its concern to be with how readers may have both contemplation and active life.[18] Even the *Cloud* prologue, for all its emphasis on the exclusiveness of contemplation, can envisage some benefit to readers not wholly removed from active life (p. 70), and it is a token of how contemplation might be perceived that brief accounts are to be found in the broader context of various works of moral and ascetic instruction.

In his *De Lectione* to a solitary, Hilton refers back to a recent talk between them: 'You are very singular and high-flown in your thoughts. . . . You are very elaborate in explaining what you feel – so strange as to be almost unintelligible. I do not condemn this entirely, but I am uneasy about it.'[19] Hilton's disquiet here at singularity and unusual language represents that aesthetic discipline observed more largely by the English medieval mystics in their own writings about contemplation: rarely elaborate, never unintelligible, shunning 'singularity'. Writing after Rolle, the later English mystics warn against simplification, self-willed impulsiveness and excess; and in favour of restraint and qualification. Excessive zeal in asceticism is always checked (e.g. *Cloud*, ch. 12; *Scale*, I, 22, 72). Moderation and patience are urged upon the eager. Shrewd advice is offered on distrusting visions and revelations;[20] and on disesteeming physical sensations, or incantatory raptures and fervours.[21] Acquiescence in the advice of a spiritual director and in the tenets of traditional teaching is recurrently commended. This proves a pervasive theme for the English mystics, implyng that some would-be contemplatives, confident of a special vocation, grew restive with any direction but their own. The *Cloud*-author notes drily how some always complain that they can find no one who really understands them (ch. 51). Hilton is highly sensitive to possibilities of error and heresy in any such 'liberty of spirit', warning against it in the third of the *Eight Chapters on Perfection* (pp. 141–2). Comparable warnings recur in *Qui Habitat*, *De Lectione*, and in Book II of *The Scale*,[22] where there are also parallels between Hilton's themes (II, 35–7, 40) and the glosses interpolated by the English translator of *The Mirrour of Simple Soules* to counteract disturbing implications of 'liberty of spirit' in the French original.

The influence of Rolle, continental works of mysticism available in English translation, uneasy relations with authority: all are brought together in *The Book of Margery Kempe*, the uniquely revealing testimony of one 'consumer' of the mystical literature circulating in late medieval England. Margery's inability to read for herself did not deny her access to books on contemplation. She tells Richard of Caister that the Trinity spoke to her soul more exaltedly about the love of God than any book she had ever heard read ('neythyr Hyltons boke, ne Bridis boke, ne *Stimulus Amoris*, ne *Incendium Amoris*, ne non other', p. 230), and when later recalling how a young priest would read to her she names the same four books 'and swech other' (ch. 58). By 'Hyltons boke' Margery may perhaps mean Book I of *The Scale*, and her familiarity with Rolle's characteristic ideas is suggested by her sensation of fire burning in her breast (p. 234). It was perhaps in part its Passion meditations that attracted Margery to the *Stimulus Amoris*, which at one point she quotes from and names in English as 'The Prykke of Lofe' (ch. 62). Margery's friend, the Carmelite Alan of Lynn,

the revelations of St Bridget of Sweden or 'Bridis boke', which –
circulating in various English versions, much excerpted and anthologized
– was widely influential. St Bridget's life and works – visionary and
pilgrim, married woman and Bride of Christ – offered a compelling
model to Margery Kempe, who visited in Rome the scenes of the saint's
life. Other saintly women's biographies and visions from the continent
– those of Mary of Oignies and Elizabeth of Hungary – are named by
Margery in her *Book* when cited to her by those who had read them,
perhaps in the kind of anthologies of spiritual reading in which Middle
English versions of both texts are still extant.[23]

   Although their works may be found conscientiously transcribed
in their entirety, in a manuscript culture the writings of the medieval
English mystics were also extensively anthologized from an early stage.
Selective copying and selective reading are represented by spiritual
miscellanies assembled according to the tastes and uses of various
consumers, religious and lay, teachers and pupils. Although the
Cloud-author had admonished his readers to read everything and in
the order presented (p. 69), consumers of mystical literature – in so far
as extant manuscripts embody their interests and demands – took a
different view of what might be copied and what read of the mystics'
work. Parts of the writings of Rolle and Hilton were repackaged and
recycled, in manuscript and later in print, within a burgeoning
literature of composite works of spiritual counsel. Even so short a
work as the *Eight Chapters on Perfection* was subject to excerpting,
with individual chapters anthologized (p. 281, n. 1). The only extant
medieval copy of any part of Julian's longer text is a late fifteenth-century
anthology of extracts from her *Revelations* (Westminster Cathedral
Treasury MS 4), and an anthology of excerpts from *The Book of
Margery Kempe*, printed *c*.1501, reflects a comparable consumer
demand. Despite his animadversions the *Cloud*-author was not safe
from being read selectively: two extant tracts each comprise a tissue of
extracts reassembled from the *Cloud* corpus and from Hilton, and
arranged according to the purgative, illuminative and unitive way of
contemplation. Both tracts – *Of Active Life and Contemplative
Declaration* (in BL MS Add. 37049) and *Via ad Contemplationem* (in
BL MS Add. 37790)[24] – survive in Carthusian productions, and it is
clear that the Carthusians had a signal influence, along with the
Briggitine order, on the transmission of contemplative writings in
England.[25]

Medieval English taste for mystical literature may be represented at its most ambitious by the compendium in BL MS Add. 37790 (the 'Amherst' manuscript).²⁶ This draws together the legacy of Rolle's teachings on contemplation, some synthesis in the *Via ad Contemplationem* of teaching from Hilton and the *Cloud* corpus, and Julian's shewings ('I sawe my saule swa large as it ware a kyngdome', p. 209). To the English mystics the manuscript adds a select library of translations from continental mysticism, ranging from the relatively accessible (like St Bridget or Suso in their English redactions) to the arguably heretical *Mirrour of Simple Soules* and the demanding *Treatise of Perfection* (with its account of 'the impacient hungre, besylye goynge, as a floode swyftly rynnynge . . . to wante it is intollerable, to folowe it impossible', p. 263). As a mystical 'reader' from the period, the Amherst collection can offer a guide to selection of pieces in the present volume on the English mystics of the Middle Ages, which focusses on the four major figures (with extracts from Margery Kempe), but includes some associated and translated works. Preference has been given to including whole works where possible: Rolle's English epistles, the *Cloud*-author's *Book of Privy Counselling*, three of Hilton's shorter works, the Amherst version of Julian's *Revelations*. These are accompanied by extracts from each author's longer works, and from some writings associated with them. There follow selected works by anonymous translators, illustrating the adaptation for English use of a range of texts on contemplation, including those of Ruusbroec and Suso. At the close of this book comes a work by Richard Methley who – both as a student of the English mystics before him and as a mystical writer himself – stands near the close of medieval English writings about what the *Cloud*-author termed 'the eendles merveilous miracle of love, the whiche schal never take eende' (p. 72).

RICHARD ROLLE
(*c.* 1300–1349)

1 *The Fire of Love*

Richard Rolle, 'Richard Hermit of Hampole', is the first, easily the most controversial, and probably the most widely influential of the English mystical writers of the fourteenth and fifteenth centuries. Of all the prolific writings in various genres that Rolle produced – and many more were later attributed to him – it is the Latin prose *Incendium Amoris* (*The Fire of Love*), with its vivid moments of autobiographical recollection and its rhapsodic, exultant spirituality, that establishes the singular persona that is such a central part of Rolle's strategy as a mystical artist: idiosyncratic, ingenuous, impassioned, he is exuberantly lyrical, winsome and sensual. The *Incendium*'s prologue catches the surprise in Rolle's still-amazed memory of first feeling the fire of love in his breast (even in this literal English version of 1435 by the Carmelite Richard Misyn):

Mor have I mervayled then I schewe, forsoth, when I felt fyrst my herte wax warme and – truly, not ymagyn[yn]gly, bot als it were with sensibill fier – byrned! I was forsoth mervaylde as the byrnynge in my saule byrst up, and of an unwonte solas. For uncuthnes of slike helefull habundance oftymes have I gropyd my breste, sekandly whedyr this byrnynge were of any bodely cause utwardly. But when I knewe that onely it was kyndylte of gostely caus inwardlye – and that this brynnynge was nought of fleschly lufe ne concupiscens – in this Y consayvyd it was the gyfte of my makar: glad therfor I am moltyn into the desyre of grettyr luf.[1] (BL MS Add. 37790, fol. 19r)

Through the whole work – an apologia for the mystic-author, and in praise of the solitary, eremitical life – Rolle evokes the three graces of his mystical experience: *fervor*, *dulcor* and *canor* (heat, sweetness and song). Neither the classical, threefold mystic way (purgative, illuminative, unitive), nor the triad of the three degrees of love which recurs in *Emendatio Vitae* and Rolle's English epistles, can easily be made to fit with this triad, for which *Incendium,* chapter 14 offers some definition:

Heet sothely I calle, when mynde treuly is kyndylde in lufe everlastynge, and the harte on the same maner to byrn not hopinglye bot verraly is felte. The harte treuly turnyd into fyre gyfis felynge of byrnynge lufe. Songe I calle, when in a plentevus saulle swetnes of everlastynge lovynge with byrnynge is takun, and thoyth into songe inturnyd, and mynde into fulle swete sounde is changyd. This to in ydilnes ar not gettyn, bot in hie devocion; of the whilke the thyrde, that is to say swetnes untrowyd, is nere. Heet truly and songe in the sawle causes a mervellus swetnes; and also of fulle grete swetnes thay may be causyd.[2] (fol. 42r)

In Rolle's various expositions the order of reception in this triad differs and the attributes overlap, but in chapter 15 Rolle recalls a key moment of transition where the mystic's thought, after earlier ardent feelings of *fervor*, turns into a kind of exalted spiritual harmony:

Whils treuly in the same chapelle I satt, and in the nyght before sopar als I myght sal[m]ys I songe, als were the noyes of redars or rather syngars abowen me I behelde. Whilst also prayande to hevyns with alle desyre I toke hede, on whate maner I wote not sodanly in me noys of songe I felte, and likyngest melody hevynly I toke, with me dwellynge in mynde. Forsoth my t[h]oyth continuly to myrth of songe was chaungid, and als were loveynge I had thynkande, and in prayers and sal[m]ys sayande the same sounde I scheuyd, and so forth to synge that before I sayde for plente off inwarde swetnes I bryst oute, forsoth prively, for allonly before my makar.[3] (fol. 44r–44v)

Fittingly, prose therefore gives way recurrently to poetry in Rolle's writings, and in the concluding chapter of the *Incendium* Rolle likens his spiritual singing of mystical love to the nightingale's song (chapter 42).[4]

Rolle's experience is his material and his authority. But his experience made such exceptional claims that his role and authority seem to have remained problematic. His various writings suggest both Rolle's touchy intolerance of criticism and his truculent defiance of detractors, convinced of the inevitable rightness of his individual calling. Yet the nature of that calling was apparently irregular, in so far as Rolle's career can now be reconstructed from the two, very partial, remaining sources: the (defensive and self-justifying) autobiographical allusions in his own writing, and the *Officium* compiled around 1380 in hopes of Rolle's canonization. In the *Officium*'s glowingly romantic narrative of the saint's early vocation, the young Rolle is a bright lad from Thornton-le-Dale (near Pickering, North Yorkshire), sent up to Oxford by a benefactor. At eighteen he rejects further study in order to turn from the world, fashioning a makeshift hermit's habit for himself from two of his sister's tunics and his father's rainhood before fleeing from home; he is then supported as a hermit by a local patron. There is no mention of his ever being ordained priest, and much of the implied criticism of Rolle centres on the alleged irregularity and instability of his life as a hermit (that he moved about too much to suit himself, picking and choosing patrons ungratefully, insufficiently given to an ascetic life and not unmindful of creature comforts).

One of the few facts about Rolle's life known independently of the calculated presentation of that life by himself and by his admirers is that he died at Michaelmas 1349, in the vicinity of the Cistercian nunnery of Hampole, near Doncaster, where he acted as a spiritual guide to various women disciples. For such recipients Rolle's three English epistles were composed and – in view of his candid confessions in the *Incendium* of how attracted he was to women – there is an achieved authority in the tact and wisdom with which Rolle translates some of his mystical understanding into these vernacular letters of spiritual counsel to his female pupils.

Although Rolle may well have been a 'difficult' man, one criticism of his example as a mystic has always been that it was not 'difficult' enough. Was he a true mystic, or simply subject to an intense enthusiasm accompanied by physical symptoms and phenomena? For Rolle his *fervor, dulcor* and *canor* may be spiritual, but his subjective, repetitious style of evoking their attributes risks confusing them with physical, sensory experience, while providing no structured step-by-step programme for a pupil's progressive advance. The characteristic absence of caution and self-criticism from the mystic's persona in Rolle's writings could be a misleading model, and Rolle's example might encourage his readers all too easily to mistake merely sensory experience for mystical. Subsequent medieval English writers on contemplation were concerned to qualify the influence of Rolle, who had become one of the most widely read of English authors. It was through his writings indeed, or those attributed to him, that meditations on the Passion,[5] and devotion to the Holy Name of Jesus,[6] came to have their influence on readers in later medieval England. The *Incendium* prologue ends with a characteristic direction of his book to the kind of reader Rolle intends:

> Qwharefore this boke I offyr to be sene, nought to philosophirs nor wyes men of this warlde, ne to grete devyens lappyd in questions infenyte, bot unto boystus and untaught, more besy to con lufe God then many thynges to knawe. For treuly, not desputynge bot wyrkande it is kunde and loffande. For treuly, I trowe thies thynges here contenyd, of thies questionaries – in all sciens moste hy in connynge, bot in the lufe of Cryste moste lawe – may nought be undyrstandid. Therfore to thame I have not written, bot if – all thynges forgettyn and putt o-bak that to this warlde is longynge – onely to the desires of oure maker thay to lufe onely be gifen. . . .[7] (fol. 20r)

2 *The Mendynge of Lyfe*

(Chapter 12)

Emendatio Vitae was probably Rolle's last work in Latin and written for a member of the secular clergy. Over one hundred manuscripts survive either in Latin or in seven distinct English versions (none by Rolle).[1] The *Emendatio*'s twelve chapters chart a path from conversion to contemplation.[2] The eleventh chapter – drawing on Richard of St Victor's *De Quattuor Gradibus Violentae Caritatis* – describes the three grades of love: insuperable, inseparable, singular (but Rolle passes over Richard's fourth grade of *amor insatiabilis*, where the soul realizes that its desire is unattainable in this life). Rolle's twelfth chapter defines approaches to contemplation, in which his notion of spiritual song has its place. Inclusive, systematic, useful: the *Emendatio* accessibly distils mystical teaching within a style and presentation that bespeaks, without expanding upon, the author's experience.

Base manuscript: CUL MS Ff. 5. 30 (Ff), fols. 161r–164v. Also cited: Bodleian Library MS Douce 322 (D).

(12) *Of contemplacioun*

Contemplacioun or contemplatyf lyf hath thre partes. The firste is redinge, the secunde preyinge, and the thridde is meditacioun. In redinge speketh God to us; in preyere we speken with God. In meditacioun aungeles comen doun to us and techen us that we erren not; in preyere thei styen up and offren oure preyeres unto God, enjoyinge of oure profite, the whiche ben messangeres now bitwixe God and us. Preyere is a meeke affeccioun of the soule directe into God, the whiche – whan it cometh to him – it hath delite and it cometh not from him but constreyned. Meditacioun of God is to be taken after redinge and preyere, where the halsinge of Rachel is.[3] To redinge pertineth resoun and seekinge and inquisicioun of soothfastnesse, the whiche is free lyht ypreented upon us. To preyere pertineth loovinge ympne, biholdinge, overpassinge and wunderinge. And thus is contemplacioun in preyere. To meditacioun pertineth inspiracioun of God, understondinge, wysdom, and sighinge or moornynge.

If thou aske what contemplacioun is, it is hard for to telle or utterly diffine. Summe seyn (and wel) that contemplacioun is a knowynge of hidde thinges for to come, or elles a cesinge fro alle worldly occupaciouns, or studye of holy writte. Oothere seyn (and bettere) that contemplacioun is a wunderful joyinge of hevenli thinges. The thridde seyn (and best) that contemplacioun is a wunderful joye of an upreysed soule, deth of alle fleschly affecciouns. Soothly me thinketh that contemplacioun is a wunderful joye of Goddes love, conceyved in the soule with swetnesse of aungeles lovinge. This wunderful joyinge is ende of parfyte preyere and of hyest devocioun. This is a joyinge of the soule, had for hire endeles loved, brestinge out bi voys into song. And soothli this werk is a fulfillinge and most parfyte of alle oothere werkes in this lyf. And therfore seith the prophete: 'Blissed is that folk that knoweth wunderful joyinge';[4] that is, the contemplacioun of God. Soothly no man that is straunge ne ferre fro God thoruh sinne may thus enjoye in Jhesu, ne feele the swetnesse of his love. And therfore he that desireth bisily to be kyndeled with the fyre of eendeles love for to be enoorned with pacience, meekenesse and myldenesse, and with alle manere clennesse of bodi and soule, to be fulfilled with gostly oynementes and to be reised up in contemplacioun – lete him seeke uncesingely heleful vertues, with the whiche he may in this lyf be maad free from sinne, and in that oother from al peyne, joyinge in blisful lyf. And if he doo thus, thanne shal he mown come thus in this lyf to this wunderful joyinge of contemplacioun.

And therfore irke he nouht for to yive him to preyeres and wakinges, and to use himself in holi meditaciouns. For soothly with swich manere gostly travayles, with moornynges and weepinges of inwardly conpunccioun is the love of Jhesu Crist kindeled, and also alle oothere vertues and the yiftes of the Holy Gost ben yette into the soule. Therfore biginne he thoruh wilful poverte, that he coveyte no thing of this world, that he may lyve soberly, meekely and rihtwysly bifore God and man. For to have nouht cometh sumtime of neede. But for to wole nouht have cometh of gret vertu. We may have many thinges and yit wilne to have riht nouht, whan we holde that we have to oure neede, nouht to oure luste. Riht as he sumtime that hath nouht coveyteth to have many thinges, riht so he that seemeth to have many thinges hath riht nouht, for he that hath it loveth it nouht but oonly for

his bodily neede. Hise necessaries bihooveth the most parfyte man to
take, for elles were he not parfyte if he forsooke that thing the whiche
him bihooved to live by. And therfore this manere is to be kept in
parfite men: that thei despise for Goddes sake alle eertheli goodes and
yit of the same shal thei take here mete and here clothes and oothere
necessaries. And if thei any time faile or wante, he shal not grucche, but
thanke God of al, and al outrage shal he forsake in that that in hym is.

The more a man is brent with the fyre of endeles light, so michel
more strong and pacient shal he be in alle adversitees. He also is maad
meeke withouten feynynge that holdeth him despicable and nouht, and
is not stired to ire or wraththe for noon harme or no reprove that man
may sey or do to him. Wherfore he yiveth him to continuel meditacioun,
and therfore him is yoven of God to come to hevenly contemplacioun,
and wunderfulli, sweetely and brennyngly for to enjoye in inward
joyinge. And with the eye of his soule purifyed as michel as his dedly
freelte may suffre, he seeth and knoweth God. Soothly whan he is sette
in this degree, he fleeth not ne renneth not aboute for to gete outward
thinges, ne he goth not any time with prowd foot or feelinge, but he
hath oonly his joye and his mirthe in hevenly thinges, and therfore is he
ravisshed in the swetnesse of Goddes love. And so ravisshed, he is
wunderfully gladed. Soothly swich is lyf contemplatyf if it be taken in
due manere. Thoruh long exercise of gostli werkinge come we to
contemplacioun of thinges of hevene. The sight of the soule is taken up
and biholdeth gostli thinges as it were in a schadewe and not cleerly.
For as longe as we gon bi feith we seen not but as it were thoruh a
mirrour and a liknesse.[5] For thouh the eye of understondinge be bisy
for to biholde gostly light, nevertheles the light as it is in itself he may
not yit see. And yit he feeleth wel that he hath ben there as longe as he
holdeth the savour and the fervour of the light with him. And therfore
seith the prophete: 'As his derknesse, so is his lyght.'[6] Thouh al
derkenesse of sinne be ravisshed awey fro an holi soule and blake
clowdes ben withdrawen, and the mynde that was unclene be poorged,
yit neverthelattere, as longe as it is constreyned to dwelle in this dedly
flesh, it may not see that unspekable joye as it is in itself.

Holy and contemplatyf men biholden the joye of God thoruh
revelacioun,[7] and that is either thoruh openynge of here gostly witte for
to understonde holi writ,[8] or elles the dore of hevene opened unto
hem,[9] that is more, that as it were alle obstacles bitwixe God and hem
doon awey, with the eye of here soule clensed, thei biholden hevenly

citizines. Summe men han taken bothe. And therfore riht as whil we ben in derknesse of sinne we mowen not see gostly light, the whiche a cleene soule seeth in contemplacioun, riht so in contemplacioun whiche lighteneth oure [sowle]*a* cesably we may not see that light cleerly that we shul see in blisse. For Crist putteth derknesse his hidinge place and he speketh to us yit in a clowde,[10] but notforthanne it is ful sweete that is feeled. And soothly in that is shewed parfite love, whan a man livinge in dedly flesh can not joyen but in God, ne no thing wilne or coveyte but God or for God. Heerfore it is wel shewed that holinesse stondeth not in sobbinge or sighinge or roumynge of herte in teeres or in any outward werkinge, but it stondeth specially in swetnesse of parfite love and hygh contemplacioun; for manye have be molten in teres and afterward have fallen ayen into sinne. But ther was nevere noon that evere wolde fowle him eftsoones with worldly bisines after that he hadde oones soothfastly tasted the swetnesse of eendeles love. For to weepe and sorwe falleth to hem that ben newely turned, and biginneres and profiteres. But for to wunderfully joye in contemplacioun falleth oonly to hem that ben parfite. Therfore what man so evere feeleth bitinge and remorse of conscience for his sinne that is passed, thouh he have long time doon penaunce, wite he wel that he dide not yit parfite penaunce. And therfore in the mene time be hise teres to hym breed dai and niht, for wite he wel that he may not come to the swetnesse of contemplacioun but if he first travaile himself with weepinges and sighinges of verry compunccioun.

The swetnesse of contemplacioun may not be geten but with huge travailes. But whan it is had, it is sovereyn gladnesse and endeles counfort. Ye! and shortly to sey, it cometh not thoruh merite ne diserte of man, but oonly of the free yifte of God. And soothly ther was nevere man fro the biginnynge of the world unto this day that evere mihte be ravished into contemplacioun of endeles love, but if he bifore forsook parfytly al worldly vanite. And ferthermor hym bihooved to yive himself lastingly to holi meditacioun and devowt preyere, er he mihte come to hevenly contemplacioun. Contemplacioun is a travaile, but it is sweete, softe and desirable: this travaile maketh a man glad and not hevy. This may no man have but joyinge; and not whan it cometh, but whan it goth awey, he is wery. O goode travaile, to the which men in dedly bodies ordeyne hem! O noble bisynesse, which sitteres and

---

a sowle] D; Ff *om.*

resteres most parfitely fulfillest! For him needeth to be in gret reste of
bodi and soule, whom the fyre of the Holi Gost verrily enflawmeth.
Ther ben manye that kunne not holde haliday ne make saterdai in hir
soule, ne putte out veyne thouhtes fro hire mynde. Thei may not fulfille
that the prophete biddeth, seyinge these woordes: 'Cese ye, and seeth
how sweete oure Lord is.'[11] Nouht men cesinge in body but in soule
deserven to taste and to see how sweete oure Lord is, and how sweete
the heyghte of contemplacioun is.

Eche contemplatyf man loveth oonlynesse, that he may soo
michel more freely and fervently use hymself in hise affecciouns and in
his gostly werkinge, that he is not letted with no man withoute
counforte. Therfore sithe it is certeyn contemplatyf lyf to ben more
wurthi and more meritorie than actyf lyf, alle contemplatyf men –
thoruh the stiringe of the love of God, lovinge solitude for the
swetnesse of contemplacioun – ben cheefly brennynge in love. It
sheweth that solitarie men, thoruh the yifte of contemplacioun maad
high, atteyneth to the hiyeste and most sovereyn degree of perfeccioun.
But if it be soo that summe ben in that degree and state, that on the side
thei have cauht thoruh grace the heighte of contemplatyf lyf, and yit
thei fulfille on that oother side the office of prechinge: these passen
solitarie men, thouh thei be most high in contemplacioun and of
grettest perfeccioun, in that that thei shule have al oother thing liche a
special meede in hevene that is called aureole for here prechinge.

A verry contemplatyf man is ofte ravished in so gret desire into
that gostli unseable liht that he is deemed of men as a fool and
unsensible; and that is for the soule is so fully enflawmed in the love of
Jhesu Crist that it utterly chaungeth the bodily g[e]stur[e],[b] and is
twinned and departed from alle eerthely and bodily werkinges, so that
he is maad as it were al anoother man. Soothly on this manere the soule
is gadered togidere in oon swetnesse of eendeles love, holdinge hym
withinne bisily, nomore goinge aboute seekinge bodily and eerthely
delices. And therfore for she is so delicatly fed al with inward delices,
no wunder thouh she be reised up in desire and seye: 'Who shal yive me
thee, my brother, that I may fynde thee withoute and kisse thee?'[12]
That is: That I mai be departed fro this dedly flesh, and so fynde thee,
and seen thee face to face, and be festened to thee withoute ende; and
thanne shal no man despise me.

[b] gesture] D; gustur FF.

A devoute soule that is yoven to contemplatyf lyf and filled with love of endelesnesse despiseth al the veyn joye of this world, and, in Jhesu alloone wunderfulli joyinge, it coveiteth to dye and be with Crist; the which, for as miche as she is despised and nouht set bi of the world, gretliche languisheth in love and hugely desireth that she mihte be sette with theese queeres of aungeles in blisful joye, where no worldly disese shal mown dere hire. Therfore soothly ther is nothing more profitable ne more merye thanne is grace of contemplacioun, the whiche reiseth us up above alle eertheli thinges and presenteth us unto God. What is grace of contemplacioun but a biginnynge of endeles joye? Nouht elles. And what is perfeccioun of this joye but a fulfillinge of this grace? In the which is cleped to us a gloriows gladnesse, ablest, everelastinge, and joye withouten ende: to live with seyntes, to dwelle with aungeles, and, that is above al this, to knowe God fully, to love him perfytly, to see the brightnesse of his gloriowse majestee, and with unspekable and wunderful joyinge and melodie to loove him withouten ende – to whom be honour, wurshipe and endeles blisse in world of worldes withouten ende. Amen.

Heere eendeth the twelve chapitres of Richard Heremite of Hampool.

3 Ego Dormio

Named by modern editors after its opening text, *Ego Dormio* is usually considered the earliest of Rolle's English epistles and is an exposition of 'thre degrees of lufe', the third being 'contemplatife lyfe'. According to CUL MS Dd. 5. 64 it was written for a nun of Yedingham Priory (near Pickering, North Yorkshire), and modern opinion has been divided on whether the exhortations against worldliness point to a laywoman reader (who may have been considering becoming a nun, or became one after the epistle's composition), or whether the opening and the emphasis on the second degree of love imply an intended reader who is already a nun. Whoever the recipient, there is a striking intimacy of address in the opening paragraph's identification with wooing for another and with a 'messanger to bryng the to hys bed', as also in the declaration 'Til the I write specialy . . . .' Such a reader may at least aspire to the third degree of love, in which 'kyndelde with fyre of Cristes lufe . . . and feland lufe, joy, and swetnes . . . thi prayers turnes intil joyful sange'. Rolle's account of the three degrees of love is hence fittingly punctuated by lyric passages: the first degree closes with some unrhymed alliterative lines ('Alle perisches and passes . . . '); the second degree is closed by a Passion Meditation lyric, which may serve as a means of transition to the third degree (although 'I say noght that thou, or another that redes this, sal do it all'); the third degree closes with a love lyric to Jesus, offered, like the Passion lyric, for the reader's devotional use. In the account of the third degree in Longleat MS 29 is preserved a unique and evidently authentic passage on the mystic's attitude to death, which is included below within square brackets (see p. 31).

Base manuscript: CUL MS Dd. 5. 64 (Dd), fols. 22v–29r. Also cited: Bodleian Library MS Rawlinson A 389 (R), and Longleat House (The Marquess of Bath) MS 29 (L).

Ego dormio et cor meum vigilat.[1] Thai that lyste lufe, herken, and here of luf. In the sang of luf it es writen: 'I slepe, and my hert wakes.' Mykel lufe he schewes, that never es irk to lufe, bot ay standand, sittand, gangand, or wirkand, es ay his lufe thynkand, and oftsyth tharof es dremande. Forthi that I lufe, I wow the, that I myght have the als I walde, noght to me, bot to my Lorde. I wil become that messanger to

bryng the to hys bed, that hase made the and boght the, Criste, the
keyng sonn of heven. For he wil with the dwelle, if thou will lufe hym:
he askes the na mare bot thi lufe. And my dere syster in Criste, my wil
thou dose if thou lufe hym. Criste covaytes noght els, bot at thou do his
wil, and enforce the day and nyght that thou leve al fleschly lufe, and al
lykyng that lettes the til lofe Jhesu Crist verraly. For ay, whils thi hert es
heldand til lufe any bodely thyng, thou may not perfitely be coupuld
with God.

In [heven]*a* er neyn orders of aungels,[2] that er contened in thre
ierarchies. The lawest ierarchi contenes aungels, archaungels, and
vertues; the mydel ierarchi contenes principates, potestates, and
dominacions; the heest ierarchi, that neest es to God, contenes thronos,
cherubyn, and seraphyn. The lawest es aungels, the heest es seraphyn;
and that order, that leste es bryght, es seven sythe sa bryght als the sonn
es bryghtar than a kandele, the kandel bryghtar than the mone, the
mone bryghtar than a sterne. Also er the orders in heven ilk ane
bryghter than other, fra aungels to seraphyn. This I say to kyndel thi
hert for to covayte the felichip of aungels. For al that er gude and haly,
when thai passe owt of this worlde, sal be taken intil thies orders: some
intil the lawest, that hase lufed mykel; some intil the mydelmest, that
hase lufed mare; other intil the heest, that maste lufed God and
brynandest es in hys lufe. Seraphyn es at say 'brynand'; til the whilk
order thai er receyved that leest covaytes in this worlde, and maste
swetnes feles in God, and brynandest hertes hase in his lufe

Til the I write specialy, for I hope mare godenes in the than in
another, and [that]*b* thou wil gyf thi thoght to fulfil in dede that thou
says es maste prophetabel for thi sawle, and that lyf gif the til [in]*c* the
whilk thow may halyest offer thi hert to Jhesu Criste and leste be in
bisynes of this worlde. For if thow stabil thi lufe, and be byrnande
whils thou lyfes here, withowten dowte thi settel es ordaynde ful hegh
in heven and joyful before Goddes face amang his haly aungels. For in
the self degre their prowde devels fel downe fra, er meke men and
wymen, Criste dowves, sett, to have rest and joy withowten ende, for a
litel schort penance and travel that thai have sufferd for Goddes lufe.
The thynk peraventure hard to gife thi hert fra al erthly thynges, fra al
ydel speche and vayne, and fra al fleschly lufe, and to be alane, to
wa[ke]*d* and pray and thynk of the joy of heven and of the passyon of

Jhesu Criste, and to ymagyn the payne of hell that es ordande for
synful man. Bot wyterly, fra thou be used tharin, the wil thynk it
lyghter and swetter than thou dyd any erthly thyng or solace. Als
sone als thi hert es towched with the swetnes of heven, the wil lytel
lyst the myrth of this worlde; and when thou feles joy in Criste lufe,
the wil lathe with the joy and the comforth of this worlde and erthly
gamen. For al melody and al riches and delites, that al men in this
world kan ordayne or thynk, sownes bot noy and anger til a mans
hert that verraly es byrnand in the lufe of God; for he hase myrth and
joy and melody in aungels sang, als thou may wele wyt. If thou leve al
thyng that thi fleschly lufe list, for the lufe of God, and have na
thoght on syb frendes, bot forsake al for Goddes lufe, and anely gyf
thi hert to coveyte Goddes lufe and pay hym, mare joy sal thou have
and fynd in hym than I can on thynk. How myght thou than wyt it? I
wate never, if any man be in swilk lufe; for ay the hegher the lyfe es,
the fewer folowers it hase here. For many thynges drawes man fra
Goddes lufe, that thow may here and se; and God comfortes his
lufers mare than thai wene that lufes hym noght. Forthi, thof we seme
in penance withowten, we sal have mykel joy within, if we ordayne
us wysely to Goddes servyce, and sett in hym al owre thoghtes, and
forsake al vanyte of this worlde.

Gyf thien entent til understand this wrytyng; and if thou have sett
al thi desyre til lufe God, here thies thre degrees of lufe, sa that thou
may rise fra ane til another, to thou be in the heest. For I wil noght
layne fra the, that I hope may turne the til halynes. The fyrst degre of
lufe es, when a man haldes the ten commandementes, and kepes hym
fra the seven dedely synnes, and es stabyl in the trowth of hali kyrke;
and when a man wil noght for any erthly thyng wreth God, bot trewly
standes in his servyce, and lastes tharin til his lyves ende. This degre of
lufe behoves ilk man have, that wil be safe; for na man may com til
heven, bot if he lufe God and his neghbor withowten pride, ire, envy, or
bakbityng, and withowten al other venemus synne, glotony, lichery,
and covayties; for thies vices slaes the saule, and makes it to depart fra
God, withowten wham na creature may lyf. For als a man pusonde of a
swete morcell takes venome that slase his body, sa dose a synful wreche
in likyng and luste of hys flesch: destrues his sawle, and brynges it to
dede withowten end. Men thynk it swete to synne; bot thaire mede,
that es ordand for tham, es bitterer than the gall, sowrar than the atter,
war than al the waa that we may here se or fele.

[Alle perisches and passes that we with eghe see];*e* it wanes into wrechednes, the welth of this worlde. Robes and ritches rotes in dike; prowde payntyng slakes into sorow. Delites and drewryse stynk sal ful sone; thair golde and thaire tresoure drawes tham til dede. Al the wikked of this worlde drawes til a dale, that thai may se thare sorowyng, whare waa es ever stabel. Bot he may syng of solace, that lufes Jhesu Criste; the wretchesse fra wele falles into hell.

Bot when th[ou]*f* have wele leved in the ten comandementes of God, and styfly put th[e]*g* fra al dedely synnes, and payes God in that degre, umbethynk the that thou wil plese God mare, and do better with thi sawle, and become perfyte. Than enters thou into the tother degre of lufe, that es to forsake al the worlde, thi fader and thi moder, and al thi kyn, and folow Criste in poverte. In this degre thou sal stody how clene thou be in hert, and how chaste in body; and gife the til mekenes, suffryng, and buxumnes; and loke how fayre thou may make thi saule in vertues and hate al vices, so that thi lyf be gastly and noght fleschly. Never mare speke evyl of thi neghbor, ne gyf any evel worde for another; bot al that men says, evel or gude, suffer it mekeli in thi hert, withowten styrryng of wreth; and than sal thou be in rest within and withowte, and so lyghtly sal thou come to the gastly lyfe, that thou sal fynde swettar than any erthly thyng.

Perfite life and gastly es, to despise the worlde, and covete the joy of heven, and destroy thorow Goddes grace al wicked desyres of the flesch, and forgete the solace and the lykyng of thi kynredyn and lufe noght bot in God: whethir thai dy or lyfe, or be pore or riche, or seke, or in wa or in hele, thank thou ay God, and blisse hym in al thi werkis. For his domes er so pryve, that na creature may comprehend tham. And oftsithes some haves thar likyng and thair wil in this worlde, and hell in the tother; and some men er in pyne and persecucion and anguysch in this lyfe, and hase heven to thair mede. Forthi, if thi frendes be ay in thaire ese and hele and welth of this worlde, thou and thai bath may have the mare drede that thai lose noght the joy of heven withouten ende. If thai be in penance and sekenes, or if thai lyf rightwisly, thai may trayste to come til the blysse. Forthi in this degre of lufe thou sal be fulfilde with the grace of the Haly Gaste, that thou sal noght have na sorow ne grutchyng bot for gastly thyng, als for thi synnes and other mennes, and after the lufe of Jhesu Criste, and in

e Alle . . . see] R; Dd *om.*   *f* thou] R; thai Dd.   *g* the] R; tham Dd.

thynkyng of his passyon. And I wil that thou have it mykel in mynde, for it wyll kyndel thi hert to sett at noght al the gudes of this worlde and the joy tharof, and to desyre byrnandly the lyght of heven with aungels and halowes. And when thi hert es haly ordande to the service of God, and al worldly thoghtes put oute, than wil the liste stele by the alane, to thynk on Criste, and to be in mykel praying. For thorow gode thoghtes and hali prayers thi hert sal be made byrnand in the lufe of Jhesu Criste, and than sal thow fele swetnes and gastely joy bath in praying and in thynkyng. And when thou ert by the alane, gyf the mykel to say the psalmes of the psauter and Pater noster and Ave Maria; and take na tent that thou say many, bot that thou say tham wele, with al the devocion that thow may, liftand up thi thoght til heven. Better it es to say seven psalmes wyth desyre of Crystes lufe, havand thi hert o[n]^b thi praying, than seven hundreth thowsand suffrand thi thoght passe in vanitees of bodyli thynges. What gude, hopes thou, may come tharof, if thou lat thi tonge blaber on the boke and thi hert ren abowte in sere stedes in the worlde? Forthi sett thi thoght in Criste, and he sal rewle it til hym. And halde the fra the venome of the worldly bisynesse.

And I pray the, als thou covaytes to be Goddes lufer, that thou lufe this name Jhesu, and thynk it in thi hert, sa that thou forget it never, whareso thou be. And sothely I say the, that thou sal fynd mykel joy and comforth tharin; and for the lufe that thou lufes Jhesu, so tenderly and so specialy, thou sal be fulfild of grace in erth, and be Criste dere servande in heven. For na thyng pays God swa mykel als verray lufe of this nam Jhesu. If thou luf it ryght and lastandely, and never let, for na thyng that men may do or say, thou sal be receyved intil a heghar lyfe than thou can covete. His godenes es sa mykel, thar we inwardely aske hym ane, he wil gyf fyfe, so wele payde es he when we wil sett al oure hert to lufe hym.

In this degre of lufe thou sal overcome thi enmyse, the worlde, the devel, and thi flesche. Bot never-the-latter thou sal ever have feghtyng whils thou lyfes. Til thou dye, the behoves to be bysy to stande, that thou fal noght intil delites, ne in evel thoghtes, ne in evel wordes, ne in evel warke. Forthi grete aght thi yernyng be that thou lufe Criste verrayly. Thi flesche sal thou overcome with haldyng of thi maydenhede, for Goddes lufe anely; or if thou be na mayden, thorow chaste lyvyng and resonabel in thoght and dede, and thorow discrete abstinence. The

^{b} on] R; of Dd.

worlde thou sal overcom thorow covaytyng of Cristes lufe and
thynkyng on this swete name Jhesu, and desyre til heven. For als sone
als thou feles savoure in Jhesu, the wil thynk al the worlde noght bot
vanyte and noy for men sawles. Thow will noght covayte than to be
riche, to have many mantels and fayre, many kyrtels and drewryse; bot
al thou wil sett at noght, and despise it als noght it ware, and take na
mare than the nedes. The wil thynk twa mantels or ane inogh; thow
that hase fyve or sex, gyf some til Criste, that gase naked in a pore
wede; and halde noght all, for thou wate noght if thow lif til thai be half
gane. The devell es overcome when thou standes stabely agaynes al his
fandyngys in sothefast charite and mekenes.

I wil that thow never be ydel, bot ay owther speke of God, or
wirke som notabil warke, or thynk on hym principaly, that thi thoght
be ay havand hym in mynde. And thynk oft on his passyon:

Meditacio de passione Christi [3]

My keyng, that water grette and blode swette;
Sythen ful sare bette, so that hys blode hym wette,
When thair scowrges mette.
Ful fast thai gan hym dyng and at the pyler swyng,
And his fayre face defowlyng with spittyng.
The thorne crownes the keyng; ful sare es that prickyng.
Alas! my joy and my swetyng es demed to hyng,
Nayled was his handes, nayled was hys fete,
And thyrled was hys syde, so semely and so swete.
Naked es his whit breste, and rede es his blody syde;
Wan was his fayre hew, his wowndes depe and wyde.
In fyve stedes of his flesch the blode gan downe glyde
Als stremes of the strande; hys pyne es noght to hyde.
This to see es grete pyte, how he es demed to the dede
And nayled on the rode tre, the bryght aungels brede.
Dryven he was to dole, that es owre gastly gude,
And alsso in the blys of heven es al the aungels fude.
A wonder it es to se, wha sa understude,
How God of mageste was dyand on the rude.
Bot suth than es it sayde that lufe ledes the ryng;
That hym sa law hase layde bot lufe it was na thyng.

Jhesu, receyve my hert, and to thi lufe me bryng;
Al my desyre thou ert, [I]*ⁱ* covete thi comyng.
Thow make me clene of synne, and lat us never twyn.
Kyndel me fire within, that I thi lufe may wyn,
And se thi face, Jhesu, in joy that never sal blyn.
Jhesu, my saule thou mend; thi lufe into me send,
That I may with the lend in joy withowten end.
In lufe thow wownde my thoght, and lyft my hert to the.
My sawle thou dere hase boght; thi lufer make it to be.
The I covete, this worlde noght, and for it I fle.
Thou ert that I have soght, thi face when may I see?
Thow make my sawle clere, for lufe chawnges my chere.
How lang sal I be here?
[When mai I negh the nere, thi melody to here,]*ʲ*
Oft to here sang,
That es lastand so lang?
Thou be my lufyng,
That I lufe may syng.

If thou wil thynk this ilk day, thou sal fynde swetnes that sal draw thi hert up, that sal gar the fal in gretyng and in grete langyng til Jhesu, and thi thoght sal al be on Jhesu, and so be receyved aboven all erthly thyng, aboven the firmament and the sternes, so that the egh of thi hert may loke intil heven.

And than enters thow into the thirde degre of lufe, in the whilk thou sal have grete delyte and comforth, if thow may get grace to com thartill. For I say noght that thou, or another that redes this, sal do it all; for it es at Goddes will to chese wham he will, to do that here es sayde, or els another thyng on another maner, als he gifes men grace til have thaire hele. For sere men takes seer grace of oure Lorde Jhesu Criste; and al sal be sett in the joy of heven, that endes in charite. Wha sa es in this degre, wisdom he hase, and discrecion, to luf at Goddes will.

This degre es called contemplatife lyfe, that lufes to be anely, withowten ryngyng or dyn or syngyng or criyng. At the begynyng, when thou comes thartil, thi gastly egh es taken up intil the blysse of heven, and thar lyghtned with grace and kyndelde with fyre of Cristes lufe, sa that thou sal verraly fele the bernyng of lufe in thi hert ever mare and mare, liftand thi thoght to God, and feland lufe, joy, and swetnes so mykel that na sekenes, anguys, ne schame, ne penance may greve the, bot al thi lyf sal turne intyl joy; and tha[n]^k fore heghnesse of thi hert [thi]^l prayers turnes intil joyful sange, and thi thoghtes to melody. Than es Jhesu al thi desyre, al thi delyte, al thi joy, al thi solace, al thi comforth; al I wate that on hym ever be thi sang, in hym all thi rest. Then may thow say: 'I slepe, and my hert wakes. Wha sall tyll my lemman say: For hys lufe me langes ay?' All that lufes vanytees and specials of this warlde, and settes thaire hert on any other thynges than of God, intyll this degre thai may noght come, ne intyll [the]^m other degre of lufe before nevynd. And tharfore all worldely solace the behoves forsake, that thi hert be heldande til na lufe of any creature, ne til na bysynes in erth, that thou may be in sylence, be ay stabilly and stalwortly with thi hert in Goddes lufe and hys drede.

[Ful entierly the behoveth gif thi hert to Jhesu, if thou wil cum to this degre of love. Fro thou be therin, thou hast no nede afterward of no lykynge, of no liggynge, ne of bed, ne of worldes solace, bot ever the wil list sit, that thou be ever lovynge thy Lord. In this degre of love thou wil covait the deth, and be joyful when thou hirest men name deth, for that love maketh the as siker of hevyn when thou deyest as thou now art of deile, for the fyre of love hath brent away al the roust of syn. And I wene, fro thou or I or another be broght in to this joy of love, we mow nat lyve longe after as other men doth, bot as we lyve in love, also we shal dey in joy, and passe to hym that we have loved. In this degre of love al drede, al sorow, al wo, al ydel joy and al wicked delites is put fro us, and we lyve in swetnesse of hevyn. Thynk ever to lest, and to be bettyr and better, and that wil gif the grace to love hym as he doth another].^{n}

Owre Lorde gyfes noght to men fairehede, ritchesse, and delytes for to sette thaire hertes on and dispend tham in synne, bot for thai sulde knaw hym and lufe hym and thank hym of al hys gyftes. The mare es thaire schame, if thai wreth hym that hase gyfen tham gyftes in body and in saule. Forthi, if we covayte to fle the payne of purgatory, us behoves restreyne us perfitely fra the lust and the likyng and al the il delytes and wikked drede of this worlde, and that worldely sorow be noght in us, bot that we halde owre hope faste in Jhesu Criste, and stande manly agaynes al temptacions.

---

^{k} than] R; thar Dd. ^{l} thi] R; in Dd. ^{m} the] R; Dd *om.*
^{n} Ful entierly . . . another] L; Dd *om.*

Now I wryte a sang of lufe, that thou sal delyte in when thow ert lufand Jhesu Criste:

Cantus amoris

My sange es in syhtyng, my lyfe es in langynge,
Til I the se, my keyng, so fayre in thi schynyng,
So fayre in thi fayrehede.[4]
Intil thi lyght me lede, and in thi lufe me fede,
In lufe make me to spede, that thou be ever my mede.
When wil thou come, Jhesu my joy,
And cover me of kare,
And gyf me the, that I may se,
Lifand evermare?
Al my coveytyng war commen, if I myght til the fare.
I wil na thyng bot anely the, that all my will ware.
Jhesu my savyoure, Jhesu my comfortoure,
Of al my fayrnes flowre, my helpe and my sokoure,
When may I se thi towre?
When wil thou me kall? me langes to thi hall,
To se the than al; thi luf, lat it not fal.
My hert payntes the pall that steds us in stal.[5]
Now wax I pale and wan for luf of my lemman.
Jhesu, bath God and man, thi luf thou lerd me than
When I to the fast ran; forthi now I lufe kan.
I sytt and syng of luf langyng that in my breste es bredde.
Jhesu, Jhesu, Jhesu, when war I to the ledde?
Full wele I wate, thou sees my state; in lufe my thoght es stedde.
When I the se, and dwels with the, than I am fylde and fedde.
Jhesu, thi lufe es fest, and me to lufe thynk best.
My hert, when may it brest to come to the, my rest?
Jhesu, Jhesu, Jhesu, til the it es that I morne
For my lyfe and my lyvyng. When may I hethen torne?
Jhesu, my dere and my drewry, delyte ert thou to syng.
Jhesu, my myrth and melody, when will thow com, my keyng?
Jhesu, my hele and my hony, my whart and my comfortyng,
Jhesu, I covayte for to dy when it es thi payng.
Langyng es in me lent that my lufe hase me sent.
Al wa es fra me went, sen that my hert es brent
In Criste lufe sa swete that never I wil lete,

Bot ever to luf I hete; for lufe my bale may bete,
And til hys blis me bryng, and gyf me my yernyng,
Jhesu, my lufe, my swetyng.
Langyng es in me lyght, that byndes me, day and nyght,
Til I it hafe in syght, his face sa fayre and bryght.
Jhesu, my hope, my hele, my joy ever ilk a dele,
Thi luf lat it noght kele, that I thi luf may fele
And won with the in wele.
Jhesu, with the I byg and belde; lever me war to dy
Than al this worlde to welde and hafe it in maystry.
When wil thou rew on me, Jhesu, that I myght with the be,
To lufe and lok on the?
My setell ordayne for me, and sett thou me tharin;
For then moun we never twyn.
And I thi lufe sal syng thorow syght of thi schynyng
In heven withowten endyng. Amen.

Explicit tractatus Ricardi heremite de Hampole, scriptus cuidam moniali de Yedyngham.

4 *The Commandment*

Written, according to CUL MS Dd. 5. 64 for a nun of Hampole, *The Commandment* begins with an exposition of the first great commandment (Matthew 22: 37–8). There are no exhortations here to spiritual development drawn from Rolle's own experience, and this epistle discourses on love through a mixture of reworkings from Rolle's earlier works with passages borrowed from other texts on affective meditation, combining evocations of passionate love with admonitions against sin.

Base manuscript: CUL MS Dd. 5. 64 (Dd), fols. 29r–34r. Also cited: CUL MS Ii. 6. 40 (Ii).

The comawndement of God es, that we lufe oure Lorde in al oure hert, in all oure saule, in al oure thoght. In al oure hert: that es in al oure understandyng, withowten erryng. In al owre sawle: that es, in al oure will, withowten gaynsaiyng. In al oure thoght: that es, that we thynk on hym, withowten forgetyng. In this maner es verray lufe and trew, that es werk of mans will. For lufe es a wilful stiryng of owre thoght intil God, sa that it receyve na thyng that es agaynes the lufe of Jhesu Crist, and tharwith that it be lastand in swetnes of devocion; and this es the perfeccion of this lyfe, til the whilk al dedely syn es contrary and enmy, bot noght venyall syn. For venial syn dose noght away charite, bot anly lettes the usce and the byrnyng tharof. Forthi all that wil lufe God perfitely, thaim behoves noght alanly fle al dedly synnes, bot alsa, als mykel als thai may, all venial syn, in thoght and worde and dede; and namly, to be of lytel speche. And that sylens be in occupacion of gode thoghtes, it helpes gretely to Goddes lufe; for jangelers and bakbyters, that appayres other mens lyfe with wikked wordes, and all that roses thar awne state before all other, or that despises any state in the whilke a man may be safe, thai have na mare syght of the lufe of God in thaire sawle then the egh of a bak has of the sonne. For vayne speche and ill wordes er syngne of a vayne hert and ill, that es withowten grace of God; and he that spekes ay the gode, and haldes ilk a man better than hymselfe, he schewes wele that he es stabel in godenes in hys hert, and ful of charite til God and til his neghbor.

And that thou may wynne til the swetnes of Goddes lufe, I sett here thre degres of lufe, in the whilk thou be ay waxand. The fyrst degre es called insuperabel, the secunde inseparabel, the thyrd singuler.[1] Thi luf es insuperabel, when na thyng may overcome hit, that es, nowther wele ne waa, ese ne anguys, lust of flesch ne likyng of this worlde; bot ay it lastes in gode thoght, if it wer temped gretely, and it hates all syn, sa that na thyng may slokken that lufe. Thi lufe es inseparabel, when al thi thoghtes and thi willes er gederd togeder and festend haly in Jhesu Criste, swa that thou may na tyme forgete hym, bot ay thou thynkes on hym. And forthi it es called inseparabel, for it may noght be departed fra the thoght of Jhesu Criste. Thi luf es singuler, when al thi delyte es in Jhesu Cryste, and in nane other thyng fyndes joy and comforth. In this degre es lufe stalworth as dede, and hard as hell; for als dede slas al lyvand thyng in this worlde, sa perfite lufe slas in a mans sawle all fleschly desyres and erthly covaytise; and als hell spares noght til dede men, bot tormentes al that commes thartill, alswa a man that es in this degre of lufe, noght anly he forsakes the wretched solace of this lyf, bot alswa he covaytes to sofer pynes for Goddes lufe.

Tharfore, if the lyst lufe any thyng, lufe Jhesu Criste, that es the fayrest, richest, and wysest, whas lufe lastes in joy endles. For al erthly lufe es passand, and wytes sone away. If thou be covetose after gode, luf hym, and thou sal have al gode. Desyre hym trewly, and the sal wante na thyng. If delites like the, lufe hym, for he gyfes delites til hys lovers, that never may perisch. Bot al the delytes of this world er faynt and fals and fayland in maste nede; thai bygyn in swettnes, and thair endyng es bitterer than the gall. If thou kan noght lyf withowten felichip, lyft thi thoght til heven, that thou may fynd comforth with aungels and halows, the whilke wil helpe the til God and noght lett the, als thi fleschly frendes dos. Restreyn thi will a while fra al lust and lykyng of syn, and thou sall have efterwarde al thi will; for it sal be clensed, and made sa fre that the lyst do na thyng bot that that es payng of God. If the lyste speke, forbere it at the begynnyng, for Goddes lufe; for when thi hert feles delyte in Criste, the wil not liste to speke, ne jangell, bot of Criste. If thow may not dreghe to syt by thi nane, use the stalworthly in hys lufe; and he sal sa stabyly sett the, that al the solace of this worlde sal noght remove the, for the will noght list tharof. When thow ert be thiself, be ay, till slepe come, owther in prayer or in gode

meditacioun; and ordan[e]^a thi prayng and thi wakyng and thi fastyng
that it be in discrecion, noght over mykel na over litel. Bot thynk ay
that of all thyng maste coveytes God the lufe of mans hert; and forthi
seke mare to lufe hym than to do any penance. For unskylful penance es
litel worth, or noght; bot lufe es ay the best, whether thou do penance
mykel or lytel. Be abowtwarde in thi myght, that thou war swa
inwardly gyven til the lufe of Jhesu Criste, that for gastly joy of thi
sawle na thyng that men may do or say make the sary; swa that thi
thoght within be fed anly in the swetnes of Cristes lufe, and noght in
delyte of erthly ese, ne in lovyng of men, when thai begyn to speke gode
of the in ydel joy. Trayst in God, that he wil gif til the that thou prayse
hym skilfully.

Skylful prayer es, til Cristen mans sawle, to seke and aske nyght
and day the lufe of Jhesu Criste, that it may lufe hym verraly, feland
comforth and delyte in hym, owtkastyng worldes thoghtes and il
bysynes. And sykir be thou, if thou covayte his lufe trewly and
lastandly, swa that na lufe of thi flesche, ne angers of the worlde, ne
speche, ne hatreden of men draw the agayne and caste the noght in
bisynes of bodily thyng; thou sal have his lufe and fynd and fele that it
es delitabeler in an owre than al the welthe that we here se may til
domesday. And if thou fayle and fall for temptacions, or for angers, or
for over mykel luf of thi frendes, it es na wonder if he halde fra the
thyng that thow covaytes noght trewly. He says that 'he lufes tham that
lufes hym, and thai that arely wakes til hym sal fynde hym'.^{2} Thow ert
arely wakand oftsythe, why than fyndes thou hym noght? Certes, if
thou seke hym ryght, thou sall fynde hym. Bot ay whiles thou sekes
erthly joy, if thou wake never sa arely, Criste may thou noght fynde.
For he es noght funden in thair lande that lyves in fleschly lustes. Hys
moder, whan he was willed fra hyr, scho soght hym gretand arely and
late ymang his kynredyn and hirs; bot scho fand hym noght, for al hyr
sekyng, til at the laste scho come intil the tempyl, and thare scho fand
hym syttand ymange the maysters, herand and answerand. Swa
behoves the do, if thou wil fynd hym: seke hym inwardly, in trouth and
hope and charite of haly kyrk, castand owt al syn, hatand it in al thi
hert: for that haldes hym fra the, and lettes the, that thou may noght
fynd hym. The herdes, that hym soght, fand hym lyand in a krybbe
bytwyx twa bestes – that thou knawes. If thou seke hym verraly, the

---

^{a} ordane] ɪi; ordand ᴅᴅ.

behoves ga in the way of povert and noght of riches. The sterne led the thre keynges intil Bedlem, thar thai fand Criste swedeld in clowtes sympely, as a pore barne. Tharby understand, whils thou ert in pryde and vanyte, thou fyndes hym noght. How may thou for schame, that es bot servand, with many clathes and riche folow thi spowse and thi Lorde, that yhede in a kyrtel, and thou trayles als mykel behynd the as al that he had on? Forthi, I rede that thou parte with hym ar thou and he mete, that he reprove the noght of outrage; for he wil that thow have that thou hase mister of, and na mare. He sayde til his discipyls that thai sulde noght have als many clathes as twa myght be sustend with; for to traveyle thareabowte es owtrage bisynes, that he forbedes.

The lufe of Jhesu Criste es ful dere tresure, ful delytabyl joy, and ful syker to trayst man on. Forthi he wil not gyf it to folys, that kan noght hald it and kepe it tenderly; bot til thaim he gese it, the whilk nowther for wele ne for wa wil lat it passe fra tham, bot are thai wil dye or thai wolde wrath Jhesu Criste. And na wyse man dose precyous lycor in a stynkand vessell, bot in a clene; als Criste dose noght his lufe in a foule hert in syn and bownden in wile lust of flesche, bot in a hert that es fayre and clene in vertues. Noght forthi, a fowle vessel may be made sa clene, that a ful dere thyng savely may be done tharin. And Jhesu Criste oftsythes purges many synfull mans sawle, and makes it abyl, thurgh his grace, to receyve the delitabel swetnes of hys luf, and to be his wonnyng-stede in halynes; and ay the clennar it waxes, the mare joy and solace of heven Criste settes tharin. Forthi, at the fyrst tyme when a man es turned to God he may not fele that swete lycor, til he have bene wele used in Goddes servys, and his hert be purged thorow prayers and penance and gode thoghtes in God. For he that es slaw in Goddes servyce may noght be byrnand in lufe, bot if he do al his myght and travell, nyght and day, to fulfill Goddes will. And when that blyssed lufe es in a mans hert, it will not suffer hym be ydel, bot ay it stirres hym to do some gode that myght be lykand til God, as in praying, or in wirkyng profitabel thynges, or in spekyng of Cristes passyon; and principally in thoght that the mynde of Jhesu Criste passe noght fra his thoght. For if thou lufe hym trewly, thou wil glad the in hym, and noght in other thyng. And thou [wil]*b* thynk on hym, kastand away al other thoghtes. Bot if thou be fals, and take other than hym, and delyte the in erthly thyng agaynes his wille, wit thou

b wil] ii; Dd *om.*

wele, he will forsake the, as thou hase done hyme, and dampne the for thi synne.

Wharfore, that thou may lufe hym trewly, understand that his lufe es proved in thre thynges: in thynkyng, in spekyng, in wirkyng. Chaunge thi thoght fra the worlde, and kast it haly on hym; and he sall norysche the. Chaunge thi mowth fra unnayte and warldes speche, and speke of hym; and he sall comforth the. Chaunge thi hend fra the warkes of vanitese, and lyft tham in his name, and wyrke anly for hys lufe; and he sall receyve the. Do thus, and than lufes thou trewly, and gase in the way of perfitenes. Delyte the sa in hym, that thi hert receyve nowther worldes joy ne worldes sorow, and drede no anguys ne noy that may befalle bodyly on the, or on any of thi frendes; bot betake all intil Goddes will, and thank hym ay of all hys sandes, swa that thou may have rest and savowre in hys lufe. For if thi hert owther be ledde with worldes drede or worldes solace, thou ert full fer fra the swetnes of Cristes lufe. And loke wele, that thou seme not ane withowten and be another wythin, als ypocrites dose, the whilk er like til a sepulker that es paynted richely withowten, and wythin rotes stynkand banes. If thou have delyte in the name of religion, loke that thou have mare delyte in dede that falles til religion. Thyne abett says that thou hase forsaken the world, that thou ert gyven till Goddes servys, that thou delyte the noght in erthly thyng. Lok than, that it be in thi hert, als it semes in men syght. For na thyng may make the religious, bot vertues and clennes of sawle in charite. If thi body be cled wythowten as thine order wille, loke that thi sawle be noght naked within, that thine order forbedes. Bot naked be thi sawle fra all vices, and warme happed in lufe and mekenes. Drede the domes of God, sa that thou wrath hym noght. Stabel thi thoght in hys lufe, and helld owt of the al synnes. Kast away slawnes. Use the manly in godenes. Be deboner and meke til al men. Lat na thyng bryng the til ire or envy. Dyght thi sawle fayre, and make tharin a towre of lufe til Goddes sone, and gar thi will be covaytous to receyve hym als gladly as thou walde be at the commyng of a thyng that thou lufed mast of al thyng. Wasche thi thoght clene wyth lufe teres and brennand yernyng, that he fynd na thyng fowle in the. For his joy es that thou be fayre and lufsom in his eghen. Fayrehede of thi sawle, that he covaytes, es that thou be chaste and meke, mylde and sufferand, never irk to do his wille, ay hatand all wykkednes. In al that thou dose, thynk ay to come to the syght of his fairehede, and sett al thine entent tharin, that thow may come thartil at thine endyng. For that aght to be the ende of al oure traveyle, that we evermare, whils we lyve here, desyre that syght in all oure hert, and that we thynk ay lang thartill.

Alssa festen in thi hert the mynd of his passyon and of his woundes: grete delyte and swetnes sal thou fele, if thou halde thi thoght in mynde of the pyne that Cryst sufferd for the. If thou traveyle right in hys lufe, and desyre hym brennandly, all temptacyons and dredes of ill thou sall overcom, and deful under thi fote, thorow his grace. For al that he sees in gode will to luf hym, he helpes tham agaynes all thar enmys, and rayses thar thoght aboven all erthly thyng, swa that thai may have savoure and solace in the swetnes of heven. Purches the the welle of gretyng, and cees noght till thou have hym. For in the hert whare teres sprynges, thar wil the fyre of the Haly Gaste be kyndelde; and sythen the fyre of lufe, that sal byrn in thi hert, wil bryn til noght al the rust of syn, and purge thi sawle of al fylth, als clene as the golde that es proved in the fournes. I wate na thyng, that swa inwardly sal take thi hert to covayte Goddes lufe, and to desyre the joy of heven, and to despyse the vanitees of this worlde, as stedfast thynkyng of the myscheves and grevous woundes of the dede of Jhesu Criste. It wil rayse thi thoght aboven erthly lykyng, and make thi hert brennand in Cristes lufe, and pur[ch]es^c in thi sawle delitabelte and savoure of heven.

Bot peraunter thou will say: 'I may noght despyse the worlde; I may not fynd it in my hert to pyne my body; and me behoves lufe my fleschly frendes, and take ese when it comes.' If thou be temped with swilk thoghtes, I pray the that thou umbethynk the, fra the begynnyng of this worlde, whare the worldes lovers er now, and whare the lovers er of God. Certes, thai war men and wymen as we er, and ete and drank and logh; and the wreches that lofed this worlde toke ese til thair body, and lyved as tham lyst in likyng of thair wikked will, and led thair dayes in lust and delyces; and in a poynt thai fel intil hell.[3] Now may thou see that thai wer foles, and fowle glotons, that in a few yeres wasted endles joy that was ordand for tham, if thai walde have done penance for thair synnes. Thou sese that al the ryches of this world and delytes vanys away, and commes til noght. Sothely, swa dose al the lofers tharof; for na thyng may stande stabely on a fals gronde. Thair bodys er gyn til wormes in erth, and thair sawles til the devels of hell. Bot all that forsakes the pompe and the vanite of this lyfe, and stode stalworthly agaynes all temptacions, and ended in the lufe of God, thai

^{c} purches] Ii; purges Dd.

ar now in joy, and hase the erytage of heven, thar to won withowten end, restand in the delyces of Goddes syght: for here thai soght na mare rest ne ese til thair body then thai had nede of.

A thyng I rede the, that thou forgete noght his name Jhesu, bot thynk it in thi hert, nyght and day, as thi speciall and thi dere tresowre. Lufe it mare than thi lyfe. Rute it in thi mynde. Lufe Jhesu, for he made the, and boght the ful dere. Gyf thi hert till hym, for it es his dette. Forthi set thi lufe on hys name Jhesu, that es 'hele'. Ther may na ill thyng have dwellying in the hert thar Jhesu es halden in mynde trewly. For it chaces devels, and destroyes temptacions, and puttes away wykked dredes and vices, and clenses the thoght. Whasa lofes it verraly es full of Goddes grace and vertues; in gastly comforth in this lyfe, and when thai dye, thai er taken up intil the orders of awngels, to se hym in endles joy that thai have lufed. Amen.

Explicit tractatus Ricardi Hampole, scriptus cuidam sorori de Hampole.

5 *The Form of Living*

Addressed in many of its manuscripts to 'Margaret' and in Longleat MS 29 to 'Margareta de Kyrkby', *The Form of Living* almost certainly dates from the last year of Rolle's life (1348–9) and is addressed to a young woman recluse, probably at the beginning of her enclosure as an anchoress. The *Officium* refers to a disciple of Rolle's called 'Margareta' (*lectio viijta*); a 'Margaret la Boteler nun of Hampole' is recorded in December 1348 as being enclosed at East Layton (near Richmond, North Yorkshire); and a 'Margaret de Kirkeby recluse' is recorded in January 1357 as being allowed to remove her enclosure from East Layton to Ainderby. Such evidence for a date late in Rolle's career accords with *The Form*'s maturity in its spiritual direction to the female solitary. The first six chapters linger over general admonitions which perhaps betray Rolle's anxiety about his young pupil (especially in the warnings against over-abstinence). With chapter 7, beginning *Amore langueo* ('I languish for love . . .'), Rolle passes on to devote the second half of *The Form* to a consideration of spiritual love and contemplative life, directed to a reader whose life was to be devoted to contemplation. Here – in a rhapsodic style and rhythm – are: an exposition, expanded from *Emendatio Vitae*, of the three degrees of love; definitions in reply to questions about love (ch. 10); and a conclusion on contemplative life (ch. 12). Here too *The Form* (as in ch. 8) circles back on the experiences in *Incendium Amoris*: the fire of love burns in the soul 'als thou may fele thi fynger byrn, if thou putt it in the fyre'; thought turns into song; death seems sweeter than honey; and the mystic's soul is 'as the nyghttyngale, that lufes sang and melody and fayles for mykel lufe'.

Base manuscript: CUL MS Dd. 5. 64 (Dd), fols. 1r–22v. Also cited: Bodleian Library MS Rawlinson C 285 (R); Longleat MS 29 (L); Lincoln Cathedral Library MS 91, the 'Thornton Manuscript' (T); BL MS Arundel 507 (A).

Incipit forma vivendi scripta a beato Ricardo heremita ad Margaretam anachoritam, suam dilectam discipulam.

(1)

In ilk a synful man or woman, that es bunden in dedly syn, er thre wrechednes, the wylk brynges tham to the dede of hell. The first es defaute of gastly strenght, that thai er sa wayke within thair hert that thai may nouther stand agaynes the fandynges of the fende, ne thai may lyft thair will to yerne the lofe of God and folow thartill. The secund es use of fleschly desyres: for thai have na will ne myght to stand, thai fall in lustes and likynges of this worlde; and for thai thynk tham swete, thai dwell in tham still, many tyll thaire lyves ende; and sa thai come to the thrid wrechednes. The thred wrechednes es chaungyng of lastand gode for a passande delite: als swa say, thai gif joy endles for a litell joy of this lyfe. If thai will torn tham, and ryse till penance, God will ordeyne thair wonyng with awngels and with haly men. Bot for thai chese the vile syn of this world, and hase mare delite in the fylth of thaire flesch than in the fairhede of heven, thai lose bath the worlde and heven. For he that hase noght Jhesu Criste, he tynes all that he has, and all that he es, and all that he myght gete; he ne es worthy the lyfe, ne to be fedde with swynes mete. All creaturs sal be styrde in his vengaunce at the day of dome.

Thiere wrechednes, that I have of talde, er noght anely in worldly men or women, that uses gluttry or litcheri and other apert synnes, bot thai er alswa in other, that semes in penance and in gode lyf. For the devyll, that es enmy till all mankynde, when he sees a man or a woman ymang a thousand turne haly to God, and forsake all the vanytees and ryches that men that lufes this [world]^a covaytise, and sek[e]^b the joy lastand, a thousand wiles he has on what maner he may desayve tham. And when he may noght bryng tham intill swylk synnes, the whylk myght gar all men wonder on tham, that knew tham, he begyles many swa prively that thai kan noght oft syth fele the trap that has taken thaime. Some he takes with errour that he puttes tham yn; som wyth singulere witt, when he gars thaime wene that the thyng that thai sai or do es best, and forthi thai wyll na counsell have of other that es better and conander then thai; and this es a foule stynkand pryde, for he wolde sett his witt before all other. Some the devell deceyves thurgh vayne glory, that es ydil joy: when any has pryde and delyte in thamself of the penance that thai suffer, of gode dedes that thai do, of any vertu that thai have; es glad when men loves tham, sari when men lackes tham, haves envy to tham that es spokyn mare gode of than of tham; thai halde thairself so gloriouse, and swa fer passand the lyf that other men ledes, that thai thynk that nane suld reprehend tham in any thyng

---

^{a} world] R; worldes DD. ^{b} seke] R; sekes DD.

that thai do or say; an[d]^c dispises synfull men and other, the whilk will not do als thai byd tham. How may thow fynd a synfuller wretche than swilk ane? And sa mykell es he the wer, that he wate noght that he es yll, and es halden and honord of men als wyse and hali. Some er deceyved with over mykell lust and likyng in mete and drynk, when thai passe mesure and com intill outrage and has delyte tharein, and wenes that thai synn noght; and forthi thai amend tham noght, and swa thai destruye vertues of saule. Some er begylde with ovre mikell abstinens of mete and drynk and slepe, that es of the temptacion of the devell, for to gar tham fall in myddes thair werk, swa that thai bryng it till nane endyng, als thai suld have done if thai had knawne skyll and halden discrecion; and swa thai tyne thaire merit for thaire frawerdnes.

This gylder layes oure enmy to take us with, when we begyn to hate wyckednes and turne us till God. Then many begynnes the thyng that thai may nevermare bryng till ende; then thai wene that thai may do what so thair hert es sett on. Bot oft thai fall or thai come ymyd gate; and that thyng, that thai wend war for tham, es lettyng till tham. For we have a lange way till heven; and als many gode dedys [als]^d we do, als many prayers als we make, and als many gode thoghtes als we thynk in trouth and hope and charite, als many paces ga we till hevenward. Than if we make us sa wayke and so febyll, that we may nouther wyrk ne pray als we suld do ne thynk, er we noght gretly at blame, that fayles when we had maste nede to be stalworth? And wele I wate, it es noght Goddys will that we sa do. For the prophete says: 'Lorde, I sall kepe my strengh to the',[1] so that he myght susten Goddys servys till his dede day, and noght in a litill and in a schort tyme waste it, and than lygge wanand and granand be the wall. And it es mykel mare peryll than men wenes. For Saynt Jerome says that he makys of ravyn offerand, that outragely tourmentis his body in ovre lytel mete or slepe; and Saynt Bernarde sais: 'Fastyng and wakyng lettis noght gastly godes, bot helpes, if thai be done with discrecion; withouten that, thai er vices.'[2] Forthi it es noght gode to pyne us so mykell, and sithen have unthank for oure dede.

Thare hase bene many, and er, that wenes that it es noght all that thai do, bot if thai be in sa mikell abstinence and fastyng, that all men speke of tham that knawes tham. Bot oftsythes it befalles that ay the mare joy and wonduryng thai have withouten of the lovyng of men, ay

---

^{c} and] an DD. ^{d} als] R; DD *om.*

the les joy thai have within of the luf of God. At my dome, thai sulde pay
Jhesu Criste mikell mare, if thai toke for his love, in thankyng and
lovyng of hym, for to sustan thar body in his servyse and to halde tham
fra mikell speche of men, what so God send for the tyme and the stede,
and gaf tham sithen enterely and perfitely to the luf and the lovyng of
that Lorde Jhesu Criste, that will stalworthly be lufed and lastandly be
served; so that thaire halynes war mare sene in Goddes egh then in
mans. For ay the better thou ert, and the les speche thou has of men, the
mare es thi joy before God. Ha! What it es mykell, to be worthi lovyng,
and be noght loved! And what wrechednes it es, to have the name and
the habet of halynes, and be noght so, bot cover pride, ire, or envy under
the clathes of Criste barnhede! A foule thyng it es to hafe lykyng and
delite in mens wordes, that can na mare deme what we er in oure saule,
then thai wate what we thynk. For oftsithe thai say that he or scho es in
the hegher degre that es in the lawer; and that thai say es in the lawer, es
in the hegher. Forthi I halde it bot wodnes to be gladder or sarier,
whethir thai say gude or ill. If we be aboutewarde to hyde us fra speche
and lovyng of this worlde, God wyll schew us till hys lovyng and oure
joy. For that es his joy, when we er strenghfull to stande agaynes the
pryve and the aperte fandyng of the devell, and sekes na thyng bot the
honoure and the lovyng of hym, and that we myght enterely love hym.
And that aght to be oure desyre, oure prayer, and oure entent, nyght and
day, that the fyre of hys lufe kyndell oure hert and the swetnes of hys
grace be oure comfort and oure solace in wele and wo.

  Thow hase now herd a party how the fende deceyves, wyth hys
sotell craftes and whaynt, men and women. And if thou will do be gode
cownsel and folow haly lare, als I hope that thou will, thou sall destroy
his trappes, and bryn in the fyre of luf all the bandes that he walde bynd
the with; and all his malys sall turne the til joy, and hym till mare
sorow. God suffers hym to tempe gode men for thaire profete, that thai
may be the hegher crownde when thai thurgh his helpe hase overcomne
sa cruell an enmy, that oftsythes both in body and in saule confowndes
many man. In thre maners the devell has power to be in a man. On a
maner: hurtande the godes that thai have of kynde, als in dome men
and in other, blemysand thair thoght. On another maner: revande the
godes whilk thai have of grace; and so he es in synfull men, the whilk he
hase deceyved thurgh delyte of the worlde and of thair flesche, and
ledes tham with hym till hell. On the third maner: he tourmentes a
mans body, als we rede that he has done Job. Bot wytt thou wele, if he

begyle the noght within, the thar noght drede what he may do the withouten, for he may do na mare than God gyfs hym leve for to do.

(2) For that thou has forsakyn the solace and the joy of this world, and taken the to solitary lyf, for Gods luf to suffer tribulacion and anguys here, and sithen com to that blys that nevermare blynnes, I trowe treuly that the comforth of Jhesu Criste and the swetnes of his love, with the fire of the Haly Gast, that purges all syn, sall be in the and with the, ledand the, and lerand the how thou sall thynk, how thou sall pray, what thou sall wyrk; so that in a few yers thou sall have mare delyte to be by thi nane, and speke till thi luf and to thi spows Jhesu Crist, that hegh es in heven, than if thou war lady here of a thowsand worldes. Men wenes that we er in pyne and in penance grete, bot we have mare joy and mare verray delyte in a day, than thai have in the worlde all thar lyve. Thai se oure body; bot thai se noght oure hert, whare oure solace es. If thai saw that, many of tham wold forsake all that thai have, for to folow us. Forthi be comford and stalworth,[3] and drede na noye ne angwysch; bot fest all thyne entent in Jhesu, that thi lyf be gode and wheme. And loke that there be na thyng in the, that suld be myspayand till hym, that thou ne sone amend itt.

The state that thou ert in, that es solitude, es maste abyll of all othyr til revelacion of the Haly Gaste. For when Saynt Jone was in the yle of Pathmos, than God schewed hym his pryvytees.[4] The godenes of God it es, that he comfortes tham wondyrfully, that has na comforth of the worlde, if thai gyf thair hert enterly till hym, and covayts noght, ne sekes, bot hym; then he gyves hymself till thaime in swetnes and delyte, in byrnyng of luf, and in joy and melody, and dwelles ay with tham in thaire saule, sa that the comforth of hym departes never fra tham. And if thai any tym begyn till erre, thurgh ignorance or freelte, sone he wysses tham the right way; and all that thai have nede of, he leres tham. Na man till swylk revelacion and grace on the first day may kom, bot thurgh lang travell and bysines to love Jhesu Criste, als thou sall here afterward.

Noght forthi than he suffers tham to be temped on sere maners, both wakand and slepand. For ay the ma temptacions, and the grevoser, thai stande agayne and overcomes, the mare sall thai joy in his luf when thai er passed. Wakand thai er umwhile tempyd wyth foule thoghtys, vile lustes, wicked delites, with pryde, ire, envy, despaire, presumpcion, and other many. Bot thaire remedy sall be prayer, gretyng, fastyng, wakyng. Thire thynges, if thai be done with

discrecion, thai put away syn and filth fra the saule, and makes it clene
to receyve the luf of Jhesu Criste, that may noght be loved bot in clennes.

Also umwhile the fende tempes men and women, that er solitary
by tham ane, on a qwaynt maner and a sotell. He transfigurs hym in the
lyknes of an awngel of lyght, and apers till tham, and sayes that he es
ane of Goddes awngels comen to comforth tham; and swa he deceyves
foles. Bot thai that er wys, and wil not tyte trow till all spirites, bot
askes cownsel of conand men, he may not begyle tham.[5] Als I fynd
writen of a recluse, that was a gude woman, til the whilk the ill awngell
oftsythes aperde in the forme of a gode awngel, and sayd that he was
comen to bryng hir to heven. Wharfore scho was right glad and joyful.
Bot never-the-latter scho talde it til hir schryft-fader; and he, als wyse
man and war, gaf hir this counsell. 'When he comes,' he sayde, 'byd
hym that he schew the oure Lady Saynt Mary. When he has done swa,
say Ave Maria.' Scho dyd sa. The fende sayde: 'Thou has na nede to se
hyr; my presence suffyse to the.' And scho sayde, on all maner scho suld
se hyr. He saw that hym behoved outher do hir wyll, or scho walde
despyse hym. Als tyte he broght forth the fayrest woman that myght
be, als to hyr syght, and schewed til hyr. And scho sett hir on hir knees,
and sayde 'Ave Maria'. And als tyte all vanyst away; and for scham
never sithen come he at hir. This I say, not for I hope that he sal have
leve to tempe the on this maner, bot for I will that thou be war, if any
[s]wy[l]k[e] temptacions befall the, slepand or wakand, that thou trow
not ovre tyte, til thou knaw the soth.

Mare privilyer he transfigurs hym in the forme of an awngel of
lyght,[6] that comonli al men ar temped with, when he hydes ill under the
liknes of gode; and that es in twa maneres. Ane es, when he egges us til
ovre mykel ees and rest of body and softnes til oure flesche, undir
ne[d]e[f] to susteyne oure kynde. For swilk thoghtes he puttes in us: bot
if we ete wele, and drynk wele, and slepe wele, and lygge soft, and sytt
warme, we may not serve God, ne last in the travell that we have
begonn. Bot he thynkes to bryng us till over mykel lust.

Another es, when under the lyknes of gastly gode he entices us til
scharp and ovre mikel penance, for to destroye oureself; and says thus:
'Thou wate wele, that he that suffers mast penance for Goddes lufe, he
sall have maste mede. Forthi ete litell and febyl mete, and drynk lesse;
the thynnest drynk es gode ynogh till the. Recke noght of slepe; were

_e_ swylk] R; wyk Dd.   _f_ nede] L; nethe Dd.

the hayre and the habirion. All thyng that es affliccion for thi flesche, do it, so that thare be nane that may passe the in penance.' He that says the thus es aboute to sla the with ovre mykel abstinence, als he that sayde the tother to sla the with ovre lytell. Forthi, if we will be right disposed, us behoves sett us in a gude mene, and that we may destroy oure vices and halde oure flesche under; and never-the-latter that it be stalworth in the servyse of Jhesu Criste.

Alsswa oure enmy will noght suffer us to be in rest when we slepe; bot than he es aboute to begyle us in many maners. Umwhile with uggly ymages, for to make us radde and make us lathe with oure state. Umwhile with faire ymages, fayre syghtes and that semes confortabell, for to make us glad in vayne, and gar us wene that we er better than we er. Umwhile tels us that we er haly and gode, for to bryng us intill pryde. Bot he, that es ordiner of all thyng, suffers noght that oure slepe be withowten mede til us, if we dresse oure lyfe till his will. And wyt thow wele, thou syns noght slepand, if thou be evermare wakande withouten outrage of mete and drynk and withouten ill thoghtes. Bot many ane the devel hase deceyved thurgh dremes, when he haves gart tham sett thair hert on tham. For he hase schewed tham some sothe, and sethyn begylt tham with ane that was fals. Forthi says the wyse man, that many besynes folowes dremes; an[d]^g thai fell, that hoped in tham.^{7}

Wharfore, that thou be not begylde with tham, I will that thou witt that ther er sex maners of dremes. Twa er, that na man, haly ne other, may eschape. Thai er, if thair wambe be ovre tome, or ovre full; than many vanitees in seer maners befalles tham slepande. The thryd es, of illusyons of oure enmy. The ferth es, of thoght before, and illusion folouand. And the fyft, thorow the revelacion of the Hali Gast, that es done on many a maner. The sext es, of thoghtes before that falles to Criste or hali kyrk, revelacion comand after. In thus many maners touches the ymage of dremes men when thai slepe. Bot sa mykell we sall latlyer gyf fayth till any dreme, that we may not sone wyt whilk es soth, whilk es fals, whilk es of oure enmy, whilk es of the Hali Gaste. For whare many dremes er, thare er many vanitees. And many thai may make to erre; for thai hegh unwhaynt men, and swa deceyves tham.

---

^{g} and] an Dd.

(3)   Knawe that thi lyfe es gyven to the servyce of God. Than es it
schame til the, bot if thou be als gode, or better, within in thi sawle, als
thou ert semand at the syght of men. Turne forthi thi thoghtes perfitely
till God, als it semes that thou hase done thi body. For I will not that
thou wene that all er hali that hase the abet of halynes, and er noght
ocupyed with the worlde; ne that all er ill that melles tham with erthly
bysines. Bot thai er anly hali, what state or degre thai be in, the whilk
despises all erthly thyng, that es at say, lufs it noght, and byrnes in the
luf of Jhesu Criste, and al thair desires er sett til the joy of heven, and
hates al synn, and ceses noght of gode werkys, and feles a swetnes in
thaire hert of the lufe withouten ende. And never-the-latter thai thynk
thamself vylest of all, and haldes tham wretchedest, leste, and lawest.
This es hali mens lyf; folow it and be haly. And if thou will be in mede
with apostels, thynk noght what thou forsoke, bot what thou despyses.
For als mykell thai forsake, that foloues Jhesu Criste in wilfull povert,
and in mekenes, and in charite, and in paciens, als thai may covayte
that folows hym noght. And thynk with how mykel and how gude will
thou presentes thi vowes before hym; for till that he hase hys egh. And
if thou with gret desyre offer thi praiers, with grete fervoure covayte to
se hym, and seke na erthly comforth bot the savoure of heven; and in
contemplacion therof have thi delyte. Wondurfulli Jhesu wirkes in hys
lovers, the whilk he reves fra the lust of flesch and of blode thorow
tender lufe. He makes tham to will na erthly thyng, and dose tham ryse
into the solace of hym, and to forgete vanytees and fleschely lufe of the
worlde, and to drede na sorow that may fall. To lathe with over mykel
bodili ees, to suffer for his luf, tham thynk it joy; and to be solitary thai
have grete comforth, that thai be noght lettyd of that devocyon.

     Now may thou se that many er war than thai seme, and many er
better than thai seme, and namely amang thase that hase the habett of
halynes. Forthi afforce the, in all that thow may, that thou be noght
wer than thou semes. And if thou will do als I lere the in this schort
forme of lyvyng, I hope, thorou the grace of God, that if men halde the
gude, thou sall be wele better.

(4)   At the begynnyng turne the enterely to thi Lorde Jhesu Criste.
That turnyng till Jhesu es noght els bot turnyng fra all the covaytyse
and the likyng and the occupacions and bisynes of worldly thynges and
of fleschly lust and vayne luf, swa that thi thoght, that was ay donward,
modeland in the erth, whils thou was in the worlde, now be ay

upwarde, als fire, sekand the heghest place in heven, right til thi spows, thare he syttes in hys blys. Til hym thou ert turned, when his grace illumyns thi hert, and [it]*ᵇ* forsakes all vices, and conformes it til vertues and gude thewes, and til all maner of debonerte and mekenes.

And that thou may last and wax in gudenes that thou hase begon, withowten slawnes and sarynes and irkyng of thi lyf, fowre thyngs sall thou have in thi thoght, til thou be in perfyte lufe. For when thou ert commen thartill, thi joy and desyre will ay be byrnand in Criste. Ane es: the mesur of thi lyf here, that sa schort es, that unnethis es it oght. For we lyve bot in a poynt, that es the leste thyng that may be. And sothely oure lyfe es les than a poynt, if we liken it to the lyfe that lastes ay. Another es: uncertente of owre endyng. For we wate never when we sal dye, ne whare we sal dye, ne how we sal dye, ne whider we sal ga when we er dede; and that God wil that this be uncertayn til us, for he will that we be ay redy to dye. The thyrd es: that we sall answer before the ryghtwys juge of all the tyme that we have bene here: how we have lyved, what oure occupacioun hase bene, and why, and what gude we myght have done when we have bene ydel. Forthi sayde the prophete: 'He hase calde the tyme agayn me',*⁸* that ilk day he hase lent us here for to despende in gude use, and in penance, and in Gods servys. If we waste it in erthly lufe and in vanitees, ful grevosly mon we be demed and punyst, for that es ane of the maste sorow that may be, bot we afforce us manly in the lufe of God, and do gude til all that we may, whil oure schort tyme lastes. And ilk tyme that we thynk not on God, we may cownt it als the thyng that we have tynt. The ferth es: that we thynk how mykell the joy es that thai have, the whilk lastes in Goddes lufe til thair endyng. For thai sal be brether and felaws with awngels and haly men, lufand and thankand, lovand and seand the kyng of joy in the fayrhede and in the schynyng of his majeste; the whilk syght sall be mede and mete and al delytes that any creature may thynk, and mare than any may tell, till all hys lovers withouten ende. It es mikel lightar to come to that blys than for to tell it. Alsswa thynk on what pyne and what sorow and tormentyng thai sall have, the whilk lufs noght God over all other thynges that man sees in this world, bot files thare bodi and thair sawle in lust and letchery of this lyfe, in pryde and covaytes and other synnes. Thai sall byrne in the fyre of hell, with the devell wham thai served, als lang as God es in heven with his servandes, that es evermare.

ᵇ it] so that it ʀ; ᴅᴅ *om.*

(5)   [I]*i* wyll that thou be ay clymbande tyll Jhesu-warde, and ekand thi luf and thi servys in hym; noght als foles doos: thai begyn in the heyest degre, and coms downe till the lawest. I say noght, for I will that if thou have begune unskylfull abstinence, that thou halde it; bot for many that was byrnand at the begynnyng and abyll til the luf of Jhesu Criste, for owre mykel penans thai have lettyd thamself, and made tham sa febel that thai may noght lufe God as thai sulde. In the whilk luf that thow wax ay mare and mare es my covaytyng and my amonestyng. I halde the never of the lesse meryt yf thou be noght in swa mykel abstinence; bot if thou sett al thi thoght how thou may luf thi spouse Jhesu Criste mare than thou has done, than dar I say that thi mede es waxand and noght wanande.

(6)   Wharfore, that thou be ryght disposed, bath for thi saule and thi body, thou sall understande fowre thynges. The fyrst thyng es: what thyng fyles a man. The tother thyng: what makys hym clene. The thyrd: what haldes hym in clennes. The ferth: what thyng drawes hym for to ordayne his will all at Goddes will. For the fyrst, wyt thou that we synne in thre thynges that makes us fo[wl]e,*j* that es, wyth hert, and mouth, and dede.[9]

        The synnes of the hert er thir: ill thoght, ill delyte, assent till synne, desyre of ill, wikked will, ill suspecion, undevocion (if thou lat thi hert any tyme be ydell, withouten occupacion of the lufe of the lovyng of God); ill drede, ill lufe, errour, fleschely affeccioun till thi frendes, or till other that thou lufes, joy in any mens ill fare (whethir thai be enmy or nane); despyte of pure or of synfull men, to honor ryche men for thaire rytches, unconabyll joy of any worldes vanite, sorow of the worlde, untholmodnes, perplexite (that es, dowt what es to do and what noght, for ilk a man aght for to be syker what he sall do and what he sall leve); obstinacion in ill, noy to do gude, anger to serve God, sorow that he dyd na mare ill, or that he dyd noght that luste or that will of his flesche, the whilk he myght have done, unstabylnes of thoght, pyne of penance, ypocrisy, lufe to plees to men, drede to dysplees tham, schame of gude dede, joy of ill dede, synguler witt, covaytyse of honoure or of dignite, or to be halden better than other, or rycher, or fayrer, or to be mare dred, vayne glory of any godes of kynde, or of happe, or of grace, schame with pore frendes, pryde of thi

---

i I] ʀ; ᴅᴅ *om.*   *j* fowle] ʀ; folowe ᴅᴅ.

riche kynne or of gentyl (for all we er ilike fre befor Gods face, bot if owre dedes make any better or wers than other); despyte of gude counsell and of gude techynge.

The synnes of the mowthe er thir: to swere oftsyth, forsweryng, sclaunder of Criste, or of any of his halows, to neven his name withouten reverence, agaynsaiyng and strife agayne sothfastnes, grotchyng agayns God for any angwys, or noy, or tribulacioun that may befall in erth, to say Goddes servys undevowtly and withouten reverence, bakbityng, flateryng, lesyng, missaiyng, wariyng, defamyng, flytyng, manasyng, sawyng of discorde, treson, fals wytnes, ill cownsell, hethyng, unboxumnes with worde; to turne gude dedes to ill, for to gar tham be halden ill that dose tham (we aght to lappe oure neghboure dedes in the beste, noght in the warst); excityng of any man till ire, to reprehende in another that he dose hymself, vayne speche, mykel speche, fowle speche; to speke ydell wordes, or wordes that er na nede; rusyng, polysyng of wordes, defendyng of synne, criyng of laghter, mowe-makyng on any man; to syng seculere sanges and lufe tham; to prayse ill dedes; to syng mare for lovyng of men than of God.

The synnes of dede er thir: glotony, letchery, drunkynhede, symony, wytchecraft, brekyn[g]^k of the haly dayes, sacrileghe; to receyve Goddes body in dedely synn; brekyng of vowes, apostasy, dissolucioun in Goddes servys; to gyf ensawmpyl of il dede; to hurt any man in his body or in his godes or in hys fame; theft, ravyn, usur, desayte; sellyng of ryghtwysnes; to herken ill; to gyf to herlotes; to withhalde necessaries fra thi body, or to gyf it to owtrage; to begyn a thyng that es abowen oure myght; custom to syn; fallyng oft to syn; fenyng of mare gude than we have, for to seme halyer, or conander, or wiser than we er; to halde the office that we suffice noght till, or that that may noght be halden withouten syn; to lede karols; to bryng up new gyse; to be rebell agayne hys soverayns; to defoule tham that er lesse; to syn in syght, in heryng, in smellyng, in towchyng, in handelyng, in swell[ow]yng,^{l} in gyftes, in wayes, sygnes, bydynges, writynges; to receyve the circumstance, that er, tyme, stede, maner, nowmber, person, dwellyng, conyng, elde (thir makes the syn mare or lesse); to covayte to syn or he be temped; to constreyne hym till syn.

Other many syns thar er of omission, that es, of levyng of gude undone, when men leves the gude that thai suld do: noght thynkand on

---

^{k} brekyng] R; brekyn DD. ^{l} swellowyng] L; swellyng DD; schewyng R.

God, ne dredand ne lovand hym, ne thankand hym of his benefices; to do noght all that he doos for Goddes lufe; to sorow noght for hys syn as he sulde do; to dispoos hym noght to receyve grace, and if he have taken grace, to use it noght als hym aght, ne to kepe it noght; t[o]^*m* turne noght at the inspiracion of God; to conforme noght his will to Gods will, to gyf noght entent till his prayers, bot rabill on, and rek never bot thai be sayde; to do necligently that he es bownden till thorow a vowe, or comawnded, or es enjoynde in penance; to draw on lengh that es at do sone; havand na joy of his neghbur prophet als of his awne; noght sorowand for his ill fare; standand noght agayne temptacions; forgifand noght tham that hase done hym harme; kepand noght trouth to his neghbur, als he walde that he dyd till hym; and yheldand hym noght a gude dede for another if he may; amendand noght tham that synnes before his ene; peesand noght stryves; lerand noght tham that er noght conand; comfortand noght tham that er in sorow, or in sekenes, or in povert, or in penance, or in pryson. Thir synnes, and many other, makes men foule.

The thynges that clenses us of that filth er thre,[10] agaynes thase thre maners of synnes. The fyrst es: sorow of hert, agayne the syn of thoght. Ant it behoves be perfyte, that thou will never syn mare, and that thou have sorow of all thi synnes, and that all joy and solace, bot of God and in God, be put out of thi hert. The tother es: schryft of mouth, agayn the syn of mouth. And that salle be hasty withouten delaying, naked withouten excusyng, hale withowten partyng, als for to tell a syn till a preste and another till another (say all that thow wate till ane, or els thi schryft es noght worth). The third es: satisfaccion. That has thre partyes, fastyng, prayer, and almos-dede (noght anly to gif pore men mete and drynk, bot for to forgyf tham that dose the wrange, and prai for tham, and enforme tham how thai sall do, that er in poynt to perisch).

For the thyrd thyng, thou sall wyt that clennes behoves be keped in hert, and in mouth, and in werk. Clennes of hert thre thynges kepes. Ane es waker thoght and stabel of God. Another es bisynes to kepe thi fyve wittes, sa that all the wyked styryngs of tham be closed out of the flesche. The third, honest occupacion and prophetabyll. Alswa clennes of mouth kepes thre thynges. Ane es, that thow umthynk the before or thou speke. Another es, that thou be not of mikel speche, but of litel,

---

^*m* to] tu Dd.

and namly ay til thi hert be stabeld in the luf of Jhesu Cryst, swa that
the thynk that thou lokes ay on hym, whether thou speke or noght. Bot
swilk a grace may thou noght have in the fyrst day, bot with lang travell
and grete bysines to lof hym with custom, so that the egh of thi hert be
ay upwarde, sall thou com thartill. The thyrd, that thou for na thyng,
ne for na mekenes, lye on any man. For ilk a lee es syn, and il, and noght
Goddes will. The thar noght tell all the soth ay, bot if thow will; bot al
lees hate. Yf thou say a thyng of thiself that semes thi lovyng, and thou
say it to the lovyng of God and help of other, thou dos noght unwisely,
for thou spekes sothfastnes. Bot if thou will have oght pryve, tel it til
nane bot swylk ane, that thou be syker that it sulde noght be schewed,
bot anly til the lovyng of God, of wham es all gudenes, and that makes
some better than other, and gifes tham special grace, noght anely for
thamself, bot alswa for tham that wil do wele after thaire ensawmpell.

Clennes of werk thre thynges keps. Ane es: a bysi thoght of dede.
For the wyse man says: 'Umbethynk the of thi last endyng, and thou
sall noght syn.'[11] Another: Fle fra ill felyschypp, that gyfs mare
ensawmpel to luf the worlde than God, erth than heven, filth of body
than clennes of saule. The third es: Temperance and discrecion in mete
and drynk, that it be nowther til owtrage, ne beneth skilwys sustinance
for thi body. For both comes til an ende, owtrage and over mykel
fastyng; for nowther es Gods will. And that many wil noght wene, for
noght that man may say. Yf thou take sustenance of swilk gude als God
sendys for the tyme and the day, what it be (I owt-take na maner of
mete that Cristen men uses), with discrecion and mesur, thou dose
wele; for sa dyd Criste hymself and hys apostels. Yf thou leve many
metes that men has, noght dispysand the mete that God has made till
mannes helpe, bot for the thynk that thou hase na nede tharof, thou
dose wele, if thou se that thow ert stalworth to serve God, and that it
brekes noght thi stomake. For if thou have broken it with ovre mikel
abstynence, the es reft appetyte of mete, and oft sal thou be in qwathes,
als thou war redy to gyf the gast; and wit thou wele, thou synned in that
dede.

And thou may not witt sone whethir thi abstinence be agayne the
or with the. For the tyme that thou ert yong, I rede that thou ete and
drynk better and war als it comes, that thou be noght begylt; and
afterwarde, when thou has proved many thynges and overcommen
many temptacions, and knawes better thiself and God than thou dyd,
than, if thou se that it be at do, thou mai take til mare abstinence. And

whils thou may, do pryve penance, that al men thar noght wyt.
Ryghtwysnes es noght al in fastyng, ne in etyng: bot thou ert ryghtwys,
if all ilyke be to the, despyte and lovyng, povert and rytches, hunger
and nede, als delytes and dayntes. If thou take thir with a lowyng of
God, I halde the blyssed, and hee before Jhesu. Men that comes til the,
thai luf the for thai se thi grete abstinens, and for thai se the enclosed.
Bot I may not love the so lyghtly, for oght that I se the do withowten;
bot if thi wil be conformed enterely to Goddes will. And sett noght by
thar lovyng ne thar lackyng, and gyf thou never tale, if thai speke lesse
gode of the than thai dyd; bot that thou be byrnander in Goddes luf
than thou was. For a thyng warne I the: I hope that God has na perfyte
servand in erth withouten ennemyes of som men; for anely wretchednes
has na enmy.

    For to draw us, that we conforme oure will till Goddes will er thre
thynges. Ane es: ensawmpel of haly men and haly wymen, the whilk
war ententife nyght and day to serve God and drede hym and luf hym.
And we folow tham in erth, we moun be with tham in heven. Another
es: the godenes of oure Lorde, that despises nane, bot gladly receyves
all that comes till hys mercy; and he es hamlyer to tham than brother or
syster, or any frende that thai maste luf or maste treystes on. The thyrd
es: the wonderfull joy of the kyngdom of heven, that es mare than tong
may tell, or hert mai thynk, or egh may se, or ere may here. It es swa
mykel, that als in hel myght na thyng lyve for mykel pyne, bot at the
myght of God suffers tham noght to dye, swa the joy in the syght of
Jhesu in his Godhede es swa mykel that thai mond dye for joy, if it ne
war his godenes, that will that his lovers be lyvand ay in blys, als his
ryghtwysnes wil that al that lufed hym noght be ay lyvand in fyre that
es horribel till any man at thynk, loke then what it es to fele. Bot thai
that will not thynk it and drede it now, thai sal suffer it evermare.

    Now hase thow herd how thou may dispose thi lyfe, and rewle it
to Goddes will. Bot I vate wele that thou desyres to here some special
poynt of the luf of Jhesu Criste, and of contemplatyf lyfe, the whilk
thou hase taken the till at mens syght. Als I have grace and konnyng, I
will lere the.

(7)   *Amore langueo*.[12] Thir twa wordes er wryten in the Boke of Lufe,
that es kalled the Sang of Lufe, or the Sang of Sanges. For he that mykel
lufes, hym lyst oft syng of his luf, for joy that he or scho hase when thai
thynk on that that thai lufe, namely if thair lover be trew and lufand.

And this es the Inglisch of thies twa wordes: 'I languysch for lufe.'

Sere men in erth has sere gyftes and graces of God; bot the special gift of thas that ledes solitary lyf es for to lufe Jhesu Criste. Thow says me: 'All men lufes hym that haldes his comawndementes.' Soth it es. Bot all men that kepes hys byddyngs, kepes noght also hys cownsayle; and all that dos his cownsell er noght also fulfyld of the swetnes of his lufe, ne feles noght the fyre of byrnand luf of hert. Forthi, the diversite of lufe makes the diversite of halynes and of mede. In heven, the awngels that er byrnandest in lufe er nerrest God. Also men and women that maste has of Goddes lufe, whether thai do penance or nane, thai sall be in the heghest degre in heven; thai that lufes hym lesse, in the lawer order. If thou lufe hym mykel, mykel joy and swetnes and byrnyng thou feles in his lufe, that es thi comforth and strengh nyght and day. If thi lufe be not byrnand in hym, litel es thi delyte. For hym may na man fele in joy and swetnes, bot if thai be clene and fylled with his lufe; and thartill sal thou com with grete travayle in praier and thynkyng, havand swilk meditacions that er al in the lufe and in the lovyng of God.

And when thou ert at thi mete, love ay God in thi thoght at ilk a morsel, and say thus in thi hert: 'Loved be thou, keyng, and thanked be thou, keyng, and blyssed be thou, keyng, Jhesu, all my joyng, of all thi giftes gude, that for me spylt thi blude and died on the rode; thou gyf me grace to syng the sang of thi lovyng.' And thynk it noght anely whils thou etes, bot bath before and after, ay bot when thou prayes or spekes. Or if thou have other thoghtes that thou has mare swetnes in and devocion than in thase that I lere the, thou may thynk [tham].[n] For I hope that God will do swilk thoghtes in thi hert, als he es payde of, and als thou ert ordaynde for. When thou prayes, loke noght how mykel thou says, bot how wele: that the lofe of thi hert be ay upwarde, and thy thoght on that thou sayes, als mykel als thow may. If thou be in prayers and meditacions al the day, I wate wele that thou mon wax gretely in the lufe of Jhesu Cryste, and mikel fele of delyte, and within schort tyme.

(8)   Thre degrees of lufe I sal tell the, for I walde that thou moght wyn to the heest. The fyrst degre es called insuperabel; the secund, inseparabel; the thyrd es syngulere. Thi luf es insuperabel, when na thyng that es contrary til Gods lufe overcomes it, bot es stalworth

---

[n] tham] R; Dd *om.*

agayns al fandyngs, and stabel, whether thou be in ese or in angwys, or
in hele or in sekenes; swa that the thynk that thow walde noght for all
the worlde, to have it withowten ende, wreth God any tyme; and the
war lever, if outher sulde be, to suffer al the pyne and waa that myght
com til any creature, or thou wald do the thyng that suld myspay hym.
On this maner sal thi lufe be insuperabel, that na thyng may downe
bryng, bot spryngand on heght. Blyssed es he or scho that es in this
degre; bot yitt er thai blyssedar, that myght halde this degre and wyn
intil the tother, that es inseparabel.

Inseparabel es thi lufe, when al thi hert and thi thoght and thi
myght es swa haly, swa enterely, and swa perfytely festend, sett, and
stabeld in Jhesu Cryste, that thi thoght comes never of hym, never
departyd fra hym, outaken slepyng; and als sone als thou wackens, thi
hert es on hym, sayand 'Ave Maria', or 'Gloria tibi Domine', or 'Pater
noster', or 'Miserere mei Deus', if thou have bene temped in thi slepe,
or thynkand on his lufe and his lovyng, als thou dyd wakand; when
thou may na tyme forgete hym, what sa thou dose or says, than es thi
lufe inseparabel. Ful mykel grace have thai that es in this degre of lufe,
and me thynk thou, that hase noght els at do bot for to lufe God, may
com thartill, if any may gete it.

The thyrd degre es heest, and maste ferly to wyn, that es calde
synguler, for it hase na pere. Singuler lufe es, when all comforth and
solace es closed owt of thi hert, bot of Jhesu Cryste alane. Other joy
lyst it noght, for the swetnes of hym in this degre es swa comfortand
and lastand in his lufe, sa byrnand and gladand, that he or scho, that es
in this degre, mai als wele fele the fyre of lufe byrnand in thaire saule,
als thou may fele thi fynger byrn, if thou putt it in the fyre. Bot that fire,
if it be hate, es swa delitabell and wondyrful that I kan noght tell it.
Than thi sawle es Jhesu lufand, Jhesu thynkand, Jhesu desirand, anly
in the covayties of hym anedande, til hym syngand, of hym byrnand, in
hym restand. Than the sange of lovyng and of lufe es commen, than thi
thoght turnes intil sang and intil melody, than the behoves syng the
psalmes that thou before sayde, than thou mon be lang abowte few
psalmes, than the wil thynk the deed swettar than hony, for than thou
ert ful syker to se hym that thou lufes; than may thou hardely say: 'I
languysch for lufe'; than may thou say: 'I slepe, and my hert wakes.'

In the first degre, men may say: 'I languysch for lufe', or 'Me
langes in lufe'; and in the tother degre alswa, for languysyng es when
men fayles for sekenes. And thai that er in thire twa degrees fayles fra al

the covayties of this worlde, and fra lust and lykyng of synful lyfe, and settes thair entent and thair hert to the lufe of God. Forthi thai may say: 'I languysch for lufe.' And mykel mare, that er in the secund degre, than in the fyrst. Bot the sawle that es in the thyrd degre es als byrnand fyre, and as the nyghttyngale, that lufes sang and melody and fayles for mykel lufe; swa that the saule es [anely][o] comforted in lovyng and lufyng of God, and til the dede com es syngand gastly til Jhesu, and in Jhesu, and Jhesu, noght [bodyly c]ryand[p] wyth mouth – of that maner of syng[yng spe]ke[p] I noght, for that sang hase bath g[ude and ill; and][p] this maner of sang hase nane, bot if thai be in this thyrd degre of lufe, til the whilk degre it es impossibel to com, bot in a grete multitude of lufe. Forthi, if thou will wytt whatkyn joy that sang has, I say the that na man wate, bot he or scho that feles it, that has it, and that loves God, syngand tharwyth. A thyng tel I the: it es of heven; and God gyfes it til wham he wil, bot noght withouten grete grace comand before. Wha hase it, hym thynk al the sang and al the mynstralcy of erth noght bot sorow and wa thartil. In soverayne rest sal thai be, that may gete it. Gangrels and jangelers, and kepers of comers and gangars arely and late, nyght and day, or any that es takked with any syn wilfully and wittandly, or that has delyte in any erthly thyng, thai er als far tharfra, als es fra heven to erth. In the fyrst degre er many, in the tother degre er ful faa, bot in the thyrde degre unnethes er any; for ay the mare that the perfeccion es, the faer folowers it has. In the fyrst degre er [men][q] lickend to the sternes; in the tother, till the mone; in the thyrd, til the sonne. Forthi says Saynt Paule: 'Other of the sonne, other of the mone, other of the sternes';[13] swa it es of the lufers of God. In this third degre, if thou may wyn thartill, thou sall witt of mare joy than I have talde the yitt. And ymang other affeccions and sanges thou [may in thi][r] langyng syng this in thi hert til thi Lorde Jhesu, [when][r] thou covaytes hys comyng and thi gangyng:

Cantus amoris

When will thow com to comforth me and bryng me owt of care,
And gyf me the, that I may se, havand evermare?
Thi lufe es ay swettest of al that ever war.
My hert, when sal it brest for lufe? Than languyst I na mare.
For lufe my thoght has fest, and I am fayne to fare.

[o] anely] R; swa mykel Dd. [p] bodyly . . . yng . . . spe . . . gude . . . and] Dd *badly stained*.
[q] men] R; many Dd. [r] may in thi . . . when] Dd *stained*.

I stand in still mowrnyng. Of all lufelyst of lare
Es lufe langyng, it drawes me til my day,
The band of swete byrnyng, for it haldes me ay
Fra place and fra plaiyng til that I get may
The syght of my swetyng, that wendes never away.
In welth bees oure wakyng wythowten noy or nyght.
My lufe es in lastyng, and langes to that syght.

(9)   If thou wil be wele with God, and have grace to rewle thi lyf, and
com til the joy of luf, this name J H E S U, fest it swa fast in thi hert, that it
com never owt of thi thoght. And when thou spekes til hym and says
'Jhesu' thurgh custom, it sal be in thi ere joy, in thi mouth hony, and in
thi hert melody.[14] For the sall thynk joy to here that name be nevened,
swetnes to speke it, myrth and sang to thynk it. If thou thynk Jhesu
contynuly, and halde it stabely, it purges thi syn, and kyndels thi hert; it
clarifies thi sawle, it removes anger, and dose away slawnes; it
woundes in lufe, and fulfilles of charite; it chaces the devel, and puttes
oute drede; it opens heven, and makes a contemplatif man. Have in
mynde Jhesu; for al vices and fantomes it puttes owte fra the lover. And
haylce oft Mary, bath day and nyght. Mikel lufe and joy sal thou fele, if
thou wil do aftyr this lare. The thare noght covayte gretely many
bokes; halde lufe in hert and in werke, and thou hase al that we may say
or wryte. For fulnes of the law es charite;[15] in that hynges all.

(10)   But now may thou ask me, and say: 'Thou spekes sa mykel of
lufe, tel me, what es lufe? An[d]^s whar es lufe? And how I sal lufe God
verrayly? And how that I may knaw that I lufe hym? And in what state I
may maste lufe hym?' Thir er hard questyons to lere til a febyll man and
a fleschly, als I am. Bot never-the-latter tharfore I sal noght lette that I
ne sall schew my wytt, and als me thynk that it may be; for I hope in the
helpe of Jhesu, that es wel of lufe and pees and swetnes.
        The fyrst askyng es: What es lufe?[16] And I answer: Love es a
byrnand yernyng in God, with a wonderfull delyte and sykernes. God
es lyght and byrnyng. Lyght clarifies oure skyll; byrnyng kyndels oure
covayties, that we desyre noght bot hym. Lufe es a lyf, copuland
togedyr the lufand and the lufed. For mekenes makes us swete to God;
purete joynes us tyll God; lufe ma[kes]^t us ane with God. Luf es
fayrhede of al vertues. Luf es thyng, thurgh the whilk God lufes us, and

we God, and ilk ane of us other. Lufe es desyre of the hert, ay thynkand til that that it lufes; and when it hase that it lufes, than it joyes, and na thyng may make it sary. Lufe es a st[i]ryng" of the saule, for to luf God for hymself, and all other thyng for God; the whilk lufe, when it es ordaynde in God, it dose away all inordinate lufe in any thyng that es noght gude. Bot al dedely syn es inordynate lufe in a thyng that es noght; than lufe puttes out al dedely syn. Luf es a vertu, that es rightest affeccion of man saule. Trowth may be withouten lufe, bot it may noght helpe withouten it. Lufe es perfeccion of letters, vertu of prophecy, frute of trowth, help of sacramentes, stablyng of witt and conyng, rytches of pure men, lyfe of dyand men. Se how gude lufe es. If we suffer to be slayne, if we gyf al that we have til beggar staf, if we kan als mykel als al men kan in erth, til al this, withouten lufe, es noght bot sorow ordande and torment.[17] If thou will aske how gode es he or scho, ask how mykel lufes he or scho; and that kan na man tel, for I hald it bot foly to deme a mans hert, that nane knawes bot God. Lufe es a ryghtwis turnyng fra al ertly thynges, and es joynd til God withouten departyng, and kyndelde with the fire of the Haly Gaste, fer fra fylyng, fer fra corrupcion, oblyst till na vice of this lyfe, hegh aboven all fleschely lustes, ay redy and gredy til contemplacion of God, in all thynges noght overcomen, the sowme of al gude affeccyons, hele of gude maners, ende of comawndementes of God, dede of synnes, lyf of vertues, vertu whils feghtyng lastes, crowne of overcomers, mirynes til haly thoghtes. Withouten that, na man may pay God; with that, na man synnes. For if we luf God in al oure hert, thar es na thyng in us thurgh the whilk we serve to syn. Verray luf clenses the saule, and delyvers it fra the pyne of hell, and of the foule servys of syn, and of the ugly felyschip of the devels; and of the fendes sone makes God sonn, and parcenel of the heritage of heven. We sall afforce at cleth us in lufe, als the yren or the cole dose in the fyre, als the ayer dose in the sone, als the woll dose in the hewe. The cole swa clethes it in the fyre, that al es fyre; [the ayre swa clethes it in the son, that al es ligth];" and the woll swa substancialy takes the hewe, that it es lik it. In this maner sall a trewe lufar of Jhesu Criste do; his hert sal swa byrne in lufe, that it sal be turned intil fyre of lufe, and be als it war al fire, and he sal sa schyne in vertues, that in na parte of hym he be myrke in vices.

The tother askyng es: Whare es lufe? And I answer: Lufe es in the

---

" stiryng] stryng Dd.   " the ayre . . . ligth] R; Dd *om*.

hert and in the will of mane; noght in hys hand, ne in his mouth, that es at say, noght in hys wark, bot in his sawle. For many spekes gode, and dose gode, and many lufes noght God; als ypocrites, the whilk suffers grete penance, and semes haly at mens syght, bot for thai seke lovyng and honoure of men and favoure, thai have lost thar mede, and in the syght of God er the devel sons and ravysand w[o]lves.^{w18} Bot if a man gyf almose-dede, and take hym til povert, and do penance, it es signe that he lufes God; bot tharfore lufes he hym noght, bot when he forsakes the worlde anly for Goddes lufe, and settes al his thoght on God, and lufes al men als hymself, and al the gude dedes that he may do, he dose tham in entent for to pay Jhesu Criste and to cum til the rest of heven. Than he lufes God, and that luf es in his saule, and sa his dedes schewes withouten. If thou speke the gude, and do the gude, men supposes that thou lufes God. Forthi loke wele that thi thoght be in God, or elles thou dampnes thiselfe, and deceyves the men. Na thyng that I do withowten proves that I lufe God; for a wicked man myght do als mykel penance in body, als mykel wake and faste, als I do. How may I than wene that I lufe, or halde me better for that, that ilk a man may do? Certes mi hert, whethir it lufe my God or noght, wate na man bot God, for noght that thai may se me do. Wharfore luf es in will verraily, noght in warke, bot [als]^{x} a signe of lufe. For he that says he lufes God, and wil noght do in dede that in hym es to schew lufe, say hym that he lyghes. Lufe wil noght be ydel: it es wirkand som gude evermare. If it sesse of wirkyng, wit thou that it keles and wytes away.

The thirde askyng es: How sal I verrayli lufe God? I answer: Verray lufe es, to lufe hym in al thi myght stalwortly, in al thi hert wysely, in al thi sawle devowtely and swetely. Stalwortly may na man lufe hym, bot he be stalworth. He es stalworth, that es meke; for al gastly strengh comes of mekenes, on whame restes the Haly Gaste in a meke sawle.^{19} Mekenes governes us, and kepes us in al oure temptacions, swa that thai overcome us noght. Bot the devel deceyves many that er meke, thorow tribulacions and reproves and bakebitynges. Bot if thou be wrath for any anguys of this worlde, or for any worde that men says of the, or for oght that men says til the, thou ert noght meke, ne thou may swa lufe God stalwortly; for luf es stalworth als the dede,^{20} that slaes al lyvand thyng in erth, and hard als hell, that spares noght till tham that er dede. And he that lufes God perfitely, he greves

---

^{w} wolves] R; wlves DD. ^{x} als] L; in DD.

hym noght, what schame or angwys that he suffers; bot he hase delyte and covaytes that he war worthy for to suffer torment and payne for Crystes lufe. And he hase joy that men reproves hym and spekes ill of hym: als a dede man, what sa men dos or sayes, he answers noght. Ryght swa, wha sa lufes God perfitely, thai er not stirred for any worde that man may say. For he or scho kan noght lufe, that may noght suffer payne and anger for thair frendes lufe; for wha sa lufes, thai have na pyne. Prowde men or women lufes noght stalworthly; for thai er swa wayke, that thai fall at ilk a styryng of the wynde, that es temptacion. Thai seke heghar stede than Cryste; for thai wil have thair wil done, whethir it be with right or with wrang, and Cryst will nathyng be done bot wele, and withouten harme of othir men. Bot wha sa es verrayly meke, thai wil noght have thair wil in this worlde, bot that thai may have it in the tother plenarly. In na thyng may men sonar overcom the devel than in mekenes, that he mykel hates; for he may wake and faste and suffer pyne mare than any other creature may. Bot mekenes and lufe may he noght have.

Alswa the behoves luf God wysely; and that may thou noght do, bot if thou be wyse. Thou ert wyse, when thou ert pore, withowten covaytyse of this world, and dispyses thiselfe for the lufe of Jhesu Cryste, and dispendes al thi witte and al thi myght in hys servys. For sum that semes wysest er maste foles, for al thar wysdom thai spyll in covayties and bisynes abowte the world. If thou saw a man have preciouse stanes, that he myght by a kyngdom wyth, if he gaf tham for an appyl, als a barne wil do, ryghtwysly moght thou say that he war noght wyse, bot a grete fole. Alsswa, if we wyl, we have preciouse stanes, povert and penance and gastly travayle, with the whilk we may by the kyngdome of heven; for if thou lufe povert, and dispyse riches and delytes of this worlde, and halde thiself vyle and pure, and thynk that thou hase noght of thiself bot syn, for this povert thou sall have rytches withouten ende. And if thou have sorowe for thi synnes, and for thou ert swa lang in exile owte of thi contre, and forsakes the solace of this lyfe, thou sal have for this sorow the joy of heven. And if thou be in travayle, and punysche thi body skilwisly and wisely in wakyns, fastyngs, and in prayers and meditacions, and suffer hete and calde, hunger and thyrst, myses and anguys for the lufe of Jhesu Cryste, for this travel thou sal com till reste that lastes ay, and syt in a setel of joy with aungels. Bot som er, that lufes noght wysely, like til barnes, that lufes mare an appel than a castel. Swa dose many: thai gyf the joy of heven for a litel delyte of thar flesche, that es noght worth a plowme. Now may thow se that wha sa will lufe wysely, hym behoves lufe lastand thyng lastandly, and passand thyng passandly; swa that his hert be sette and festend in na thyng bot in God. And if thou will lufe Jhesu verraly, thow sal noght anly lufe hym stalwortly and wysely, bot also devowtly and swetely. Swete lufe es, when thi body es chaste and thi thoght clene. Devowte luf es, when thou offers thi prayers and thi thogtes til God with gastly joy and byrnand hert in the hete of the Haly Gaste, swa that the thynk that thi saule es, als it war, drunken for delyte and solace of the swetnes of Jhesu; and thi hert conceyves sa mykel of Goddes helpe that the thynk that thow may never be fra hym departyd. And than thou comes intil swilk rest and pees in sawle, and quiete withowten thoghtes of vanitese [or]^y of vices, als thou war in sylence and slepe and sette in Noe schyppe, that na thyng may lette the of devocion and byrnyng of swete lufe. Fra thou have getyn this lufe, all thi lyf til dede come es joy and comforth, and [thou es]^z verrayli Cristes lufer, and he restes in the, whas stede es maked in pees.^{21}

The ferth askyng was: How thou moght knaw that thou war in lufe and charite? I answer, that na man wate in erth that thai er in charite, bot if it be thorow any privelege or special grace that God hase gifen til any man or woman, that al other may noght take ensawmpel by. Haly men and women trowes that thai have trowth and hope and charite, and in that dose als wele as thai may, and hopes certaynly that thai sal be safe. Thai wate it not als tyte; for if thai wiste, thair merit war the lesse. And Salomon says that it er rightwys men and wyse men, and thair warkes er in Goddes hand.^{22} And noght forthi man wate noght whethir he be worthi hateredyn or lufe; bot al es reserved uncertayne til another worlde. Never-the-latter, if any had grace that he moght wyn til the thirde degre of lufe, that es called syngulere, he sulde knaw that he war in lufe; bot in that maner his knawyng es, that he moght never bere hym the hegher, ne be in the lesse bisynes to lufe God. Bot sa mykel the mare that he es siker of lufe, wil he be bisy to lufe hym, and drede hym, that hase made hym swilk, and done that godenes til hym. And he that es swa hee, he wil noght halde hymself worthier than the synfullest man that gaas on erth.

Alsswa, seven experimentes er, that a man be in charite. The fyrst es, when al covatise of ertly thyng es slokkend in hym. For whare sa

^{y} or] R; Dd om. ^{z} thou es] L; Dd om.

covaityse es, thare es na lufe of Cryste; than if he have na covaytyse, signe es that he hase lufe. The secunde es, byrnand yernyng of heven. For when men hase feled oght of that savoure, the mare thai have the mare thai covayte; and he that noght hase feled, noght he desires. Forthi, when any es swa mykel gyfen til the luf tharof that he kan fynd na joy in this lyfe, taken he hase that he es in charite. The thyrd es, if his tung be chawngyd, that was [wone]^a to speke of the erth now spekes of God, and of the lyf that lastes ay. The feerth es, exercise of gastly profet, als if any man or woman gyf tham enterely to Goddes servyes, and entermetes tham of nane erthly bisynes. The fift es, when the thyng that es hard in itselfe semes lyght for to do; the whilk luf makes. For als Austyne says, 'Lufreden es that bryngs the thyng that es farre nerehande, and impossibel til possibel apertly.'^{23} The sext es, hardynes of thoght, to suffer all anguyses and noyes that comes. Withowten this, al the other suffices noght. For it sal noght make a ryghtwys man sary, what sa falles hym; for he that es ryghtwys, he hates noght bot syn, he lufes noght bot God [and]^b for God, he dredes noght bot to wreth God. The sevent es, delitabilite in sawle when he es in tribulacion, and makes lovyng to God in ilk anger that he suffers; and this schewes wele that he lufes God, when na sorow may bryng hym downe. For many lufes God whils thai er in ese, and in adversitee thai grotche and falles in swa mykel sarynes that unneth may any man comforth tham; and swa sclawnder thai God, flytand and feghtand agayne his domes. And that es a caytif lovyng, that any welth of the worlde makes; bot that lovyng es of mykel pryce, that na violence of sorow may do away. The fifte askyng was: In what state men may maste lufe God? I answer: In swilk state sa it be, that men er in maste rest of body and sawle, and leest occupied with any nedes or bisynes of this worlde. For the thoght of the lufe of Jhesu Criste, and of the joy that lastes ay, sekes rest wythowten, that it be noght lettyd with comers and gangers and occupacion of worldely thynges; and it sekes within grete sylence fra the noyes of covayties and of vanitees and of ertly thoghtes. And namely, al that lufes contemplatyfe lyf, thai seke rest in body and in saule. For a grete doctor says that thai er Goddes trone, that dwelles still in a stede, and er noght abowte rennand, bot in swetnes of Cristes lufe er stabyld. And I have lufed for to sytt, for na penance, ne for na fantasy that I wild men spak of me, ne for na swylk thyng; bot anly for I knew that I loved God

---

^{a} wone] R; Dd *om.* ^{b} and] L; Dd *om.*

mare, and langar lasted within the comforth of lufe, than gangand or standand or kneleand. For sittand am I in maste rest, and my hert maste upwarde. Bot tharfore peraventure es it noght the best til another at sitte, als I did, and wil do til my dede, bot if he war disposed als I was in his sawle.

(11) Seven gyftes of the Hali Gaste er in men and wymen that er ordaynd til the joy of heven, and ledes thaire life in this worlde rightwisly. Thies thai er: wysdome, understandyng, cownsayle, strengh, connyng, pyte, and the drede of God. Begynne we at cownsel, for tharof es maste nede at the begynnyng of owre werkes, that us myslike noght afterwarde. With thier seven gyftes the Haly Gaste towches sere men serely. Cownsel es, doyng away of worldes rytches and of delytes and of al thynges that man may be ta[gild]^c with in thoght or dede; and tharwith be drawne inwardely til contemplacion of God. Understandyng es, to knaw what es for to do and what for to leve; and that, that sal be gifen, to gif it til tham that hase nede, noght til other that hase na myster. Wysdom es, forgetyng of ertly thynges, and thynkyng of heven with discrecion in al mens dedes. In this gyft schynes contemplacion, that es, a[ls]^d Saynt Austyn says, 'A gastely dede of fleschly affeccions, thorow the joy of a raysed thoght.' Strengh es, lastyng to fulfill gude purpose, that it be noght left for wele ne for wa. Pyte es, that a man be mylde, and agayne-say noght haly writte when it smytes his synnes, whethir he understand it or noght; bot in al his myght purge he the vilete of syn in hym and in other. Connyng es, that makes a man in gude hope, noght rusand hym of his rightwisnes, but sorowand of his syn; and that man geder erthly godes anely to the honoure of God, and prow til other men mare than til his self. The drede of God es, that we turne noght agayne til oure syn thorou any il eggyng; and than es drede perfyte in us and haly, when we drede to wreth God in the leste syn that we may knaw and flees it as venym.

(12) Twa lyves thar er that Cristen men lyfes. Ane es called actyve lyfe; for it es in mare bodili warke. Another, contemplatyve lyfe; for it es in mare swetnes gastely. Actife lyfe es mykel owteward, and in mare travel, and in mare peryle for the temptacions that er in the worlde. Contemplatyfe lyfe es mykel inwarde; and forthi it es lastandar and

---

^{c} tagild] T; tacit DD (cit *over erasure*). ^{d} als] A; at DD.

sykerar, restfuller, delitabiler, luflyer, and mare medeful. For it hase joy in Goddes lufe, and savowre in the lyf that lastes ay, in this present tyme if it be right ledde. And that felyng of joy in the lufe of Jhesu passes al other merites in erth; for it es swa harde to com to, for the freelte of oure flesch and the many temptacions that we er umsett with, that lettes us nyght and day. Al other thynges er lyght at come to in regarde tharof, for that may na man deserve, bot anely it es gifen of Goddes godenes til tham that verrayli gifes tham to contemplacion and til quiete for Cristes luf.

Til men or wymen that takes tham til actife lyfe, twa thynges falles. Ane, for to ordayne thair meyne in drede and in the lufe of God, and fynd tham thaire necessaries, and thamself kepe enterely the comandementes of God, doand til thar neghbur als thai wil that thai do til tham. Another es, that thai do at thar power the seven werkes of mercy: the whilk es, to fede the hungry, to gyf the thirsti a drynk, to cleth the naked, to herbar hym that hase na howsyng, to viset the seke, to comforth tham that er in prysoun, and to grave dede men. Al that [mai and hase]*e* cost: thai may noght be qwyt with ane or twa of thir, bot tham behoves do tham al, if thai wil have the benyson on domes day, that Jhesu sal til al gyf that dose tham; or els may thai drede the malysoun that al mon have that wil noght do tham, when thai had godes to do tham wyth.

Contemplatife lyf hase twa partyes, a lower and a heer. The lower party es meditacion of haly wrytyng, that es Goddes wordes, and in other gude thoghtes and swete, that men hase of the grace of God abowt the lufe of Jhesu Criste, and also in lovyng of God in psalmes and ympnes, or in prayers. The hegher party of contemplacion es behaldyng and yernyng of the thynges of heven, and joy in the Haly Gaste, that men hase oft. And if it be swa that thai be noght prayand with the mowth, bot anely thynkand of God and of the fairehede of aungels and haly sawles. Than may I say that contemplacion es a wonderful joy of Goddes luf, the whilk joy es lovyng of God, that may noght be talde; and that wonderful lovyng es in the saule, and for abundance of joy and swettenes it ascendes intil the mouth, swa that the hert and the tonge acordes in ane, and body and sawle joyes in God lyvand.

A man or woman that es ordaynd til contemplatife lyfe first God

---

e mai and hase] R; h.a.m. Dd.

enspires tham to forsake this worlde and al the vanite and the covayties and the vile luste tharof. Sythen he ledes tham by thar ane, and spekes til thar hert, and als the prophete says, 'He gifes tham at sowke the swetnes of the begynnyng of lufe.'[24] And than he settes tham in wil to gyf tham haly to prayers and meditacions and teres. Sithen, when thai have sufferd many temptacions, and foule noyes of thoghtes that er ydel, and of vanitees, the whilk wil comber tham, that can noght destroy tham, er passand away, he gars tham geder til tham thair hert, and fest anely in hym; and opens til the egh of thair sawls the gates of heven, swa that the ilk egh lokes intil heven. And than the fire of lufe verrali ligges in thair hert and byrnes tharin, and makes clene of al erthly filth. And sithen forward thai er contemplatife men, and ravyst in lufe. For contemplacion es a syght, and thai se intil heven with thar gastly egh. Bot thou sal witt, that na man hase perfite syght of heven whils thai er lifand bodili here; bot als sone als thai dye, thai er broght before God, and sese hym face til face and egh til egh, and wones with hym withouten ende. For hym thai soght, and hym thai covayted, and hym thai lufed in al thar myght.

Loo, Margarete, I have schortly sayde the the forme of lyvyng, and how thou may come til perfeccion, and to lufe hym that thou hase taken the til. If it do the gude, and profit til the, thank God, and pray for me. The grace of Jhesu Criste be with the and kepe the.[25] Amen.

Explicit forma vivendi.

ANONYMOUS

6 *The Cloud of Unknowing*

(Prologue and chapters 3–7)

'A book of contemplacyon, þe whiche is clepyd þe Clowde of Vnknowyng, in þe whiche a soule is onyd wiþ God' is the rubric of this mystical treatise in seventy-five short chapters, an heir to the *Mystica Theologia* of Pseudo-Dionysius the Areopagite (*c.* 500 AD). Certainly fittingly – and perhaps deliberately – this Middle English exposition of the Dionysian *via negativa*, the negative way to God, remains anonymous. Any pointers to the author's state of life can only be inferred from his writings: he apparently lives as a recluse; his assimilated theological learning suggests a university graduate; like a priest, he gives the blessing at the end of *The Cloud*.[1] On linguistic evidence *The Cloud* derives from the north-east Midlands in the last quarter of the fourteenth century, and hence the *Cloud*-author and Walter Hilton were living and writing in much the same area and period, with parallel passages in their writings suggesting that one or both knew the other's work. *The Book of Privy Counselling* refers to 'other diverse places of myn owne writyng' (see below, p. 93), mentioning *The Cloud*, *The Epistle on Prayer*, and an English translation of *Mystica Theologia*, the *Hid Divinite*. Of this, the prologue refers to 'a book wretin before, the whiche is clepid *The Cloude of Unknowing*', and also acknowledges 'a worthi expositour' of Dionysius, that is Thomas Gallus (d. 1246), whose influence on *The Cloud* has been detected.[2] To this group of acknowledged works by the *Cloud*-author are usually added three related treatises on aspects of the spiritual life: *The Pistle of Discrecioun of Stirings*, *The Tretyse of the Stodye of Wysdome that Men Clepen Benjamyn* (an abridged paraphrase of Richard of St Victor's *Benjamin Minor*), and *The Tretis of Discrescyon of Spirites* (drawing on two of St Bernard's sermons).

Referring to Pseudo-Dionysius, *The Cloud* declares 'Who-so wil loke Denis bookes, he schal fynde þat his wordes wilen cleerly aferme al þat I haue seyde' (ch. 70), and also 'Seynte Denis seyde: "Þe moste goodly knowyng of God is þat, þe whiche is knowyn bi vnknowyng"'. God himself is unknowable, and there always intervenes between God and the soul 'a derknes, and as it were a cloude of unknowing, thou wost never what', although God may 'sum tyme parauenture seend oute a beme of goostly liȝt, peersyng þis cloude of vnknowing þat is bitwix þee & hym, & schewe þee sum of his priuite' (ch. 26). The first half or so of *The Cloud* recurs to its key idea of the contemplative soul as placed between two clouds: the cloud of unknowing always remaining between it and God, and the cloud of forgetting, down into which the soul should suppress every recollection of worldly things and thoughts. Much of *The Cloud*'s teaching deals with overcoming difficulties intrinsic to the very nature of human psychology (analysed in chs. 63–7) and to the use of language itself ('Beware that thou conceyve not bodely that that is mente goostly, thof al it be spokyn in bodely wordes . . . ' ch. 61), although the author is a master of the strategic, startling use of imaginative language. With the past forgotten and the attention cleared of all sensory and intellectual distractions, with the imagination checked and all discursive thought superseded, the contemplative's whole life must be one of unceasing and undeflected longing for God – sought in his undifferentiated and absolute nature – who remains incomprehensible to every created intellect, but not to love. To love without knowing is the business of that strenuous contemplative 'werk' enjoined repeatedly by the *Cloud*-author, for whom love is man's supreme cognitive power ('Loue may reche to God in þis liif, bot not knowing', ch. 8). To that 'blind' and 'nakid' intent, an outreaching longing, with its prerequisite humility, the text insistently spurs its reader in pithy, terse English, although mindful that the initiative rests with God ('Be þou bot þe tre, & lat it be þe wriȝt; be þou bot þe hous, & lat it be þe hosbonde wonyng þer-in,' ch. 34). All progress depends on grace, although none capable of receiving it will lack such grace, and tips are offered on testing one's vocation ('alle holy desires growen bi delaies . . . ' ch. 75). What the contemplative may through grace attain is however carefully defined: 'þof al it may be seide in maner þat in þis tyme God & þou ben not two bot one in spirit – in so moche þat þou or anoþer for soche onheed þat feleþ þe perfeccion of þis werk may soþfastly, bi witnes of Scripture, be clepid a God – neuerþeles ȝit þou arte bineþe hym' (ch. 67).

As chapter 4 reveals, *The Cloud* is addressed to a particular twenty-four year old disciple, a solitary who is on the threshold of unitive prayer, and its teaching is intended solely for those 'in the sovereinnest pointe of contemplatife leving' (p. 69; also ch. 74). The author is justifiably anxious lest the book's teaching be read selectively and out of context by those whom it may mislead. Unapologetically directed towards the needs of a specialist readership, *The Cloud* begins a long way on from the beginning in the spiritual life, takes much for granted, and is focused intently, even narrowly, on the initial attainment of contemplation and the means to that end. Written with wry and candid informality, as if to a known recipient, *The Cloud* speaks with unfailing panache in an unforgettably individual voice. Firm and clear in edification, sinuous in persuasion, feline in sense of pace it coaches its pupil, sometimes through vivid imaginary dialogues where the reader's question is anticipated and his understanding transcended by some staggering reply. 'Wirche more wiþ a list [craft, tactics], þen wiþ any liþer [brute] strengþe' (ch. 46) cites a proverb that matches well with *The Cloud*'s wisdom. But the author's own mystical experience, although implicit in his guidance towards contemplation, remains as undescribed in the text as the attainment of the contemplative goal. *The Cloud* is for use – a means, an instrument, a map – and in the early chapters the author sets out his distinctive way.

Base manuscript: BL MS Harley 674 (H), fols. 17v–18v, 24v–31v. Also cited: CUL MS Kk. 6. 26 (Kk).

Here biginneth the prolog.

In the name of the Fader and of the Sone and of the Holy Goost.

I charge thee and I beseche thee, with as moche power and vertewe as the bonde of charite is sufficient to suffre, whatsoever thou be that this book schalt have in possession – outher bi propirte outher by keping, by bering as messenger or elles bi borowing – that in as moche as in thee is by wille and avisement, neither thou rede it, ne write it, ne speke it, ne yit suffre it be red, wretyn, or spokyn, of any or to any, bot yif it be of soche one or to soche one that hath (bi thi supposing) in a trewe wille and by an hole entent, purposed him to be a parfite folower of Criste, not only in actyve levyng, bot in the sovereinnest pointe of contemplatife leving the whiche is possible by grace for to be comen to in this present liif of a parfite soule yit abiding in this deedly body; and therto that doth that in him is, and bi thi supposing, hath do longe tyme before, for to able him to contemplative levyng by the vertuous menes of active levyng. For elles it acordeth nothing to him.

And, over this, I charge thee and I beseche thee bi the autorite of charite, that yif any soche schal rede it, write it, or speke it, or elles here it be red or spokin, that thou charge hem, as I do thee, for to take hem tyme to rede it, speke it, write it, or here it, al over. For paraventure ther is som mater therin, in the beginnyng or in the middel, the whiche is hanging and not fully declared ther it stondeth; and yif it be not there, it is sone after, or elles in the ende. Wherfore, yif a man saw o mater and not another, paraventure he might lightly be led into errour. And therfore, in eschewing of this errour bothe in thiself and in alle other, I preye thee par charite do as I sey thee.

Fleschely janglers, opyn preisers and blamers of hemself or of any other, tithing tellers, rouners and tutilers of tales, and alle maner of pinchers: kept I never that thei sawe this book. For myn entent was never to write soche thing unto hem. And therfore I wolde that thei medel not therwith, neither thei ne any of thees corious lettred or lewed men. Ye, though al that thei be ful good men of active levyng, yit this mater acordeth nothing to hem; bot yif it be to thoo men the whiche, [th]ough*a* al thei stonde in actyvete bi outward forme of levyng, nevertheles yit bi inward stering after the prive sperit of God, whos domes ben hid, thei ben ful graciously disposid, not contynowely as it is propre to verrey contemplatyves, bot than and than to be parceners in the hieghst pointe of this contemplative acte: yif soche men might se it, thei schuld by the grace of God be greetly counforted therby. . . .

(3)   Lift up thin herte unto God with a meek steryng of love; and mene himself, and none of his goodes. And therto loke thee lothe to thenk on ought bot on hymself, so that nought worche in thi witte ne in thi wille bot only himself. And do that in thee is to forgete alle the creat[u]res*b* that ever God maad and the werkes of hem, so that thi thought ne thi desire be not directe ne streche to any of hem, neither in general ne in special. Bot lat hem be, and take no kepe to hem.

This is the werk of the soule that moste plesith God. Alle seintes and aungelles han joie of this werk, and hasten hem to helpe it in al here might. Alle feendes ben wood whan thou thus doste, and proven for to felle it in alle that thei kun. Alle men levyng in erthe ben wonderfuli holpen of this werk, thou wost not how. Ye, the soules in purgatori ben esed of theire peine by vertewe of this werk. Thiself arte clensid and maad vertewos by no werk so mochel. And yit it is the lightest werk of alle, when a soule is holpen with grace in sensible liste, and sonnest done. Bot elles it is hard and wonderful to thee for to do.

Lette not therfore, bot travayle therin tyl thou fele lyst. For at the first tyme when thou dost it, thou fyndest bot a derknes, and as it were a cloude of unknowyng, thou wost never what, savyng that thou felist in thi wille a nakid entent unto God. This derknes and this cloude is, howsoever thou dost, bitwix thee and thi God, and letteth thee that thou maist not see him cleerly by light of understonding in thi reson, ne fele him in swetnes of love in thin affeccion. And therfore schap thee to

---

a though] ʒouʒ H.   *b* creatures] creatres H.

bide in this derknes as longe as thou maist, evermore criing after him that thou lovest; for yif ever schalt thou fele him or see him, as it may be here, it behoveth alweis be in this cloude and in this derknes.[3] And yif thou wilte besily travayle as I bid thee, I triste in his mercy that thou schalt come therto.

(4) But forthi that thou schalt not erre in this worching, and wene that it be otherwise then it is, I schal telle thee a lityl more therof, as me thinketh. This werk asketh no longe tyme er it be ones treulich done, as sum men wenen; for it is the schortest werke of alle that man may ymagyn. It is neither lenger ne schorter then is an athomus;[4] the whiche athomus, by the diffinicion of trewe philisophres in the sciens of astronomye, is the leest partie of tyme. And it is so litil that, for the littilnes of it, it is undepartable and neighhonde incomprehensible. This is that tyme of the whiche it is wretyn: Alle tyme that is yoven to thee, it schal be askid of thee how thou haste dispendid it. And skilful thing it is that thou yeve acompte of it; for it is neither lenger ne schorter, bot even acording to one only steryng that is withinne the principal worching might of thi soule, the whiche is thi wille. For even so many willinges or desiringes – and no mo ne no fewer – may be and aren in one oure in thi wille, as aren athomus in one oure. And yif thou were reformid bi grace to the first state of mans soule, as it was bifore sinne,[5] than thou schuldest evermore, bi help of that grace, be lorde of that stering or of thoo sterynges; so that none yede forby, bot alle thei schulde streche into the soverein desirable and into the heighest wilnable thing, the whiche is God.

For he is even mete to oure soule by mesuring of his Godheed; and oure soule even mete unto him bi worthines of oure creacion to his ymage and to his licnes. And he by himself withouten moo, and none bot he, is sufficient at the fulle, and mochel more, to fulfille the wille and the desire of oure soule. And oure soule, bi vertewe of this reformyng grace, is mad sufficient at the fulle to comprehende al him by love, the whiche is incomprehensible to alle create knowable might, as is aungel and mans soule. (I mene by theire knowyng and not by theire lovyng, and therfore I clepe hem in this caas knowable mightes).

Bot s[e]th:[c] alle resonable creatures, aungel and man, hath in

---

[c] seth] кk; sith н.

hem, ilchone by hemself, o principal worching might, the whiche is clepid a knowable might, and another principal worching might, the whiche is clepid a lovyng might: of the whiche two mightes, to the first, the whiche is a knowyng might, God, that is the maker of hem, is evermore incomprehensible; and to the secound, the whiche is the lovyng myght, in ilch one diversly he is al comprehensible at the fulle, in so mochel that o lovyng soule only in itself, by vertewe of love, schuld comprehende in it hym that is sufficient at the fulle – and mochel more, withoute comparison – to fille alle the soules and aungelles that ever may be. And this is the eendles merveilous miracle of love, the whiche schal never take eende; for ever schal he do it, and never schal he seese for to do it. See, who bi grace see may, for the felyng of this is eendles blisse; and the contrary is eendles pyne.

And therfore whoso were refourmyd by grace thus to continow in keping of the sterynges of the wille, schuld never be in this liif – as he may not be withouten thees sterynges in kynde – withouten som taast of the eendles swetnes; and in the blisse of heven withouten the fulle food. And therfore have no wonder thof I stere thee to this werk. For this is the werk, as thou schalt here after, in the whiche man schuld have contynowed yif he never had synned, and to the whiche worching man was maad, and alle thing for man, to help him and forther him therto, and by the whiche a man schal be reparailed ayein. And for the defaylyng in this worching a man falleth depper and depper in synne, and ferther and ferther fro God. And by kepyng and contynowel worching in this werk only, withouten mo, a man evermore riseth hier and hier fro synne, and nerer and nerer unto God.

And therfore take good keep into tyme, how that thou dispendist it. For nothing is more precious than tyme. In oo litel tyme, as litel as it is, may heven be wonne and lost. A token it is that time is precious: for God, that is yever of tyme, yeveth never two tymes togeder, bot ich one after other. And this he doth for he wil not reverse the ordre or the ordinel cours in the cause of his creacion. For tyme is maad for man, and not man for tyme. And therfore God, that is the rewler of kynde, wil not in the yevyng of tyme go before the steryng of kynde in a mans soule; the whiche is even acordyng to o tyme only. So that man schal have none excusacion ayens God in the dome and at the yevyng of acompte of dispendyng of tyme, seiing: 'Thou yevest two tymes at ones, and I have bot o steryng at ones.'

Bot soroufuly thou seist now: 'How schal I do? And sith this is

soth that thou seist, how schal I yeve acompte of iche [tyme]*d* diversly; I
that into this day, now of foure and twenty yere age, never toke hede of
tyme? Yif I wolde now amende it, thou wost wel, bi verrey reson of thi
wordes wretyn before, it may not be after the cours of kynde ne of
comoun grace, that I schuld mowe kepe or elles make aseeth to any mo
tymes than to thoo that ben for to come. Ye, and moreover wel I wote,
bi verrey proef, that of thoo that ben to come I schal on no wise, for
habundaunce of freelte and slownes of sperite, mowe kepe one of an
hondred; so that I am verrely conclude in theese resons. Help me now,
for the love of Jhesu!'

   'Right wel hast thou seide 'for the love of Jhesu'. For in the love of
Jhesu there schal be thin help. Love is soche a might that it makith alle
thing comoun. Love therfore Jhesu, and alle thing that he hath it is thin.
He by his Godheed is maker and yever of tyme. He bi his manheed is the
verrey keper of tyme. And he, bi his Godheed and his manheed togeders,
is the trewist domesman and the asker of acompte of dispending of
tyme. Knyt thee therfore bi him by love and by beleve; and than by
vertewe of that knot thou schalt be comoun parcener with him and with
alle that by love so ben knittyd unto him; that is to sey, with oure Lady
Seinte Mary, that ful was of alle grace in kepyng of tyme, with alle the
aungelles of heven that never may lese tyme, and with alle the seintes in
heven and in erthe, that by the grace of Jhesu kepen tyme ful justly in
vertewe of love. Loo! here lith counforte; construe thou cleerly and pike
thee sum profite. Bot of oo thing I warne thee amonges alle other: I
cannot see who may trewliche chalenge comunite thus with Jhesu and
his just moder, his highe aungelles and also with his seyntes, bot yif it be
soche one that doth that in hym is, with helping of grace, in kepyng of
tyme; so that he be seen to be a profiter on his partye, so litil as is, unto
the comunite, as ich one of hem doth on his.

   And therfore take kepe to this werk and to the merveylous maner
of it withinne in thi soule. For yif it be trewlich conceyved, it is bot a
sodeyn steryng, and as it were unavisid, speedly springing unto God as
sparcle fro the cole. And it is merveylous to noumbre the sterynges that
may be in one oure wrought in a soule that is disposid to this werk. And
yit, in o steryng of alle theese, he may have sodenly and parfitely
foryeten alle create thing. Bot fast after iche steryng, for corupcion of
the flesche, it falleth doune ayein to som thought or to some done or

d tyme] кк; thing н.

undone dede. Bot what therof? For fast after, it riseth ayen as sodenly as it did bifore.

And here mowe men schortly conceyve the maner of this worching, and cleerly knowe that it is fer fro any fantasie, or any fals ymaginacion, or queynte opinion; the whiche ben brought in, not by soche a devoute and a meek blynde stering of love, bot by a proude, coryous and an ymaginatiif witte. Soche a proude, corious witte behoveth algates be born doun and stifly troden doun under fote, yif this werke schal trewly be conceyvid in purete of spirite. For whoso herith this werke outher be red or spoken, and weneth that it may or schuld be comen to by travayle in theire wittes – and therfore thei sitte and sechin in theire wittes how that it may be, and in this coriouste thei travayle theire ymaginacion paraventure ayens cours of kynde, and thei feyne a maner of worching, the whiche is neither bodily ne goostly – trewly this man, whatsoever he be, is perilously disseyvid; in so mochel that, bot yif God of his grete goodnes schewe his mercyful myracle and make hym sone to leve werk and meek hym to counsel of provid worchers, he schal falle outher into frenesies, or elles into other grete mischeves of goostly sinnes and devels disseites; thorow the whiche he may lightly be lorne, bothe liif and soule, withouten any eende. And therfore for Goddes love beware in this werk, and travayle not in thi wittes ne in thin ymaginacion on no wise. For I telle thee trewly, it may not be comen to by travaile in theim; and therfore leve theim and worche not with theim.

And wene not, for I clepe it a derknes or a cloude, that it be any cloude congelid of the humours that fleen in the ayre, ne yit any derknes soche as is in thin house on nightes, when thi candel is oute. For soche a derknes and soche a cloude maist thou ymagin with coriouste of witte, for to bere before thin ighen in the lightest day of somer; and also ayenswarde in the derkist night of wynter thou mayst ymagin a clere schinyng light. Lat be soche falsheed; I mene not thus. For when I sey derknes, I mene a lackyng of knowyng; as alle that thing that thou knowest not, or elles that thou hast foryetyn, it is derk to thee, for thou seest it not with thi goostly ighe. And for this skile it is not clepid a cloude of the eire, bot a cloude of unknowyng, that is bitwix thee and thi God.

(5)   And yif ever thou schalt come to this cloude and wone and worche therin as I bid thee, thee byhoveth, as this cloude of

unknowyng is aboven thee, bitwix thee and thi God, right so put a cloude of forgetyng bineth thee, bitwix thee and alle the cretures that ever ben maad. Thee thinketh, paraventure, that thou arte ful fer fro God, forthi that this cloude of unknowing is bitwix thee and thi God; bot sekirly, and it be wel conseyved, thou arte wel ferther fro hym when thou hast no cloude of foryetyng bitwix thee and alle the creatures that ever ben maad. As ofte as I sey 'alle the creatures that ever ben maad', as ofte I mene, not only the self creatures, bot also alle the werkes and the condicions of the same creatures. I oute-take not o creature, whether thei ben bodily creatures or goostly, ne yit any condicion or werk of any creature, whether thei be good or ivel; bot schortly to sey, alle schuld be hid under the cloude of foryetyng in this caas.

For thof al it be ful profitable sumtyme to think of certeyne condicions and dedes of sum certein special creatures, nevertheles yit in this werke it profiteth lityl or nought. For why mynde or thinkyng of any creature that ever God maad, or of any of theire dedes outher, it is a maner of goostly light; for the ighe of thi soule is openid on it and even ficchid therapon, as the ighe of a schoter is apon the prik that he schoteth to. And o thing I telle thee, that alle thing that thou thinkest apon it is aboven thee for the tyme, and bitwix thee and thi God. And in so mochel thou arte the ferther fro God, that ought is in thi mynde bot only God. Ye, and yif it be cortesye and semely to sey, in this werk it profiteth litil or nought to think of the kyndenes or the worthines of God, ne on oure Lady, ne on the seintes or aungelles in heven, ne yit on the joies in heven: that is to say, with a special beholding to hem, as thou woldest bi that beholding fede and encrees thi purpos. I trowe that on no wise it schuld be so in this caas and in this werk. For thof al it be good to think [a]pon*e* the kindenes of God, and to love hym and preise him for hem: yit it is fer betyr to think apon the nakid beyng of him, and to love him and preise him for himself.

(6) But now thou askest me and seiest: 'How schal I think on himself, and what is hee?' And to this I cannot answere thee bot thus: 'I wote never.' For thou hast brought me with thi question into that same derknes, and into that same cloude of unknowyng that I wolde thou were in thiself. For of alle other creatures and theire werkes – ye, and of

---

e apon] кk; onpon н.

the werkes of God self – may a man thorou grace have fulheed of
knowing, and wel to kon thinke on hem; bot of God himself can no
man thinke. And therfore I wole leve al that thing that I can think, and
chese to my love that thing that I cannot think. For whi he may wel be
loved, bot not thought. By love may he be getyn and holden; bot bi
thought neither. And therfore, thof al it be good sumtyme to think of
the kyndnes and the worthines of God in special, and thof al it be a light
and a party of contemplacion: nevertheles in this werk it schal be
casten down and keverid with a cloude of foryetyng. And thou schalt
step aboven it stalworthly, bot listely, with a devoute and a plesing
stering of love, and fonde for to peerse that derknes aboven thee. And
smyte apon that thicke cloude of unknowyng with a scharp darte of
longing love, and go not thens for thing that befalleth.

(7)   And yif any thought rise and wil prees algates aboven thee,
bitwix thee and that derknes, and asche thee seiing: 'What sekist thou,
and what woldest thou have?' sey thou that it is God that thou woldest
have. 'Him I coveite, him I seche, and noght bot him.' And yif he ascke
thee what is that God, sey thou that it is God that maad thee and
bought thee, and that graciously hath clepid thee to his love. 'And in
him,' sei thou, 'kanst no skile.' And therfore sey: 'Go thou down ayein.'
And treed him fast doun with a steryng of [love],[f] thof he seme to thee
right holy, and seme to thee as he wolde help thee to seke hym.

     For paraventure he wil bryng to thi minde diverse ful feire and
wonderful pointes of his kyndnes, and sey that he is ful swete and ful
lovyng, ful gracious and ful mercyful. And yif thou wilt here him, he
coveiteth no beter; for at the last he wil thus jangle ever more and more
til he bring thee lower to the mynde of his passion. And there wol he lat
the see the wonderful kyndnes of God; and if thou here him, he kepeth
no beter. For sone after he wil lat thee see thin olde wrechid leving; and
paraventure, in seing and thinkyng therof, he wil bryng to thi mynde
som place that thou hast wonid in before this tyme. So that at the last,
er ever wite thou, thou schalt be scaterid thou wost never where. The
cause of this scateryng is that thou herddist him first wilfuly,
answeredist him, resceivedist him and letest him allone.

     And yit, nevertheles, the thing that he seide was bothe good and
holy; ye, and so holy, that what man or womman that wenith to come

---

[f] love] for add. H.

to contemplacion withoutyn many soche swete meditacions of theire owne wrechidnes, the passion, the kyndenes and the grete goodnes and the worthines of God comyng before, sekirly he schal erre and faile of his purpos. And yit, nevertheles, it behoveth a man or a womman, that hath longe tyme ben usid in theese meditacions, algates leve hem, and put hem and holde hem fer doun under the cloude of foryetyng, yif ever schal he peerse the cloude of unknowyng bitwix him and his God.

Therfore, what tyme that thou purposest thee to this werk, and felest bi grace that thou arte clepid of God, lift than up thin herte unto God with a meek steryng of love. And mene [God]^g that maad thee, and bought thee, and that graciousli hath clepid thee to this werk; and resseive none other thought of God. And yit not alle theese, bot thee list; for it suffiseth inough a naked entent directe unto God, withouten any other cause then himself.

And yif thee list have this entent lappid and foulden in o worde, for thou schuldest have betir holde therapon, take thee bot a litil worde of o silable; for so it is betir then of two, for ever the schorter it is, the betir it acordeth with the werk of the spirite. And soche a worde is this worde GOD or this worde LOVE. Cheese thee whether thou wilt, or another as the list: whiche that thee liketh best of o silable. And fasten this worde to thin herte, so that it never go thens for thing that bifalleth.

This worde schal be thi scheeld and thi spere, whether thou ridest on pees or on werre. With this worde thou schalt bete on this cloude and this derknes aboven thee. With this worde thou schalt smite doun al maner thought under the cloude of forgeting; in so mochel that yif any thought prees apon thee to aske thee what thou woldest have, answere him with no mo wordes bot with this o worde. And yif he profre thee of his grete clergie to expoune thee that worde and to telle thee the condicions of that worde, sey him that thou wilt have it al hole, and not broken ne undon. And yif thow wilt holde thee fast on this purpos, sekir be thou he wil no while abide. And whi? For thou wilt not late him fede him on soche swete meditacions touchid before. . . .

^{g} God] love *add*. H.

7 The Book of Privy Counselling

'& ȝif þee þenk þat þer be any mater þer-in þat þou woldest haue more openid þan it is, late me wetyn whiche it is and & þi conceyte þer-apon; & at my simple kunnyng it schal be amendid ȝif I kan' (*Cloud*, ch. 74). To such an offer *The Book of Privy Counselling* may well represent the outcome, perhaps written some years later, and addressed to a particular 'goostly frende'. Imputations that the author's spiritual counsel is too abstruse are briskly dismissed, and in less than half the length the *Privy Counselling* distils *The Cloud*'s essential themes, developing some in more detail, insisting on the 'nakid entent' and the disciplined 'werk' of contemplation. If the manner of instruction is concentrated, the mood is sober; the sparkle of *The Cloud* occurs more intermittently, although unmistakably. Differences from *The Cloud* in pace, tone and content reflect the recipient's intellectual and spiritual development. This is discourse between two specialists in advanced contemplation: the recipient can now be instructed with scriptural quotation,[1] and the whole epistle sustains its argument to the reader with a determined and unemotional cogency, as urgently focused and undispersed as that loving longing for God that it commends.

Base manuscript: BL MS Harley 674 (H), fols. 92r–110v. Also cited: CUL MS Kk. 6. 26 (Kk).

Goostly freende in God, as touching thin inward ocupacion as me think thee disposid, I speke at this tyme in specyal to thiself, and not to alle thoo that this writyng scholen here in general. For yif I schuld write unto alle, than I must write thing that were acordyng to alle generaly. Bot sith I at this tyme schal write unto thee in special, therfore I write none other thing bot soche as me think that is moste speedful and acording to thin disposicion only. If eny other be so disposid as thou arte, to whom this writing may profite as unto thee, in so moche the betir, for I am wel apaied. Nevertheles, at this tyme thin owne inward disposicion is only by itself, as I may conceive it, the poynte and the prik of my beholdyng. And therfore to thee, in persone of alle other liche unto thee, I sei thus:

Whan thou comyst bi thiself thenk not before what thou schalt do after, bot forsake as wel good thoughtes as ivel thoughtes. And prey not with thi mouth bot thee list right wel; and than, yif thou ought schalt sey, loke not how mochel ne how litil that it be, ne charge not what it is ne what it bemenith, be it orison, be it psalm, ympne or antime, or any other preyer, general or specyal, mental withinne enditid bi thought or vocale withouten by pronounsyng of worde. And loke that nothing leve in thi worching mynde bot a nakid entent streching into God, not clothid in any specyal thought of God in hymself, how he is in himself or in any of his werkes, bot only that he is as he is. Lat hym be so, I prey thee, and make him on none other wise. Seche no ferther in hym by sotiltee of witte. That byleve b[e]^a thi grounde. This nakid entent, freely fastenid and groundid in verrey beleve, schal be nought elles to thi thought and to thi felyng bot a nakid thought and a blynde feling of thin owne beyng: as yif thou seidist thus unto God withinne in thi menyng, 'That at I am, Lorde, I offre unto thee, withoutyn any lokyng to eny qualite of thi beyng, bot only that thou arte as thou arte, withouten any more.'

That meek derknes be thi mirour^2 and thi mynde hole. Thenk no ferther of thiself than I bid thee do of thi God, so that thou be on with hym in spirit as thus, withoutyn departyng and scatering of mynde. For he is thi being, and in him thou arte that at thou arte, not only bi cause and bi beyng, bot also he is in thee bothe thi cause and thi beyng. And therfore thenk on God as in this werk as thou dost on thiself, and on thiself as thou dost on God, that he is as he is and thou arte as thou arte, so that thi thought be not scaterid ne departid, bot onid in hym that is al; evermore savyng this difference bitwix thee and him, that he is thi being and thou not his. For thof it be so that alle thinges ben in hym bi cause and bi beyng and he be in alle thinges here cause and here being, yit in himself only he is his owne cause and his owne being. For as nothing may be withoutyn him, so may he not be withoutyn himself. He is being bothe to himself and to alle. And in that he is only departid from alle that he is being bothe of hymself and of alle; and in that he is one in alle and alle in him that alle thinges han her beinges in him and he is being of alle. Thus schal thi thought and thi feling be onid with hym in grace withoutyn departing, alle corious sechinges in the queinte qualitees of thi blinde beyng or of his fer put bac; that thi thought be nakid and thi felyng nothing defoulid, and thou, nakidly as thou arte,

---

^{a} be] ⱪⱪ; by ⱨ.

with the touching of grace be prively fed in thi felyng only with hym as he is; bot blyndly and in partie, as it may be here in this liif, that thi longing desire be evermore worching.

Loke up than lightly and sey to thi Lorde, outher with mouth or mening of hert: 'That at I am, Lorde, I offre unto thee, for thou it arte.' And thenk nakidly, pleynly and boistously that thou arte as thou arte, withoutyn any maner of coriouste. This is litil maistrie for to think, yif it were bodyn to the lewdist man or womman that levith in the comounist wit of kynde in this liif, as me thenkith. And therfore softely, mornyngly and smylingly I merveyle me somtyme whan I here sum men sey (I mene not simple lewid men and wommen, bot clerkes [and men]^b of grete kunnyng) that my writyng to thee and to other is so harde and so heigh, and so curious and so queinte, that unnethes it may be conceivid of the sotelist clerk or wittid man or womman in this liif, as thei seyn. Bot to thees men most I answere and sey that it is moche worthi to be sorowid, and of God and his lovers to be mercyfuly scornid and bitterly reprovid, that now thees dayes not only a fewe folkes, bot generaly nighhond alle (bot yif it be one or two in a contrey of the specyal chosen of God) ben so bleendid in here coryous kunnyng of clergie and of kynde that the trewe conceite of this light werk, thorow the whiche the boistousest mans soule or wommans in this liif is verely in lovely meeknes onyd to God in parfite charite, may no more, ne yit so moche, be conceyvid of hem in sothfastnes of spirit, for her blyndnes and here corioustee, then may the kunnyng of the grettest clerk in scole of a yong childe at his A.B.C. And for this blyndnes erryngly thei clepin soche simple teching coriouste of witte, whan, yif it be witterly lokyd, it schal be founden bot a symple and a light lesson of a lewid man.

For I holde him to lewyd and to boistous that kan not thenk and fele that himself is, not what himself is bot that hymself is. For this is pleynli proprid to the lewdist kow or to the moste unresonable beest (yif it might be seide, as it may not, that one were lewder or more unresonable then another) for to fele the owne propre beyng. Moche more than it is proprid to man, the whiche is singulerly endowid with reson aboven alle other beestes, for to thenk and for to fele his owne propre beyng.

And therfore com doun into the lowest poynte of thi witte, the

_____
^{b} and men] кк; н _om._

whiche sum man holdeth by verrey preof that it is the highest, and
thenk on the lewedest maner, bot bi sum man the wisest, not what
thiself is, bot that thiself is. Forwhi to thee for to thenk what thou arte
in alle propirte longeth moche crafte of clergie and of kunnyng and
moche sotil seching in thi kyndely wittys. And this hast thou done now
many day with help of grace, so that thou wost now as in partye, and as
I suppose it is profitable to thee for the tyme, what thou arte: a man in
kind and a foule stinking wreche by synne. Thou knowest wel how;
and paraventure thee thenkith sumtyme to wele alle the filthis that
folowen and fallen to a wreche. Fy on hem! Late hem go, I prey thee.
Stire no ferther in hem for ferde of stynche. Bot for to thenk that thou
arte, mayst thou have of thi lewydnes and thi boistouste withoutyn any
grete kunning of clergie or of kynde.

And therfore, I prey thee, do no more now in this caas bot thenk
boistously that thou arte as thou arte, be thou never so foule ne so
wrechid; so that thou have beforetymes (as I suppose thou hast) ben
lawefuly amendid of alle thi sinnes in special and in general, after the
trewe counseil of holi chirche; for elles schalt thou never ne none other
by my consent be so bolde to take apon yow this werk. Bot yif thou fele
that thou hast done that in thee is, than schalt thou set thee to this
werk. And thof al thou fele thiself yit than so vile and so wrechid that
for kombraunce of thiself thou wost not thiself what is best thee for to
do with thiself, this than schalt thou do as I sei thee:

Take good gracyous God as he is, plat and pleyn as a plastre, and
legge it to thi seek self as thou arte. Or – yif I otherwise schal sey – bere
up thi seek self as thou arte and fonde for to touche bi desire good
gracious God as he is, the touching of whome is eendeles helthe by
witnes of the womman in the gospel: *Si tetigero vel fimbriam
vestimenti eius, salva ero.*[3] 'If I touche bot the hemme of his clothing, I
schal be saa[f].'[c] Miche more schalt thou than be maad hole of thi
seeknes for this heighe hevenly touching of his owne beyng, him owne
dere self. Step up than stifly and taast of that triacle; bere up thi seek
self as thou arte unto gracious God as he is, withoutyn any corious or
special beholdyng to eny of alle the qualitees that longyn to the beyng
of thiself or of God, whether thei be clene or wrechid, gracyous or
kyndely, godli or manly. It chargeth not now in thee bot that thi blynde
beholdyng of thi nakid beyng be gladli born up in listines of love, to be

[c] saaf] kk; saak h.

knittid and onid in grace and in spirit to the precious beyng of God in himself only as he is, withouten more.

And thof al that thi wantoun seching wittys kon finde no mete unto hem in this maner of doyng, and therfore grochingly thei wilen bid thee algates to leve of that werk and do sum good on here corious maner (for it semeth to hem that it is no thing worth that thou dost, and al is for thei kan no skile therapon), bot I wolde love it the betir, for bi that it semith that it is more worthi then thei ben. And whi schuld I not than love it the betir, and namely whan ther is [no]^d werk that I may do, ne that may be wrought in the coriouste of any of my wittis, bodely or goostly, that might bring me so ny unto God and so fer fro the woreld as this nakid litil felyng and offring up of my blynde beyng wold do? And therfore, althof thi wittis kon fynde no mete unto hem in this werk, and therfore thei wolde have thee awey, yit loke that thou leve not for hem, bot be thou here maystre. And go not bak in fedyng of hem, be thei never so wode. Than gost thou bak in fedyng of thi wittes whan thou suffrest hem seche in the diverse corious meditacions of the qualitees of thi beyng; the whiche medi[t]acions,^{e} thof al thei be ful good and ful profitable, nevertheles, in comparison of this blynde felyng and offring up of thi beyng, thei ben ful diverse and scateryng from the perfeccion of onheed, the whiche fallith for to be bitwix God and thi soule. And therfore holde thee before in the first poynt of thi spirit, the whiche is thi beyng; and go not bak for nokyns thing, seme it never so good ne so holy the thing that thi wittis wolde lede thee unto.

And fulfille the counseil and the teching of Salamon, seiing thus to his son: *Honora Dominum de tua substancia et de primiciis frugum tuarum da pauperibus: et inplebuntur horrea tua saturitate et vino torcularia redundabunt.*^{4} 'Worschip thi Lorde with thi substaunce, and with the first of thi frutes fede thou the pore: and thi bernes scholen be fillid with fulheed and thi grape stockes schul rebounde ful of wyne.' This is the text that Salamon spake to his sone bodely, as yif he had seyde to thin understondyng, as I schal sey in his persone unto thee goostly: 'Thou goostly frende in God, loke that alle corious seching in thi kyndely wittys left, thou do hole worschip to thi Lorde God with thi substaunce, offring up unto him pleinly and holy thin owne self, al that thou arte and soche as thou arte, bot generaly and not specyaly, (that is, withouten specyal beholdyng to that that thou arte), that thi sight be

^{d} no] κκ; н *om.* ^{e} meditacions] medidacions н.

not scaterid ne thi felyng defoulid, the whiche wolde make thee les on with thi God in purete of spirit. And with the first of thi frutes fede thou the pore; that is with the first of thi goostly or bodely qualitees, the whiche ben growen up with thee fro the first byginnyng of thi makyng into this day.'

Alle the yiftes of kynde and of grace that ever God yave thee, I clepe hem thi frutes, with the whiche thou art holden to fostre and fede in this liif, bothe bodely and goostly, as wel alle thi brethren and sistren in kynde and in grace as thou arte thin owne propre self. The first of thees yiftes clepe I the first of thi frutes. The first yift in iche creature is only the being of the same creature. For thof it be so that the qualitees of thi beyng ben so fast onyd to the self beyng as thei ben withoutyn departyng, yit, for thei hangen alle upon it, verely it may be clepid, as it is, the first of thi yiftes. And thus it is only thi beyng that is the first of thi frutes. For yif thou breide oute the corious beholdyng of thin hert to eny or to alle the sotil qualitees and the worthi condicions that fallen to the being of man, the whiche is the nobelist beyng of maad thinges, evermore thou schalt fynde that the first poynte and the pricke of thi beholdyng, whatsoever it be, is thi nakid being. As yif thou seidest thus in thiself in ich one of thi beholdynges, stering thiself by the menes of this beholdyng to the love and the preising of thi Lorde God that not only yave thee to be, bot so nobli to be as the qualitees of thi beyng wolen witnes in thi beholdyng, seiing thus: 'I am and I see and fele that I am, and not only I am, bot so I am and so and so and so and so,' rekenyng up in thi beholdyng alle the qualitees of thi beyng in special. And than, that more then al this is, lap up alle this in general and sey thus: 'That at I am and how that I am, as in kynde and in grace, alle I have it of thee, Lord, and thou it arte. And al I offre it unto thee principaly to the preising of thee, for the help of alle myn evyn-Cristen and of me.' And thus maist thou se that the first and the poynte of thi beholding is moste substancialy set in the nakid sight and the blynde felyng of thin owne being. And thus it is only thi being that is the first of thi frutes.

Bot thof al it be the first of ich one of thi frutes, and thof al that the other frutes hangyn alle upon it, yit it spedith not now in this caas to lap ne to clothe thi beholdyng to it in eny or in alle the corious qualitees of it, the whiche I clepe thi frutes and in whiche thou hast ben travailid before this tyme. Bot it suffisith now unto thee to do hole worschip unto God with thi substaunce and for to offre up thi nakid beyng, the whiche is the first of thi frutes, in contynowel sacrifiye of preising of God, bothe for thiself and for alle other as charite askith, unclothid with eny qualite or special beholdyng that on eny maner fallith or may falle unto the beyng of thiself or of any other, as thou woldest by that beholding help the nede, forther the spede, or encrese the profite to perfeccion of thiself or of eny other. Lat be this: it wil not be thus in this caas trewly. For it profitith more soche a blynde comoun beholding to the nede, the spede, and the perfeccion of thiself and of alle other in purete of spirit then any special beholdyng that eny man may have, seme it nevir so holy.

This is soth by witnes of scripture, bi ensaumple of Crist and bi quik reson. For as alle men weren lost in Adam, for he fel fro this onyng affeccion, and as alle, that with werk acordyng to here clepyng wol witnes here wille of salvacion, ben savid and schul be by the vertewe of the passion of only Crist, offring himself up in verreiest sacrifiye, al that he was in general and not in specyal, withoutyn special beholdyng to any o man in this liif, bot generaly and in comon for alle: right so a verey and a parfite sacrifier of himself thus by a comon entent unto alle doth that in him is to knit alle men to God as effectuely as himself is. And more charite may no man do then thus to sacrifice himself for alle his brethren and sistren in grace and in kynde. For as the soule is more worthi then the body, so the knittyng of the soule to God (the liif of it) by the hevenly fode of charite is betir than the knittyng of the body to the soule (the liif of it) bi eny erthli fode in this liif. This is good for to do bi itself bot withoutyn the tother it is never weel done. This and the tother is the betir; bot the tother by itself is the best. For this bi itself deserveth never salvacion; bot the tother bi itself, where the plente of this defailith, deservith not only salvacion bot ledeth to the grettist perfeccion.

For it nedith not now in encrese of thi perfeccion to go bak in fedyng of thi wittys, as it is in beholdyng of the qualitees of thi beyng, so that thou mightest by soche beholdyng fede and fille thin affeccion with lovely and likyng felynges in God and goostly thinges, and thin understondyng with goostly wisdome of holy meditacions in seching after the knowyng of God. For, yif thou wilt holde thee besily, as thou maist by grace, evermore contynowly in the first poynte of thi spirit, offring up unto God that nakid blynde felyng of thin owne beyng, the whiche I clepe the first of thi frutes, sekir be thou that the tother hynder ende of Salamons lesson schal be ful verrely fulfillid as he hoteth, withouten besines of thiself in corious seching and ransakyng with thi goostly wittis amonges eny of the qualitees that longin not only to the beyng of thiself bot also to the beyng of God.

For wite thou right wel that in this werk thou schalt no more beholdyng have to the qualitees of the being of God than to the qualitees of the beyng of thiself. For ther is no name, ne felyng ne beholdyng more, ne so moche, acordyng unto everlastyngnes, the whiche is God, as is that the whiche may be had, seen and felt in the blinde and the lovely beholding of this worde IS.[5] For yif thou sey 'Good' or 'Faire Lorde', or 'Swete', 'Merciful' or 'Rightwise', 'Wise' or 'Alwitty', 'Mighti' or 'Almighti', 'Witte' or 'Wisdome', 'Mighte' or 'Strengthe', 'Love' or 'Charite', or what other soche thing that thou sey of God: al it is hid and enstorid in this litel worde IS. For that same is to him only to be, that is alle thees for to be. And yif thou put to an hundrid thousand soche swete wordes as ben thees – good, faire and alle thees other – yit yedest thou not fro this worde IS. And yif thou sey hem alle, thou puttest not to it. And yif thou sey right none, thou takist not fro it. And therfore be as blynde in the lovely beholdyng of the beyng of thi God as in the nakid beholdyng of the beyng of thiself, withoutyn eny corious seching in thi wittys to loke after eny qualite that longeth to his being or to thine. Bot alle coriouste left and fer put bak, do worschip to thi God with thi substaunce, al that thou arte [as][f] thou arte unto alle him that is as he is, the whiche only of himself, withoutyn moo, is the blisful being bothe of himself and of thee.

And thus schalt thou knittingly, and in a maner that is mervelous, worschip God with himself; for that thou arte thou hast of him and he it is. And thof al thou haddest a biginnyng in thi substancyal creacion, the whiche was sumtyme nought, yit hath thi being ben evermore in hym withoutyn beginnyng and evir schal be withoutyn ending, as himself is. And therfore oft I crie, and ever upon one: 'Do worschip to thi God with thi substaunce, and comoun profite to alle that ben men with the first of thi frutes; and than schul thi bernes be fulfillid with fulheed.' That is: than schal thi gostly affeccion be fillid with the fulheed of love and of vertuous levyng in God, thi grounde and thi purete of spirit. 'And thi grape-stockes scholen rebounde ful of wyne.' That is: thin inward goostly wittis, the whiche thou arte wonte for to streine and presse togeders bi diverse corious meditacions and

[f] as] kk; that H.

resonable investigacions abouten the goostly knowing of God and
thiself in beholding of his qualitees and of thine, scholen than rebounde
ful of wyne. By the whiche wine in holy scripture is verrely and mistely
understonden goostly wisdome in verrey contemplacion and heigh
savour of the Godheed. And al this schal be done sodenly, listely and
gracyously, withoutyn besines or travaile of thiself, only by the
mynistracion of aungelles thorow vertewe of this lovely blinde werk.
For unto it alle aungelles knowing done special servise as the maiden
unto the lady.

In grete comendacion of this listi sleig[h]ᵍ worching, the whiche
in itself is the heigh wisdom of the Godheed graciousli descendyng into
mans soule, knitting it and onyng it unto himself in goostly sleight and
prudence of spirit, the wise man Salamon brestith up and seith: *Beatus
homo qui invenit sapienciam et qui affluit prudencia. Melior est
adquisicio eius negociacione auri et argenti. Primi et purissimi fructus
eius. Custodi, fili mi, legem atque consilium; et erit vita anime tue et
gracia faucibus tuis. Tunc ambulabis fiducialiter in via tua, et pes tuus
non inpinget. Si dormieris, non timebis; quiesces et suavis erit sompnus
tuus. Ne paveas repentino terrore, et irruent[e]sʰ tibi potencias
impiorum, quia Dominus erit in latere tuo et custodiet pedem tuum ne
capiaris.*⁶ Alle this is to thin understondyng thus: He is a blisful man
that may fynde this onyng wisdom and that may abounde in his goostly
worching with this lovely sleight and prudence of spirit, in offring up of
his owne blynde feling of his owne beyng, alle corious kunnyng of
clergie and of kynde fer put bak. The purchasing of this goostly
wisdom and this sleigh worching is betir than the getyng of golde or of
silver. By the whiche gold and silver is moraly understonden al other
bodely and goostly knowyng, the whiche is getyn bi corious seching
and worching in oure kyndely wittis benethe us, withinne us or even
with us, in beholdyng of eny of the qualitees that longyn to the beyng of
God or of eny create thing. And whi is it beter, he putteth to the cause
and seith: for *primi et purissimi eius.* That is: 'for first and purest ben
the frutes of it'. And no wonder, for whi the frute of this worching is
highe goostly wisdom, sodenly and frely riftid of the spirit inly in itself
and unformid, ful fer fro fantasie, inpossible to be streinid or to falle
under the worching of naturele witte. The whiche naturele witte, be it
never so sotyl ne so holy, may be clepid in comparison of this bot feynid

---

ᵍ sleigh] sleight H.   ʰ *irruentes*] *irruentas* H.

foly formyd in fantome, as fer fro the verrey sothfastnes whan the
goostly sonne schinith as is the derknes of the moneschine in a mist at
midwinters night fro the brightnesse of the sonnebeme in the clerest
tyme of missomer day.

'Kepe, my sone', he seith, 'this lawe and this counseil' in the
whiche alle the comaundementes and the counselle, as wel of the Olde
Testament as of the Newe, ben verely and parfitely fulfillid, withoutyn
any special beholdyng to any one singulerly in itself. And on other wise
is not this maner of worching clepid a lawe, bot for it conteneth in it
fully alle the braunches and the frutes of the lawe. For yif it be witterly
lokid, the grounde and the strengthe of this worching schal be seen
nought elles bot the glorious yifte of love, in the whiche, by the teching
of the apostle, alle the lawe is fulfillid: *Plenitudo legis est dileccio.*[7] 'The
fulheed of the lawe is love.' And this lovely lawe and this lively
counseil, yif thou kepe it, as Salamon seith, 'schal be liif to thi soule'
withinne in softnes of love to thi God, 'and grace to thi chekes'
withoutyn in the trewest teching and the semeliest governaunce of thi
bodely beryng in outward forme of leving to thin evyn-Cristen. And in
thees two, the tone withinne and the tother withoutyn, by the teching
of Crist, 'hangeth alle the lawe and the profesies': *In hiis enim
duob[u]s[i] tota lex pendet et prophete: scilicet dileccio dei et proximi.*[8]

And therfore, whan thou arte maad thus parfite in thi worching
bothe withinne and withoutyn, then schalt thou goo tristely groundid
in grace, the gide of thi goostly wey, loveli liftyng up thi nakid blinde
beyng to the blisful beyng of thi God, the whiche ben bot one in grace
thof al ye ben diverse in kynde. 'And the fote of thi love schal not
sporne.'[9] That is to sey: from thou have the preve of thi goostly werk in
continowaunce of spirit, than schalt thou not so lightly be lettyd and
drawen bac by the corious questions of thi sotil wittys, as thou arte
now in thi begynnyng. Or elles thus: then schal the fote of thi love
neither snapir ne sporne on eni maner of fantasie causid of thi corious
seching in thi wittys. For whi utterly in this werk, as it is seide before, is
al corious seching in any of thi kyndeli wittis fer put bak and fully
foryeten for ferde of fantasie or any feinid falsheed that may falle in this
liif, the whiche in this werk might defoule the nakid felyng of thi blynde
beyng and drawe thee awey fro the worthines of this werk.

For yif eny maner of special thought of any thing, bot only of thi

[i] *duobus*] *duobis* H.

nakyd blinde beyng (the whiche is thi God and thin entent), come in thi
mynde, then arte thou awey and drawen bac to worche in the sleight
and the coriouste of wittys, in scatering and departyng of thee and of
thi mynde bothe fro thee and thi God. And therfore holde thee hole and
unscaterid as forth as thou maist bi grace and bi sleight of goostly
contynowaunce. For in this blinde beholdyng of thi nakid beyng, thus
onyd to God as I telle thee, schalt thou do al that thou schalt do: ete and
drink, sleep and wake, go and sit, speke and be stille, ligge and rise,
stonde and knele, renne and ride, travaile and rest. This schalt thou
iche day offre up unto God as for the moste precious offring that thou
canst make. And it schal be the cheef of alle thi doynges, [in alle thi
doynges,]^j whether thei be actyve or contemplatyve. For, as Salamon
seith in this processe, 'yif thou slepe' in this blynde beholdyng from al
the noise and the steryng of the fel fende, the fals woreld and the freel
flessche, 'thou schalt not drede any peril' ne any deceyte of the feende.
For whi utterly in this werk he is masid and maad blynde in a peynful
unknowyng and a wood wondryng to wite what thou doost. Bot no
force therof, for 'thou schalt gracyously rest' in this lovely onheed of
God and thi soule; 'and thi sleep schal be ful softe', for it schal be
goostly fode and inly strengthe, as wel to thi body as to thi soule. As
this same Salamon seith sone after: *Universe carni sanitas est.*[10] 'It is
helthe to al the freelte and the seeknes of flesche.' And worthely; for
sith al seeknes and corupcion fel into the flesche whan the soule fel fro
this werk, than schal alle helthe come to the flesche whan the soule bi
the grace of Jhesu, the whiche is the cheef worcher, riseth to this same
werk agein. And this schalt thou hope only to have by the mercy of
Jhesu and thi lovely consent. And therfore I preie thee, with Salamon
here in this processe, that thou stonde stifly in this werk, evermore
beryng up unto hym thi lovely consent in listines of love. *Et ne paveas
repentino terrore et irruentes tibi potencias impiorum.*[11] 'And be not
astonyed' with any unrestful drede, thof the feend (as he wol) come
'with a sodeyn feerdnes', bussching and betyng on the walles of thin
house there thou sittest, or thof he stire any of his mighty lemys to rise
and 'to renne in apon thee' sodenly, as it is withoutyn any avysement.
Thus schal it be, wite thou right wel, thou whatsoever that thou be that
settyst thee to worche trewly in this werk, thou schalt verrely see and
fele, or elles smel, taste or here som astoniing maad by the feende in

^{j} in . . . doynges] ĸĸ; ʜ *om.*

some of thi fyve wittys withoutyn. And al is done for to drawe thee
downe fro the height of this precious worching. And therfore take
good kepe of thin herte in tyme of this tourment, and lene with a tristi
listines to the love of oure Lorde.

   *Quia Dominus erit in latere tuo, et custodiet pedem tuum ne
capiaris.*[12] That is: 'for oure Lorde schal be in thi side', redy and neigh
to thin help, 'and he schal kepe thi fote', that is, the stiing up of thi love
bi the whiche thou gost to God, 'so that thou schalt not be takyn' by no
sleight ne gile of thin enemyes, the feend and his fautours, the woreld
and thi flessche. Lo! frende, thus schal oure Lorde and oure love
mightely, wisely and goodly sokoure, kepe and defende alle thoo that
for love-trist that thei fele in hym wylen utterly forsake the kepyng of
hemself.

   Bot where schal soche a soule be founden so frely fastnyd and
foundid in the feith, so fully mekid in noughtnyng of itself and so lovely
led and fed in the love of oure Lorde, with ful knowing and felyng of his
almightyheed, his unwetyn wisdom and his glorious goodnes: hou he is
one in alle and alle in hym, in so mochil that, withouty[n] ful yeeldyng
up unto hym al that of hym is, by hym and in hym, a lovyng soule is
nevermore verely mekyd in ful noughtnyng of itself; so that for this
nobil noughtnyng of itself in verrey meeknes and this hyghe allyng of
God in parfite charite, it deserveth to have God (in whos love it is
deeply drenchid in ful and in fynal forsakyng of itself as nought or
lesse, yif lesse myght be) mightely, wisely and goodly sokouryng it and
kepyng it and defendyng it fro alle adversitees, bodyly and goostly,
withoutyn besynes or travayle, rewarde or avisement of itself?

   Lateth be youre manly obieccions, ye half-mekyd soulys, and
seith not in youre resonable trasing that soche a meek and an utter
forsakyng of the kepyng of a mans self, whan he felith hym thus
touchid bi grace, is any temtyng of God, for ye fele in youre reson that
ye dor not do so yowreself. N[o],[k] holde yow payed with youre parte,
for it suffiseth to the savyng of youre soules in actyve degree, and late
other contemplatyve soulis alone that doren. And muse ye not and
merveyle you not of here wordes and of here werkes, thof al you thenk
hem passe the cours and the comoun dome of youre reson.

   O, for schame! hou ofte schul ye rede and here, and neither yeve
feith ne credence therto? I mene the thing that alle oure olde Faders han

---

[k] No] κκ; ne н.

wretyn and taught before us, and the thing whiche is the frute and the floure of alle holy scripture. Outher it semith that ye ben blynde and mowen not with bileve se that ye rede or here; or elles ye ben touchid with sum prive spice of envye, that ye mowe not trist so grete good to falle to youre brethren for ye lackith it youreself. It is good ye beware, for youre enmye is sotyl and in purpose to make yow to yeve more feith to youre owne witte than to olde teching of trewe Faders or to the worching of grace and the wille of oure Lorde.

How ofte have ye red and herde, and of hou many bothe holy, wise and trewe, that as sone as Benjamyn was borne his moder Rachel deied? By Benjamyn contemplacion, by Rachel we understonden reson. And as sone as a soule is touchid with verrey contemplacion, as it is in this noble noughtnyng of itself and this highe allyng of God, sekerly and verrely than diyeth alle mans reson. And sithen ye reden this so ofte, not only of one or of two bot of ful many ful holy and ful worthi, whi belevyn ye not it? And yif ye belevyn it, how dore ye than ransake and seche with youre reson in the wordes and the dedes of Benjamyn? By the whiche Benjamyn ben understonden alle thoo that in excesse of love ben ravisc[h]id*l* aboven mynde, the prophete seiing thus: *Ibi Benjamyn adol[es]centulus*^m *in mentis excessu.*¹³ That is to sey: 'There is Benjamyn, a yong childe, in excesse of mynde.' Loke therfore that ye be not liche to thoo wrechid wommen in body that sleen here owne children whan thei ben newe borne. Beeth ware, it is good, and setteth not the poynte of youre presumptuous spere at the might, the witte and the wille of oure Lorde, stifly in that that in yow is, and for blyndenes and lackyng of experience, as ye wolde bere hym down whan ye wene best to holde him up.

For sith in the first biginnyng of holy chirche in the tyme of persecucion, dyverse soules and many weren so merveylously touchid in sodeynte of grace that sodenly, withoutyn menes of other werkes comyng before, thei kasten here instrumentes, men of craftes, of here hondes, children here tables in the scole, and ronnen withoutyn ransakyng of reson to the martirdom with seintes: whi schul men not trowe now, in the tyme of pees, that God may, kan and wile and doth – ye! touche diverse soules as sodenly with the grace of contemplacion? And this I trowe he wil do ful gracyously in chosyn soulis. For he wol worthely be knowen in the eende, to the wondryng of alle the woreld.

---

l ravischid] raviscid H.   *m adolescentulus*] *adolocentulus* H.

For soche a soule, thus loveliche noughtnyng itself and thus heily allyng his God, schal ful gracyously be kept from alle castyng doun of his goostly or bodely enemyes, withoutyn besines and travaile of itself, only by the goodnes of God; as the godly reson askith, that he trewly kepe alle thoo that for besines aboute hys love forsakith and list not kepe hemself. And no wonder thof thei be mervelously kept, for thei ben so fully mekyd in booldnes and strengthheed of love.

And whoso dar not do this [and seith ayens this],[n] outher the devil is in his brest and revith him the love-trist that he schuld have to his God and the weel-wilnes that he schuld have to his even-Cristen; or elles he is not yit as parfitely mekid as hym nedid to be, I mene yif he purpose to that liif that is verrey contemplatyve. And therfore be thou not abasched thus to be mekid to thi Lorde, ne thus for to slepe in this blynde beholdyng of God as he is, from alle the noise of this wickid woreld, the fals feende and thi frele flesche; for oure Lorde schal be redy to help thee and kepe thi fote that thou be not takyn.

And wel is this werk licnyd to a slepe. For as in the slepe the use of the bodely wittys is cesid, that the body may take his ful rest in fedyng and in strengthing of the bodyly kynde; right so in this goostly sleep the wantoun questyons of the wilde goostly wittys, ymaginatyve resons, ben fast bounden and utterly voidid, so that the sely soule may softely sleep and rest in the lovely beholdyng of God as he is, in ful fedyng and strengthing of the goostly kynde.

And therfore bynde in thi wittys in offryng up of this nakid blynde felyng of thin owne beyng. And loke ever, as I ofte sey, that it be nakyd and not clad with any qualite of thi beyng. For yif thou clothe it with any qualite, as with the worthines of thi beyng or with any other prive condycion that fallith to the beyng of man forby the beyng of eny other creature, than as fast thou yevest mete to thi wittys, by the whiche thei han occasyon and a strengthe to drawe thee to many thinges, and so to be scaterid, thou woste never how. Beware bi this disceite, I prey thee.

Bot now, paraventure, at the sotil examinacion of thi corious wittys, bicause thei kun no skyle in this werk, thou merveylist thee in maner of this werk, and hast it suspecte. And that is no wonder; for thou hast ben yit hedirtoward over wise in thi wittys to kun any skyle of any soche doyng. And paraventure thou askyst in thin herte how thou schuldest wite whether this werk were plesyng to God or not; or, yif it be plesaunt, how that it may be that it is so plesaunt as I sey that it is. To this I answere and sey that this questyon is moved of a corious witte, the whiche wil on no wise late thee consent to this werk er the tyme be that ther be maad aseeth to the coriouste therof by sum feire skile.

And herfore schal I not lette; bot I schal in party make me liche to thee, favoring thi proude witte, that thou be aftirward liche unto me, folowing my counseil withoutyn settyng of merkes in thi meeknes. For, as witnessith Seinte Bernard:[14] Parfite meeknes settith no merkes. Than settist thou merkes in thi meeknes whan thou wilt not fulfille the counseil of thi sovereyn goostly, bot yif thi witte se that it be to do. Lo! here maist thou see that I coveite sovereinte of thee. And trewly so I do, and I wol have it. I trowe love sterith me therto more then any abilnes that I fele in myself in any height of kunnyng, or yit of worching, or degree of my levyng. God amende that is amys, for he wote fully, and I bot in party!

Bot now (for to make aseeth to thi proude witte) in comendyng of this werk, trewly I telle thee that yif a soule, that is thus ocupied, had tonge and langage to sey as it felith, than alle the clerkes of Cristendome schuld wondre on that wisdam. Ye! and in comparison of it, al here grete clergie schuld seme apeerte foly. And therfore no wondre thof I kan not telle thee the worthines of this werk with my boystouse beestly tonge. And God forbede that it scholde be so defoulid in itself for to be streynid under the steringes of a fleschly tonge! Nay, it may not be, and certes it wil not be, and God forbede that I schuld coveyte it! For al that is spokyn of it is not it, bot of it. Bot now, sithen we mowe not speke it, lat us speke of it, in confusion of proude wittys, and namely of thine, the whiche is only, occasionly at the leest, the cause of this writyng at this tyme.

At the first, I aske of thee what is perfeccion of mans soule and whiche ben the propirtees that fallyn to this perfeccion. I answere in thi persone, and I sey that perfeccion of mans soule is not elles bot an oneheed maad bitwix God and it in parfite charitee. This perfeccion is so heigh and so pure in itself, aboven the understondyng of man, that it may not be knowen ne perceyvid in itself. Bot there where the propirtees that fallen to this perfeccion ben verely seen and perceyvid, there it is liche that the substaunce is aboundyng. And forthi it is to wite here wheche ben the propirtees that fallyn to perfeccion, in declaryng of the nobilte of this goostly excersise before alle other. The propirtees that fallyn to perfeccion, the which iche parfyte soule falleth to have, ben vertewes. And than, yif thou wilt verrely beholde to this werk in thi soule and to the propertee and the condicion of iche vertewe diversely, thou schalt fynde that alle vertewes ben cleerly and parfitely comprehendid in it, withoutyn any crokyng or corupcion of the entent.

I touche no vertewe here in specyal, for it nedith not; thou hast hem touchid in maner in other diverse places of myn owne writyng. For this same werk, yif it be verrely conceyvid, is that reverent affeccion and the frute departid fro the tre that I speke of in thi lityl *Pistle of Preier*.[15] This is the *Cloude of Unknowyng*; this is that prive love put in purete of spirit; this is the 'Arke of the Testament'. This is *Denis Devinite*, his wisdom and his drewry,[16] his lighty derknes and his unknowyn kunnynges. This is it that settith thee in silence as wele fro thoughtes as fro wordes. This makith thi preier ful schorte. In this thou arte lernid to forsake the woreld and to dispise it.

And that more is, in this thou arte lernid to forsake and dispise thin owne self, after the teching of Crist in the gospel, seiing thus: *Si quis vult venire post me, abneget semetipsum; tollat crucem suam et sequatur me.* [17] That is: 'Whoso wole come after me, late hym forsake hymself, late hym bere his cros and folow me.' As if he seide thus to thin understondyng acordyng to oure mater: 'Whoso wil come meekly, not with me bot after me, to the blis of heven or to the mounte of perfeccion.' For Crist yede before bi kynde, and we comyn after bi grace. His kynde is more worthi then grace, and grace is more worthi then oure kynde. And in this he lateth us wetyn fully that we mowen on no wise folow hym to the mounte of perfeccion, as it fallith to be in the use of this werk, bot yif it be only sterid and led by grace.

And that is ful sothe. For wite thou right wel, and alle liche unto thee that this writyng scholen outher rede or here, that thof al I bid thee thus pleynly and thus booldly set thee to this werk, nevertheles yit I fele verely, withoutyn errour or doute, that Almighty God with his grace behoveth algates be the cheef sterer and worcher, outher with mene or withoutyn; and thou only, or eny other liche unto thee, bot the consenter and suffrer: savyng that this consent and this suffring schal be, in the tyme of this werk, actuely disposid and ablid to this werk in purete of spirit, and semely borne up to thi sovereyn, as thou mayst be lernid by the proef in the goostly sight of thi spirit.

And sith so is that God of his goodnes sterith and touchith diverse soulis diversely, as it is som with mene and som withoutyn, who dar than seie that God stereth not thee in this writyng, or eny other liche unto thee that this schal outher rede or here, only by me mene, thof I be unworthi, savyng his worschipful wille, that hym likith to do as hym likith? I suppose it schal be thus: the werk schal witnes whan the proef worchith. And therfore, I preie thee, dispose thee for to receyve this grace of thi Lorde, and here what he seith. 'Whoso wil come after me' (in the maner before seide) 'late hym forsake hymself.' I prey thee, how may a man more forsake himself and the woreld, and more dispise himself and the woreld, then for to dedein for to think of eny qualite of here beinges?

For wite thou wel for certeyn that, thof al I bid thee foryete alle thinges bot the blynde felyng of thi nakid beyng, yit nevertheles my wille is, and that was myn entent in the biginning, that thou schuldest foryete the felyng of the beyng of thiself as for the felyng of the beyng of God. And for this skyle I provid thee in the bigynnyng that God is thi beyng. Bot for me thought that thou were not yit abil sodenly to be liftid up to the goostly felyng of the being of God for rudenes in thi goostly felyng, therfore, to late thee climbe therto by degree, I bad thee first gnawe on the nakid blinde felyng of thin owne being, unto the tyme that thou mightest be maad able to the highe felyng of God bi goostly contynowaunce of this prive werk. For thin entent and thi desire schal be ever to fele God in this worching. For thof al I bid thee in the biginnyng, bicause of thi boistouste and thi goostly rudenes, lappe and clothe the felyng of thi God in the felyng of thiself, yit schalt thou after whan thou arte maad by contynowaunce more sleigh in clennes of spirit, nakyn, spoyle and utterly unclothe thiself of al maner of felyng of thiself, that thou be able to be clothid with the gracyous felyng of God self.

And this is the trewe condicion of a parfite lover, only and utterly to spoyle hymself of himself for that thing that he lovith, and not admit ne suffre to be clothed bot only in that thing that he lovith; and that not only for a tyme, bot eendlesly to be umbilappid therin, in ful and fynal foryetyng of hymself. This is the werk of love that none may knowe bot he that felith it. This is the lesson of oure Lorde whan he seith: 'Whoso wil love me, late hym forsake himself'; as who seith: 'Late him spoyle hymself of himself yif he wil be verely clothid in me, that am the side garnement of love and of lastyng that never schal have eende.'

And therfore, ever whan thou beholdest to thi worchyng, and seest and felest that it is thiself that thou felest and not God, then schalt thou make sorow ernestly, and hertely longe after the felyng of God, evirmore desiryng withoutyn cesyng to forgo the woful wetyng and the foule felyng of thi blynde beyng; and coveite to fle fro thiself as from venym. And than forsakyst thou thiself and dispisest thee ful felly, as thi Lorde biddeth thee. And than, whan thou coveitest so streitly, not for to unbe – for that were woodnes and dispite unto God – bot to forgo the wetyng and the felyng of thi beyng (the whiche behovith algates be, yif Goddes love schal parfitely be felt as it may be here) and seest and felest that on no wise thou maist come to thi purpose, for ther wil algates folow and go with thi doyng a nakid felyng of thi blynde beyng, be thou never so besy (bot yif it be any seeldom schort tyme whan God wol late thee fele hymself in habundaunce of love) the whiche nakyd felyng of thi blynde beyng wol evyrmore prees aboven thee, bitwix thee and thi God, as wolen in thi begynnyng the qualitees of thi beyng bitwix thee and thiself: than wol thee thenk it a wel hevy and a ful peynful birthen of thiself. Ye! Jhesu help thee thanne, for than hast thou nede. For alle the woo that may be withoutyn that is not a poynte to that. For than arte thiself a cros to thiself. And this is trewe worching and wey to oure Lorde, as himself seith: 'Late hym bere his cros,' first in the peynfulnes of hymself, and sith 'folow me' into blis or into the mounte of perfeccion, taastyng the softenes of my love in godly felyng of myself. Lo! here mayst thou see that thee behovith soroufuly desire to forgo the felyng of thiself, and peynfuly bere the birthin of thiself as a cros, er thou maist be onyd to God in goostly felyng of himself, the whiche is parfite charite. And here mayst thou se sumwhat and in partye fele, al after that thou arte touchid and goostly merkid with this grace, the worthines of this werk before alle other.

And, I preie thee, how schuldest thou com to this worching by the use of thi wittys? Sekirly never; ne yit by thi faire wise, thi sotyle and thi queinte ymaginacions and meditacions, ye, thof thei be of thi wrechid levyng, the passion of Criste, the joies of oure Lady, or of alle the seintes and aungelles of heven, or yit of eny qualite or sotilte or condicion that perteynith to the beyng of thiself or of God. Sekirly me had lever have soche a nakid blynde felyng of myself as I touchid before (not of my doynges bot of myself. Many men clepen here doynges hemself, and it is not so; for one am I that do, and another aren my dedes that ben done. And the same it is of God; for one is he in himself, and another ben his werkes). And rather it schuld breke myn herte in teres for lackyng of felyng of God and for the peinful birthin of myself,

and kyndil my desire in love and desiryng after the felyng of God, than
alle the sotyle and the queynte ymaginacions or meditacions that man
kan telle or may fynde wretyn in book, be thei never so holy ne schewe
thei never so feire to the sotyle ighe of thi corious witte.

Nevertheles yit ben thees faire meditacions the trewest wey that a
synner may have in his begynnyng to the goostly felyng of himself and
of God. And me wolde thenk that it were inpossible to mans
understondyng – thof al God may do what he wil – that a synner schuld
com to be restful in the goostly felyng of himself and of God, bot yif he
first sawe and felt by ymaginacion and meditacion the bodely doynges
of hymself and of God, and therto sorowed for that that were to
sorowen, and maad joie for that that were to joien. And whoso cometh
not in bi this weye, he cometh not trewly; and therfore he mote stonde
theroute, and doth so whan he weneth that he is best therin. For many
weneth that thei ben withinne the goostly dore, and yit stonden thei
theroute, and scholen do unto the tyme that they sechen meekly the
dore. And somme ther ben that fynden the dore sone, and comen inne
rather then somme; and that is longe on the porter pleynly, withoutyn
prees or deseert of hemself.

It is a merveilous housholde, goostlines, for whi the Lorde is not
only portour hymself, bot also he is the dore: the porter he is bi his
Godheed, and the dore he is by his manheed. Thus seith hymself in the
gospel: *Ego sum ostium. Per me si quis introierit, salvabitur; et sive
egredietur sive ingredietur, pascua inveniet. Qui vero non intrat per
ostium sed assendit aliunde, ipse fur est et latro.*[18] That is to thin
understondyng as yif he seide thus acordyng to oure mater: 'I that am
almighty by my Godheed and may levefuly as porter late in whom I
wol, and bi what wey that I wol, yit, for I wol that ther be a comoun
pleyne wey and an open entre to alle that wolen come, so that none be
excusid by unknowyng of the wey, I have clothid me in the comoun
kynde of man, and maad me so opyn that I am the dore by my
manheed, and whoso entreth by me, he schal be saaf.'

Thei entren by the dore, that in beholdyng of the passion of
Criste sorowen here wickydnes, the whiche ben cause of that passion,
with bitter reprovyng of hemself, that deservid and not suffrid, and pite
and compassion of that worthi Lorde, that so vili suffrid and nothing
deservid; and sithen lifte up here hertes to the love and the goodnes of
his Godheed, in the whiche he voucheth-saaf to meke hym so lowe in
oure deedly manheed. Alle thees entren bi the dore, and thei scholen be

saaf. And whether thei gon inne, in the beholdyng of the love and the goodnes of his Godheed, or oute, in beholdyng of the peyne of his manheed, thei scholen fynde goostly fode of devocion inowgh, soffisaunt and aboundyng to the helthe and savyng of here soules, thof al thei comen never ferther inwardes in this liif.

   And whoso entreth not by this dore, bot clymbeth otherwise to perfeccion by the sotil seching and the corious fantastic worchyng in his wilde wantoun wittis, levyng this comoun pleyn entre touchid before and the trewe counseil of goostly faders: he, that whatsoever he be, is not only a night theef bot a day skulker. A night theef he is, for he goth in the derknes of synne, more lenyng in his presumpcion to the syngulerte of his owne witte and his wille then to any trewe counseil or to this comon pleyn wey touchid before. A day skulker he is, for, under colour of clere goostly levyng, prively he pikith the outward signes and wordes of contemplacion and hath not the frute. And thus for he felith in him sumtyme a [liking]⁰ longing, so lityl as it is, to come nere God, therfore, bleendid under colour of this, he wenith al be good inowgh that he doth, whan it is the perilousest purpose that may be, a yong man to folow the feersnes of his desire unrewlid bi counseil; and namely whan it is singulerly set to climben in highe thinges, not only aboven himself bot aboven the comoun plein wey of Cristen men touchid before, the whiche I clepe, by the teching of Criste, the dore of devocion and the trewest entre of contemplacion that may be in this liif.

   Bot now forthe of oure mater that specialy in this writyng perteyneth unto thee, and to alle other liche unto thee in that disposicion only. What therof yif this be the dore, schal a man than whan he hath the dore ever stonde therate or therinne and com none innermore? I answere for thee, and I sey that it is good that he so do ever, til the grete rust of his boistous bodelynes be in grete party rubbid awei, his counseil and his conscience to witnes; and namely, ever to he be clepid innermore bi the prive teching of the spirit of God, the whiche techyng is the rediest and the sekerist witnes that may be had in this liif of the clepyng and the drawyng of a soule innermore to more special worching of grace.

   Evydence of this touching a man may have thus: yif he fele in his contynoweel excersise as it were a soft growyng desire to come nere God in this liif, as it may be by a specyal goostly felyng, as he herith

⁰ liking] κκ; litil н.

men speke of, or elles fyndeth wretyn in bokes. For he that felith hym not sterid in heryng and redyng of goostly worching, and namely in his iche dayes excersise by a growing desire to come nere God, lat hym stonde yit stylle at the dore, as a man clepid to salvacion bot not yit to perfeccion.

And of o thing I warne thee. Whatsoever thou be that this writyng schalt outher rede or here, and namely in this place where I make a difference bitwix hem that ben clepid to salvacion and hem that ben clepid to perfeccion, that of whether partie that thou fele is thi clepyng, loke neither that thou deme ne discusse in the dedes of God ne of man, ferther then only thiself – as whom he sterith and clepith to perfeccion and whom he clepith not; or of the schortnes of tyme, whi he clepith hym rather then hym. Yif thou wilt not erre, loke not that thou deme; bot onys here and understonde. Yif thou be clepid, yeve preisyng to God, and prey that thou falle not. And yif thou be not yit clepid, prey meekly to God that he clepe thee whan his wille is. Bot teche him not what he schal do. Late hym alone. He is mighty, witty and willy inowgh to do the best for thee and alle that hym loveth. Have pees with thi parte. Whether that thou have, thee nedeth not to pleyne thee; for thei ben bothe precious. The first is good and algates nedeth to be had. The secound is betir, gete whoso gete may; or (yif I sothelier schal sey) whoso bi grace is getyn and clepid therto of oure Lorde. Proudly mowe we prees and snapir at the eende; bot certes withoutyn him it is nought that we do, hymself seiing: *Sine me nichil potestis facere.*[19] That is to thin understondyng: 'Withoutyn me first steryng and principaly movyng, and ye only bot consentyng and suffryng, ye mowen nowght do thing that is parfiteli plesyng to me', as schuld be in maner the werk of this writyng.

And alle this I sey in confusion of here erryng presumpcion that, in the coryouste of here clergie or here kyndely witte, wolen algates be principal worchers hemself, God bot suffryng or only consentyng, whan verrely the contrary is soth in thinges contemplatyve. For only in hem ben alle corious skyles of clergie or of kyndely kunnyng fer put bak, that God be the principal. Nevertheles, in thinges leveful and actyve, mans clergye and his kyndely kunnyng schal worche with God by and by, only by his consent in spirit provid by thees thre witnes: scripture, counseil and comoun custum of kynde and degre, eelde and conpleccyon; in so moche that man schal not folow the steryng of the spirit, seme it nevir so liking ne so holy; I mene in thinges actyve – bot yif it falle under his clergial or his kyndely kunnyng, thof al it be nevir so strongly stuffid by alle or by eny of thees thre witnes touchid before. And verrely it is grete skile that man be more then his werkes. And for this it is that by the statute and the ordinaunce of holy chirche, ther schal no man be admittyd to prelacye, the whiche is the heiest degre in actyve levyng, bot yif the office of that cure wol falle under his kunnyng by testymony of trewe examynacion. So that, in thinges actyve, mans clergie and his kyndely kunnyng schal principaly abounde as in worching, God gracyously consentyng, with thees thre witnes aprovid. And skilfuly, for alle thinges actyve ben benethe and under the wisdam of man. Bot in thinges contemplatyve the heighest wisdom that may be in man [as man]*p* is fer put under, that God be the principal in worching, and man bot only consenter and suffrer.

And thus I understonde this worde of the gospel: *Sine me nichil potestis facere* – that is: 'Withoutyn me ye mowe do nothing' – on o maner in actyves and on another in contemplatyves. In actyves behoveth hym be, outher with suffring or with consent or elles with bothe, yif ought schal be done, whether it be leveful and plesaunt to hym or not: in contemplatyves, by principal worching, askyng of hem nought elles bot only sufferaunce and here consent. So that generaly to understonde: in alle oure doynges, leveful and unleveful, actyve or contemplatyve, withoutyn hym we mowe do nothing. He is with us in synne only bi suffraunce and not by consent, to oure fynal damnacion bot yif we meekly amende us. In dedes that ben actyve and leveful, he is with us bothe by suffring and consent, to oure reproef yif we go bak and oure grete mede yif we do forth. In dedes that ben contemplatyve he is with us, principaly steryng and worching, and we only bot suffring and consenting, to oure grete perfeccion and goostly onyng of oure soule unto hym in parfite charite. And thus sith alle the men of this liif mowen be devided in thre, in synners, in actyves and in contemplatyves, therfore generaly, acordyng to alle this woreld, this worde of oure Lorde may be seide unto alle: 'Withoutyn me' only suffryng and not consentyng as in synners, or elles bothe suffryng and consentyng as in actyves, or, that more than alle this is, principaly steryng and worching as in contemplatyves, 'ye mowen do nothing.'

Lo! here many wordes and lityl sentence. Nevertheles, alle this have I seide to late thee wite in whiche thinges thou schalt use the werk

p as man] kk; h *om.*

of thi wittes, and in whiche nought; and how that God is with thee in o werk and how in another. And yit, paraventure, in this knowing thow maist eschewe disceytes, in the whiche thou mightest have fallen ne had this be schewid. And therfore, sith it is seide, late it be, thof al it be bot lityl perteynyng to oure mater. Bot now forthe of oure mater.

Thou mayst aske me this questyon: By what o tokyn or mo, yif thee liste telle me, may I rathest wite withoutyn errour whether this growyng desire that I fele in myn iche dayes worching and this likyng steryng that I have in redyng and heryng of this mater be verrely a clepyng of God to a more specyal worching of grace, as is the mater of this writyng; or it is a norisching and a fedyng of my spirit to abide stylle and to worche forth in my comoun grace, this that thou clepest the dore and the comoun entre of alle Cristen men?

To this I answere so febely as I kan. Thou seest wel here that I sette thee here in this writyng two kyndes of evidences, bi the whiche thou schalt prove thi goostly clepyng of God as to this werk, one withinne, another withowten. Of the whiche two, neither may suffise in this caas fully, as me thenketh, withoutyn that other. Bot where thei bothe ben togeders one and acordyng, than is thin evidence ful inowgh withoutyn eny failing.

The first of thees two evydence, the whiche is withinne, is this growyng desire that thou felist in thin iche dayes worching. And of this desire thou schalt wite thus moche: that thof al that the desire be a werk of the soule blynde in itself – for right is the desire of the soule as gropyng and steppyng is of the body; and bothe ben groping and steppyng blynde werkes of the body, thou wost wel thiself – bot thof that the werke of this desire be never so blynde, yit nevertheles ther comouneth and folowith with it a maner of goostly sight, the whiche is in partye cause and a mene forthering this desire. Beholde than besily to thin iche dayes excersise, what it is in itself. And than yif it be the mynde of thi wrechidnes, the passyon of Criste, or eny soche that longeth to the comoun entre of Cristen men touchid before, than yif it so be that this goostly sight, that thus comouneth and foloweth with thi blynde desire, rise fro thees comoun beholdynges, sekirly than it is a tokyn to me that the growing of this desire is bot a norisching and a fedyng of thi spirit to abide stille and to worche forth in thi comoun grace, and no cleping ne stering of God to any more special grace.

Now, forthermore, the tother secounde evidence withoutyn is a likyng stering that thou felest in redyng or hering of this mater. I clepe this evidence withouten, for it comith froo withoutyn by the windowes of thi bodily wittys, as by heryng and seing in the tyme of thi redyng. Now touching the secounde evidence, yif it so be that this likyng stering, that thou felist in hering and redyng of this mater, laste ne contynew no lenger with thee bot only the tyme of thi reding or hering, bot it cesith thanne, or elles sone after, so that thou neither wakenest ne slepist therin ne therwith, and namely it foloweth thee not in thi cotidiane excersise, as it were going and presing bitwix thee and it, stering and ledyng thi desire; than it is a token verrey, in my conseit, that this likyng stering that thou felist in hering and redyng of this mater, is bot [a]*q* kyndely gladnes that iche Cristen soule hath in hering or redyng of the trewthe (and nameli of that the whiche touchith sotely and declareth verely the propirtees of perfeccion that most ben acording to the soule of man, and namely of God) and no goostly touching of grace, ne cleping of God to any other more special worching of grace then is that the whiche is the dore and the comoun entre to Cristen men.

Bot yif it so be that this likyng stering, that thou felest in redyng and hering of this mater, be so abounding in itself that it go with thee to bedde, it riseth with thee at morow, it foloweth thee forth al the day in al that thou doste, it revith thee fro thi cotidiane wonte excersise and goth bitwix it and thee, it comouneth and foloweth thi desire, in so moche that thee thenk it al bot o desire or thou wost never what, it chaungeth thi gesture and maketh thi chere semely. Lastyng it, alle thing eseth thee and nothing may greve thee. A thousand mile woldest thou renne to comoun mouthly with one that thou wist that verrely felt it; and yit, whan thou comest there, kanst thou nought sey, speke whoso speke wil, for thee list not speke bot of it. Fewe ben thi wordes, bot ful of frute and of fiir. A schorte worde of thi mouth conteneth a woreld ful of wisdam, yit semeth it bot foly to hem that wonen in here wittis. Thi silence is softe, thi speche ful speedful, thi preier is preve, thi pride ful pure, thi maners ben meek, thi mirthe ful mylde, thi list is likyng to pleye with a childe. Thou lovest to be only and sit by thiself; men wolden let thee, thee thenkith, bot yif thei wrought with thee. Thee list not rede book ne here book, bot only of it, so that thin inwarde evidence and also thin utter weren bothe acordyng and knittyng in one.

q a] & H.

Ye! and yif bothe these evidence with alle here fautours wretyn now here – fro thou have ones had hem alle or eny of hem – sese for a tyme, and thou be lefte as thou were bareyn, thee thenkith, as wel fro the felyng of this newe fervour as from thin olde wont werk, so that thee thenketh thee fallen doun bitwix two, havyng never neither bot lacking hem bothe: yit be not over hevy for this; bot suffre meekly and abide paciently the wille of oure Lorde. For now arte thou in the goostly see, to my licnes, schipping over fro bodelines into goostlines. Many grete stormes and temptacions, paraventure, scholen rise in this tyme, and thou wost never whether to renne for socour. Alle is awey fro thi feling, comoun grace and specyal. Be not over feerde, althof thou have mater as thee thenketh; bot have a love-trist in oure Lorde, so litil as thou maist gete for the tyme, for he is not fer. He schal loke up, paraventure right sone, and efte touche thee with a more fervent stering of that same grace than ever thou feltest any before. Then arte thou al hole and alle good inowgh, as thee thenketh, last while it laste may. For sodenly, er ever thou wite, alle is awey, and thou levyst bareyn in the bote, blowyn with blundryng, now heder now theder, thou wost nevir where ne wheder. Yit be not abascht, for he schal come, I behote thee, ful sone, whan hym likith [to lethe thee]^r and doughtely delyver thee of alle thi dole, fer more worthely then he ever did before. Ye! and yif he [eft]^s go, eft wol he come ayeyn; and iche tyme, yif thou wel bere thee by meek suffryng, wil he come more worthelyer and merilier then other. And alle this he doth for he wil have thee maad as pleying to his wille goostly as a roon glove to thin honde bodely.

And sith he sumtyme goth and somtyme cometh, therfore doubli in this double werk wol he prively prove thee and worche thee to his owne werk. By the withdrawyng of thi fervour, the whiche thee thenketh his goyng, thof al it be not so, wole he propirly prove thi pacyence. For wite thou right wel that, thof God sumtyme withdrawe thees sensible swetnes, thees fervent felynges and thees flaumyng desires, nevertheles he withdraweth never the rather his grace in his chosen. For sekirly I may not trowe that his special grace may ever be withdrawen fro his chosen that onys have ben touchid therwith, bot yif synne deedly were in the cause. Bot alle thees sensible swetnes, thees fervent felynges and thees flawmyng desires, the whiche in hemself ben

<hr>

^{r} to lethe thee] κκ; н *om.* ^{s} eft] κκ; н *om.*

not grace but tokenes of grace, thees ben oft-tymes withdrawyn in provyng of oure pacience, and oft-tymes for oure other many goostly profites, moo than we wene. For grace in itself is so heigh, so pure and so goostly, that it may not be felt in oure sensible partye. The tokenes therof mowen, bot not it. And thus sumtyme oure Lorde wol withdrawe thi sensible fervours bothe in bygyng and provyng of thi pacyence; and not only for this skyle, bot for many other, the whiche I set not here at this tyme. Bot forth of oure mater.

By the worthines, the oftnes and the growyng of thees sensible felynges touchid before (the whiche thee thenkith his comyng, thof al it be not so) he wol norische and fede thi spirit to last and to lyve in love and worscheping of hym. So that thus, bi paciens in absens of thees sensible felynges, the tokenes of grace, and by that lively norisching and that lovely fedyng of thi spirit in here presence, he wol make thee in bothe togedir so blithely bowyng and so plesauntly pliing to the perfeccion and the goostly onheed to his owne wille (the whiche onyng is parfite charite) that thou schalt be as glad and as blithe to forgo soche sensible felynges at his wille, as for to have hem and fele hem in contynowaunce alle thi liif-tyme.

And in this tyme is thi love bothe chaste and parfite. In this tyme it is that thou bothe seest thi God and thi love, and nakidly felist hym also bi goostly onyng to his love in the sovereyn poynte of thi spirit, as he is in hymself, bot blyndely, as it may be here, utterly spoylid of thiself and nakidly clothed in hymself as he is, unclothed and not lappid in any of thees sensible felynges (be thei never so sweet ne so holy) that mowen falle in this liif. Bot in purete of spirit propirly and parfitely he is parceyvid and felt in himself as he is, fer lengthid fro any fantasye or fals opinion that may falle in this liif. This sight and this felyng of God, thus in hymself as he is, may no more be departyd fro God in hymself (to thin understondyng that thus felist or thus seest) then may be departyd God himself fro his owne beyng, the whiche ben bot one bothe in substaunce and also in kynde. So that as God may not be fro his beyng for onheed in kynde, so may not that soule, that thus seeth and felith, be fro that thing that he thus seeth and feleth for onheed in grace.

Lo! thus and by thees tokenes maist thou sumwhat fele, and in partye prove, the maner and the worthines of thi cleping and thi steryng in grace in thi goostly worching withinne, in thi redyng or hering of this mater withouten. And than, fro the tyme be that thou, or

eny other liche unto thee as in spirit, have had verrey experience of alle
thees tokenes, or of eny of hem – for at the first tyme ther ben bot ful
fewe that ben so specialy touchid and merkyd with this grace that thei
mowen have sone or sodenly, in verrey felyng, the proef of hem alle;
nevertheles, it suffiseth to have sum one or two, thof a man have not
alle at the first tyme – and therfore, yif thou felest that thou hast trewe
experience of one or of two, provid by trewe examynacion of scripture
and of counseil and of concyence: than it is speedful to thee sumtyme
for to cees of thees queinte meditacions and thees sotyle ymaginacions
of the qualitees of thi beyng and of Goddes, and of the werkes of thiself
and of God (in the whiche thi wittes han ben fed and with the whiche
thou hast ben led from wordlines and bodelines to that abilnes of grace
that thou arte inne) and for to lerne how thou schalt be ocupied goostly
in felyng of thiself and of God, whom thou hast lernid so wel before by
thenkyng and ymagenyng of youre doynges.

Ensaumple of this schewid Criste in this liif. For whi, yif it so had
ben that ther had ben none hier perfeccion in this liif bot in beholdyng
and in lovyng of his manheed, I trowe that he wolde not than have
assendid unto heven whiles this woreld had lastid, ne withdrawen his
bodely presence from his specyal lovers in erthe. Bot for ther was an
hier perfeccion, the whiche man may have in this liif (that is to sey, a
pure goostli felyng in the love of his Godheed) therfore he seide to his
disciples, the whiche grocheden to forgo his bodely presence (as thou
doost in partie and in maner to forgo thi corious meditacions and thi
queinte sotyl wittes) that it was speedful to hem that he went bodely fro
hem: *Expedit vobis ut ego vadam.*[20] That is: 'It is speedful to yow that I
go bodely fro yow.' Uppon this worde seith the doctour[21] thus: 'That
bot yif the schap of his manheed be withdrawen from oure bodely
ighen, the love of his Godheed may not fasten in oure goostly ighen.'
And thus sey I unto thee, that it is speedful sumtyme to leve of thi
corious worching in thi wittes and leere thee to taast sumwhat, in thi
felyng goostly, of the love of thi God.

And to this felyng schalt thou come bi that wey that I telle thee, by
helpe of grace goyng before. And that is, that thou evermore withouten
cesyng lene to the nakid felyng of thiself, evermore offryng thi being
unto God as for the most precious offring that thou maist make. Bot
loke, as I ofte seide, that it be nakid for drede of disceite. Yif it be nakid,
than wol it be ful peynful to thee in the biginnyng to abide therin any
while. And that is, as I before seyde, for thi wittys fynden no mete

therin unto hem. Bot no force therof, for I wol love it the betyr. Late hem faste awhile, I preie thee, from here kyndely delite in here kunnyng; for, as it is wel seide, a man kyndely desireth for to kunne; bot certes he may not taast of goostly felyng in God bot only by grace, have he never so moche kunnyng of clergie ne of kynde. And therfore, I preie thee, seche more after felyng then after kunning; for kunnyng oft-tymes disceyvith with pride, bot meek lovely felyng may not begile. *Sciencia inflat, karitas edificat.*[22] 'In knowyng is travaile, in feling is rest.'

Bot now mayst thou seye: What rest is this that thou spekist of? For me thenkith that it is travayle, pynyng, and no rest. For whan I set me to do as thou seyst, I fynde ther pyne and batayle on alle sides. For on that o partye my wittys wolden have me awey, and I wil not; and on that other partye I wolde fele God and lake the felyng of myself, and I may not. So that batayle is on alle sides and peyne; and this thenk me a queynte rest that thou spekist of. To this I answere and sey: That thou arte not used in this werk, and therfore it is more peynful to thee. Bot yif thou were wonte therto, and knewest by experience what profite were therin, thou woldest not wilfuly come oute therof to have alle the bodely joie and rest of this woreld. And yit it is grete peyne and a travayle also. Bot in that I clepe it a rest, for the soule is not in dwere what it schal do, and also for a soule is maad sekir – I mene in the tyme of this doynge – that it schal not moche erre.

8 Mystical Prayer

Apparently the work of a reader of the *Cloud*-author, this short treatise on the early stages of mystical prayer survives uniquely, without heading, in MS Douce 262, along with copies of *The Cloud of Unknowing*, *The Book of Privy Counselling* and extracts from Latin mystical works, including the third section of Hugh of Balma's *Viae Sion Lugent* or *De Triplici Via*, which comments upon *De Mystica Theologia* of Pseudo-Dionysius. The manuscript, which belonged to the London Charterhouse, was written *c.* 1500.

Sole manuscript: Bodleian Library MS Douce 262 (D), fols. 132v–133v.

When a solle begynyth to fele grace werke in hym, he wexyt then sory for hys synne, and rememberyth hys gret unkyndnes don agenst God and in what peryll his soll ys in. Anone he wepyth and waylyth his offence, and with gret sorow and lamentacyon cryth and callyth to God for mercy. Then thus contynewing, he gettyth hym to relygyon, or at-lest-wysse to confessyon, ther purgyng hymself clene from alle rust of syn by contricyon and penance-doyng. Anone he felyth hym esyd in body and soll, and delyverd fro knawyng of consyens, wych ys the gretyst peyn in erghth. Then contynently, he felyth gret swetnes both in redyng and preyer and sermons-heryng, thynkyng that this doth all worldly solas excede, and gret conforth he felyth in that the wych not long byfore was fulle tedyosse and paynfulle to hym. Then ys he prest and redy to do alle thys that scholde pleese God, and fleyng that thyng that schold dysploese hym. Then lernyghth he meknys, dred and love, convryttyng evermore hys wylle and preyer to the wylle of Gode.

Thus contynewyng, God – seyng the good wylle and desyer of the solle – drawyth hym more nere to hymself by a swet steryng of love and compassyon; so that, wher byfore the solle weppt and sorowyd for hys syns and unkyndnis, now wayllyth he for love and compassyon; so that no conforth ne joy ys to hym bysyd the rememberans of Christes passyon and the joys of hevyn.

Thus perseveryng in puryte of consyens, in preyer and meditacyon,

sodenly God sen[dy]th^*a* into the solle a bornyng love of desyer, so
farvantly that all bodyly myghth faylyth and the coruppt body fallyth
to the erghth. Then thynkyth he of no joy ne payne, nether of syne, ne
on the passyon of Christ, ne of our Lady, nor of nothyng in hevyn, in
helle, ne in erghth, but only on God. Not what God ys in kynd and
maner, but that God ys alle hys desyer; so that for abundans of love
that ys in the hart the mowth spekyth: 'Hart, hart, hart' or 'God, God,
God'.[1] Then ys the soll in a stylle rest that he felyth God in hymself and
he in God. So glad ys the solle and body then, that mar[v]yll^*b* yt ys that
the hart of man brek not and lepp not owt of the mowth for love into
God.

Other whylle, or the solle ys rappt into God, he sekyth (at the
fyrst kyndlyng) in the strettes of hevyn amonges sayntes and angellys
whom hys hart desyeryth, not caryng for ther company and joy, for hys
mynd ys not on them, ne on no other thyng, as Y sayd byfore, but only
on God. When he hath thus sawth and fond his love, [he]^*c* ronnyth with
a mek and a fervant desyer homly to hym. Notwithstondyng, not by
and by, he enteryth not into our Lord, but ronnyth abowt hym with a
bornyng love and pytyosly stondyth byfor God hys desyer, that he may
enter to hys hert. But God – faynyng hymself ungentylle and unkurtys,
and as a man takyng no hede to hys lover – keppyth hym of.
Neverthelesse, the sely solle abydyth in a longyng desyer, trystyng to
have that he cam for. Then God with lovely cownttynance takyth the
solle and pottyth hym into the mydyst of hys hart. Then all the wor[l]d^*d*
nor, Y trow, alle hevyn and hell cannot expresse the joy that the solle
felyth in hys Lord and love. Amen.

^*a* sendyth] senth D (dy *by corrector*).   ^*b* marvyll] marwyll D (ve *over line by c.*).
^*c* he] MS *om* (*inserted by c.*).   ^*d* world] word D.

WALTER HILTON
(d. 1396)

9 *Epistle on the Mixed Life*

Colophons in various manuscripts state that Walter Hilton died as a canon of the Augustinian priory of Thurgarton in Nottinghamshire on the Eve of the Annunciation (24 March) 1396. There is also a manuscript tradition that he was an Inceptor in canon law (i.e. he qualified for the doctorate, but had not actually taken it). A Walter Hilton, Bachelor of Civil Law, is recorded at the Ely Consistory Court in 1375, and Hilton may have been linked with Cambridge and Ely circles while Thomas Arundel was Bishop of Ely (1374–88). A Walter Hilton, B.C.L., was granted the reservation of a canonry and prebend of Abergwili, Carmarthen, on 28 January 1371. To have graduated by 1370, he would have gone up to Cambridge by 1357, having therefore been born before 1343.[1]

Little is otherwise known of Hilton's life, beyond some allusions in his Latin epistles, which address a number of themes also pursued in his English works. In probably his earliest extant work, *De Imagine Peccati* (*On the Image of Sin*), Hilton writes as one solitary to another, admitting to his own lack of fulfilment in the solitary life, and beginning that theme of the renewal of the *imago Dei* that he is to sustain through his writings. *De Utilitate et Prerogativis Religionis* (*On the Usefulness and Prerogatives of Religion*) is a letter to Adam Horsley, an Exchequer official appointed Controller of the Great Roll in 1375, who joined the Charterhouse of Beauvale in 1386. Hilton encourages Horsley in his intention, but he also gives a defence of the vowed religious life against (Wycliffite?) 'heretics' who deny its validity, and mentions the possibility of himself joining a religious community. The *De Adoracione Ymaginum* (*On the Veneration of Images*) shows Hilton engaged in an orthodox contribution to contemporary controversy, while in *De Lectione, Intentione, Oratione, Meditatione, etc.* (*On Reading, Intention, Prayer, Meditation, etc.*) he writes, possibly to a contemplative, as an established spiritual guide (perhaps by now at Thurgarton), expounding orthodox practice and warning against 'singularity' and 'liberty of spirit'.[2] The *Epistola ad Quemdam Seculo Renuntiare Volentem* (*Letter to Someone Wanting to Renounce the World*) is addressed to a lawyer who has experienced a religious conversion, and Hilton mentions in passing how he has himself given up a promising legal career. Hilton's purpose is to reassure the lawyer about some points on which he has scruples, and to dissuade him from entering the religious life, for which he is unsuited. The vowed religious life in community is not for everyone: for some, like this lawyer, religion lived out in the world should be their vocation.

Such an outline of his Latin letters suggests some of the character of Hilton as a spiritual guide more widely. With a shrewd understanding of human psychology, and from experience in the world, as a solitary, and in community, he addresses himself to a range of secular or religious readers, perhaps to particular individuals in the first instance, although as the works are copied the recipients come to represent classes of reader. A mode of address at once individual yet general is also found in Hilton's English works, and there are overlaps in material between *The Scale of Perfection*, Book I, and *De Imagine, De Utilitate, De Lectione* and *Of Angels' Song;* overlaps also occur between *Scale*, Book II, and *Ad Quemdem, Eight Chapters on Perfection,* and the psalm commentary *Qui Habitat.*

Hilton's teaching on the spiritual life is pre-eminently judicious, balanced and practical. His luminous style of writing – steeped in scripture – is limpid and serene. Yet he is intent on perfection, on making his reader realize every opportunity for growth in holiness. To this end – orthodox and conservative though he may be – Hilton is original in method, modifying traditional teaching in his *Mixed Life* and effecting in *The Scale* a creative and original synthesis. The two books of *The Scale* taken as a whole may be seen as the earliest work in English to address the entire spiritual life, meeting the needs both of beginners and of advanced contemplatives. That divergences between the two books show an adapted view of who may attain to contemplation is an instance of how Hilton's writings reflect his own developing understanding, despite his disclaimers of personal experience.

Mixed Life is addressed to a wealthy layman who has all the responsibilities of a parent, master of a household and landowner, but who feels himself called to devotion. Hilton's treatise aims to dissuade its recipient from attempting to imitate the contemplative life of a vowed religious. He should instead follow the path to holiness that is practical in his position, not resenting the inevitable interruptions from his secular commitments, in which he may serve God by serving others, and accepting the boundaries to contemplative life in his circumstances. To do so is to preserve the 'order of charity' (cf. Canticles 2: 4), and Hilton's counsel in *Mixed Life* represents a remarkable adaptation of traditional teaching, which had little to say of the interior life of contemplation in relation to active works of charity, except with regard to the 'mixed life' of bishops and preachers, where a blending of action and contemplation might occur in a pastoral context. Hilton adapts for lay people principles formulated by Gregory the Great[3] for prelates and pastors: active, secular people are encouraged to live a deeper life of prayer by analogy with the state of bishops, whose outward works should be informed by their inner life of contemplation. It is an exhortation to imitate the 'mixed' life of Christ, in which Hilton offers instruction to recipients lacking both contemplative retirement and the training of a religious. At the time he wrote on such a 'mixed' life Hilton apparently thought that it might attain to a middle stage of 'devotion', while true contemplation was in principle the prerogative of the contemplative life.[4] This accords with *Scale* I, to which *Mixed Life* is closely related and complementary.

Base manuscript: Lambeth Palace Library MS 472 (L), fols. 194r–213r. Also cited: CUL MS Ff. 5. 40 (Ff); Lincoln Cathedral Library MS 91, the 'Thornton Manuscript' (T); Bodleian Library MS Eng. poet. a. 1., the 'Vernon Manuscript' (V).

Here bigynneth the book that is cleped 'Medeled Liyf', whiche is drawen oute bitwene actif liyf and liyf contemplatif.

Brothir and suster, bodili and goosteli,[5] two maner states there ben in hooli chirche, bi the whiche Cristen soules plesen God and geten hem the blis of hevene: that oon is bodili, and that othir is goostli.

Bodili wirchynge longeth principali to wordli men or women, the whiche han leufulli wordeli goodes and wilfulli usen wordeli bisynesses. Also it longeth to alle yonge, bigynnynge men, whiche comen newe oute of wordli synnes to the service of God; for to make hem able to goosteli wirkynge and for to breke doun the unbuxumnesse of the body bi reson and bi such bodili werchynge that it myght be souple and redi and not moche contrarious to the spirit [in]^a goosteli wirchinge. For as Seint Poul seith, 'As woman was maad for man and not man for woman',[6] right so bodili worchynge was maad for goosteli, and not goostli for bodili. Bodili wirchynge gooth bifore and goosteli cometh aftir, so seith Seynt Poul: *Non quod prius spirituale, sed quod prius animale, deinde spirituale.*[7] 'Goosteli werk cometh not first, but first cometh bodili werk that is doon bi the bodi, and sithen cometh goostli werk aftir.' And this is the cause whi it bihoveth to be so: for we aren born in synne and in corrupcioun of the flesch, bi the whiche we aren blynded and so overleid that we have neithir the gostli knowynge of God bi light of undirstondynge, ne goostli felynge of hym bi clene desire of lovynge. And forthi we mai not sodeynli stirte oute of this myrk pitte of this fleschli corrupcion into

---

^{a} in] Ff; L *om.*

that goostli light; for we mai not suffre it ne beere it for sikenesse of oure silf, n[o]*b* more thanne we mai with oure bodili ighen whanne thei aren sore bihoolde the [l]ight*c* of the sonne. And therfore we mosten abide and worche bi proces of tyme, first bi bodili werkes bisili unto wee ben discharged of this hevy birthene of synne the whiche letteth us fro goostli wirkynge, and to oure soule be sumwhat clensed from grete outeward synnes and abled to goosteli werk.

Bi this bodili worchynge that I speke of, mai thou undirstonde al maner of good werkes that thi soule dooth bi the wittes and the membres of thi bodi unto thi silf – as is fastynge, wakynge, and in refreynyng of thi fleschli lustis bi othir penaunce doynge – or to thyn even-Cristen bi fulfillinge of the dedes of merci bodili or goosteli, or unto God bi suffrynge of alle maner myscheves for the love of rightwisenesse. Alle thise werkes doon in trouthe bi charite plesen God, withouten the whiche thei aren nought.

Thanne whoso desireth for to be occupied goostli, it is siker and profitable to him that he be first wel assaied a longe tyme in this bodili worchynge, for thise bodili deedes aren a tokene and a schewynge of moral vertues, withouten whiche a soule is not able for to worche goostli. Breke doun first pride in bodili berynge and also withinne thyn herte, thenkynge, boostynge and rosynge of thisilf and of thi deedes, presumynge of thisilf, veyn likynge in thisilf of ony thynge that God hath sent to thee, bodili or goostli. Breke doun also envie and wrath ayens thyn even-Cristen, whethir he be riche or pore, good or badde; that thou hate him not, ne have disdeyn of hym wilfulli, nothir in word ne in deede. Also breke doun covetise of wordli good: that thou for hooldynge, of getynge, or savynge of it, offende not thi conscience, ne breke not charite to God and to thyn even-Cristene for love of no wordli good, but that thou getist to kepe it and spende it withoute love and veyn likynge of it, as resoun asketh, in worschipe of God and helpe of thyne even-Cristen. Breke doun as moche as thou mai fleschli likynges, eithir in accidie or in bodili eese, or glotonie, or leccherie, and thanne, whanne thou hast be wel traveiled and wel assaied in alle siche bodili werkes, than mai thou bi grace ordayne thee to goostli worchynge.

Grace and goodnesse of oure Lord Jhesu Crist – that he hath schewid to thee in withdrawynge of thyn herte fro love and likynge of wordeli vanite and use of fleschli synnes, and in turnynge of thi wille

b no] Ff; ne L.   *c* light] Ff; sight L.

entierli to his service and his plesaunce – bringeth into thi herte moche matier to love him and his merci. And also it stireth me greteli to strengthe thee in the good purpos and into thi good worchyng that thou haste bigunne, for to brynge it to a good eende (yif that I coude), and principalli for God and sith for tendre affeccioun of love whiche thou haste to me.

If I be a wrecche and unworthi, Y knowe weel the desire of thyn herte: that thou yernest gretli to serve oure Lord bi goostli occupacioun al holli, withoute lettynge, or trobolynge, or wordeli bisynesse, that thou myghtest come bi grace to more knowynge and goosteli feelynge of God and of goostli thynges. This desire is good, as Y hope, and of God, for it is sette unto hym in charite speciali. Neverthelees, it is for to restreyne and rulen it bi discrecion as anemptis outeward worchynge, aftir the staat that thou art inne, for charite unruled turneth sumtyme into vice. And forthi it is seid in hooli writte: *Ordinavit in me caritatem.*[8] That is to seie: 'Oure Lord, yevynge me charite, sette it in ordre and in rule', that it schulde not be lost thorugh myn undiscrecioun. Right so this charite and this desire that oure Lord hath yeven of his merci to thee is for to rulen and ordaynen hou thou schal pursue it aftir thi degree asketh and aftir the lyvynge that thou hast used bifore this tyme, and aftir the grace of vertues that thou now haste.

Thou schalt not uttirli folwen thi desire for to leven occupacioun and bisynesse of the world (whiche aren nedefull to usen in rulynge of thisilf and of alle othere that aren undir thi kepynge) and yeve thee hooli to goostli occupaciouns of preiers and meditaciouns, as it were a frere, or a monk, or anothir man that were not bounden to the world bi children and servauntes as thou art. For it falleth not to thee, and yif thou do soo thou kepest not the ordre of charite. Also, yif thou woldest leven uttirli goostli occupacion – nameli now aftir the grace that God hath yeven unto thee – and sette the hooli to the bisynesse of the world, to fulfillynge of werkes of actif liyf, as fulli as anothir man that nevere feeled devocion, thou levest the ordre of charite. For thi staat asketh for to doo bothe, eche of hem in dyvers tyme. Thou schalt meedele the werkes of actif liyf with goostli werkes of lif contemplatif, and thanne doost thou weel. For thou schalt oo tyme with Martha[9] be bisi for to rule and governe thi houshoold, thi children, thi servauntis, thi neighbores, thi tenauntes: yif thei doo weel, comfort hem therinne and helpe hem; yef thei doon yvele, for to teche hem and amende hem and chastice hem. And thou schalt also loke and knowe wiseli that thi

thynges and thi wordeli goodes be rightfully keped bi thi servauntes
governynge and truli spended, that thou myght the more plentevousli
fulfille the deedes of merci with hem unto thi even-Cristene. Also thou
schal with Maria leve bisinesse of the world, and sitten doun at the
f[ee]t^d of oure Lord bi mekenesse in praiers, and in hooli thoughtis, and
in contemplacioun of him as he yeveth thee grace. And so schalt thou
goon from the toon to the tothir medfulli and fulfille hem bothe. And
thanne kepist thou weel the ordre of charite.

Neverthelees, that thou have no wondir of this that Y seie,
therfore I schal telle and declare to thee a litil of this more openli. Thou
schalt undirstonde that theer is three maner of lyvynge: oon is actif,
another is contemplatiyf, the thredde is maad of bothe and that is
medeled. Actif liyf aloone longeth to wordeli men and women whiche
aren lewed in knowyng of goostli occupacioun, for thei feelen no
savour in devocioun bi fervour of love as othere men doon, ne thei can
no skile of it. And yit, neverthelees, thei have drede of God and of the
peynes of helle. Therfore thei fleen synne, and thei have desire for to
plese God and for to come to hevene, and thei have a good wille to her
even-Cristene. Unto thise men it is needful and spedful to usen the
werkes of actif liyf as bisili as thei mai in heelpe of hemself and of hire
even-Cristene, for thei can not ellis doon.

Contemplatif liyf aloone longeth to siche men and women that
for the love of God forsaken alle open synnes of the world and of here
flesch, and alle bisynesse, charges and governaunces of wordli goodes
and maken hemself pore and naked to the bare nede of the bodili
kynde, and fleen fro sovereynte of alle othere men to the service of God.
Unto thise men it longeth for to travaile and occupie hem inwardli, for
to gete thorugh the grace of oure Lord clennesse of herte and pees in
conscience, bi distroiynge of synne and receyvynge of vertues, and so
for to come to contemplacioun – whiche clennesse mai not be haad
withoute grete exercise of bodi and contynuel traveile of spirit in
devoute praieres, fervent desires and goostli meditacions.

The thridde liyf, that is medelid, longith speciali to men of holi
chirche – as to prelates and othire curates whiche have cure and
sovereynte over othere men for to teche and for to rule hem, bothe here
bodies and principali heer soules, in fulfillynge of the deedes of merci,
bodili and goostli. Unto thise men it longeth sumtyme [to]^e usen the

---

^{d} feet] v; foot L. ^{e} to] Ff; L *om.*

werkes of merci in actif lif, in help and sustenaunce of hemsilf and of here suggettis, and of othere also; and sumtyme for to leven al manere bisynesse outeward and yeve hem unto preieres and meditacions, redynge of hooli writ, and to othere goostli occupacions, aftir that thei feele hemsilf disposed. Also it longeth generaly [to]^f sum temporal men, þe whiche have sovereynte with moche avere of wordli goodis and haven also, as it were, lordschipe overe othere men for to governe and sustene hem – as a fadir hath over his children, a maister over his servauntes, and a lord overe his tenantes – the whiche men han also receyved of oure Lord yiftes of grace and of devocioun, and in partie savoure of goostli occupacioun. Unto thise men also longeth medeled lif that is bothe actif and contemplatif.

For yif thise men standynge the charge and the boond whiche thei han take wolen leeve uttirli the bisynesse of the world – the whiche oweth skilfulli for to be used in fulfillynge of here chaarge – and hooli yyve hem to contemplatif liyf, thei doon not weel, for thei kepen not the ordre of charite. For charite, as thou knowest weel, lieth bothe in love of God and of thin evene-Cristene. And therfore it is resonable that he that hath charite use bothe in worchynge, now the toon and now the tothir. For he that for the love of God in contemplacioun leveth the love of his even-Cristene and dooth not to hem as he oughte, whanne he is bounden therto, he fulfillith not charite. Also, on the contrarie wise, whoso hath more reward to werkes of actif liyf and to bisynesse of the world, that for the love of his even-Cristene he leeveth goostly occupacion uttirli aftir that God disposeth hym therto, he fulfilleth not fully charite. This is the seiynge of Gregor.[10] Forthi oure Lord, for to stire summe to use this medeled liyf, took upon himself the persoone of sich manere men – bothe of prelates of hooli chirche and othere sich as aren disposid, as I have seid – and yave hem ensample bi his owen worchynge that thei schulden usen this medeled liyf as he dide. O tyme he comouned with men and medeled with men, schewynge to hem his deedes of merci. For he taughte the uncouth and unkunynge bi his prechynge; he vesited the sike and heeled hem of here sooris; he fedde the hongry, and he comforted the sori. And another tyme he lefte the conversacioun of alle wordeli men and of his disciples and 'wente into dissert upon the hillis and contynued alle the nyght in praieres aloone', as the gospel seith.[11] This medeled liyf schewed oure Lord to ensample of alle othere that han

^{f} to] Ff; L om.

taken the charge of this medeled liyf, that thei schulde oon tyme yeve hem to bisynesse of wordli thynges at resonable neede, and to the werkes of actif liyf in profite of here even-Cristene whiche thei have cure of, and anothir tyme yeve hem hooli to devocion and to contemplacion in praieres and in meditacioun.

This liyf ledden and usiden thise hooli bischopis bifore, whiche hadden cure of mennys soulis and mynistracioun of temporal goodes. For thise hooli men leften not uttirli the ministracioun, and the lokynge, and the dispendynge of wordli goodes, and yaf hem hooli to contemplacioun – as moche grace of contemplacioun as thei hadden – but thei lefte ful ofte here owen reste in contemplacioun, whanne thei hadde ful lyvere have be stille therat, for love of hire evene-Cristene, and entirmeted hem with wordli bisynesse in helpynge of heer suggettis. And sotheli that was charite. For wiseli and discreteli thei departed here lyvynge in two. O tyme thei fulfilleden the lowere part of charite bi weies of actif lif, for thei were bounden therto bi takynge of hire prelacies. And anothir, thei fulfilleden the highere partie of charite in contemplacioun of God and of goosteli thynges bi praieres and meditacions. And so thei hadden charite to God and to hire evene-Cristen, bothe in affeccioun of soule withinne and also with schewynge of bodili deedes withouten. Other men that weren oonli contemplatif and oonly weren free from alle cures and prelacie, thei hadden ful charite to God and to here evene-Cristene, but it was oonli in affeccioun of hire soule and not in outeward scheewynge. And in haap so moche it was the more ful inward that it was not lettid bi outward deedis, for thei myghten not, ne it nedid not, ne it fil not for hem. But thise men that were in prelacie, and othere also that weren oonli temporal men, hadden ful charite in affeccioun withinne, and also in worchynge withoute. And that is propirly medlid lyf that is maad bothe of actif and of contemplatif lif.

And soothli, for siche a man that is in spiritual sovereynte (as prelacie, in cure, governaunce of othere, as prelates and curates ben), or in temporal sovereynte (as wordeli lordes or maistris aren), I hoolde this liyf medeled best and most bihoofful to hem as longe as thei are bounden therto. But to othere that aren free, not bounden to temporal ministracioun ne to spiritual, I hope that lif contemplatif aloone, yif thei myghten come therto sothfasteli, were best, moste spedefulle, most [me]edfulle,[g] most fair, most worthi of hem for to use, and for to

---

[g] meedfulle] Ff; nedfulle L.

hoolde, and not for to leve it wilfulli for noon outeward wirchynge of actif lif, but yif it were in gret nede – as grete relevynge and comfortynge of othir men, eithir of here bodi or of heere soule. And thanne – yif nede aske it, at the praiere and instaunce of othere, or elles atte biddynge of his sovereyne – I hope it be good to hem for to schewe outeward werkes of actif liyf for a tyme, in helpynge of heer evene-Cristene.

Bi this that I have seid thou mai a parti undirstonde whiche is oon and whiche is othir, and whiche acordeth most to thi staat in lyvynge. And soothli, as me thenketh, this medeled liyf accordeth moost to thee, sithen oure Lord hath ordeyned thee and sette the in the staat of sovereynte over othir men as moche as it is, and lente the habundaunce of wordeli goodis for to rulen and sustene speciali alle thise that arn undir thi governaunce and thi lordschipe, of thi myght and kunnynge. And also withal that thou hast receyved grace – of the merci of oure Lord – for to knowe thiself and goosteli desire and savour of his love, I hope that this lif that is medeled is the beste and acordeth moste to thee for to traveile inne. And therfor departe wiisli thi lyvyng in two: o tyme to oon, another tyme to that othere. For, wite thou weel, yif thou leve nedefull bisynesse of actif liyf, and be reklees, and take noo keep of thi wordli goodes, hou thei aren spendid and keped, ne haste no force of thi suggettis and of thyne evene-Cristene bicause of wille and desire that thou hast onli to yeve thee to goosteli occupacion, wenynge that thou art bi that excused – yif thou do soo, thou doost not wiseli.

What aren alle thyn werkes worth, whethir thei ben bodili or goosteli, but yif thei ben doon rightwiseli and resonabli to the worschipe of God and at his biddynge? Sothli, right nought. Thanne yif thou leve that thynge that thou art bounden to bi wai of charite, of right and of resoun, and wolt hooli yeve the to anothir thynge wilfulli – as it were to more plesaunce of God – whiche thou art not fulli bounden to, thou doost no worschipe discreteli to him. Thou art bisi to worschipe his heed and his face,[12] and araie it faire and curioseli, but thou levest his bodi, his armes and his feete ragged and rente, and takest noo keep thereof, and there thou worschipest hym nought. For it is velanye and no worschipe a man to be curiouseli arraied upon his heed with perre and precious stoones, and al his bodi be naked and baare, as it were a beggere. Right so goosteli, it is no worschipe to God to croune his heed and leve his bodi baare.

Thou schalt undirstonde that oure Lord Jhesu Crist as man is heed of al the goosteli bodi whiche is holi chirche. The membres of this bodi aren alle Cristene men: summe aren armes and summe feet, and summe aren othere membres, aftir sundri wirchynges that thei usen in heere lyvynge. Thanne yif that thou be bisi with al thi wirching and thi myghte for to arraie his heed – that is for to worschipe hymsilf by mynde of his passion and of his othere werkes in his manheed bi devocioun and meditacioun of him – and foryetest his feet – that aren thyn children and thi servauntes, thi tenauntes – and alle thyn evene-Cristen spille for defaute of kepynge, unaraied, unkeped, and not tended to as thei aught for to be: thou plesest him not. Thou doost noo worschipe to him. Thou makest thee for to kisse his mouth bi devocion and goosteli praier, but thou tredest upon his feet and defoulest hem, in as moche as thou wolt not tende to hem – for negligence of thisilf – whiche thou haste take the cure of. Thus thenketh me. Neverethelees, yif thou thenke that it is not sooth, for it were a faire office to worschipe the heed of him (as for to be al dai occupied in the meditacioun of his manhede), thanne for to go lowere to othere werkes and make clene his feet (as for to be bysi bothe in word and in deede aboute the heelpe of thyn even-Cristene in tyme) me thenketh not soo as unto the. For sothli, he wole the more thanke for the meke waschynge of his feet whan thei are right foule and stynken upon thee, than for al the precious peyntynge and araiynge that thou can make aboute his heed bi mynde of his manhed, for it is fair inowgh and nedeth not to be araied of thee moche. But his feet and his other membris – that aren thi sogettis and thin even-Cristen – are sumtyme yvel araied and hadde nede to be loked and holpin bi thee, nameli sithen thou art bounden therto. And for hem wole he konne thee more thanke, yif thou wilt mekeli and tendirli loke to hem.

For the more lowe service that thou hast to thi Lord for love of him or to ony of hise membris whan nede and rightwisenesse asketh it, with a glaad meke herte, the more plesist thou him, thenkenge that it were inowgh to thee for to be at the leste degre and lowest staat, sithen it is his wille that it be soo. For it semeth to me, sithen he hath put thee in that staat for to traveile and serve othere men, that it is his wil that thou schuldest fullfille it on thi myght. This ensample I seie to thee, not for thou doost not thus as I seie (for I hoope that thou dost thus and betere), but I wolde that thou schuldest doo thus gladli, and not thenke looth for to leve sumtyme goostli occupacion and entirmete thee with wordli bisynesse, in wise kepynge and spendynge of thi wordli goodes, in good rulynge of thi servauntes and thi tenauntes, and in othere good werkes wirkynge to alle thyn even-Cristene of thi myght. But that thou schuldest doo bothe werkes in divers tymes and with as good wille that oon as that othir (yif thou myght). As, yif thou hadde praied and been ocupied goostli, thou schalt aftir certayn tyme breke of that, and thanne schalt thou bisili and gladli occupie thee in sum bodili occupacion to thyn even-Cristene. Also, whanne thou hast ben bisi outward a while with thi servauntis or with othir men profitabli, thou schalt breke of and turne ayen to thi praieres and thi devociouns aftir God yeveth the grace. And so schalt thou putte awei bi grace of oure Lord sleuthe, ydelnesse and veyn reste that cometh of thi flesch undir colour of contemplacion and letteth the sumtyme fro meedfulle and spedeful occupacion in outeward bisinesse, and thou schalt be ai wel occupied eithir bodili or goosteli. And therfore, yif thou wilt doo weel, thou schalt doo goostli as Jacob dide bodili.

Holi writ[13] seith that Jacob, whan he bigan to serve his maister Laban, he coveited Rachel, his maistris doughter, to his wif for hire fairheed, and for hire he served. But whan he wende for to have hadde hire to his wif, he took first Lia, the tothir doughtir, in the stide of Rachel. And aftirward he took Rachel, and so he hadde bothe atte laste.

Bi Jacob in hooli writ is undirstonde an overgoere of synnes. Bi thise two wymmen are undirstonden, as Seynt Gregor seith,[14] two lyves in hooli chirche: actif liyf and contemplatif liyf. Lia is as moche for to seie as travelous, and it bitokeneth actif liyf. Rachel is as moche for to seie as sight of bigynnynge that is God, and bitokeneth liyf contemplatif. Lia was fruteful, but sche was soor-ighed.[15] Rachel was fair and loveli, but sche was barayne. Thanne, right as Jacob coveited Rachel for hire faireheed and neverthelees he hadde hir not whanne he wolde, but first he took Lia and aftirward hire suster – right so every man t[urn]id[b] bi grace of compunccioun sothfasteli f[ro][i] synnes of the world and of the flesch unto the service of God and clennesse of good lyvynge hath grete desire and greet longynge for to have Rachel: that is for to have reste in goosteli swettenesse, in devocioun and contemplacion, for it is so fair and so loveli, and in hope for to have that liyf oonli he disposeth him for to serve oure Lord with al his myght. But often whanne he wenede for to have had Rachel (that is reeste in devocion) oure Lord suffreth

---

[b] turnid] TV; travelid L.   [i] fro] TV; for L.

him first to be assaied wel and traveiled with Lia (that is, eithir with temptacions of the world, or elles of the devel, or elles with othir wordli besynesse, bodili or goosteli, in heelpynge of his evene-Cristene). And whanne he is weel traveiled with Lia, and nerhande oovercomen, thanne oure Lord yeveth him Rachel (that is grace of devocioun and reste in conscience) and thanne hath he bothe Rachel and Lia.

So schalt thou doo aftir the ensample of Jacob: take thise two lyves, actif and contemplatif, sithen God hath sent the bothe and use hem bothe, that toon with that tothir. Bi that oon liyf schal thou bringe forth frute of many good deedis in helpe of thyn even-Cristene, and that is bi actif liyf. And bi that othir thou schalt be maked fair, clene and bright in the sovereyne brightnesse that is God, bigynnere and endere of al that is maad; and thanne schaltou be soothfasteli Jacob, and overgoere and overcomere of alle synnes. And aftir this bi grace of God thi name schal be chaungid as Jacobis name was and turned into Israel. Israel is as moche for to seie as a man seynge God. Thanne yif thou be first Jacob and discreteli wole use thise two lyves in tyme, thou schalt aftir be Israel (that is verri contemplatif) eithir in this liyf, yif he wole delyvere thee and make thee free from chargees and bisynesses the whiche thou art bounden to, or ellis aftir this liyf fulle in the blisse of hevene whanne thou comest thider.

Liyf contemplatif is fair and medefulle and therfore thou schalte ai have it in thi mynde and in thy desire. But thou schalt have in usynge liyf actif, for it is so needful and so speedfulle. Therfore yif thou be putte fro reste in devocioun whan thou were levest be stille therat – eithir [bi]*i* thi children or thi servauntes, or bi ony of thyn evene-Cristene for here profite or ese of heertes skilfulli asked – be not angri with hem, ne hevy, ne dredefulle, as yif God wolde bee wroth with thee that thou levest him for ony other thynge, for it is not sooth. Leve of lighteli thi devocioun, whethir it be in praiere or in meditacioun, and goo doo thi dette and thi service to thyne evene-Cristene as redili as oure Lord himsilf badde thee doo so. And suffre mekeli for his love withouten grucching (if thou may doo) bothe withoute disese and trobelynge of thin herte bicause of medelynge of siche bisynesse.

For it mai falle sumtyme that the more trobeled that thou haste ben outward with actif werkes, the more brennynge desire thou schal have to God, and the more cleer sight of gosteli thinges bi grace of oure

i bi] Ff; L *om.*

Lord in devocioun whanne thou comest therto. For it fareth heerebi as
yif thou hadde a litil cole and thou wolde make a fier therwith and
make it to brenne. Thou woldest first lei to stikkes and overhile the
cole, [and though it semed for a tyme that thou schuldest quenche the
cole]^k with the stikkes, neverthelees, whanne thou haste abiden a while
and aftirward blowest a litil, anoon schal springe oute a gre[t]e^l flawme
of fiere, for the stikkes aren turned alle to fier. Right so is goostli the
wille and the desire that thou hast to God. It is as hit were a litil coole of
fire in thi soule, for it yeveth to the sumwhat of light and of goostli
heete. But it is ful litil, for ofte it wexeth coold and turneth to flesschli
reste, and sumtyme to ydelnesse. Forthi it is good that thou putte therto
stikkes, that aren good werkes of actif liyf. And though it be so that
thise werkes, as it semeth, for a tyme lette thi desire, that it mai not bee
so cleene ne so fervent as thou woldest, be not to dredefulle therfore.
But abide and suffre a while, and so blow at the fire: that is, first goo do
thi werkes, and go thanne aloone to thi praiers and to thi meditaciouns,
and lift up thyn herte to God, and praie him of his goodnesse that he
wole accepte thi werkes that thou doost to his plesaunce.

Holde the thanne as nought in thin owen sight, but oonli at the
merci of hym. Be acknowe mekeli thi wrecchidnesse and thi freelte, and
arette sothfasteli thi good deedes al to him in as moche as thei aren
goode; and in as moche as thei aren badde, and not doon discreteli with
alle circumstance that aren needfulle to a good deede, for defaute of
discrecioun – putte hem to thisilf. And thanne for this mekenesse schal
alle thi good deedis torne into a flawme of fire, as stikkes leid upon a
coole, and thanne schal thi gode deedes outeward not hyndre thi
devocioun but rather make it more.

Oure Lord seith in hooli writte thus: *Ignis in altari meo semper
ardebit, et sacerdos surgens mane subicie[t]^m ligna ut ignis non
extinguatur.*[16] 'Fier schal brenne ai in my awter, and the preest risynge
at morne schal putte under stikkes that it be not quenched.' This fier is
love and desire to God in a soule, whiche love [nede]th^n for to be
norischid and kepid bi leiynge to of stikkes that it goo not oute. Thise
stikkes aren of divers matir: sum are of oo tree and summe of anothir.
A man that is lettered and hath undirstondynge of hooli writte, yif he
have this fier of devocioun in his herte, it is good unto him for to gete
him stikkes of hooli ensamples and seiynges of oure Lord bi redynge in

---

^{k} and . . . cole] TV; L *om.* ^{l} grete] FF; grene L. ^{m} subiciet] subiciens L.
^{n} love nedeth] TV; loveth L.

hooli writte and norissch the fier with hem. Another man, unlettered, mai not so redili have at his hand hooli writ ne dottoures seiynges, and forthi it nedeth unto him for to doo many goode deedes outewarde to his evene-Cristene and kendele the fier of love with hem. And so it is good that eche man in his degree, after that he is disposid, that he gete him stikkes of o thing other of other – eithir of preieres, or of good meditaciouns, or reding in hooli writte, or good bodili worchynge – for to norische the fier of love in his soule, that it be not quenchid. For the affeccioun of love is tendre and lightli wole vanysche awai, but yif it be wel kepid, and bi good deedis bodili or goostli continueli norisched.

Now thanne, sithen oure Lord hath sent into thyn herte a litil sparcle of this blissid fier that is himsilf – as hooli writ seith: *Deus noster ignis consumens est*:[17] 'Oure Lord God is fier wastynge' (for, as bodili fier wasteth alle bodili thynges that mai be wasted, right so goosteli fier, that is God himsilf, wastith al maner of synne where-so it falleth, and forthi oure Lord is likened to fier wastynge) – I praie thee norische this fier. This fier is not ellis but love and charite. This hath he sent into the erthe, as he seith in the goospel: *Ignem veni mittere in terram et ad qu[i]d° nisi ut ardeat.*[18] 'I am come to sende fier into the erthe, and wharto not but that it schulde brenne?' That is: God hath sent fier of love, of good desire and grete wille for to plese him, into mannys soule, and unto this ende: that aftir that a man schal knowe it, kepe it, and norische it, and strengthe it, and be saved therbi. The more desire that thou hast to him and for him, the more is the fier of love in thee; and the lasse that this desire is in thee, the lasse is the fier. The mesure of this desire, hou moche it is, neither in thisilf ne in non other, knowest thou nought, ne no man of himsilf, but God oonli that yeveth it. And forthi dispute not with thisilf, as yif thou woldest knowe hou myche thi desire is. Be thou bisi for to desire as moche as thou mai, but not for to wite the mesure of thi desire.

Seynt Austyn seith that the liyf of eche good Cristen man is a continuel desire to God;[19] and that is of grete vertu, for it is a greet criynge in the eeris of God. The more thou desirest, the higher thou criest, the betere thou praiest, the wiseliere thou thenkest. And what is this desire? Sotheli, [no thinge][p] but a lothynge of al this wordlis blisse, of this fleschli likynge in thyn herte, and a wondirful longynge with a trustfull yernynge of endelees blisse and heveneli desire and joie. This

thenketh me mai be called a desire to God for himself. Yif thou have
this desire, as I hope sikirli that thou hast, I praie thee kepe it weel and
norisch it wiseli. And whanne thou schalt praie or thenke, make this
desire bigynnynge and ende of al thi werk, for to encrese it. Loke aftir
noon othir feelynge in thi bodili wittes; ne seke after noon other bodili
suettenesse, neither sownyng, ne savoryng, ne wondirful light, ne
angelis sight; ne though oure Lord himsilf (as unto thi sight) wolde
appere bodili to thee, charge it but a litil. But that al thi besynesse be:
that thou myght feele soothfasteli in thi thought a lothynge and a ful
forsakynge of alle manere of synne and of al manere of unclennesse,
with a goostli sight of it, hou foule, hou ugli and hou peynfulle it is; and
that thou have a myghti desire to vertues, to mekenesse, to charite, and
to the blis of hevene. This thenketh me were goostli comfort and
goostli suettenesse in mannys soule: as for to have clennesse in
conscience fro wikkednesse of alle wordli vanite, with stable thought,
meke hope and ful desire to God, hou so evere it be of othere comfortes
and swettenesses.

   Me thenketh that swettenesse is siker and sothfast that is feeled in
clennesse of conscience bi myghti forsaking and lothinge of alle synne,
and with inward sight, with fervent desire of goostli thinges. Alle
othere comfortes and swettenessis of ony manere of felynge – but yif
thei helpe and lede to this ende (that is, to clennesse of conscience and
goostli desire of God) – aren not siker to reste in.

   But now askest thou whether this desire be love to God? As unto
this, I seie that this desire is not propirli love, but it is a bigynnynge and
a taastynge of love. For love propirli is a ful couplynge of the lovynge
and the loved togidre, as God and a soule into oon. This couplynge mai
not be fulli hadde in this liyf, but oonli in desire and longynge therto, as
bi this ensample. As, if a man love anothir man whiche is absent, he
desireth greteli his presence for to have the use of his love and his
lyking. Right so goostly, as long as we aren in this liyf, oure Lord is
absent fro us, that we mai neithir see him, ne heere him, ne feele [him][q]
as he is. And therfore we mai not have the use of his fulle love heere in
fulle likynge, but we mai have a desire and a grete yeernynge for to be
present to him, for to see him in his blisse, and fulli for to be oned to
him in love. This desire mai we have of his yifte in this liyf, bi the wiche
we schalle be saaf, for it is love unto him as it mai be haad heere. Thus

[q] him] Ff; L _om._

seith Seynt Poul: *Scientes quoniam dum sumus in hoc corpore peregrinamur a domino, per fidem [enim]ʳ ambulamus et non per speciem; audemus autem et bonam voluntatem habemus magis peregrinari a corpore et praesentes esse ad deum, et ideo contendimus sive absentes sive praesentes placere illi.*[20] Seynt Poul seith: 'That as longe as we aren in this bodi we aren pilgrimes fro oure Lord.' That is: we aren absent from hevene in this exile. 'We goo bi trouthe, not bi sight.' That is: we lyven in trouthe, not in bodili feelynge. 'We daar and have gode wille to be absent fro the bodi and be present to God.' That is: we, for clennesse in conscience and siker trust of savacion, daar desire partyng fro oure bodi bi bodili deeth and be present to oure Lord. 'Neverthelees, for we mai not yit, therfore we stryven, whethir we ben absent or present, for to plese him.' That is: we stryven ayenes synnes of the world and likynge of the flesch bi desire to him, for to brennen in this desire al thing that letteth us from him.

But yit askest thou me, 'Mai a man have this desire in his herte continueli? Me thenketh nai.' As unto this, I mai seie as me thenketh: that this desire mai be haad as for vertu and profite of it in habite contynueli, but not in wirkynge ne in usynge, as bi this ensample. Yif thou were sike and thou schulde have, as eche man hath, a kendeli desire of bodili heele continueli in thyn herte, what thou dide, whethir thou slepe or thou wake, but not ai iliche; for yif thou slepe, or ellis wake and thenkest on sum wordli thinge, thanne thou hast this desire in habite oonli and not in worchinge, but whanne thou thenkest on thi sikenesse and of thi bodili heele, thanne hast thou it in usynge. Right so it is goostli of desire to God. He that hath this desire, of yift of God, yif he slepe or elles thenke not on God but on wordli thinges, yit he hath this desire in habite of his soule until he synne deedli. But anoon, as he thenketh on God or on clennesse of lyvynge, or of the joies of hevene, thanne worchith his desire to God, as longe as he kepith his thought and his entent to plese God, eithir in praier or in meditacioun, or in ony other good deede of actif lif. Than is it good that al oure bisynesse be for to stire this desire, to use it bi discrecioun, now in oo deede, now in anothir, aftir we aren disposyd and have grace therto. This desire is rote of al thi wirkynge, yif it be meedful; for wite thou weel, what good deede that thou dost for God, bodili or goostli, it is an usynge of this desire.

ʳ *enim*] L *om.*

And therfore whan thou doost a good deede or praiest or thenkest on God, thenke not in thyn herte, doutynge whethir thou desirest or noon, for thi deede scheweth thi desire. Summe aren unconnynge and wenen that thei desiren not God but yif thei be evere criynge on God with wordes of heere mouth or elles in heer herte, as yif thei seiden thus, 'A, Lord, bringe me to thi blisse; Lord, make me saaf,' or elles siche othere. Thise wordes aren goode whethir thei ben seid with mouth or formed in the herte, for thei stire a mannys herte to desirynge of God. But neverthelees, withouten ony siche wordes, a clene thought of God or of ony goostli thing – as of vertues or of the manhede of Crist, or of the joies of hevene, or of undirstondynge of hooli writ with love – mai be betere than siche wordes. For a clene thought of God is sothfast desire to him; and the more gostli that the thought is, the more is the desire. And forthi, be thou nought in doute ne in dwere whan thou praiest or thenkest on God, or ellis whanne thou doost othere outward good deedes to thyn even-Cristene, whethir thou desirest him or not, for thi dedes schewen it.

Neverthelees, though it be soo that alle thi good deedes bodili and goostli aren a schewynge of thi desire to God, yit is there a diversite bitwene goostli and bodili dedis. For dedis of contemplatif lif aren propirli and kyndeli the wirchinge of this desire, but outeward deedes aren not so. And forthi, whan thou praiest or thenkest on God, thi desire to God is more hool, more fervent and more goostli than whanne thou dost othere, outward, good dedis unto thin even-Cristen.

Now yif thou aske hou thou schalt kepe this desire and norisch it, a litil schal I telle thee: nought that thou schalt use the same foorme alwei that I seie, but that thou schulde have therbi, yif nede be, sum warnynge and wissynge for to rule thee in thin occupacioun. For I mai not, ne Y can not, telle thee fulli what is beste to thee for to use, but I schal seie sumwhat to the as me thenketh.

In nyghtes aftir thi slepe, yif thou wolt rise for to praie and serve thi Lord, thou schalt feele thisilf first fleschli, hevy, and sumtyme lusti. Than schalt thou dispose thee for to praie or for to thenke sum gode thought, for to quickene thyn herte to God, and sette al thi besynesse first for to drawe up thi thought from wordli vanitees and from veyn imaginacions that fallen into thi mynde, that thou mai feele sum devocioun in thi seiynge. Or ellis, yif thou wole thenke on goostli thinges, that thou be not letted with siche veyne thoughtes of the world or of the flesch in thi thenkynges. Ther aren mani maner th[enk]inges:[s] which aren best to thee, can I not seie. But I hope that that thought bi which thou feelist savour and most reste for the tyme is best for thee. Thou mai, yif thou wil, sumtyme thenke on thy synnes bifore doon, and of thi freeltees that thou fallest inne eche dai, and aske merci and foryyvenesse for hem. Also, aftir this, thou mai thenke of the freeltes, the synnes and the wrechidnessis of thyn even-Cristene, bodili and goostli, with pite and compassioun of hem. And crie merci and foryevenesse for hem as tendirli as for thisilf and as thei were thyn owen, and that is a good thought. For I telle thee, forsothe, thou mai make of othir mennes synnes a precious oynement for to heele thyn owen soule, whan thou hast mynde of hem with compassion and sorwe of hem.

This oynement is precious, though the spicery be not clene, for it is maad of venym for to distroie venym. That is for to seie, thyn owen synnes and othere mennys also, brought into thi mynde, yif thou bete hem weel with sorwe of [herte],[t] pite and compassioun, thei turne into triacle whiche maketh thi soule hool from pride and envie, and bringeth in love and charite to thyn evene-Cristene. This thought is good sumtyme for to have.

Also thou mai have mynde of the manhede of oure Lord in his birthe and in his passioun, or in ony of his werkes, and feede thi thought with goostli ymaginacions of it, for to stire thyne affecciouns more to the love of him. This thought is good and spedeful, nameli whan it cometh freeli of Goddis yifte, with devocioun and fervour of the spirit: elles a man mai not lightli have savour ne devocioun in it. I hoolde it not spedeful to a man for to prese thanne to moche therupon, as yif he wolde gete it bi maistrie, for he schal mowe breke his heed and his bodi, and he schal nevere be the neer. Forthi, me thenketh, unto thee it is good for to have in mynde his manheede sumtyme. And yif devocion come withal, and savour, kepe it and folowe it for a tyme. But leve of sone, and hange not to longe therupon. Also, yif devocion come not with mynde of the passioun, stryve not ne prese not to moche theraftir, and take esili that wolen come and goo forth to sum othir thought.

Also othere thoghtis there ben that aren more goostli: as for to thenken on vertues; and for to see bi light of undirstondynge the vertu

---

[s] thenkinges] Ff; thinges L.   [t] herte] Ff; L *om.*

of mekenesse, what it is, and hou a man schulde be meke; and also
what is pacience and clennesse, rightwisenesse, charite, chastite and
sobirte, and sich othere; and hou a man schulde gete alle thise vertues;
and bi sich thoughtes for to have grete desire and longynge to thise
vertues for to have hem; and also for to have a goosteli sight of the
principal vertues – as truthe, hope and charite. Bi the sight and the
desire of thise vertues a soule schulde mowe fele gret comfort, if he had
grace of oure Lord, withoute which grace a mannys thought is half
blynd, withouten savour or goosteli swettenesse.

Also for to thenke on seyntis of oure Lord, as on apostelis,
martires, confessours and hooli virginis: bihoold inwardli the hooli
lyvynge, the grace and the vertues that oure Lord yaaf hem heere
lyvynge. And bi this mynde stire thyn owen herte to take ensample of
hem unto betere lyvynge.

Also the mynde of oure Ladi, Seynt Marie, aboven all othere
seyntis: for to see bi goosteli ighe the habundance of grace in hire hooli
soule whan sche was heere lyvynge, that oure Lord yaaf hire aloone,
passyng alle creatures. For in hire was fulhede of alle vertues withouten
weem of synne, schewynge ful mekenesse and perfite charite, and fulli
with thise the beaute of alle othere vertues, so hooli and fully that there
myght noo stirynge of pride, ne envie, ne wraththe, ne fleschli likynge,
ne of no maner synne, entre into here herte ne defoule the soule in noo
partie of it. The bihooldynge of the fairheed of this blissid soule
schulde stire a mannys herte into goostli comforte greteli.

And moche more thanne above this the thenkyng of the soule of
oure Lord Jhesu, whiche was fulli ooned to the Godhede, passinge
withouten comparisoun oure Ladi and alle othere creatures. For in the
persone of Jhesu aren two kyndes, that is, God and man, fulli ooned
togidere. Bi the vertu of this blissid oonynge, which mai not be seid ne
conceived bi mannes wit, the soule of Jhesu receyved the fulheed of
wisdoom and love and al goodnesse. As the apostel seith: *Plenitudo
divinitatis inhabitavit in [ipso]*[u] *corporaliter*.[21] That is: the Godhede
was ooned fulli to the manhede in the soule of Jhesu, and so bi the soule
dwellide in the bodi. The mynde of the manhede of oure Lord upon this
wise – that is, for to bihoolden the vertues and the overpassinge grace
of the soule of Jhesu – schulde be comfortable to a mannys soule

Also mynde of the myght, the wisdom and the goodnesse of oure

[u] *ipso*] *cristo* L.

Lord in his creatures. For in as moche as we mai not see God fulli in himsilf heere lyvynge, forthi we schulde [bi]holde[v] him, loven him, drede him, and wondre his myght and his wisdom, and his goodnesse in his werkes and in his creatures.

Also for to thenke of the merci of oure Lord that he hath schewid to me and to thee, and to alle synfulle caityves that hath ben combred in synne, spered in the develes prisoun – hou oure Lord pacientli suffride us lyve in oure synne, and took no vengeaunce of us, as he myght have don ryghtfulli and putte us to helle, yif his love hadde not letted him. But for love he sparide us, he hadde pite on us and sette his grace into oure hertis and callide us oute of oure synnes, and bi his grace hath turned oure wille holi to him and for to have him, and for his love forsake al manere of synne. The mynde of his merci and of his goodnesse, maad with othir circumstaunce more than I can or mai reherce now, may bring into a soule gret truste of oure Lord and ful hope of savacioun, and kendeleth the desire of love myghtili to the joies of hevene.

Also for to thenke of the wrecchidnesse, myscheves and perilis bodili and goostli that fallen in this liyf; and aftir that for to thenke of the joies of hevene, hou moche blisse there is and joie. For there is neither synne ne sorwe, ne passioun ne peyne, hongir ne thriste, soore ne sikenesse, doute ne drede, schame ne schenschipe, ne defaute of might, ne lakkynge of light, ne wantynge of wille.

But there is sovereigne fairhede, strengthe, heele, likynge ai lastande, wisdom, love, pees, worschipe, sikernesse, reste, joie, and blisse inowgh, ai withouten ende. The more that thou thenkest and felist the wrecchidnes of this liif, the more ferventli schal thou desire the joie and the reste of the blisse of heven.

Many men aren covetous of wordli worschipes and ertheli richesse, dremyng and wakyng, and thenk howe and by what meenes thei myghte come therto. And forthi thei forgeten the mynde of hemself, the peynes of helle, the joies of hevene. Sothli, thei aren not wise. Thei aren like to children that rennen aftir botirflies, and, for thei loke not to her feet, thei falle sumtyme doun and breken here legges. What is al the pompe and the worschipe of this world in richesse or in jolite, but a botirflie? Sothli, not elles, and yit moche lasse. Therfore I praie thee, be thou covetous of the joies of hevene, and thou schalt have worschipes and richesses that evere schal laste. For at the last ende, whanne worldli covetous men bringen noo good in hire handes, for alle here worschipes and her richesse aren torned into nought, save sorwe and peyne, than schal heveneli covetous men that forsaken truli alle veyne worschipes and richesse of this world – or ellis, yif thei have richesse and worschipes, thei setten not bi hem, ne here love ne heer likynge in hem, but leven ai in drede, and in mekenesse, and in hope, and in sorwe sumtyme, and abiden the merci of God pacienteli – thei schullen thanne have fulli that thei heere coveitede, for thei schul be crowned as kynges and stie up with oure Lord Jhesu into the blisse of hevene.

Also there are many other meditacions, moo than I can seie, whiche that God putteth into mannys mynde for to stire the affeccion and the resoun of a mannys soule to lothe vanitees of this world and for to desire the joies of hevene. Thise wordis I seie not to thee as I hadde fulli schewed the maneres of meditaciouns as thei aren wrought in a mannes soule. But I touche hem to thee a litil, that thou schuldest bi this litil undirstondynge have the more.

Notforthi me thenketh it is good unto thee that whanne thou disposest thee for to thenke on God, as I have bifore seide or on othir wise, and thou fyndest no savour ne devocioun for to thenke, but oonli a naked desire and a weike wille, that thou woldest fayn thenke on God, but thou can not: thanne I hope it is good to thee that thou stryve not to moche with thiself, as thou woldest with thyn owen myght overcome thisilf, for thou myght lightli falle so into more mirkenesse, but yif thou were more sleigh in thi worchinge. And forthi I holde it most siker unto thee for to seie thi Pater Noster, or thyn Ave, or ellis thi mateyns, or ellis for to rede upon thi sautir. For that is evermore a siker standard that wole not faile: whoso mai cleve therto, he schal not erre. And yif thou mai bi thi praiere gete devocion, loke than this devocion be oonli in affeccioun – that is to seie, in grete desire to God with goostli delite. Hoold forth thi seiynge and breke not lightli of. For ofte it falleth that preiynge with the mouth geteth and kepeth devocioun, and yif a man ceese of seiynge, devocioun vanesch[eth][w] awei. Neverthelees, yif devocioun of praiere bringe into thin herte a thought of the goosteli manhede of oure Lord, or of ony othir biforeseid, and this thought schuld be letted bi the seiynge, thanne mai thou ceese of thi

[w] vanescheth] V; vanesch L.

seiynge and occupie thee in meditacions until it passe awai.

But of certayn thynges thee bihooveth to be-waar in thi meditacioun. Summe schal I telle thee. On is: whan thou hast had a goostli thought, eithir ymagynynge of the manhede of oure Lord, or of siche bodilich thinges, and thi soule hath be comforted and feed therwith, and it passeth awai bi itsilf – be not to bisi to kepe it stille bi maistrie, for it schal thanne turne to peyne and to bittirnesse. Also, yif it passe not, but dwelleth stille in thi mynde withouten ony travaile of thisilf, and thou for comfort of it wole not leve it, and therfore it reveth thee fro thi sleep on nyghtes or elles on daies from othire good deedes, or elles for grete fervour of it thi bodi or thyn heed falleth into grete feblenesse, [this is not wel].[x] Thanne thou schal wilfulli breke of whan tyme cometh, sumtyme whanne thou hast most devocion and were lothest for to leve it – as whanne it passeth resonable tyme, or ellis it torneth to disese of thyn evene-Cristene, but yif thou doo so. Elles doost thou nought weel, as me thenketh, ne wiseli neither.

A wordli man or woman that feelith not peraventure devocion twies in a yeer, yif he feele bi the grace of oure Lord Jhesu grete compunccioun for his synnes, or elles a mynde of the passion of oure Lord – yif he were put fro his sleep and his reste a nyght, or two, or thre, until his heed werk, it is no fors, for it cometh to hem but seeldom. But to thee or to another man that hath th[is][y] manere of wirchynge in custoom, as it were eche othir dai, it is spedefulle for to have discrecioun in youre wirchynge, not fully falle therto for to folwe it as moche as wole come. And I holde that it is good to thee for to usen this maner in what devocioun that thou be, that thou hange not to longe therupon, eithir for to putte thee longe fro thi mete, or fro thi sleep in tyme, [or][z] for to disese ony othir man unskilfulli. The wise man seith thus: *Omnia tempus habent.*[22] 'Alle thinge hath tyme.'

Another thinge is this that thee bihoveth to have: to be waar if thin thought be occupied in the ymaginacioun of the manheed of oure Lord, or in ony sich othir, and after this thou art bisi with al thi desire of thyn herte for to seke knowynge or feelynge more goosteli of the Godhede. Prese not to moche therin, ne suffre not thin herte falle fro thi deseyr, as yif thou were abidynge after sum queynte stirynge with thi bodi, or sum wondirfulle feelynge other than thou hast had. Thou schal not do so. It is ynowgh to thee and to me for to have a desire and a

---

[x] this . . . wel] TV; L *om.*   [y] this] TV; the L.   [z] or] TV; L *om.*

longynge to oure Lord. And yif he wole, of his free grace, over this desire, sende us of his goostli light, and openen oure goostli ighen for to se and knowe more of him than we have had tofore bi comone travaile, thanke we him therof.[23] And yif he wole not, for we aren not meke inowgh, or ellis we are not disposid bi clennesse of lyvynge in othir sides for to receyve that grace: thanne schal we mekeli knowe oure owen wrecchidnesse, and holde us paid with the desire that we have to hym and with othire comen thoughtis that mai lightli falle undir oure imaginacioun – as of oure owen synnes, or Cristis passioun, or siche othere, or ellis with praiers of the sautier or sum othir – and loven him with al oure herte that he wole yeve us that. Yif thou doo othirwise, thou mai be bigiled bi the spirit of errour. For it is presumcion a man bi his owen witte for to prese so moche into knowynge of goostli thinges, but yif he feeled plente of grace. For the wise man seith thus: *Scrutator maiestatis opprimetur a gloria.*[24] That is to seie: 'Ransakere of the myght of God and of his majeste withouten gr[et]e[a] clennesse and mekenesse schal be overleid and overpressid of himself.'

And therfore the wise man seith in anothir place thus: *Altiora te ne quaesieris et fortiora te ne scrutatus fueris.*[25] That is to seie: 'High thinges that aren above thi myght, wit and thi resoun, seke not; and grettere thynges that aren aboven thi myght, ransake not.' Bi thise wordes the wise man forbedeth not uttirli for to seke and ransake goostli and heveneli thinges. But he forbedeth us that as longe as we aren fleschli and boistous, not clensid from veyn love of the world, that we take not upon us bi oure owen traveile ne bi oure owen wit for to ransake or feele goosteli thinges. Ne though we feele goostli thinges and grete fervour of the love of God, so moche that we sette at nought alle erthli thinges, and us thenketh that we wolde forsake for Goddis love alle the joies and alle the welth of this world, yit aren we not as tite able and redi for to seke and biholde goostli thinges that aren aboven us, until oure soule be maad sotil and til hit be maad saad and stablid in vertues bi processe of tyme and encresynge of grace. For as Seynt Gregor[26] seith, 'No man sodeynli is maad sovereyne in grace, but fro litil he bigynneth, and bi processe wexeth, until he come to the moste.' And so graunt us to do, the Fadir and Sone and the Holi Goost. Amen.

And thus this mater is endid and red.

---

[a] grete] TV; grace L.

Of six extant manuscripts, only one (the early sixteenth-century Bodley MS 576) and Pepwell's printed edition of 1521 attribute this tract to Hilton, but the opening recalls those of other Hilton works, and there are parallels throughout in thought and style with his writings (cf. *Scale*, I, 10–12). The work responds to a question about the status of angels' song, and apparently counsels the reader against too simple an understanding of Rolle's notion of *canor* or song. The 'ende and the soverante of perfeccioun' lies in union with God by charity, and spiritual reforming may be accompanied by 'savours, swetnesses, and wonderful felyngs'. To hear angelic song is another comfort: it is spiritual 'and aboven al maner ymaginacioun and resoun', but secondary to 'the soveran and the essencial joy' in love of God for himself. It may not be heard unless a soul be in perfect charity. Hilton warns against illusion and presumption, gives advice on devotion to the Holy Name, and towards the close seems to warn of danger inherent in *The Cloud*'s theme of the 'naked mynde' of God.

Base manuscript: BL MS Add. 27592 (A), fols. 57v–61v. Also cited: Lincoln Cathedral Library MS 91, the 'Thornton Manuscript' (T), and CUL MS Dd. 5. 55 (Dd).

Dere brother in Crist, I have understanden be thin awen speche and alsso be tellyng of another man that thou yernes gretly for to have mare knawyng and wyssyng than thu has of angels song and hevenly sowne; what it es, and on what wise it is persayved and feled in a mans saule, and how a man may be syker that it is trew and noght feyned, and how it es made be presence of the gode aungel and noght be inputtyng of the ille aungel. This thing thou wald wit of me. Bot sothly I can noght telle the for syker the sothnes of this mater. Never-the-latter sumwhat als me thynk shal I shew the in a schort word.

Wit thou wele that the ende and the soverante of perfeccioun standes in a verra anhede of God and of mans saule be perfit charite. This anhede than es verraly made, when the mygtes of the saule er refourmed be grace to the dignite and the stat of the fyrst condicioun; that es, when the mynd es stabyld sadly, withouten chaungyng and vagacion, in God and gastly thyngs; and when the reson es clered fra al werdly and fleschly behaldyngs and fra al bodyly ymaginaciouns, figurs and fantasis of creaturs, and illumynd es be grace to behald God and gastly things; and when the wyl and the affeccion es purged and clensed fra al fleschly and kyndly and werdly luf, and es inflawmed with brennand luf of the haly gast.

Thys wonderful anhede ne may noght be fulfild perfitely, continuely, haly in this life, for corrupcioun of the fleshe, bot anly in the blis of heven. Never-the-latter, the ner that a saule in this presente life may come to this anhede, the mare perfit it es. For the mare that it es refourmed be grace til the ymage and the lyknes of his creatur her on this maner wyse, the mare joy and blis sal it have in heven. Oure Lord is an endles beyng withouten chaun[g]yng,[a] almightihede withoutyn faillyng, soveran wysdom, lyght, sothnes withoutyn errour or myrknes, soverayne godenes, luf, pes, and swetnes. Than the mare that a saule is aned, festynd, confourmed and joyned to our Lord, the mare stabil and myghti it es; the mare wys and cler, gode and peysible, lufand and mare vertuous it is; and so it is mare perfite. For a saule that has, be grace of Jhesu and lang travayl of bodeli and gastli exercice, overcomen and destroyd concupiscens, and passiouns, and unskylful styryngs within itselfe, and withoutyn in the sensualite,[1] and es clethed alle in vertus – als in meknes and in myldnes, in paciens and softnes, in gastli stryngh and ryghtwysnes, in continence, and wysdom, in trouthe, hope, and charite – than it es made perfit als it may be in this life.

Mykil comforth it resayves of our Lord, noght anly inwardly in hys awne pryve substance, be vertu of the anhede to our Lord that lys in knawyng and lufyng [of][b] God, in lyght and gastly brennyng of hym, in transfourmyng of the saule in the Godhede, bot alsso many other comforthes, savours, swetnesses, and wonderful felyngs on ser maners, eftir our Lord vouches-safe to visit his creaturs her in erth, and eftir the saule profites and waxes in charite. Sum saule, be vertue of charite that God gyves it, is clensed so that al creaturs, and al that he heres, or sese, or felis be any of his wittis, turnes hym to comforth and gladnes, and the sensualite resayves newe savour and swetnes in al creaturs. And ryght [als before][c] the lykyngs in the sensualite ware fleschly, vayn and vicious, [for][d] the payne of the origenal syn, right so now thai er made gastly and clene, withoutyn biternes and bytyng of conscience.

This es the godnes of oure Lord, that, sen the saule es punysched

---

[a] chaungyng] T; chaunchyng A.   [b] of] T; in A.   [c] als before] T; b.a. A.   [d] for] A bis.

in the sensualite and the flesche es parcener of payn, that eftirward the saule be comforthed in sensualite, and the flesch be felow in joy and comforth with the saule, noght fleschly bot gastly, als he was felow in tribulacion and payne. This is the fredom and the lordship, dignite, and the worship that a mans saule has over al creaturs, the whilk dignite he may recure be grace here, that ilk a creature savours to hym als it es. [And that es]*e* when be grace he sese, he heres, he felis anly God in al creaturs. In this maner wyse a saule es mad gastli in the sensualite be habundaunce of charite that es in the substance of the saule.

Also oure Lord comforteth a saule be angel[s]*f* sange. What that sang es, it may noght be discried be na bodely liknes, for it es gastly, and aboven al maner ymaginacioun and resoun. It may be feled and persayved in a saule, but it may noght be schewed. Never-the-latter I spek tharof to the als me think. When a saule es purified be luf of God, illumynd be wysdom, stabild be the myght of God, than es the egh of the saule opynd to behalde gastly things, and vertus, and angels, and haly saules, and hevenly thyngs. Than es the saule abil, because of clennes, to fele the touchyng, the spekyng of goode aungels. Thys touchyng and spekyng, it is gastly, noght bodele: for when the saule es lyft and ravisched oute of the sensualite, and oute of mynde of any erthly thyngs, than it is in gret fervour of luf and lyght of God; if oure Lord vouche-safe, the saule may here and fele hevenly sowne, made be the presence of aungels in lovyng of God.

Noght that this sang of angels es the soveran joy of the saule; bot for the difference that es betwyx a mans saule in flesch and ane aungel, because of unclennes, a saule may noght her it bot be ravischyng in luf, and nedis for to be purified wel clene and fulfilled of mykel charite, or it were abil for to here hevenly soun. For the soveran and the essencial joy es in luf of God be hymselfe and [for hymselfe, and the]*g* secundarie es in communyng and behaldyng of angels and gastly creaturs. For ryght als a saule in understandyng of gastly thyngs es oftsith touched and kenned thurgh bodele ymaginacioun, be wyrkyng of aungels – als Ezechiel the prophete saw in bodely ymaginacioun the sothfastnes of Gods privetis – right so in the luf of God, a saule be the presence of angels es ravisched oute of mynde of al erthli and fleschly thyngs into a hevenly joy, to here aungels sang and hevenly soun, eftir that the charite es mare or les.

---

e And that es] T; A *om.*   *f* angels] T; angel A.   *g* for hymselfe and the] T; A *om.*

Now, than, thynks me that ther may na saule fele verraly aungel[s]*b* sang ne hevenly soun bot he be in perfit charite. And noght forthi al that er in perfit charite ne has noght feled it, bot anly that saule that es so pouried in the fyr of luf, that al erthly savour es brent oute of it, and al mene lettyn[g]e*i* betwix the saule and the clennes of aungels es broken and put oway fra it. Than sothly may [he]*j* synge a new sang, and sothly may he here a blisful hevenly soun and aungels sang, withoutyn desayte or feynyng. Oure Lord wate whare that saule es that, for abundaunce of brennand luf, es worthi til here aungels sang. Whaso than wil here angels sang, and noght be desayved be feynyng ne be ymaginacioun of himself, ne be illusioun of the enemy, hym byhoves for to have perfit charite. And that es, when al vayn luf and drede, vayn joy and sorw, es castyn oute of the herte, that he lofs nathing bot God, ne dredes nathyng bot God, ne joys ne sorwys nathyng bot in God or for God. Whaso mygth be grace of God ga this way, he suld noght er. Never-the-latter, sum men er desayved be thar awn ymaginacioun, or be illusioun of the enemy in this mater. Sum man when he has longe traveld bodili and gastli in destroyng of syns and getyng of vertus, an[d]*k* peraventure has getyn be grace a sumdele rest and a clerte in conscience, anon he leves prayers, redyngs of haly wryt, and meditacions of the passion of Crist, and the mynde of his wrechednes; and, or he be called of God, he gadres his wittis be violence to sekyn and to byhalde hevenly thyngs, or his egh be mad gastly be grace, and overtravels be ymaginacioun his wittis, and be undiscrete travelyng turnes the braynes in his heved, and forbrekis the myghtis and the wittis of the saule and of body. And than, for febilnes of the brayn, him thynk that he heres wonderful sownes and sangs; and that is nathyng els bot a fantasy, caused o trublyng of the brayn: als a man that es in a fransy, hym thynk that he heres and sese that nan other man dos, and al es bot a vanite and a fantasy of the heved, or els it es be wirkyng of the enemy that feynes swylk soun in his heryng.

For if a man have any presumpcioun in his fantasys and in his wyrkyng, and tharbe falles to undiscrete ymaginacioun, als it ware in a fransy, and es noght kenned ne rewled of grace, ne comforthed be gastly strengh, the devel entyrs man be fals illuminaciouns, and fals sownes, and swetnes, [and]*l* desayves a mans saule. And of this fals ground springes errours and heresys, fals prophecies, presumpciouns,

---

b aungels] T; aungel A.   *i* lettynge] Dd; lettynde A.   *j* he] T; A *om.*   *k* and] T; ans A.
l and] T; A *om.*

and fals roysyngs, blasphemes, and sclaunderyngs, and many other myscheves. And tharfore, if thou se any man gastly occupied fal in any of thar synnes and there desaytes, or in fransys, wit thou wel that he never herde ne felde aungels sang, ne hevenly soun. For, sothly, he that verraly heres aungels sang, he es made sa wys that he sal nevere er be fantasy, ne be undiscrecioun, ne be na sleght of wyrkyng of the devel.

Also sum men felis in thair hertis als it ware a gastly soun and swete sangs on dyvers maners, and this es communly god, and sumtyme it may turne til desayte. This soun es feled in this wyse: sum man settis the thoght of his herte anly in the name of Jhesu, and stedefastli haldes it tharto, and in short tyme him thynk that name turnes til him til gret comforth and swetnes, and him think that the name sownes [in his herte]^m delectabili, als it ware a sang, and the vertu of this lykyng es so myghti that it drawes in al the wittes of the saule therto. Hoso may fele this soun and this swetnes verrali in his herte, wit he wel that [it]^n es of God, and als lange os he es mek he sal noght be desayved. Bot this es noght angels sang, bot it is a sang of the saule be vertu of the name, and be touchyng of the god aungel. For when a saule offers him to Jhesu treweli and mekli, puttyng al his trayst and his desire in him, and besyle kepis him in his mynd, oure Lord Jhesu, when he wol, pourge[s]^o the affeccioun of the saule, and fillis it, and fedis it with swetnes of himself, and makes his name in the felyng of the saule als hony, and als sang, and als any thyng that es delitabil; that it likes the saule evermare for to cry, 'Jhesu, Jhesu, Jhesu'. And noght anly he has comforth in this, bot also in psalmes and ympnes and antymps of haly kyrk, that the herte synges tham swetly, devotly and frely, withoutyn any travel of the saule or byternes, in the same tyme, and notis that haly kyrk oyses. Thys es god, and [of]^p the gyft of God, for the substance of this felyng lys in the luf of Jhesu, wilk es fed and lyghtned with swilk maner of sangs. Never-the-latter, in this maner of felyng a saule may be desayved be vayn glorie, noght in that tyme that the affeccioun synges to Jhesu and loves Jhesu in swetnes of hym, bot eftirward, when it sesys and the herte kelys of luf of Jhesu, than it entris in vayn glorie.

Also sum man es desayved on this wyse: he heres wel say that it es god til have Jhesu in hys mynde, or any other god word of God, than he straynes hys herte myghtily to that name, and be a custom he has it

^{m} in his herte] T; A *om.* ^{n} it] T; A *om.* ^{o} pourges] Dd; pourge A. ^{p} of] T; A *om.*

nerhand alway in hys mynde. Noght forthi he felis nouther tharbe in his affeccioun, swetnes, ne lyght of knawyng in resoun, bot anly a naked mynde of God, or of Jhesu, or of Marie, or of any other god word. He may be desayved, noght for it es il for to have Jhesu in mynde on this wyse, bot if he this felyng and this mynde, that es anly his awen wyrkyng be custum, hald it a special visitacioun of oure Lord and thynk it mare than it es. For wyt thou wele that a naked mynde or a nakid ymaginacioun of Jhesu or of any gastly thing, withoutyn swetnes of luf in the affeccioun, or withoutyn light of knawyng in resoun, it es bot a blyndnes, and a way to dissayte, if a man hald it in hys awen syght mare than it es. Tharfore I hald it syker that he be mek in his awen felyng, and hald this mynde in regard noght, til he may, be custum and oysyng of this mynde, fele the fere of luf in his affeccioun, and the lyght of knawyng in his resoun.

Lo, I have told the in this mater a litel als me thynk; noght affermand that this suffys, ne that this es the sothfastnes in this mater. Bot if the thynk it otherwyse, or els any other man savour be grace the contrary herto, leve this saying and gyve stede to hym. It suffys to me for to lif in trouth principali, and noght in felyng.

11 *Eight Chapters on Perfection*

Hilton is identified in five of the seven complete manuscripts as translator into English of the *Eight Chapters* 'founden in Maister Lowis de Fontibus book at Cantebrigge'; Hilton's source does not survive.[1] Lluis de Font, an Aragonese Franciscan friar, was assigned to read the *Sentences* at Cambridge in 1383, and if his university career followed the normal course, his regency as a Master or Doctor in Theology may be dated to 1391–3 or 1392–4.[2] Hilton's version has been suggested to show parallels with *The Scale*, Book II, and may date from the later years of his life at Thurgarton.

Base manuscript: Lambeth Palace Library MS 472 (L), fols. 213v–223v. Also cited: Bibliothèque Nationale, Paris, fonds anglais 41 (P).

> *Here bigynnen viii chapiteres necessarie for men that geven hem to perfeccion, whiche weren founden in Maister Lowis de Fontibus book at Cantebrigge, and turned into Engelisch bi Maister Watier Hilton de Turbaton.*

[1] *Of tokenes and wirkyngis of love.*

The first tokene of love is that the lovere submitte fulli his wil to the wil of him that he loveth, and this special love hath three wirkynges. The first is, yif he that is loved be simple and pore, meke and in dispite, thanne he that loveth coveiteth to be vile, pore and meke, and to be in repreef, like to him that he loveth. The secunde, that it maketh a man to leve alle manere affeccioun or frendschipe that is contrarie to this love, and so it maketh him forsake fadir and alle othere affecciouns in as mykil as thei are contrarie to the wille of him that he loveth. The thridde is, that there is nothinge hid in that toones herte that he ne wole schewe it to that othir, and this is a special tokene of high love bitwix two persones, and this is the fulfillynge of thise othere wirkynges aforeseid. Forwhi thorugh this schewynge of privetees here hertis aren opened so that thei are togedre more perfightli bounden.

137

[2]   *Of withdrawynge of devocioun, how a man schal doo.*

Yyf thou wilt continueli stien up to perfeccioun and in the weie of
God which thou art entred, evere profite more and more and encrese
from vertu to vertu. Thou schalt nevere praie the lasse, whanne grace
of devocioun is withdrawen, and temptacions and tribulacions comen
upon thee, thanne whanne thou hast grace of devocion withoute
temptacioun. But than it is most acceptable and most queemful to God:
whanne in withdrawinge of devocioun thou art in tribulacion and
discomfort, and yit neverethelees thou praiest and wakest and doost
alle othere good deedes. And so therfore doo thou thiself alle good
deedis withouten devocioun, the whiche thou didest bifore with
devocioun. Wherfore, yif ther come sumtyme temptaciouns and
tribulaciouns the whiche aren ordeyned for to ponyschen and for to
clense Goddis children, and devocioun be withdrawen, strengthe the
thanne not the lesse to preie, not the lasse to wake ne to faste, and not
the lesse in othere good werkes for to stonde. So that thorugh
contynuaunce in praieres with the teeres of thyn ighen unceesabeli
exercise thee, that thou myght, as it were, constreyne God to yeve the
fervour and heete of holi devocioun. W[h]oso*a* wole ben perfite and
lyven aftir this chapitre, do as Caton seith: *Cum recte vivas, non cures
verba malorum.*[3] Do thou that longeth to thee, and thi loved deere
Jhesu Crist schal weel doo that pertineth to him.

Praier that is maad with grete enfors, whan the slow flesch wolde
bee unlusti, is to God acceptable. Forwhi it dryveth the loved Jhesu
Crist for to yeelden and for to eken to thee grace and devocioun, and in
temptacion grete profite. Preie thanne continueli yif thou wole
purchace thee grace of devocioun, and for to profite in the wai of Crist.
And for no tribulacioun ne for no temptacioun, leve nevere praiere,
neither in wirchinge of wordli werk, neither in beed neither oute of
bed, in companye neither solitarie. For if thou be in tribulacioun or in
temptacioun and praiest lastendli, grace and devocioun schal ben
eeked. And newe confort schal be yeven to thee of Jhesu Crist, thi
loved. And though the feend putte in thyn hert that it is nought that
thou praiest, despice and defie hym with mouth and with herte, and
evere praie. And the more that thy tribulacioun and thyne affliccioun
is, the more schal be thi confort whanne grace of devocion is yyven to
thee. Praie thanne contynueli, redynge in the book of liyf, that is in the

---

a Whoso] P; Woso L.

lif of Jhesu Crist, the whiche was poverte, mekenesse, sorwe, despite, affliccioun and soothfast obedience. And whanne thou art weel entreed in this wai, thanne many temptacions and tribulaciouns of the feend, of the world, and of thee flesch, schal in many wise disese thee and hugeli tormente thee and discomfort thee. But yif thou wolt overcome al, stifli praie and pacientli abide thi loved Jhesu Crist. And he schal sende the helpe and conforte unspecable, that noo tunge mai telle hou moche it is.

Whanne thou art tormented with tribulacioun or with temptacioun, use also often with thi praier confessioun, in the whiche thou schalt schewen with al the contricioun of thyn herte to thi confessour entierli and playnli alle the woundes of thi conscience more and lasse, also ferforth as thou woldest schewe hem to thyn owen angil. And that is a sovereigne medicyn to putte alle temptaciouns and tribulaciouns awai, and for to purchace moche grace of Goddis comfort. Forwhi the feend, that is ful of pride, mai not suffre the mekenesse of pure confessioun, ne the fervour of continuel orisoun, thorugh whiche werkes speciali oure suete Lord Jhesu Crist is, as it were, thorugh violence drawen into a lovende soule and so constreyned for to conforte it. Sette thanne al thi studie and thi besinesse for to make redi a place and a prevei chambre to thi Lord Jhesu Crist – thi spouse in thi soule – bi swete meditacioun, bi continuel orisons, and bi ofte confessions maad eche dai or ellis eche thridde dai yif a man mai have leiseer, so that the lest hour of thi tyme be not foryeten, in the whiche thou hast in many thynges offended thi worthi Lord and loved Jhesu Crist. For thorugh thise thre forseid werkes – meditacioun, orisoun, and confessioun – many a man cometh to restful clennesse of conscience.

But be-waar that thou thorugh reccheleschipe yyve no place to thyne enemyes, continueli bisegynge thee, and that thou doost whanne for vanyte or for idelnesse thou levest thi praieres. Therfore the more thou art tempted and traveiled, the more stabli dwelle in thi praiere and leve it not lightli, but if it be for feblenesse of the heed or of thi brayn. Forwhi feblenesse of brayn wil sumtyme falle of unmesurable contynuaunce in praier, or in wakynge, or excesse in fastynge, and thanne is it good to stynte a while. Forwhi Sent Jerom seith: 'He erres not a litil but mykil, that preferres the lasse good to the more good'; as he dooth that setteth more price be fastynge thanne bi deedis of charite; and he that setteth wakynge bifore hoolinesse of brayn, of wit and of resoun. And he also erris greteli that, bi unmesurable and undiscret seiyng or syngynge of psalmes or of ympnes, falleth into frenasie, or into wodenesse, or into bittir hevynesse. Therfore it is good thanne for to stinten fro multitude of wordis, and thenke oonli in thin herte as eseli as thou maist. And so thorugh vertu of continuel praiere usid, what in mouth, what in herte, schalt thou be delyvered and eesed of thi temptaciouns.

Bi contynuaunce in praiere is light of grace yeven to a soule, whiche cleereth the conscience and setteth it groundli in deep soothfastnesse of mekenesse. And thorugh continuel lokynge and reedynge in the book of liyf, that is on the blissid persone Jhesu Crist and on his liyf, is the soule rooted and groundid in pacience and in charite. Forwhi in that lokynge mai thou be kenned and enformed of al that thee nedeth for to knowe. And thorugh that thou schalt mowe have siche pacience that thou schalt wille to receyve gladli al maner of tribulacioun and disese as for a greet confort. Forwhi thorugh hem thou schalt feele and see thiself sumwhat like to thi Lord Jhesu Crist, him that thou lovest. Yhe, thou shalt holde thisilf so unwise and so unworthi in Goddes sight that it is no disese to thee whatsoevere thou mai suffre. Forwhi withouten conparsoun he suffrid more for thee. Neverthelees, yit schalt thou truste and hope that – as thou art felawe with him in peyne and in disese, litil yif it be – so schalt thou be felawe with him in his joie and in his blisse. For as the apostil seith: 'Yif we be felawes of Cristis passions, we schal be felawes of his blissid consolacions.'⁴ Wherfore it semeth that there is no more dignite ne worthinesse that a man mai come to than for to have tribulacioun for Cristis love, bi the whiche a man is maad Cristes felaw heere in this liyf and in the blisse of hevene withouten ende. Amen.

[3]   *Of periles that aren to eschewe to a goostli man.*

Be-waar first that thou yeve not thisilf, ne thi ful affeccioun, ne thi ful hoomli frendschipe to no persone, but yif thou first have receyved the yifte and the spirit of discrecioun, bi the which thou maist knowe fro whiche thou schalt flee and which thou schalt drawe to. Until the tyme thou come to this, kepe thee ai playn and comoun, to eche man half straunge, savynge evere the boond of charite. Also be-waar speciali of hem that han swete plesant wordis in heere spekynges, and haveth noon hoolynesse in vertu ne swetnesse in herte, but a liknesse of holynesse oonli in the tunge and in the habite: thise that schewen of hemsilf and avaunten hemsilf of visions and of revelaciouns, or of queynte maner feelynges, or of singuler doynges or wittes, or undirstondynges over othir men, thorugh whiche thei are wondrid and over moche preised and worschiped of hem that thei speken to. For siche manere men aren ofte sithes snares of disceites to hem that aren not wise.

First avise thee of hem, and looke hem and bringe hem in thi mynde to the presence of Jhesu Crist – as yif thou woldest take a thynge oute of a myrke place for to knowe what it is, and ley it and loke it in the light. Right so Jhesu Crist is light, and there is no light of grace ne of soothfastnesse but he and in him. And therfore siche manere of men and alle othere, yhe and thisilf with hem, bringe in thi praieres and in thi mynde to Jhesu Crist. And there schal thei be seen what thei aren. There schal thei be tried. There schalt thou, thorugh biholdynge of him and of his liyf, see who is like to him and who is unlike to him. But yit be-waar that thou deme not a man fulli what he is aftir thi sight, but al cometh as a thinge uncertayn in the privete of Goddis doom. Nevertheles, thou mai bi that sight of Cristis liyf folwe and rule thyn owen conscience in this poynt: whom thou schalt folwe, and whom refuse, and with whom thou maist be homli, and with whom thou schalt be straunge. And that maner demynge is bihoofli for the.

Also be-waar of fervours, as yif thou feele the spirit of fervour greteli fallen upon thee. Thenke first and avise the weel or thanne thou folwe fulli it in wirkynge, what is the bigynnynge of it, and whereof is it causid, and thenke upon the myddis and also what ende wole folwe of it. And than folwe it as mykil as thou mai undirstande, bi grace and conceil and bi hooli writte, that is acordynge to sothfast vertu of discrecioun and to the liyf of Crist. The whiche lif of Crist thou schalt make thi myrour, thi rule and thi sampler, for to doon after it. And forthi this liyf of Crist schaltou more rewarden aftir the innere vertu of Crist thanne aftir the uttere tokenes of his lerynge.

And yit also be-war of hem that seyn hemsilf han geten the spirit of fredom and that thei have so moche grace of love that thei mai lyven as hem list. Thei thenken hem so free and so siker, that thei schal not synne. Thei maken hemsilf aboven the lawe of holi chirche and thei seyn thus as Seynt Poul seid: 'Where the spirit of God is, there is freedom.'⁵ And also thus: 'Yif ye be led with the spirit, ye are not undir lawe.'⁶ But thei menen not as Poule mente; thei understonden not his wordis. Thise men are expresseli ayens the liyf of Crist. Forwhi Crist that was maad free made himsilf thralle for us, and whan he was aboven the lawe as makere and yevere of it, yit he made him buxum under the lawe. Of thise men speketh Seynt Petir thus: 'Thei biheten to othere men fredom of spirit, and thei hemsilf aren thrallis in synne, and servauntes of fleschli corrupcioun.'[7]

[4] *Of digrees bi the whiche a soule passeth forth into contemplacioun*

The first degree is: in teeres and in sighynges and in sorwe for synnes, in compunccioun and compassioun of Cristis passioun, and in partie-feelynge of disese, and of wrecchidnesse of his even-Cristene, and in stronge stryvynge agens alle manere vices, ayens alle wikkid werkes, wikkid wordis and wikkid willes and also wikkid thoutis, with moche peyne and soor swynk of bodi and soule for to ayeenstonden hem.

The secunde degree is: greet fervour and brennande desire with continuaunce of praiere, for to plese Jhesu Crist, for to love him with al thi herte and al thi myghtes, and for to feele confort of his gracious presence. And this brennand desire wole clense the conscience from al rust of synne, bothe of that is bifore doon, and of that that he eche dai falleth in. And this werk is of grete traveile, and with wondirful bisinesse, a litil temprid with rest amonge.

The thridde degree is: a staat of wondirful swettenesse, of softenesse, of gladnesse, of rest and of cleernesse, for in that cometh the grace of the Hooli Gost doun into a soule. And than it lightneth and purifieth so the soule with oile of goostli gladnesse and turneth it al into charite of Crist, so that it thenketh that al the lymes of the bodi, and alle the makynge of the world with alle the creatures is as a melodie of the harpe. And thanne aftir this is the soule sumwhat able to goosteli halsynges of Jhesu Crist, that is here swete spouse.

The fourth degree is: in sovereyne reste of bodi and soule, and that is whan a man is deed and beried to the world and to the flesch, and slepith in pees of conscience, and riseth withoute strogelynge of veyn thoughtes, evere continueli in oure Lord Jhesu Crist.

The fifthe degre is: whan a man bigynneth for to take sothfasteli the ernest of endelees joie, and is reised up to the biholdynge of heveneli thinges. Than feeleth and perceyveth he a glymerynge of heveneli blisse; and than seeth he sumwhat of the staat of angelis and of blissid soulis; and hou that alle illuminaciouns and alle graces of charite and of goodnesse descenden oute of the blissid Trinite unspecable into Jhesu Crist, man; and hou of that glorious manheed of Crist stremen out alle graces of light and of love into angelis and into hooli soulis, and from hem comen doun to us. And than is a man maad able to revelaciouns and contemplaciouns of Jhesu Crist.

[5]   *Of periles of holi love.*

A man that was holden an high lyvere ofte was asked for to speken of gostli love, and than he bigan for to see the falshede, the periles and the disceites that ofte sithes fallen in goostli love. And he seide: 'There is nothing in al the world – neithir man, neithir feend, ne noon other thinge – that I have so moche suspect as I have the affeccioun of love; ne that I am so sore afeerd of, but yif it be weel sette. Forwhi love is so passinge a thynge and so clevynge that it synketh depper in a soule than ony othir thinge mai doon. And ther is nothinge that so fulli occupieth and byndeth and overmaistereth a mannys herte as dooth love, where it is ful had, whethir it be good love or badde. And therfore but yif a man or woman have armour of discrecioun by whiche he mai kepe and governe his love, it wole ellis lightli caste doun the soule and make it have a foul fal.

'I speke not of fleschli love that is openli yvel, the which oweth to be hated of alle Cristis loveris as a thinge most feendli, most perilous, and most contrarie to the chastite of Cristis love. But I speke of good goostli love, that is and oweth to be bitwixe God and man, and man and man, and man and woman. Forwhi that love that a soule hath conceyved thorugh grace of Jhesu Crist, but yif it be ordeyned and ruled with grete mekenesse and with grete discrecioun, and that the fervour be resonabli ordeyned, sothli or it lasteth not, but sone faileth and vanyscheth awai, or ellis it maketh a man to bigynne summe werkes so overpassingeli that he mai not continue in hem and so is he fayn to flee therfro.

'Also the love that is bitwix man and man, and man and woman, as is atwixe devoute men and devoute women, that is in God and set for God. But yif it be right weel looked to and ruled with armours of discrecioun, eithir it turneth into fleschli love and into leccherie, or elles it maketh moche of here tyme be loste and wasted, thorugh veyn speche and in here comone conversacioun, bi chesoun that here hertis aren undiscreteli festned togidre in love.

'And ofte-sithis falleth that to persoones, be it men or women, love togidre. But specialli most perilous it is whanne man and woman loven togidre with also good atent as thei can hemself devysen. And

thei looven hertili togedire in good manere and in honest, that hem
thenken that thei wolden nevere departen. And thei have togidre grete
affeccions singulere for the goodnesse that eche of hem seeth in othir,
and that maketh eche of hem to othir doon many service and grete
esynges. And what eche of hem dooth to othir, it is al of love of herte –
yhe, overmoche of herte! For hem thenketh that thei wolden ai be
togedere; and what soo oon liketh, the tothir liketh; and what so
mysliketh the toon, mysliketh the other. This love is ful perilous and ful
moche blameworthi, though it seme good, and so moche it is the more
perilous that the peril is not knowe therof. Forwhi it wole writhe al to
flesch, but yif it be ruled and governed with armours of discrecioun.'

[6]   *Of perfite love of Crist, withoute whiche al othir love is
       suspecte.*

       The best love and truest is whanne a soule is reised and lightned
into knowynge of the beynge of God in Crist, as whanne the soule
seeth hou eche creature hath his beynge of him that is sovereyn
beynge, that is God, and it seeth that nothynge is sothfast beynge but
God. Of this knowynge the soule receyveth a wondirfulle savour and
a grete understandynge that, what so is of that sovereyne beynge, it is
good, and al that he dooth is best doon. This knowinge stireth and
reiseth up a love in the soule, answerynge to that goosteli bihooldynge
of the beynge of Crist. And this knowynge maketh a man to love al
that hath beynge of him, that is alle creatures, resonable and
unresonable, for his love that yeveth beynge to alle creaturis. And
speciali it stireth the soule to love resonable creatures, and most hem
the whiche it perceyveth most loved of Crist. For as the soule seeth
Jhesu Crist enclyned to the love of alle creatures, so it is enclyned.
And than is the soule kenned for to love creatures more or lasse aftir
the mesure and the qualite of Cristis love to hem and of here love into
him. And the grace of Crist kepith the soule so in that manere that it
schal not passe mesure.
       And therfore, til thou feele this manere love sadli grounded in
thyn herte, the whiche is had of the goosteli knowynge of the beynge of
Crist, holde al thi love suspect and be aferid. But whanne thou maist
come to that poynt, that thou mai holde the sight of thi soule on this
blessid persone, Jhesu Crist, and on his sovereyne beynge, stabli in
weele and in woo, in eese and in uneese, withoutin grete blenklyng

awey fro him – thanne that wondirfulle love that is causid of this knowynge and of this bihooldynge is sufficient for to ayeynstonde the venemous daartes of alle fleschli loves, and for to putte oute heer malice fro the mynde of the soule.

[7]   *Of transformynge of the soule into the love of Jhesu Crist.*

There is thre manere transformynge of the soule. On is whanne the soule is maad meke and buxum to the wille of God, so that it schapeth himsilf in al that it mai for to be like to him, folwynge hise werkes, and for to transfiguren and turnen and have it in itself Cristis passion, with suffrynge of alle schames and repreves as Crist suffride, so that it hadde lyvere be like to Crist thorugh suffraunce of tribulacioun thanne for to have al the mirthe of the world. Another ther is, for to be transformed with God, and that is whanne his soule is ooned with Crist, and right hoomli with him. And the soule hath thanne grete feelynge of Cristis love, and often receyveth privei swettenesse of his inspiracioun, and many grete confortis and delectacions. But thei aren not so grete but that thei may bi thought and bi wordes ben schewed. The thridde transformynge is whan Jhesu Crist and a soule aren so perfighteli, so unpartabli, and so acordabli ooned and bounden togidre that Crist is in the soule and the soule is in him, so fulli as yif thei bothe were but oo spirit, as Seynt Poul seith: 'Whoso cleeveth to God, he is oo spirit with him.'[8] Thanne feeleth the soule high thynges and privei of Crist Jhesu, and of his Fadir, and of the Hooli Spirit. And it takith siche delectacions of Cristis charite, that thei mai not fulli be conceyved with thoughtis of mannys resoun, ne declared forth with wordis of mannys tonge.

The first transformyng is not sufficient for to rule and governe the affeccioun of mannys herte, ne the secunde neither. Forwhi the fervour of the affeccioun, whether it be seette actuelli in God or in man, is ofte sithis myghtiere, more egre, and more maistirful than is the wisdom of discrecioun of the soule. And therfore whiles it is so, the love mai snapere and stumble and erre, either bi over moche or bi over litil. But bi the thridde is helid and yoten into the soule sich a wisdoom and sich a deep knowynge thorugh that wondirful medelynge and oonynge of Cristis light lightenynge and of the soule lightned, that the soule is kenned bi the spirit of discrecioun hou it schal be ruled and governe the love that it hath in Crist; and hou it schal receyve goostli feelynges and

privei swettenesse and delectaciouns in Crist; and hou it schal ordeyne,
rule and mesuren the fervours of Cristis love and the visitaciouns of his
gracious presence so wiseli and so priveili and so sobirli, that it schal
mow lasten esili and continueli in the feelynges and in the goostli
comfortis of Cristis love, not discoverynge itsilf in sight of othere men,
neighther bi lawghwynge ne bi sobbynge, ne bi no queynte tokene of
berynge of the bodi. Also bi the same spirit of discrecion, the soule is
kenned hou wiseli, hou sobirli, hou chastli, hou mekeli and hou loueli
it schal have itsilf ayens his evene-Cristen man and woman, and hou
gladli, benigneli, for to condescende whan it seeth tyme, persone and
chesoun whi and whanne it is for to condescende whanne it seeth tyme
to hem. And whanne he seeth that it is not for to condescende to hem,
thanne wole he not in no wise condescende to hem. But it is wondir stif,
streight and stronge, as a thinge that myght not be stired ne chaunged
ne bowed on no side. And the skile is this: God is in himself
unchaungeable, and a soule is chaungeable of itself. But thanne,
whanne the soule is ooned to Crist bi love, the more that it is ooned to
him, the more unchaungeable it is and the lasse it hath of unchaun-
geablete. Forwhi the wisdom and the kunnynge, the sadnesse and the
light of discrecioun that the soule hath bi the vertu of this onheed in
love, yyveth the soule love and myght that it may with thise armours
rulen the affeccioun of love to God and to his even-Cristene withouten
errour or falsehed.

And therfore, he that nevere feelid this yift of discrecioun and of
wisdom and of grace in his herte, it is spedeful to him that he suffre not
his affeccioun fulli to be bounden to no creature, neithir man ne
woman, singulerli ne priveli ne passingeli, for periles that lightli mai
falle therof; but that he be playn and comone to alle and not ful hoomli
with noon, til he mai thorugh this light of discrecioun knowe bi
experience whos conversacioun and comonynge he schal flee as noious
to him and unprofitable, whos conversacioun and affeccioun he schal
coveite, as to him eesi and comfortable.

[8]   *Hou goostli love is turned into fleschli love.*

It falleth ofte tyme that a devoute man loveth anothir devoute
man or a devoute woman in good honest love and for God with good
entente. And aftir this love encreseth so moche bitwixe hem that eche
of hem desireth the presence of othir unmesurabli, so ferforth, yif thei

may not have presence at wille, thei wexen hevy and sikeli. And sumtyme whanne thei comen togidre, here affeccioun evere wexeth, so that thei are more sikli. And that byndeth hem togidere into sich an hoomli aqueyntaunce of hertes, that what so that toon wole, that tothir wole; and what so liketh [or mysliketh]*b* that toon, liketh or mysliketh that tothir, be it good, be it yvel.

And this is ful perilous bitwix man and woman whanne thei are thus bothe deepli wounded with the affeccion of love. Forwhi whan here hertis aren thus homli acordynge togidere, nedes hem most schewe outeward sumtyme bi other tokenes that semeth not moche yvel what the herte meeneth. And thus bi wordis and bi tokenes whan eche of hem scheweth to othir hou weel eche of hem loveth othir, thus is the love more encresed and more chaunged from goostlinesse into fleschlinesse. But yit thei aren bisi for to coloure and hiden the fleschli affeccioun undir clennesse of charite, and of goostli profite, and of edificacioun of soule. For thus thei seien, eche of hem to othir, that thei menen not but gode. And so undir sikirnesse of that menynge, and of that fals wenynge, thei coveiten eche of hem to handle and feele othir, and kisse othir, as semeth to hem as it were devocioun and good love. But in sothfastnesse it is sleynge of devocioun and leccherous love, and grete hindringe and harmynge to the soule that wolde and schulde feele Cristis love.

Neverthelees, in the bigynnynge here resoun grucchith sumwhat ayein it, and the conscience ayenseith it ofte. Forwhi the resoun is not yit thorugh costomable comonynge slayn ne straungeled al fulli. But whan it is ofte had in custom sich maner doynge, than is resoun blyndid and straungeled, and the conscience falsli eesed, so that hem thenketh that thei mai usen siche spekynges and sich lokynges, touchynges, handelynges, kissynges, and sich tokenes of fleschli love withouten peril. And sumtyme thei seien that thei mai doon thus, and 'though it be a synne, yit it is no gret synne'. And thus, ai bi litil and litil, goostli love falleth and dieth, and flesschli love wexeth and quekeneth. And aftir this, bi processe of tyme, the fervour of love wexeth so moche that it bynemeth awei here tunges and alle the myghtes of heere soules so ferforth that neither of hem wole ayenseyn othir for displesynge of either othir in ony thinge that either of hem wil doon, though it were deedli synne. And whanne it is thus ferthforthe brought, thanne mai

b or mysliketh] P; L *om.*

neithir wordis, ne touchinges, ne handelynges, ne kissinges, ne bodili
presence maken a ful seeth to here love. And thanne be thei stired ful to
temptaciouns of the feend, for to consenten to the deede of leccherie,
and fulli to performe it, yif that thei myght have leiser.

And for as moche as this peril mai lightli fallen of mysrulynge of
love, therfore it is good to thee for to have suspect and drede in thisilf
alle manere love, whan it is priveli and singulerli sette into ony oo
persone, man or woman. For though it be first good and goostli, and
bigynneth in God and goodenesse, neverthelees, often it falleth that it is
afterward badde and fleschli, and endeth in the werkes of the feend –
from whiche love and perilis of love, the armours of discrecioun, geten
bi the woundes of Crist in the manere bifore seid, save us and alle
Cristen men [and wommen].[c9] Amen.

[c] and wommen] P; L *om.*

12 *The Scale of Perfection*, Book I

(Chapters 44, 45, 46)

'This hevenly boke more precyous than golde' is the description of *The Scale of Perfection* in Wynkyn de Worde's edition of 1494, the first printed text of English mystical writing and published at the behest of Lady Margaret Beaufort, mother of Henry VII. The title seems ill-suited, in that imagery of a ladder (Latin: *scala*) is not the unifying concept, and other titles in the manuscripts include: *De Vita Contemplativa* (BL MS Add. 11748), and *The Reformyng of Mannys Soule* (BL MS Harley 2397).[1] Whether the two books were intended as one work remains an open question: each assumes a different readership and, after an opening casting itself as a continuation, Book II scarcely refers back to Book I. Forty-one extant copies of Book I, as against twenty-five of Book II, point to the wider popularity of the more practical earlier work; only two manuscripts have Book II alone, while two further manuscripts include both books, but separated by other material.[2] It may well be that Books I and II are separated by some years, and that they should be regarded more as two separate works than as two parts of the same work.

Book I of *The Scale* is written as if to an anchoress, and assumes that contemplative life is reserved to those vowed to the contemplative religious state. Hilton recurrently disclaims any mystical experience of his own, and in Book I the experience of contemplation remains, as it were, beyond the horizon. Hilton begins at the beginning with moral and ascetic teaching, expounding the attainment of the requisite virtues for those aspiring to contemplation, especially humility and charity. Early chapters (2–9) describe the active life and then the three parts of contemplation: a rational knowledge of the truths of the faith; 'affection' with sensible feelings of 'devotion', in turn distinguished into lower and higher degrees, i.e. occasional feelings of fervour, and a more settled 'rest of hert . . . for to alwey preye to God, and to thynk on our Lord' (I, 7); and finally, 'very contemplation'. As the contemplative advances, consolations of meditation on Christ revealed in his humanity through the bodily senses and imagination will eventually be withdrawn, to be superseded by a more directly spiritual knowledge of Christ. 'Very contemplation' is hence firmly distinguished from all sensible feelings of 'devotion', and from the effects of such religious enthusiasm as Rolle's example and writings might produce.

In *Scale*, I, 44 the section on the Holy Name of Jesus, from the words 'Bot now seist thou' to the chapter's end, may represent an added clarification by Hilton on a subject particularly associated with Rolle. The passage (now generally accepted as Hilton's work) has been sewn in on two extra leaves in BL MS Harley 6579, a mid fifteenth-century manuscript which belonged to the London Charterhouse and apparently served as a working exemplar. The many interpolations into this and other manuscripts of shorter passages – often characterized as 'Christocentric' – are not now generally thought to be authorial. To illustrate such 'Christocentric' interpolation, some examples from MS Harley 6579 have been included within square brackets in the following extract, which is based on CUL MS Add. 6686, an early and relatively uncontaminated manuscript of Book I. Some manuscripts of Book I of *The Scale* contain both the passage on the Holy Name and the interpolations, some contain neither feature and some contain one and not the other, in a variety that reflects a complex process of transmission and reception.

Base manuscript: CUL MS Add. 6686 (c), pp. 315–20. Also cited: BL MS Harley 6579 (h).

(44)   *How ilk man may be saved by the passioun of Crist, be he*
       never so wrecched, if he ask it.

And therfor if thou thynk that I have herbifor spoken over-heghe to the, for thou may noght take it ne fulfill it as I have seid or schal sey, I will fall doun to the als lowghe as thou wilt, als wel for my profite as for thin. And then sey I thus: that be thou never so mykel a wrecche, hast thou don never so mykel synne, forsake thiself and all thi werkes gode and badd. Crie mercie, and ask only savacioun by the vertue of this preciouse passioun mekely and treistily, and withouten doute thou schalt have it. And fro this original synne and all other that thou has don, thou schalt be saufe. Yee, and thou schalt be saufe as anker incluse, and noght only thou bot all Cristen soules whilk treisten upon his passioun and meken hemself, knowlechand her wrecchednes, askand mercie and forgyvenes, and the frute of this preciouse passioun only, lowghand hemself to the sacramentes of holy kirk. Thogh it be so that thei have ben encombred with synne all her lyfe tyme, and haden never felyng of gostly savour, or swetnes, or gostly knowyng of God, thei schuln in this feith and in her gode will, by vertue of this preciouse passioun of our Lord Jhesu Crist, be saufe and come to the blisse of heven. All this knowest thou wel, bot yit me liketh for to sey it.

Se her the endles mercy of our Lord, how lowghe he falleth to the and to me and to all synfull caityves. Ask mercie, and have it. Thus seid the prophet in the persoun of our Lord: *Omnis enim qui invocaverit nomen Domini, salvus erit.*[3] Ilke man, what that he be, call the name of Jhesu, that is to sey, ask savacioun by Jhesu and by his passioun, and he schal be saufe. This curtesie of our Lord summe men taken wel and ben saved therby; and summe, in treist of mercie and of this curtesie, lien still in her synne and wenen for to have it when hem list. And then moun thei noght, for thei ar taken or thei witen, and so thei dampnen hemself.

Bot now seist thou: 'If this be soth, then wonder I gretly for that I fynde writen in summe holy mennes sawghes. Summe seyn as I understond, that he that can noght love this blissed name Jhesu, ne fynde ne fele in it gostly joye and delitabletie, with wonderfull swetnes in this life her – fro the sovereyn joye and gostly suetnes in the blisse of heven he schal be alien and never schal he come therto. Sothly thise wordes when I hem rede stoneth me and maketh me gretly ferde. For I hope as thou seist that mony by the mercie of our Lord schal be saufe by the kepyng of his commaundmentz and by verrey repentaunce for her yvell lyfe bifor don, the whilk feled never gostly swetnes ne inly savour in the name of Jhesu or in the love of Jhesu. And forthi I mervaile me the mor that thei sey contrarie herto als it semeth'.

As unto this, I may sey as me thynketh, that her seyng if it be wel understonden is soth, ne it is noght contrarie to that that I have seid. For this name Jhesu is noght elles for to sey upon Englisch bot 'heler' or 'hele'. Now everilk man that lyveth in this wrecched lyfe is gostly seke, for ther is no man that lyveth withouten synne, the whilk is gostly sekenes, as Seint John seith of hymself and of other perfite men thus: *Si dixerimus quia peccatum non habemus, ipsi nos seducimus, et veritas in nobis non est.*[4] 'If we sey that we han no synne we bigyle ourself and ther is no sothfastnes in us.' And forthi he may never fele ne come to the joyes of heven until he be first made hole of this gostly sekenes. Bot this gostly hele may no man have that has use of resoun, bot if he desir it, and love it, and have delite therinne, in als mykel as he hopeth for to gete it. Now the name of Jhesu is nothyng elles bot this gostly hele. Wherfor it is soth that thei seyn, that ther may no man be saufe bot if he love and like in the name of Jhesu, for ther may no man be gostly hole bot if he love and desir gostly hele. For right as if a man wer bodily seke, ther wer non erthly thyng so dere ne so nedefull to hym, ne so mykel schuld be desired of hym so bodily hele. For thogh thou woldest yyve hym all the ryches and the worschipes of this world, and noght make hym hole if that thou myghtest, thou plesest hym noght. Right so it is to a man that is seke gostly, and feleth the peyn of gostly sekenes. Nothyng is so dere, so nedefull, ne so mykel coveited of hym so is gostly hele – and that is Jhesu, withouten whilk all the joyes of heven may noght like hym. And this is the skill, as I hope, whi our Lord, when he toke mankynd for our savacioun, he wold noght be called by no name that betokned his endles beyng, or his myght, or his wisdom, or his ryghtwisnes, bot only by that that bitokned the cause of his comyng: and that was savacioun of mannes soule, whilk savacioun was most dere and most nedefull to man. And this savacioun bitokneth this name Jhesu. Then bi this semeth it soth that ther schal no man be saufe, bot if he love [Jhesu, for there may no man be saved, bot if he love]^a savacioun, whilk love he may have that lyveth and dyeth in the lowghest degre of charite.

Also I may sey on another maner, that he that can noght love this blissed name Jhesu with gostly myrth, ne enjoye in it with hevenly melodie her, he schal never have ne fele in the blis of heven that fulhed of sovereyn joye, the whilk he that myght in this life by abundaunce of perfite charite enjoye in Jhesu schal fele and have. And so may her seyng be understonden. Nevertheles he schal be saufe and have full mede in the sight of God, if he in this life be in the lowghest degre of charite by kepyng of Goddes comaundmentz. For our Lord seith hymself thus: *In domo patris mei multae mansiones sunt.*^{5} 'In my Fadres house arn mony sere dwellynges.' Summe ar for perfite soules, the whilk in this life wer fulfilled of grace of the Holy Gost and songen lowvyng to God in contemplacioun of hym, with wonderfull swetnes and hevenly savor. Thise soules, for thei haden most charite, schuln have heghest mede in the blisse of heven, for thise ar called Goddes derlynges. Other soules that ar in this life inperfite and ar noght disposed to contemplacioun of God, ne hade noght the fulhed of charite as apostles and martires haden in the biginnyng of holy kirk, the[i]^b schul have the lowgher mede in the blisse of heven, for thise ar called Goddes frendes. Thus calleth our Lord in holy writt chosen soules, seyand thus: *Comedite, amici, et inebriamini, carissimi.*^{6} 'My frendes, ete ye: and my derlynges, be ye drunken.' As if our Lord seyd thus: Ye that ar my frendes – for ye keped my commaundmentz and sett my love bifor the love of the world, and loved me mor then any

^{a} Jhesu . . . love] H; C *om.* ^{b} thei] H; the C.

erthly thyng – ye schuln be fedd with gostly fode of the brede of life. Bot ye that ar my derlynges – that noght only keped my commaundmentz, bot also of your oun fre will fulfilled my counseils, and over that ye loved me only and enterly with all the myghtes of your soule, and brenned in my love with gostly delite, as did principaly the apostles and martires and all other soules that myght by grace come to the yift of perfeccioun – ye schul be made drunken with the heghest and the freschest wyn in my celer: that is, the sovereyn joye of love in the blis of heven.

(45) *That a man schuld be bisye to recover ageyn his worthines, and reforme in hym the ymage of the Trinite.*

Nevertheles thogh this be soth of the endeles mercy of God unto the and me and all mankynde, we schul noght therfor in treist of this be the mor rekles wilfully in our livyng, bot mor bisie unto plese hym; namly now syn we arn restored ayeyn in hope by this passioun of our Lord to the dignite and the blis whilk we hade lorn by Adam synne. And thogh we myght never gete it here fully, yit we schul desir that we myght recover her lyvand a figure and a liknes of that dignite, that our soule myght be reformed as it wer in a schadue by grace, to the ymage of the Trinite whilk we haden by kynde and after schuln have fully in blisse. For that is the life whilk is verreile contemplatif unto bigynne her, in that felyng of love and gostly knowyng of Godd by openyng of the gostly eghe, whilk schal never be lost ne be taken awey, bot the same schal be filled otherwise in the blisse of heven. This byheght our Lord to Marie Magdalene, whilk was contemplatif, and seid thus of hyr: *Maria optimam partem elegit, quae non auferetur ab ea.*[7] That Marie hade chosen the best partie, that is the love of God in contemplacioun, for it schal never be taken awey fro hir. I sey noght that thou may, her lyvand, recover so hole ne so perfite clennes, innocence, knowyng and lovyng of God as thou hadest first, ne as thou schalt have. Ne thou may noght escape all the wrecchednes and the peynes of synne, ne thou (lyvand in flesch dedly) may destrue and quench all holly the fals vein love of thiself, ne fle all veinal synnes that thei ne will – bot if thei be stopped by grete fervor of charite – alwey spryng out of thi hert as water renneth out fro a stinkand well. I wold, if thou myght noght fully quenche it, that thou myght sumwhat slek it, and come to that clennes als ner as thou may. For our Lord beheght the chyldre of Israel when he ledd hem into the londe of beheste, and in figur of hem to all Cristen men thus: *Omnis locus, quem calcaverit pes tuus tuum erit.*[8] That is for to sey, als mykel as thou may trede upon with thi fote of verrey desir here, so mykel schalt thou have in the londe of behest, that is, in the blisse of heven when thou comest thider.

(46) *How Jhesu schal be soght, desired, and founden.*

Seke then that thou has lost, that thou myght fynde it. Wel I wote, whoso myght ones have an inward syght a litel of that dignite and that gostly fairnes whilk a soule hade by kynde and schal have by grace, he schuld lothe and despise in his hert al the blis, the likyng, and the fairnes of al this world as stynk of carioun. And he schuld never have will to do other dede nyght ne day – savand the freltie and the bare nede of the bodily kynde – bot desir, mourne, and preye and seke how he myght come ageyn therto. Nevertheles in als mykel as thou has noght yit fully seen what it is, for thi gostly eghe is noght yit opened, I schal tell one word for al whilk thou schalt seke, desir and fynde, for in that word is all that thou has lost. This word is Jhesu. I meene noght this word Jhesu peynted upon the wal, or writen by letters on the boke, ne fourmed by lippes in soun of the mouth, ne feyned in the hert by travaile of the mynde; for on this maner wise may a man out of charite fynde hym. Bot I meene Jhesu [Crist, that blissed persone, God and man, sone of Virgyn Marie, whom this name bitokneth; that is]*c* al godenes, endles wisdom, love and swetnes, thi joye, thi worschipe and thin ay lastand blisse, thi God, thi Lord, and thi savacioun.

Then if it be so that thou felest grete desir in thi hert to Jhesu, eithir by the mynde of this name Jhesu, or by mynde and seyng of any word or prayer, or by any dede that thou dos, whilk desir is so mykel that it putteth out as it wer by strenkth al other thoghtes and desires of the world and of thi flesch, that thei moun noght rest in thi hert, then sekest thou wel Jhesu. And when thou felest this desir to God, to Jhesu (al is one), holpen and comforted by gostly myght so mykel that it is turned into love and affeccioun, gostly savour and swetnes, into light and knowyng of sothfastnes – so mykel that for the tyme the poynt of thi thoght is sett upon no thyng that is made, ne felest no stiryng of vein glorie, ne non other yvell affeccioun, for thei moun noght apper that tyme, bot only is enclosed, rested, softed, enoynted in Jhesu – then has

---

c Crist . . . is] H; C *om.*

thou founden sumwhat of Jhesu. Noght yit hym as he is, bot a schadue of hym. For the better that thou fyndest hym, the more schalt thou desire hym. Then by what maner of prayer, or meditacioun, or occupacioun that thou may have grettest desire to hym, and have most felyng of hym: by that occupacioun, thou sekest hym best, and best fyndest hym.

Therfor if it come to thi mynde as it wer askand what has thou lost and what sekest thou, lift up [thi mende in]*d* the desir of thi hert to Jhesu [Crist],*e* thogh thou be blynde and noght may se of hy[s Godhed],*f* and sey that hym has thou lost, and hym wold thou have, and nothyng bot hym [to be with him whare he is];*g* non other joye, non other blisse in heven ne in erth bot hym. And thogh it be so that thou fele hym in devocioun, or in knowyng, or in any other yyft what it be, rest noght therinne as thogh thou hadest fully founden Jhesu, bot foryete that thou has founden, and ay be desirand after Jhesu mor and mor for to fynde hym better, as thou hade ryght noght. For witt thou wel, what that thou felest of hym, be it never so mykel – yee! thogh thou wer ravisched into the thrid heven with Paule – yit has thou noght founden Jhesu as he is. Knowe thou or fele thou never so mykel of hym her in this life, he is yit above it. And therfor if thou wilt fully fynd hym as he is in the blisse of lovyng, cese never whiles thou lyvest of gostly desiryng.

d thi . . . in] H; C *om.*   *e* Crist] H; C *om.*   *f* hys Godhed] *corrected from* hym *in* C.
g to be . . . is] H; C *om.*

13 *The Scale of Perfection,* Book II

(Chapters 21, 33, 40, 41)

Book II of *The Scale* opens as if responding to a request from the anchoress-recipient of Book I to hear more about the soul as the image of God (I, 52), and deals with expulsion from the heart of the image of sin and re-formation of the soul in the image of Christ. But this later work conceives differently of its audience, representing a shifted, deepened understanding of what constitutes contemplation, and of those who may aspire to it. Unlike the earlier work (I, 15), Book II assumes its reader may follow the Latin scriptures (cf. II, 43), and may not necessarily be enclosed. Hilton now sees contemplation as something which all rational souls created in the image of God should desire and dispose themselves to receive, whatever their state in life. With a calm assurance in utterance and in organization, Book II sets out a pondered formulation of Hilton's doctrine of contemplation in relation to theology, particularly in its concept of the progression from 'reforming in faith' to 'reforming in feeling'. These terms are apparently Hilton's own, and reforming in feeling represents the practice of contemplation, dependent on infused grace. The earlier part of Book II treats reforming in faith: baptism and penance are the means of a first reforming of the soul, which is still apt to sin. With reforming of feeling, the influence of sinful impulses is past: the soul has what Hilton terms 'a lifely feling of grace', and the sublime sequence of concluding chapters (II, 33–45) are the culmination of Hilton's teaching on the nature of contemplation, suffused with a spiritual insight that would seem the distillation of great experience. Nonetheless, Hilton's exposition in Book II of a contemplation at once more advanced yet available to all Christians seems – on the evidence of numbers of surviving texts – to have proved less popular than his teaching in Book I.

Base manuscript: BL MS Harley 6579 (H), fols. 84r–86v, 108v–110v, 123r–130r. Also cited: CUL MS Ee. 4. 30 (Ee).

[21]   *That a man that will come to Jerusalem – that is undirstonde
       the cite of pees, the wich is contemplacioun – moste holde hym
       lowe in meknes and in faith, and suffer disseses bothe bodely
       and gostly.*

Nertheles, for thu coveites for to have sum maner wirkynge by
the whilke thu mightes the rather neighen to that reformynge, I schal
say the as me thinkith, bi the grace of oure Lord Jhesu, the shortest and
the rediest helpe that I knowe in this wirkynge. And how that schal be, I
schal telle the by example of a good pilgrym, upon this wise.

Ther was a man that wold gon to Jerusalem, and for he knewe
not the weye he come to another man that he hopid knew the wey
theder, and asked whether he mighte come to that citee. That other
man seide to him that he mighte not come theder withoute grete disese
and mikel travaile, for the wey is longe, and periles are grete of thefes
and robbours, and many other lettynges ther ben that fallen to a man
in the goyng. And also ther are mony sere weies, as it semith, ledand
thederward. Bot men alday are slayn and dispoiled, and mown not
comyn to that place that thei coveiten. Nertheles, ther is o wey, the
whilke whoso takith hit and holdith it, he wolde undirtake that he
schude come to the cite of Jerusalem, and he schulde never lese his lif,
ne be slayn, ne dye for defaute. He schulde often be robbed, and yvel
betyn, and suffren mikel disese in the goynge, bot he schulde ay han
his lif safe. Than saith the pilgrym: 'If it be so that I may have my lif
safe and come to that place that I coveite, I charge not what meschef I
suffre in the goynge. And therfore say me what thu wilt, and sothly, I
bihote for to don aftir the.'

That other man answeres and says thus: 'Lo, I sette the in the
right wey. This is the wey, and that thu kepe the lerynge that I kenne
the. What so thou heres or sees or felis that schulde lette the in thi
wey, abide not with it wilfully, tary not for it restfully, behold it not,
like it not, drede it not; bot ay go forth in thi wey, and thinke that thu
woldes be at Jerusalem. For that thu coveites, that thu desires, and
noght elles bot that. And if men robbe the and dispoile the, bete the,
scorne the, and dispise the, strife not ageyn, if thu wilt han thi lif. Bot
holde the with the harme that thu has, and go forth as noght were,
that thu take no more harme. And also if men wil tary the with tales
and fede the with lesynges for to drawe the to mirthes and for to lefe

thi pilgrimage, make def ere and answer not ageyn, and sey not elles
bot [th]at*a* thu wuldes be at Jerusalem. And if men profre the yiftes,
and wil make the riche with werdly gode, tente not to hem – thinke ay
on Jerusalem. And if thu wil holde this way and don as I hafe sayde, I
undirtake thi lif – that thu schal not be slayn, bot thou schal come to
that place that thu coveites.'

Gostly, to oure purpos, Jerusalem is as mikel for to seyen as
sight of pes, and bitokneth contemplacioun in perfit luf of God. For
contemplacioun is not ellis bot a sight of Jhesu, whilk is verrey pes.
Than if thu coveite for to come to this blessid sight of verrey pees and
ben a trew pilgrym to Jerusalem-ward – thawgh it be so that I were
never there – nertheles, as ferforth as I kan, I schal sette the in the
weye thederwarde. The bygynnynge of the highe wey in the whilk thu
schalt gon is reformyng in faith, grounded mekly in the feith and in
the lawes of holy kirke, as I hafe saide beforn. For trust sikirly,
thawgh thu have synned herebifore, if thu be now reformed bi the
sacrament of penaunce aftir the lawe of holi kirke, that thu art in the
right weie. Now than, sithen thu art in the siker weye, if thu wile
spedyn in thi goynge and make gode jurnaies the bihovith to holden
these two thinges often in thi mynde: meknes and luf. That is: I am
noght, I have noght, I coveite noght, bot on. Thu schalt hafe the
menynge of these wordes in thin entent and in habite of thi soule
lastendly, thawgh thu hafe noght specialy these wordes ay formed in
thi thoughte, for that nedith not. Meknes saith: I am noght, I hafe
noght. Lufe saith: I coveite noght bot on, and that is Jhesu. These two
strenges, wel festned with the mynde of Jhesu, makith gode acorde in
the harpe of the soule, whan thei be craftly touchid with the fynger of
resoun. For the lower thu smytes upon that on, the higher sounith that
other. The lesse thu felist that thu art or that thu hast of thiself thurgh
meknes, the more thu coveites for to han of Jhesu in desire of luf. I
mene not only of that meknes that a soule felith in the sight of his own
syn or freltees and wrecchednes of this lif, or of the worthines of his
even-Cristen. For thawgh this meknes be sothfast and medycynable,
nertheles it is boistous and fleschly as in regarde, not clene, ne softe,
ne lufly. Bot I mene also this meknes that the soule felith thurwgh
grace in sight and beholdyng of the endeles beynge and the wundreful
godnes of Jhesu; and if thou mowe not seen it yit with thi gostly ighe,

---

a that] Ee; at H.

that thou trowe it. For thurwgh sight of his beynge, either in ful feith or in felyng, thu schat holden thiself not only as the most wrecche that is, bot also as noght in substaunce of thi soule, thawgh thu haddist never don syn. And that is lufly mekenes; for in reward of Jhesu, that is sothfastly al, thu art right noght. And also that thu thinke that thu hast right noght, bot art as a vessel that standith ay torne as noght were therin, as of thiself. For, doo thou never so many gode dedis outward or inward, til thu haue – and fele that thu hast – the luf of Jhesu, thu hast right noght. For with that precious licour only mai thi soule be fulfillid, and with none other. And for as mikel as that thinge alone is so precious and so wurthi, therfor what thu hast or what thu dost – holde it as noght for to resten in, withoutyn the sight and the luf of Jhesu. Keste it al bihynde the and forgete it, that thu mighte hafe that that is the best of alle.

Right as a trewe pilgrym goende to Jerusalem lefith bihynde him hows and lande, wife and childe, and makith hymself pore and bare from al that he hath, that he might go lightly withouten lettynge: right so if thu wil be a gostly pilgrym, thu schalt make thiself nakid fro al that thu hast, that are bothe gode dedis and badde, and kesten hem al bihynde the, that thu be so pore in thin owne felynge that ther be nothinge of thin owne wirkynge that thu wilt lene upon restendly, bot ay desirend more grace of luf and ay sekend the gostly presence of Jhesu. And if thu do thus, than schalt thu setten in thi herte holly and fully that thu woldest be at Jerusalem, and at none other place bot there. And that is, thu schalt setten in thin herte holly and fully that thu woldest no thinge hafe bot the lufe of Jhesu, and the gostly sight of hym as he wile schewe hym. For to that only thu art made and boghte, and that is thi bigynnynge and thin ende, thi joye and thi blisse. And therfore, whatsoevere that thu hafe, be thu never so riche in other dedis bodily and gostly, bot if thu have that, and knowe and fele that thu hast it, halde that thu hast right noght. Preente wel this resoun in the menynge of thi herte, and clefe sadly therto. And it schal safe the fro alle periles in thi goyng, that thu schalt never perischen, and it schal saf thee fro thefes and robbours, the whilk I calle unclene spirites, that thawgh thei spoile thee and bete the thurwgh divers temptaciouns, thi lif schal ay be safe. And schortly, if thu kepe it as I schal say the, thu schalt askape alle periles and meschiefs, and come to the citee of Jerusalem within schort tyme.

Now thu art in the wey and knowest what the place highte,

wheder thu schalt drawe to. Bygynne then for to gon forth in thi
jurney. Thi forthgoynge is noght elles bot gostly wirkynge, and bodily
also whan nede is; whilk thu schalt usen bi discrecioun upon this wise.
What werk that it be that thu schulde don, after the degre and the
state that thu standis in bodily or gostly, if it helpe this gracious desire
that thu haste for to lufe Jhesu, and make it more hol, more esy and
more mighty to alle vertues and to alle goodnes, that werke hald I
beste; be it prechynge, be it thinkynge, be it redyng, be it wirkynge.
And as longe as that werke strengtheth most thin herte and thi wil to
the luf of Jhesu, and ferrest drawith thin affeccioun and thi thoghte
fro werdly vanyte, it is gode for to usen it. And if it be so that –
thurwgh use – savour of that lesseth, and the thinkith another werk
savorith the more, and thu felist more grace in another, take another
and lefe that. For thawgh thi desire and the yernynge of thin herte to
Jhesu schuld be ay unchaungable, nertheles thi gostly werkes, that thu
schalt usen in praynge or thinkynge for to feden and norischen thi
desire, may be dyvers and may wel be chaunged aftir that thu felis the
disposed thurw grace in appliynge of thin own hert.

   For it farith bi werkes and bi desire, as it doth bi stikkes and bi a
fiire. For the mo stikkes arn leide to the fiire the gretter is the fire; right
so the more divers gostly wirkynge that a man hath in his thoght for
to kepe hol his disire, the mightier and the more brennand schal his
desire be to God. And therfore loke wisely what werk thu kannist best
don, and that most helpith the for to safen hole this desire to Jhesu (if
thou be free, and art not bounden bot undir the comune lawe), and
that do. Bynde the not to wilful customes unchaungebly, that sculden
let the fredom of thin hert for to luf Jhesu if grace wolde visite the
specialy. For I schal telle the whilke customes are ay gode and nedful
to be kepte. Lo, swilke custome is ay gode for to holden that stondith
in getynge of vertue and lettynge of syn, and that custome schuld
never be lefte. For thu schalt ay be meke and paciente, sobre and
chaste, if thu wel do; and so of alle other vertues. Bot the custome of
another thinge that lettith a better is for to lefen when tyme is, ther a
man may. As thus: if a man hafe in custome for to say thus many
bedis, or for to thinken this maner of thoght thus longe tyme, or for to
waken or knelen thus longe, or ony other swilk bodily dede, this
custome is for to lefen sumtyme whan resonable cause lettith, or elles
if more grace come in other side. . . .

[33] *Hou Jhesu is hevene to the soule; and why he is clepid fier.*

What is heven to a resonable soule? Sothly not elles bot Jhesu
God. For if that be heven only that is above al thinge, than is God only
heven to mannes soule. For he is only abofe the kynde of a soule. Than
if a soule may thurgh grace have knowynge of that blissid kynde of
Jhesu, sothly he seeth heven, for he seeth God.

Therfor ther are mony men that erren in undirstandynge of
summe wordes that are seide of God, for thei undirstanden hem not
gostly. Holy writynge seith that a soule that wil fynde God schal liften
upwarde the innere eghe and seke God abofe itself. Than summe men,
that wolde don aftir this seyng, undirstonden this word 'abofe hemself'
as for hieghere settynge in stede and wurthines of place, as on elemente
and on planet is abofe another in settynge and worthines of a bodily
place. Bot it is not so gostly. For a soule is above al bodily thinge not bi
settynge of stede, bot bi sotelte and worthines of kynde. Right so on the
selfe wise, God is above al bodily and gostly creatures not bi settynge of
stede bot thurgh sotelte and worthines of his unchaungeable blissid
kynde. And therfore he that wil wisely seke God and fynden him, he
schal not renne out with his thoght as he wolde clymbe aboven the
sunne and persen the firmament, and ymagynen the majeste as it were a
light of an hundred sunnes. Bot he schal rather drawe downe the sunne
and al the firmament, and forgeten it and kesten it bineth him ther he is,
and setten al this and al bodily thinge also at noght, and thenke than if
he kan gostly, both of himself and of God also. And if he do thus, than
seeth the soule above itself and than seeth it heven.

Upon this self maner schal this wurde 'withinne' be undirstande.
It is comunly seide that a soule schal see oure Lorde withinne al thinge
and withinne itself. Sooth it is that oure Lorde is withinne alle
creatures, bot not on that manere as a kirnel is hid withinne the schelle
of a nut, or as a litel bodily thinge is holden within another mikel. Bot
he is within alle creatures as holdend and kepende hem in her beenge
thurgh sotilte and thurgh might of his owne blessed kende and klennes
unseable. For right as a thinge that is most precious and most clene is
leid innerest, right so bi that liknes it is seid that the kende of God – that
is most precious, most clene and most gostly, ferrest fro bodiliched – is
hid within alle thinges. And therfor he that wil seke God within, he
schal forget first alle bodily thinge – for al that is withouten – and his

owne body; and he schal forgete thenkynge of his owne soule and thenken on that unmade kynde that is Jhesu that made him, qwikneth him, holdith him, and gifith him resoun and mende and lufe; the whilk is within him thurgh his might and sovereyn sotilte. Upon this maner schal the soule do when grace touchith it, or elles it wil bot litel availe seke Jhesu and to fyndyn him within itself and within alle creatures, as me thinketh.

Also it is seide in holy writ that God is light. So seith Seint John: *Deus lux est.*[1] That is: 'God is light.' This light schal not ben undirstanden as for bodily light, bot it is undirstandid thus. God is light. That is: God is trewth and sothfastnes, for sothfastnes is gostly light. Than he that most graciously knowith sothfastnes, best seeth God. And nertheles it is likned to bodily light; for this skil. Right as the sunne schewith to the bodily eighe itself and al bodily thinge bi it, right so sothfastnes – that is God – schewith to the resoun of the soule itself first, and by itself al othere gostly thinge that nedith to be knowen of a soule. Thus seith the prophet: *Domine, in lumine tuo videbimus lumen.*[2] 'Lord, we schul see thi light bi thi light.' That is: we schul see the that art sothfastnes bi thiself.

On the self wise it is seide that God is fire: *Deus noster ignis consumens est.*[3] That is: 'Our Lord is fir wastende.' That is for to seie: God is not fire elementarie that hetith a body and brenneth it, bot God is luf and charite. For as fiire wasteth al bodily thinge that may be wasted, right so the luf of God brennith and wastith al synne out of the soule and makith it clene, as fire makith clene al maner metal. These wordes – and al other that are spoken of oure Lorde in holy writynge bi bodily liknes – moste nedis ben undirstonden gostly, elles ther is no savour in hem. Nertheles the cause whi swilke maner wordes are seid of oure Lorde in holy writt is this: for we are so fleschly that we kun not speken of God ne undirstonden of him bot if we bi swilke wordes first ben entrid in. Nertheles when the inner eighe is opned thurgh grace for to hafe a litel sight of Jhesu, than schal the soule turne lightly inowgh alle swilke wordes of bodily thinges into gostly undirstondynge.

This gostly opnynge of the inner ighe into knowynge of the Godhed I calle reformyng in feith and in felynge. For than the soule sumwhat felith in undirstandynge of that thinge that it had bifore in nakid trowynge and that is the bigynnynge of contemplacioun, of the whilk Seynt Poul seith thus: *Non contemplantibus nobis quae videntur, sed quae non videntur; quae enim videntur, temporalia sunt, quae*

*autem non videntur, aeterna sunt.*⁴ That is: 'Oure contemplacioun is
not in thinges that are seen bot it is in thinges unseable. For thinges that
are seen are passende, bot unseable thinges are ay lastende.' To the
whilk sight everilk a soule schuld desire for to come to, bothe here in
party and in the blis of heven fully. For in that sight and in that
knowynge of Jhesu is fully the blis of a resonable soule and endles lif.
*Haec est autem vita aeterna: ut cognoscant te unum Deum, et quem
misisti Jhesum Christum.*⁵ That is: 'Fader, this is endeles lif: that thi
chosen soules knowe the and thi sone, whom thu hast sent, on sothfast
God.' . . .

[40]   *What vertues and gracis a soule resceyveth thorugh openyng of
       the innere eye into the gracious beholdyng of Jhesu; and hou it
       may not be gete only thorugh mannys traveil, but thorugh
       special grace and traveil also.*

Thus wirkith lufe outwarde in a soule, opynende the gostly eighe
into biholdynge of Jhesu bi inspiracioun of special grace, and makith it
clene, sotil and able to the werk of contemplacioun. What this opnyng
of the gostly eighe is, the grettest clerk in erth couthe not ymagyn by his
witte ne schewe fully bi his tonge. For it may not be geten be studye ne
thurgh mannes traveile only, bot principally bi grace of the Holy Gost
and with travail of man. I drede mikel to speke ought of it, for me
thinkith I kan not. It passith myn assay and my lippes are unclene.
Nertheles, for I hope luf askith and lufe biddith, therfore I schal seyen a
litel more of it, as I hope luf techith. This openynge of the gostly eighe is
that lighty mirknes and riche noght that I spake of bifore, and it may be
callid: *Purte of spirit and gostly reste, inwarde stilnes and pees of
conscience, heighenes of thoght and onlynes of soule, a lifly felynge of
grace and pryvete of herte, the waker slep of the spouse and tastyng of
hevenly savour, brynnyng in lufe and schynynge in light, entre of
contemplacioun and reformynge in felynge.* Alle these resons are saide
in holy writynge bi divers men, for ilke of hem spake of it aftir his
felynge in grace, and thawgh al thai are divers in schewynge of wordes,
nertheles thei arne alle in on sentence of sothfastnes.

For a soule that thurgh visitynge of grace hath on, hath al. Forwhi
a sighend soule to seen the face of Jhesu, whan it is touchid thorugh
special grace of the Holy Gost, it is sodenly chaunged and turned fro
the plight that it was in to another maner feling. It is wondirfully

departid and drawen first into itself fro the lufe and likynge of al erthly thinge, so mikel that it hath lost savour of the bodily life and of al thinge that is, save only Jhesu. And *than is it clene fro alle the filthe of syn*, so ferforth that the mende of it and al unordeyned affeccioun of ony creature is sodeynly weschen and wiped awey, that ther is no mene lettynde atwix Jhesu and the soule, bot only the bodily life. And *than is it in gostly reste*; forwhi alle pyneful doutes and dredes and al other temptaciouns of gostly enmys arn drifen out of the herte, that thei troblen not ne synken not therin for the tyme. It is in rest fro the noye of werdly bisynes and peynful taryinges of wikked stirynges; bot it is ful bisy in the fre gostly wirkynge of lufe; and the more it travelith so, the more rest it felith. This restful travel is ful fer fro fleschly ydelnes and fro blynde sikernes. It is ful of gostly werk; bot it is called reste, for grace losith the hevy yokke of fleschly luf fro the soule and makith it mighty and free thurgh the gifte of the gostly luf, for to wirken gladly, softly and delectably in al thinge that grace stirith it for to wirken in. And therfor is it called an holy ydelnes and a reste moste besy; and so is it, *in stilnes* fro the grete cryinge and the bestly noise of fleschly desires and unclene thoghtis.

This stilnes makith the inspiracioun of the Holy Gost, in beholdynge of Jhesu. Forwhi his vois is so swete and so mighty that it puttith silence in a soule to jangelen of alle other spekers; for it is a voys of vertue softly souned in a clene soule, of the whilk the prophete saith thus: *Vox Domini in virtute*.[6] That is: 'The voice of oure Lord Jhesu is in vertue.' This voys is a lifly worde and a spedy, as the apostel seith: *Vivus est sermo Domini et efficax, penetrabilior omni gladio*.[7] That is: 'Qwike is the worde of Jhesu and spedy, more persande then ony swerde is.' Thurgh spekynge of his worde is fleschly luf slayn, and the soule kept in silence fro alle wicked stirynges. Of this silence it is seyd in the Apocalips thus: *Factum est silentium in coelo, quasi media hora*.[8] 'Silence was made in heven, as it were an half houre.' Heven is a clene soule, thurgh grace lift up fro erthly luf to hevenly conversacioun, and so is it in silence; bot for as mikel as that silence may not lesten hole continualy, for corupcioun of the bodily kynde, therfor it is likned bot to the tyme of an half oure. A ful schorte tyme the soule thinkith that it is, be it never so longe, and therfor it is bot as an half oure. And than hath it *pees in conscience*, forwhi grace puttith out gnawyng and prikkynge, stryfyng and flytynge of synnes, and bryngith in pees and accorde, and makith Jhesu and a soule bothe at one in ful accordance of wille. Ther is non upbraydyng of synnes ne scharpe reprefynge of defautes made that tyme in a soule, for thei are kissed and frendes – al is forgifen that was misdone.

Thus felith the soule thanne with ful meek sikernes and grete gostly gladnes, and it conceifith a ful grete boldnes of salvacioun bi this acorde-makynge, for it herith a pryvey witnesynge in conscience of the Holy Gost, that he is a chosen sone to hevenly heritage. Thus Seint Poul seith: *Ipse Spiritus testimonium perhibet spiritui nostro, quod filii Dei sumus.*[9] That is: 'The Holy Gost berith witnes to oure spirit, that we arne Goddis sones.' This witnesynge of conscience, sothfastly felde thurgh grace, is the verray joie of the soule, as the apostel seith: *Gloria mea est testimonium conscienciae mea.*[10] That is: 'My joye is the witnes of my conscience', and that is whan it witnesith pees and accorde, trewe luf and frendschip atwix Jhesu and a soule. And whan it is in this pees, than is it *in heighenes of thought*.

When the soule is bounden with lufe of the werlde, then is it bineth alle creatures; for ilk a thinge overgoth it and berith it doun by maystrye, that it may not see Jhesu ne lufen him. For right as the lufe of the werlde is veyn and fleschly, right so the biholdynge and thenkynge and the usyng of creatures is fleschly; and that is a thraldom of the soule. Bot than thurgh opnynge of the gostly eighe into Jhesu, the luf is turned and the soule is reisid up after his owne kynde abofe alle bodily creatures; and than the beholdynge and thenkynge and the usynge of hem is gostly, for the luf is gostly. The soule hath than ful grete dedeyn for to be buxum to luf of bodily thinges; for it is heighe sett abofen hem thurgh grace. It settith noght bi al the world, forwhi al schal passen and perischen. Unto this heighenes of herte, whils the soule is kept therin, cometh none errour ne disceite of the fende, for Jhesu is sothfastly in sight of the soule that tyme and al thinge byneth him. Of this spekith the prophet thus: *Accedat homo ad cor altum; et exaltabitur Deus.*[11] 'Come man to heighe herte and God schal be heighed.' That is: a man that thurgh grace comith to highenes of thoght schal seen that Jhesu only is heighed abofen alle creatures and he in him.

And than is the soule alone, mikel straunged fro felaghschep of werdly lufers – thowgh here body be in middis amonge hem – ful fer departid fro fleschly affecciouns of creatures. It chargith noght thawgh it never see man ne speke with him, ne had confort of him, if it might ay be so in that gostly felynge. It felith so grete homlynes of the blissed presence of oure Lord Jhesu, and so mikel savour of him, that it may lightly for his luf forgetyn the fleschly affeccioun and the fleschly mynde of alle creatures. I sey not that it schal not lufen ne thinken of other creatures, bot I sey that it schal thinken on hem in tyme and seen hem and lufen hem gostly and frely, not fleschly and pynefully as it did bifore. Of this onlynes spekes the prophet thus: *Ducam eam in solitudinem, et loquar ad cor eius.*[12] 'I schal leden hir into onlystede, and I schal speke to hir herte.' That is: Grace of Jhesu ledith a soule fro noious companye of fleschly desires into onlynes of thoght, and makith it to forgete the likynge of the werld and sownith bi swetnes of his inspiracioun wordes of lufe in eres of the hert. Only is a soule whan it lufith Jhesu and tentith fully to him, and hath lost the savour and the confort of the werld; and that it might the better kepe this onlynes it fleeth the companye of alle men if it may, and sekith onlynes of body, for that mikel helpith to onlynes of soule and to the free wirkyng of luf. The lesse lettyng that it hath withouten of veyn jangelynge, or within of veyn thenkynge, the more free it is in gostly biholdynge, and so is it *in pryvete of hert.*

Al withouten is a soule whil it is overleid and blynded with werdly luf; it is as comune as the heighe wey. For ilk a stirynge that comith of the flesch or of the fende sinkith in, and goth thurgh it. Bot than thurgh grace it is drawen into the pryvey chambre into the sight of oure Lorde Jhesu, and hereth his privy counseilis, and is wondirfully counforted in the heryng. Of this spekith the prophet thus: *Secretum meum mihi; secretum meum mihi.*[13] 'My pryvete to me, my pryvete to me.' That is: The lufer of Jhesu, thurgh inspiracioun of his grace, taken up fro outward felynge of werdly lufe and ravisched into pryvete of gostly lufe, yeldith thankyng to him, seiend thus: *My pryvete to me.* That is: My Lord Jhesu, thi pryvete is schewde to me and pryvely hid fro alle lufers of the world, for it is called hid manna, that may lightlyer ben askid then tolde what it is. And that oure Lorde Jhesu bihetith to his lufer thus: *Dabo sibi manna absconditum, quod nemo novit, nisi qui accipit.*[14] That is: 'I schal gif manna hid that no man knowith bot he that takith it.' This manna is hevenly mete and aungels fode, as holy writ seith. For aungels arne fully fed and fillid with clere sight and brennende lufe of oure Lorde Jhesu, and that is manna. For we moun aske what it is, bot not wete what it is. Bute the lufer of Jhesu is not filled yit here, bot he is fed bi a litil tastyng of it whils he is bounden in this bodily lif.

This tastyng of manna is a lifely felynge of grace, had thurgh opnyng of the gostly eighe. And this grace is not another grace than a chosen soule felith in bigynnyng of his conversioun; bot it is the same and the self grace, bot it is otherwise felid and schewyd to a soule. Forwhi, grace wexeth with the soule and the soule wexith with grace, and the more clene that the soule is fer departid fro luf of the werld, the more mighty is the grace, more inwarde and more gostly schewend the presence of oure Lorde Jhesu. So that the same grace that turnith first hem fro synne and makith hem bigynnande and profitande bi giftes of vertues and exercice of gode werkis makith hem also perfit; and that grace is kallid *a lifly felynge of grace*, for he that hath it felith it wel and knowith wel by experience that he is in grace. It is ful lifly to him, for it quicneth the soule wondirfully and makith it so hole that it felith no peynful disese of the body, thawgh it be feble and sekely. Forwhi, than is the body mightiest, most hool, and most restful, and the soule also.

Withouten this grace the soule kan not lifen bot in peyn, for it thinkith that it might ay kepe it and no thinge schulde pute it awey. And nertheles yit it is not so, for it passith awey ful lightly; bot nertheles thawgh the sovereyn felynge passe awey and withdrawe the reliefe lefith stille and kepith the soule in sadnes and makith it for to desiren the comyng ageyn. And this is also the wakir slepe of the spouse, of the whilk holy writ seith thus: *Ego dormio, et cor meum vigilat.*[15] 'I slepe and my herte wakith.' That is: I slepe gostly, when thurgh grace the luf of the werld is slayn in me and wicked stirynges of fleschly desires are ded so mikel that unnethes I fele hem; I am not taried with hem. Myn herte is made free, and than it wakith, for it is scharpe and redy for to lufe Jhesu and seen him. The more I slepe fro outwarde thinges, the more waker am I in knowynge of Jhesu and of inward thinges. I may not wake to Jhesu bot if I slepe to the werld. And therfore the grace of the Holy Gost sperend the fleschly eighe, dothe the soule slepe fro werdly vanytee, and opnende the gostly eighe waken into the sight of Goddis majeste, hiled undir cloude of his precious manhede; as the gospel seith of the apostels when thei were with oure Lorde Jhesu in his transfiguracioun. First thei slepid, and than *vigilantes viderunt maiestatem*,[16] 'thei waknend seen his majeste.' By slepe of the apostels is undirstonden dyenge of werdly lufe thurgh inspiracioun of the Holy Gost; by here waknynge, contemplacioun of Jhesu. Thurgh this slep the soule is broght into reste fro dyn of fleschly luste; and thurgh waknynge it is reisid up into the sight of Jhesu and gostly thinges. The more that the eighen are spered in this maner slepe fro the appetite of erthli thinge, the scharper is the inner sight in lufly

beholdynge of hevenly fairhed. This slepynge and this wakynge lufe
wirkith thurgh the light of grace in the soule of the lufer of Jhesu.

[41] *Hou special grace in beholdyng of Jhesu withdrawith sumtyme
fro a soule, and hou a soule shal have hir in the absence and
presence of Jhesu, and how a soule shal desire that in it is
alwey the gracious presence of Jhesu.*

Schew me than a soule that thurgh inspiracioun of grace hath
openynge of the gostly eighe into biholdynge of Jhesu; that is departid
and drawen out fro luf of the wor[l]de*b* so fer forth that it hath *purte
and poverte of spirit, gostly rest, inward silence and pees in conscience,
heighenes of thoght, onlynes and pryvetee of herte, waker slepe of the
spouse; that hath loste lykynge and joyes of this werlde, taken with
delice of hevenly savour, ay thristand and softely sikynge the blessed
presence of Jhesu*; and I dar hardely pronuncen that this soule brennyth
al in luf and schynyth in gostely light, wurthi for to come to the name
and to the wurschip of the spouse. For it is reformed in felynge: made
able and redy to contemplacioun. These are the toknes of inspiracioun
in openynge of the gostly eighe; forwhi when the eighe is opned the
soule is in ful felynge of alle these vertues bifore-seid, for that tyme.

Nertheles it fallith ofte sithes that grace withdrawth in party, for
corrupcioun of mannys freelte, and suffrith the soule falle into itself in
fleschhed, as it was befor; and then is the soule in sorw and in peyn, for
it is blynde and unsavory and can no gode. It is weyk and unmyghty,
encumbred with the body and with alle the bodily wittes; it sekith and
desirith after the grace of Jhesu ageyn, and it may not fynde it. For holy
writt seith of oure Lorde thus: *Postquam vultum suum absconderit,
non est qui contempletur eum.*[17] That is: 'After when our Lord Jhesu
hath hid his face, ther is none that may biholden him.' When he shewth
him, the soule may not unsee him for he is light; and whan he hidith
him, it may not see him, for the soule is myrk. His hidyng is but a sotil
assaynge of the soule; his schewynge is wondir merciful goodnes in
conforte of the soule.

Have thu no wondir, thawgh the felyng of grace withdraw
sumtyme fro a lufer of Jhesu. For holy writ seith the same of the spouse,
that she farith thus: *Quesivi et non inveni illum: vocavi et non
respondit mihi.*[18] 'I seked and I fonde him not: I called and he answerid

b worlde] Ee; worde H.

not.' That is: when I falle doun to my freeltee, than grace withdrawth; for my fallynge is cause therof, and not his fleeng. Bot than fele I peyne of my wrechednes in his absence, and therfore I soghte him bi grete desirynge of hert, and he gaf to me no felable answerynge. And than I cried with alle my soule: *Revertere dilecte mi!* [19] 'Turne ageyn, thu my loved.' And yit it semed as he [h]arde*ᶜ* me not. The peynful felyng of myself and the assailyng of fleschly lufes and dredes in this tyme, and the wantyng of my gostly strength, is a continuel cryeng of my soule to Jhesu; and nertheles oure Lord makith straunge awhile and comith not, cry I never so fast. For he is sikir inowgh of his lufer, that he wil not turn ageyn to wordly luf fully; he may no savour han therin. And therfor abidith he the lenger.

Bot at the last when he wil, he comyth ageyn ful of grace and of sothfastnes, and visiteth the soule that langueshth in desire bi sikynges of luf to his presence, and touchith it and anoyntith it ful softely with the oyle of gladnes, and makith it sodeynly hool fro alle pyne. And than crieth the soule to Jhesu in gostely voyce with a gladd herte thus: *Oleum effusum nomen tuum.* [20] 'Oyle yotted is thi name', Jhesu. Thi name is Jhesu: that is, hele. Than as longe as I fele my soule sore and seke for synne, pyned with the hevy birthen of my body, sory and dredende for periles and wrecchednes of this life, so longe, Lorde Jhesu, thi name is oile sparid, not oile yottede to me. Bot whan I fele my soule sodeynly touched with the light of grace, heled and softed fro alle the filthe of synne, conforted in lufe and in light with gostly strenthe and gladnes unspekable, than may I say with lysty lovyng and gostly might to the: 'Oile yotted is thi name, Jhesu, to me. For bi the effect of thi gracious visitynge I fele wel of thi name the trewe exponyng: that art Jhesu, hele. For oonly thi presence gracious helith me fro sorowe and fro synne.' Blissed is that soule that is ay fed in felynge of luf in his presence, or is borne up bi desire to him in his absence. A wise lufer is he, and a wel taght, that sadly and reverently hath him in his presence, and lufly biholdith him withoute dissolute lightnes, and paciently and esily berith him in his absence withoute venymous despeire and over peynful bitternes.

This chaungabilite of absence and presence of Jhesu that a soule felith is not perfeccioun of the soule, ne it is not ageyns the grace of perfeccioun or of contemplacioun; bot in so mikel is perfeccioun the

---

ᶜ harde] ᴇᴇ; arde ʜ.

lesse. For the more lettynge that a soule hath of itself fro continuel felynge of grace, the lesse is the grace; and thawgh yit nertheles is the grace in itself grace of contemplacioun. This chaungabilite of absence and presence fallith as wel in stat of perfeccioun as in state of bigynnynge, bot in another maner. For right as ther is diversite of felynge in the presence of grace atwix these two states, right so is ther in the absence of grace. And therfor he that knowt not the absence of grace is redy to be desceifid; and he that kepith not the presence of grace is unkynde to the visityng, whether he be in the state of bigynners or of perfighte. Nertheles, the more stabelnes that ther is in grace, unhurt and unbroken, the luflier is the soule and more like unto him in whom is no manere chaungabilite, as the postel seith; and it is ful semely that the soule spouse be like to Jhesu spouse in manere and in vertues, ful acordant to him in stabelnes of perfit lufe. Bot that fallith seldom; nowhere bot in the special spouse.

For he that perceifith no changabilite in felyng of his grace, bot ilike hool and stable, unbroken and unhurt as him thinkith, he is outher ful perfit or ful blynde. He is perfit that is sequestred fro alle fleschly affeccions and comunyng with of alle creatures, and alle menes are broken awey of corupcioun and of synne atwix Jhesu and his soule, fully oned to him with softnes of luf. Bot this is only grace above mans kynde. He is ful blynde that feynith him in grace withouten gostly felynge of Goddis inspiracioun, and settith himself in a maner of stabelnes, as he wer ay in felynge and in wirking of special grace, demande that al is grace that he doth and felith withouten and withinnen, thenkand that whatsoevere he do or speke is grace, holdende himself unchaungeable in specialte of grace. If ther be ony sich, as I hope ther is none, he is ful blynde in feling of grace.

Bot than might thou seien thus: that we schulde lifen only in trouthe and not coveiten gostly felynges ne rewarden hem if thei comen, for the apostle seith: *Justus ex fide vivit.*[21] That is: 'The rightwis man lifith in trowth.' Unto this I sey that bodily felynges, be thei never so confortable, we schul not coveiten, ne mikel rewarden if thei comen. Bot gostly felynges swilk as I speke of nowe – if thei come in the maner as I hafe seide before – we schul ay desiren; that arne sleeng of alle werdly luf, opnyng of the gostly eighe, purtee of spirit, pees in conscience, and alle other bifore-seide. We schul coveiten to felen ay the lifly inspiracioun of grace made bi the gostly presence of Jhesu in oure soule, if that we mighten; and for to han him ay in oure sight with reverence, and ay felen the swetnes of his lufe by a wondirful homlynes of his presence. This schulde ben oure lif and oure felynge in grace, after the mesure of his gifte in whom al grace is, to summe more and to summe lesse; for his presence is feled in divers maner wise as he vouchith-safe. And in this we schulde life, and wirken that longith to us fo[r]^d to werken; for withouten this we schulde not kun lifen. For right as the soule is the lif of the body, right so Jhesu is lyfe of the soule bi his gracious presence. And nevertheles this maner felynge, be it never so mikel, it is yit bot trouth as in rewarde of that that schal ben of the self Jhesu in the blis of heven.

Loo, this felyng schul we desiren, for ilk a soule resonable owith for to coveite with alle the mightes of it neighenge to Jhesu and onyng to him, thurgh felynge of his graciouse unseable presence. How that presence is feled, it may better be knowen bi experience than bi ony writynge; for it is the lif and the lufe, the might and the light, the joie and the rest of a chosen soule. And therfore he that hath sothfastly ones feled it, he may not forberen it withouten pyne; he may not undesire it, it is so good in itself and so confortable. What is more confortable to a soule here than for to be drawe out thurgh grace fro the vile noye of wordly bisynes and filthe of desires, and fro veyn affeccioun of alle creatures into reste and softnes of gostly lufe; pryvely perceifande the gracious presence of Jhesu, felablely fed with savour of his unseable blissed face? Sothly nothinge, me thinkith. Nothinge may make the soule of a lufer ful merye, bot the gracious presence of Jhesu, as he kan schewen him to a clene soule. He is never hevy ne sory, bot whan he is with himself in fleschlynes; he is never ful glad ne mery, bot whan he is out of himself fer, as he was with Jhesu in his gostlynes. And yit is that no ful mirthe, for ay ther hongith an hevy lumpe of bodily corupcioun on his soule, and berith it doune and mikil lettith the gostly gladnes, and that mot ay be whils it is here in this life.

Bot nertheles, for I speke of chaungabilite of grace, how it comith and goth, that thu mistak it not, therfore I mene not of the comune grace that is had and felt in trowth and in gode wil to God, withouten the whilk hafenge and lastenge therin, no man may be sauf, for it is in the lest chosen soule that lifith. Bot I mene of special grace felt bi inspiracioun of the Holy Gost, in the manere as it is bifore seide. The comune grace, that is charitee, lasteth hool whatsoevere a man do, as

---

^d for] EE; fo H.

longe as his wil and his entent is trew to God, that he wulde not synne dedly, ne the dede that he wilfully doth is not forbed as for dedly synne, for this grace is not lost bot thurgh synne. And thanne is it dedly synne when his conscience witnesseth with avisement that it is dedly synne, and yit nertheles he doth it; or elles his conscience is so blynded that he holdith it no dedly synne, althawgh he do the dede wilfully the whilk is forbed of God and of holi kirke as dedly synne.

Special grace felt thurgh the unseable presence of Jhesu, that makith a soule a perfit lufer, lasteth not ay ilike hool in the heighenes of felynge, bot chaungably comith and goth as I hafe seide biforen. Thus oure Lord seith: *Spiritus ubi vult spirat; et vocem eius audis, et nescis unde veniat, aut quo vadat.*[22] 'The Holy Gost spirith where he wil, and thou herest his voice, bot thou wost not when he comith ne whider he goth.' He comith pryveily sumtyme whan thu art lest war of him, bot thu schalt wel knowen him or he go, for wondirfully he stirith and mightily he turneth thin herte into beholdynge of his godnes, and doth thin herte melte delitably as wex ageyn the fire into softnes of his lufe, and this is the voice that he sounith. Bot than he goth er thu wite it. For he withdrawith him sumwhat, not alle, bot fro excesse into sobirte; the heighenes passith bot the substance and the effect of grace dwellith stille, and that is as longe as the soule of a lufer kepith him clene and fallith not wilfully to recleshede or dissolucioun in fleschlynes, ne to outwarde vanyte, as sumtyme it doth thawgh it have no delite therin, for frelte of itself. Of this chaungabilite in grace speke I of now. . . .

14 *Qui Habitat*

(**Commentary on Psalm 90; extracts**)

Hilton's authorship of the commentary on Psalm 90 ('*Qui Habitat*'; A.V. 91: 'He that dwelleth') is not certain, but is suggested by parallels in thought and expression with *The Scale*, Book II, as in the handling of the theme of the opening of the spiritual eye.[1]

Base manuscript: Lambeth Palace Library MS 472 (L), fols. 226v–228r, 231r–232v, 238v–239v. Also cited: CUL MS Hh. i. 11 (Hh).

. . . [4] *Scapulis suis obumbrabit tibi, et sub pennis eius sperabis.* Oure Lord schal with his schuldres umbischadwe thee, and undir his fedris thou schalt hope.

    . . . The fetheris of oure Lord ben the wordis of hooli writ, endited bi the Hooli Gost in comfort of chosen soulis travailynge in myrkenesse of this liyf, the whiche wordes, yif thei ben truli fastened in a meke soule, thei beren up the soule from al ertheli filthe into heveneli conversacion, as fetheris beeren briddes up in to the eire. . . . Thou schalt thorough touchinge of thise wordis flee up fro gree unto gree, that is fro bodili exercice unto goostli, til thou come to perfeccion that thou mai see oure Lord in the mount of Syon. . . .

[5] *Scuto circumdabit te veritas eius; non timebis a timore nocturno.* His soothfastnesse schall goo aboute thee with a scheld, and thou schalt not drede the drede of the nyght.

    For oure Lord Jhesu schal not only arme thee with his schadwe of his manhede, but also he as soothfastnesse schal cumpase thee with thee scheld of his godheede, wondirfulli openyng the sight of the soule in bihooldynge of him, tendirli touchynge the affeccioun of thi soule thorough swettenesse of his liyf, schewynge to thee in grete reverence the sight of his privetees. . . . This is the scheeld of contemplacioun, that is above al armour. . . .

[8]   *Verumptamen oculis tuis considerabis; et retribucionem pec-
catorum videbis*. Sotheli with thyn yghen thou schalt bihoolden, and
the yeldynge of synnes thou schalt see.

Whan thou art turned from the love of the world to the love of
God and, thorugh long exercise in preyynge and thenkynge of God,
thou feelist thy conscience mychel clensid and wel pesid thorugh grace
from th[i]*ᵃ* doutis and thi dredes and thi fleschli desires that thou feelist
hem lasse myghti than thei were, thanne thou schalt biholde with thin
ighen – what? – sothli, God! For clene herte schal see God:² not bodili,
but goostli, and not goostli in his unchaungeable beynge, what he is or
as he is, but in his werkes. For thy innere ighe schal be opened thorugh
[light of grace]*ᵇ* for to see sumwhat of the merciful goodnesse of God
and of his wondirful wisdom, doon and schewed to thee aboute
savynge of thi soule. And thou schalt wondre on him, that he myghte
kepe thee so weel from alle thi periles. And thou schalt love him, that
he wolde helpe thee so weel. And thou schalt see that al the sorwe and
travaile that thou haste feelid was not wrathful smytynge of God, ne
worchynge of the feend principali, but it was a tendir love of him, that
he wolde drawe thee oute of synne and departe thi soule from veyn love
and fals reste that thou haddest in this world and in thi fleschlihede. For
thi silf is oonli the cause of thyn owen sorwe. Yif thou hadde in thee no
wordli love, than thou schuldest not be mykil pyned in temptacioun.
This schalt thou see, and moche more. For what maner biholdynge a
lovere schal have in God mai I not telle thee. But this I seie: that right as
a lovere of the world hath his biholdynge with likynge of love in wordli
good – sum in goold, sum in silver, summe in fair housis and highe,
summe in oo thynge, summe in another – right so the lovere of God,
that hath the ighe of his soule clensid by grace from all the filthe of
synnes, hath his biholdynge in God with swettenesse of love in gostli
good. That is, in the wondirful wirkynges of oure Lord in vertues of
soule, in the wordis of hooli writ that are opened to his sight b[o]t[he]*ᶜ*
morali and mistili, in wirkynges of mannes soule, in the blissid kynde
of angelis – and above al this, a litil in the blissid kynde of God, oonli in
schadwe. Thise thynges schal thou biholde with thyn ighen, yif thei bee
cleene from filthe of synne. Thee dar not be ydel ne hevy: thou schal
fynde inow fair and precious in the goostli contre wherewithal thou
schal mowe feede the liking of thi goostli ighe.

ᵃ thi] Hh; the L.   *ᵇ* light of grace] Hh; g.o.l. L.   *ᶜ* bothe] but L.

And yit, over this, thou schalt see [the]^d yeldynge of synnes: for as thou schalt see the mercifull goodnesse of God schewed to thee and to alle chosen soulis in hooli chirche, right so schalt thou see the streit righwisnesse of him in ponyschynge of repreved soulis and in yeeldynge pyne for here synnes at the dai of doom. But this schalt thou see bifore the doom come with thi goostli ighe, and thou schalt thenke it ful resonable. For he that ai wold lyve in synne and lustis of this liyf, and nevere have othir joie yif he myght have that, it is rightful that he be after this liyf in eendelees pyne and nevere feele joie. But of this streit doom of God, and of this endelees yeldynge of synnes, Y schal not drede. . . .

[16] *Longitudine dierum ad-implebo eum, et ostendam illi salutare meum.* In lengthe of daies Y schal fulfille him, and I schal schewe to him myn heele.

The lengthe of daies is the endeleeshede of blissid liyf, not changyng undir tyme of diverse daies, but it schal be alwai dai and oo dai. Neverthelees, this dai is likned to the lengethe of many daies, for it is lengere than alle tymeful daies. 'And with the lengthe of this dai that is ay lastynge I schal fulfille him. I schal be his light and his sonne, ful schynynge to him, for I schal thanne schewe to him fulli myn heele, that is Jhesu. Than schal I schewe to hym openli that I am Jhesu. As longe as he is in this bodi of synne he mai not see me as I am, for I schewe me not to him in my blissed beynge. He myght not suffre me and lyve, as hooli writ seith. But for he troweth in me fulli that I am as Y am, and a litil I schewe him of me hid undir a veil of fair liknesse, and bi that merke sight I drawe his love to me and make him for to love me that he seeth not: therfore I schal schewe me to him. Thanne his love toucheth me neer than his sight dooth. For whanne knowynge faileth for weykenesse of resoun, than is love myghtiest and highest in his worchynge thorugh enspirynge of my grace. And for as mychil as he desireth so moche for to see me as Y am – that I am Jhesu, savyour, sovereyne myght, sovereyne wisdom and sovereyne goodnesse – and schyneth so bright to my sight, therfore I schal schewe me to him fulli in my ful blisse and fulfille his desire. I schal speke apertli to him, not in proverbes, for whoso loveth me I schal love him, and I schal schewe me to hym.'

^{d} the] Hh; bi the L.

15 *The Prickynge of Love*

(Chapters 26 and 27)

The Prickynge is a free English translation, with both abridgement and expansion, of *Stimulus Amoris* (itself an expanded, rearranged form of a work of that name by the thirteenth-century Franciscan James of Milan, but long attributed to St Bonaventure). The influence of the *Stimulus* has been traced in *The Scale of Perfection*, but attribution of *The Prickynge* to Hilton – made by four manuscripts and some modern scholars – remains disputed.[1] Chapters 26 and 27 deal with experience of rapture or ecstasy.[2]

Base manuscript: Trinity College, Cambridge, MS B. 14. 19 (T), fols. 117v–120r. Also cited: BL MS Harley 2254 (H).

(26) *Hou a soule somtyme is maad drunken thorou contemplacioun of Crist.*

Who mai stie up to the hil of God, or who mai stonde in his hooli stide? Noon but a soule loved of Crist. A! thou soule, Cristis leef, be glad and fayn for to fulfille al that mai helpe thee for to neigh to Crist. For wel were it with thee if thou myghtist neighe him so neer, and so depeli be pryntid in him, that thou myghtist not thenke bot him. And that othere thingis than he were bitter to thee withouten him. And that thou haddist levere thi soule were departed fro thi bodi thanne thi thought were twynned fro the mynde of God and fro the biholding of him and, as thou thenkist, thou lovest not thisilf but if thou love oonli him.

A! hooli soule, herkene to Crist and turne thee al fulli into thi loved, for he is thi spouse fro whom thou maist no-gatis be twynned. Nevertheles, if he wole a litil withdrawe him for to assaie thee, loke that thou cesse not for to seke him ayen, in what wise thou maist, til thou have founde him. A! what sorowe, what wepyng and what morenyng thou schalt make whanne thi spouse is ought hid fro thee. But thanne is this a wondir thing: that whanne thee thenkith that Jhesu hadde hid him fro thee, and thou art bisi with al thin herte for to seke him, he is thanne with thee and thou woost not. But whether Jhesu, thi loved, schall evere hide him fro thee? Nai, sotheli! But he wole schewe him whanne him luste, and thou thanne whanne thou seest him whom thou hast so brennyngli sought, thou schalt thanne al turne into love. But thou schalt evere have reverence and drede. What grace and what comfort thou schalt feele, experience schal teche thee, but nevertheles, here now. Whanne thou weenest to be sikir of him, he schal efte sodenli absente him fro thi sight, and thanne schalt thou more longyng have and more brennyng desir aftir him, til thou have with mykel sekyng founde him ayen. What mai I seie? Sotheli, as ofte as he schal absente him fro thee and pleie with thee thus comyng and goyng, until thou be maad so bisi for to kepe him that thou be not siker for to holde him, but that al be suspect to thee, bothe his comyng and his goyng. This is the game on love. His absence schal make thee for to morene aftir him and lyve in longyng, and his presence schal fille thee with pyment of his swetnesse and make thee liik drunken. But what he schal yyve thee aftir this drunkenesse, bi asaie thou maist wite, if he wole. Forwhi he is wondur liberal and myche more curteis for to yive thanne men weenen. Nevertheles holde thou evere this in thin herte: that thou art vilest wrecche of alle and unable for to resseyve ony siche yiftis. But holde it the grettist grace that he wole foryyve thee thi synnes and suffre thee to be pyned with alle turmentis in this liif and make thi soule saaf. Holde thee here, and lete him yyve thee what he wole, Jhesu Crist, ful of grace and of sothfastnesse. Amen.

(27) *Hou a mannes soule bifor ravysching mai be sereli maad drunken.*

For as mykel as it is seid bifore that a soule thorou feelyng of Cristis swetnesse mai be maad liik drunken, that thou schuldist more clereli undurstonde what that meeneth, therfor I telle thee that a soule aftir manye goostli comfortis and graces, or thanne it mai come to hevenli savour or to ravyschyng, to the whiche fewe contemplatifs moun atteyne, two manere of drunkenes mai feele. The firste drunkenesse is a greet abundaunce of gladnesse and a hoge myrthe of herte that cometh sodeynli into a soule thorou a newe lightnyng of Cristis presence, aftir mykel wepyng goyng bifor or aftir a deep and an inwardli biholdyng of Cristis passioun; or ellis aftir a greet fervour or a

long desire kyndiled thorou assiduel biholdyng of Crist. These ben
sothfast enchesouns and undisseyvable. And this gladnesse, whanne it
is conseyved, encreessith so mykel withinne and reboundith into the
bodi and makith alle the lymes for to be fayn and myrie of Cristis
comfortyng. And sumtyme for oure mykel gladnesse thei stiren and
suffren no restyng, in the maner as a man were drunken. And in this
tyme the soule is so stirid thorou mykelnesse of Cristis love that hir
thenkith that sche mai fynde Crist in alle creaturis and likith for to
halse hem. But the herte is not applied to veyn delite of the creature but
oneli of Crist in the creature.

Anothere drunkenesse is this: whanne a man in contemplacioun,
aftir sothfast enchesouns goyng bifor, as it is seid, feelith his herte fillid
with a wondurful swetnesse thorou Cristis presence, and this swetnesse
so mykel aboundith in the herte that alle the lymes of the bodi taken
part of it, so ferfor[th]ᵃ that a man thenkith that al his feeling without
and withinne is swettere than hony. The firste drunkenesse that is
causid of over mykel gladnesse makith al the bodi for to stire. But this
drunkenesse that is causid of over myche swetnesse makith the bodi for
to reste in stilnesse. But yit nevertheles neither of hem withdrawith fro
a man the reisyng of his bodili wittis, but if it encrees so myche that it
mai conseyve hevenli savour. Thanne leveth a mynde of this world and
usyng of his wittis and is ravyschid into Crist, and that is the excellence
of grace in which no disseite mai be. But nevertheles in this drunkenesse
mai come no disseite. Forwhi as longe as a man hath mynde of himsilf
and feelyng and usyng of his wittis he mai be disseyved, but if he be war
and wel avised.

Of these two manere drunkenesse the secounde is the more
perelouse and neer disseit thanne the firste. Therfor a man schal not
fulli lene therto as in ful sikirnesse but evere have drede. For though it
be of Crist oneli, yit it is good for to have drede of it, leste that the fend
entre in and sowe his seed. Forwhi? The fend transfigurith himsilf into
an aungel of light and procurith wondurful swetnesse into a man, or
ellis if thei ben sothfastli fillid of Goddis grace yit wole the fend
entremete him. For he wolde that a man hadde pride and sete wel bi
himsilf for feelyng of sich swetnesse, and that he fulli fedde himsilf in
sich manere delitis as in ful reste of his soule, and so bi this manere of
weie shulde he be turned fro God, for he wolde noon othere biholdyng

---

ᵃ ferforth] H; ferfor T.

have, but oonli to feelyng of sich swetnesse. Thus ben summe
contemplatifs disseyved, and that is of the suffraunce of God, for this
enchesoun. Summe contemplatifis, whanne thei feelen ought of Crist,
anoon thei presumen of hemsilf and despisen othere men and weenen
that thei ben next God, whanne thei ben thorou pride ful fer caste fro
him. And therfor the fend, that is fadir of pride, hath sich power over
hem for to disseyve hem with siche swetnesse and with sich manere
feelyngis.

Therfor, thou that wolt not be disseyved, be meke and refuse not
al swetnesse as thei schulde be al false, but biholde wel thisilf and thi
chesoun wherof thei comen, that it be good and sothfast. And whanne
thei comen, sette evere the poynt of thi thought in Crist, and suffre not
the lokyng of thin hert go fro him, so that thou referre and yelde al thi
likyng and thi swetnesse that thou feelist into him. Forwhi though this
swetnesse be of Crist, nevertheles it is [not]*b* Crist. And therfor be ai
cleeve to Crist and honge in him, and suffre the swetnesse if it wole
cleve to thee and honge on thee. And if thou do thus, thanne schal that
swetnesse, if it be sothfastli of God, encrees and clefe betere to thee.
And if it be of the fend, it schal vanysche awei and lessen. So bi this
thou maist undurstonde that ther is no reste propirli in this liif, ne ther
is no sikirnesse, but evere doutyng and drede, for no thing that a man
mai feele, until he mai come out fro feelyng of himsilf into ravyschyng.

It is a greet yifte of God for to have feelyng of gostli swetnesse, as
it is bifor seid, but it be mekeli taken, thorou which a mannes soule is
departid fro al coveitise of the world and fro passiouns and fleischli
affecciouns of alle creaturis. But yit ful sikirnesse is it noon, but if thou
be ravyschid fro the usyng of thi bodili wittis so that alle manere
fantomes of bodili licnesse be withdrawen fro biholdyng of thi soule,
and thi mynde overpassith the comyne and the resonable maner of
thenkyng of this liif. Oneli turne thee into Crist, and thanne at erste
hast thou founden sothfast reste in this liif, withouten errour or disseit
of the fend, as longe as it lastith and no lengere. For whanne thou
comest ayen to feelyng of thisilf, be-war of the fend [thanne]*c* as thou
were bifore.

If thou weene for to fynde othere reste than this as ende of travel
or fruyt of contemplacioun or perfeccioun of Cristis love, thou errist
and makist an ende there noon is in the myddis of thi weie, and therfor

b not] H; not of T.   *c* thanne] H; thanne thou art T.

maist not thou come to the ende. And therfor thou that feelist sich swetnesse or siche comfortis withouten ravysching, that thou be not disseyved thorou presumpcioun, foond for to meke thisilf thus: thenke that for a litil thing that thou doist to God perchaunce he wole rewarde thee here in this liif, forwhi thou art not worthi to have endeles mede. Thus maist thou thenke, but deme it not as for certeyn. Also thou maist drede thus that [though]^d siche swetnesse be yoven of God for to comfort thee, thei ben [not]^e God. And so thei myght be to thee occasioun of greet fallyng, as a good medecyn unwiseli taken mai be cause of a mannes deeth. And therfor, [take hem] if [thei]^f come freli, and thanke oure Lord for his yifte. And desire more for to have sorewe and woo and travel and turmentyng with Crist crucified here in this wrecchid warde. For that is sikerere, withouten ony disseite, thanne for to be [fed]^g with siche perelous delitis that mai thorou thin owne defaute turne to thin owne deth. Coveite for to wepe for thin owne synnes, and to be revylid of alle men as it is bifor seid, and loke aftir delites in the blisse of hevene – to the which blis brynge us Jhesu Crist! Amen.

^{d} though] H; *erasure in* T. ^{e} not] H; not of T. ^{f} take hem if thei] H; if thou T.
^{g} fed] H; T *om.*

JULIAN OF NORWICH
(1342 – after 1416)

16 *Revelations of Divine Love* (shorter version)

Two versions survive of the 'Shewings' or 'Revelations' of Julian of Norwich: a longer version preserved in post-medieval copies made by English recusants; and a shorter version (the 'Amherst' text), presented here in its entirety from the unique fifteenth-century copy, of which the rubric describes Julian as 'recluse atte Norwyche and yitt ys on lyfe' in 1413. Julian was born in late 1342, for she records how she received her revelations in May 1373 when she was thirty and a half years old (Long text, ch. 2). Various wills (the latest from 1416) name Julian as a beneficiary and locate her anchorhold at St Julian's Church, Conisford, in Norwich. Whether Julian was a religious and when she became a recluse remain unknown. She may have been a widow. That her mother and friends were at her sickbed, and that her local priest was sent for, have suggested that she was not enclosed as an anchoress when she received her revelations. By the time Margery Kempe visits 'Dame Jelyan', her reputation is clearly established (see below, pp. 230–2).

The Amherst text is now accepted as an authentic early stage in Julian's composition of her text, rather than a scribal abridgement of the longer version. It reads with the immediacy and directness of a transcript of experience, as if written near to the event.[1] It already presents not only the narrative sequence of the visions – delineated with a painterly eye – but also the ground of Julian's interpretation of her sixteen revelations. Yet the presentation is sometimes tentative: Julian will not allow her being a woman to prevent her writing but disclaims the role of teacher (ch. 6[2]); she is anxious to establish the shewings' authority, without promoting herself as the medium. Evidently addressed to contemplatives (chs. 4, 13), Julian's text is humbly offered as a witness. A simple creature 'unlettyrde' or 'that cowde no letter' at the time of her shewings is how Julian describes herself (Long text, ch. 2) – perhaps meaning that she did not know Latin, or that she could not read or write – although learning as well as wisdom is manifest in her texts.

Sole manuscript: BL MS Add. 37790 (A), fols. 97r–115r. (The corrector's contribution in A is not recorded here). Also cited are MSS of the Longer Version: Bibliothèque Nationale, Paris, fonds anglais 40 (P) and BL MS Sloane 2499 (S).

*There es a vision schewed be the goodenes of God to a devoute
woman and hir name es Julyan, that is recluse atte Norwyche
and yitt ys on lyfe, anno Domini millesimo CCCCxiii, in the
whilke visyon er fulle many comfortabylle wordes and gretly
styrrande to alle thaye that desyres to be Crystes looverse.*

[1]   I desyrede thre graces be the gyfte of God. The fyrst was to have
mynde of Cryste es passion, the seconde was bodelye syekenes, and the
thryd was to have of Goddys gyfte thre woundys. For the fyrste come
to my mynde with devocyon: me thought I hadde grete felynge in the
passyon of Cryste, botte yitte I desyrede to have mare be the grace of
God. Me thought I wolde have bene that tyme with Mary Mawdeleyne³
and with othere that were Crystes loverse, that I myght have sene
bodylye the passion of oure Lorde that he sufferede for me, that I
myght have sufferede with hym as othere dyd that lovyd hym.
Notwithstandynge that, I leevyd sadlye alle the peynes of Cryste as
halye kyrke schewys and techys, and also the payntyngys of crucyfexes
that er made be the grace of God aftere the techynge of haly kyrke to
the lyknes of Crystes passyon, als farfurthe as manys witte maye reche.

Noughtwithstondynge alle this trewe beleve, I desyrede a bodylye
syght whareyn Y myght have more knawynge of bodelye paynes of
oure Lorde, oure savyoure, and of the compassyon of oure Ladye and
of alle his trewe loverse that were belevande his paynes that tyme and
sythene; for I wolde have beene one of thame and suffrede with thame.
Othere syght of Gode ne schewynge desyrede I nevere none tylle atte
the sawlle were departyd frome the bodye, for I trayste sothfastlye that
I schulde be safe, and this was my menynge; for I wolde aftyr, becawse
of that schewynge, have the more trewe mynde in the passion of Cryste.

For the seconde, come to my mynde with contricion, frelye
withowtyn any sekynge, a wylfulle desyre to hafe of Goddys gyfte a
bodelye syekenes. And I wolde that this bodylye syekenes myght have
beene so harde as to the dede, so that I myght in the sekenes take alle
my ryghtynges of halye kyrke, wenande myselfe that I schulde dye; and
that alle creatures that sawe me myght wene the same, for I wolde hafe
no comforth of no fleschlye nothere erthelye lyfe. In this sekenes I
desyrede to hafe alle manere of paynes, bodelye and gastelye, that I

schulde have yyf I schulde dye, alle the dredes and tempestes of feyndys, and alle manere of [othere]*ᵃ* paynes, safe of the owghte-passynge of the sawlle, for I hoped that it myght be to me a spede when I schulde dye, for I desyrede sone to be with my God.

This two desyres of the passyon and of the seekenes I desyrede thame with a condicyon, for me thought that it passede the comene course of prayers; and therfore I sayde, 'Lorde, thowe woote whate I wolde. Yyf it be thy wille that I have itt, grawnte itt me. And yyf it be nought thy wille, goode lorde, be nought dysplesede, for I wille nought botte as thowe wille.' This sekenes desyrede I yn my [y]ought,*ᵇ* that Y myght have it whene I were threttye yeere eelde.

For the thirde, I harde a man telle of halye kyrke of the storye of Saynte Cecylle,⁴ in the whilke schewynge I vndyrstode that sche hadde thre woundys with a swerde in the nekke, with the whilke sche pynede to the dede. By the styrrynge of this I conseyvede a myghty desyre, prayande oure Lorde God that he wolde grawnte me thre woundys in my lyfe tyme, that es to saye: the wound[e]*ᶜ* of contricyon, the wounde of compassyon, and the wounde of wylfulle langgynge to God. Ryght as I askede the othere two with a condyscyon, so I askyd the thyrde withowtyn any condyscyon. This two desyres beforesayde passed fro my mynde, and the thyrde dwellyd contynuelye.

[2]   Ande when I was thryttye wyntere alde and a halfe, God sente me a bodelye syekenes in the whilke I laye thre dayes and thre nyghttes; and on the ferthe nyght I toke alle my ryghttynges of haly kyrke, and wenyd nought tylle have lyffede tylle daye. And aftyr this Y langourede furthe two dayes and two nyghttes, and on the thyrde nyght I wenede oftetymes to hafe passede, and so wenyd thaye that were abowte me. Botte in this I was ryght sarye and lothe thought for to dye, botte for nothynge that was in erthe that me lykede to lyeve fore, nor for nothynge that I was aferde fore, for I tristyd in God. Botte it was fore I walde hafe lyevede to have lovede God better and lange tyme, that [I]*ᵈ* myght, be the grace of that lyevynge, have the more knowynge and lovynge of God in the blysse of hevene. For me thought alle the tyme that I wolde lyeve here so lytille and so schorte in the regarde of endeles blysse. I thought thus, 'Goode Lorde, maye my lyevynge be no langere

ᵃ othere] P; thayre A.   *ᵇ* yought] P; thought A.   *ᶜ* wounde] P; woundys A.
ᵈ I] P; A *om.*

to thy worschippe?' And I was aunswerde in my resone, and be the felynges of my paynes, that I schulde dye. And I asentyd fully with alle the wille of mye herte to be atte Godys wille.

Thus I endurede tille daye, and by than was my bodye dede fra the myddys downwarde, as to my felynge. Than was I styrrede to be sette uppe ryghttes, lenande with clothes to my heede for to have the mare fredome of my herte to be atte Goddes wille, and thynkynge on hym whilys my lyfe walde laste; and thay that were with me sente for the person, my curette, to be atte myne endynge. He come, and a childe with hym, and brought a crosse, and be thanne I hadde sette myne eyen and myght nought speke. The persone sette the crosse before my face and sayde, 'Dowghtter, I have brought the the ymage of thy savioure. Loke thereopon, and comforthe the therewith, in reverence of hym that dyede for the and me.'

Me thought than that Y was welle, for myne eyen ware sette upwarde into hevene, whethyr I trustede for to come. Botte neverethelesse I assendyd to sette myne eyen in the face of the crucyfixe yif Y myght, for to endure the langyr into the tyme of myn endynge; for me thought I myght langyr endure to loke evyn forthe than uppe ryght. Aftyr this my syght bygganne to fayle, and it was alle dyrke abowte me in the chaumbyr, and myrke as it hadde bene nyght, save in the ymage of the crosse there helde a comon lyght, and I wyste nevere howe. Alle that was besyde the crosse was huglye to me, as yyf it hadde bene mykylle occupyede with fendys.

Aftyr this the overe partye of my bodye begganne to dye, as to my felynge. Myne handdys felle downe on aythere syde, and also for unpowere my heede satylde downe on syde. The maste payne that I felyd was schortnes of wynde and faylynge of lyfe. Than wende I sothelye to hafe bene atte the poynte of dede. And in this sodeynlye alle my payne was awaye fro me and I was alle hole, and namelye in the overe partye of my bodye, as evere I was before or aftyr. I merveylede of this chaunge, for me thought it was a pryve wyrkynge of God, and nought of kynde. And yitte be the felynge of this ese I trystede nevere the mare that I schulde lyeve, ne the felynge of this ese was ne fulle ese to me, for me thought I hadde levere have bene delyverede of this worlde, for my herte was wilfulle thereto.

[3]   And sodeynlye come unto my mynde that I schulde desyre the seconde wounde of oure Lordes gyfte and of his grace, that he walde

fulfylle my bodye with mynde of felynge of his blessede passyon, as I
hadde before prayede, for I wolde that his paynes ware my paynes,
with compassyon, and aftyrwarde langynge to God. Thus thought me
that I myght, with his grace, have his woundys that Y hadde before
desyrede. But in this I desyrede nevere ne bodely syght, ne no manere
schewynge of God, botte compassyon, as me thought that a kynde
sawlle myght have with oure Lorde Jhesu, that for love wolde become
man dedlye. With hym Y desyrede to suffere, lyevande in dedlye bodye,
as God wolde gyffe me grace.

And in this sodaynlye I sawe the rede blode trekylle downe fro
undyr the garlande alle hate, freschlye, plentefully, and lyvelye, ryght
as me thought that it was in that tyme that the garlonde of thornys was
thyrstede on his blessede heede. Ryght so both God and man the same
sufferde for me. I conseyvede treulye and myghttyllye that itt was
hymselfe that schewyd it me withowtyn any meen,[5] and than I sayde,
'*Benedicite Dominus.*'[6] This I sayde reverentlye in my menynge, with a
myghtty voyce, and fulle gretlye I was astonnyd for wondere and
merveyle that Y had, that he wolde be so homblye with a synfulle
creature lyevande in this wrecchyd flesch[e].[e] Thus I tokede it for that
tyme that oure Lorde Jhesu of his curtayse love walde schewe me
comforthe before the tyme of my temptacyon. For me thought it myght
be welle that I schulde, be the suffyrraunce of God and with his
kepynge, be temptyd of fendys or I dyede. With this syght of his
blyssede passyon, with the Godhede that I saye in myn undyrstandynge,
I sawe that this was strengh ynowghe to me, ye, unto alle creatures
lyevande that schulde be saffe agaynes alle the feendys of helle and
agaynes alle gostelye enmyes.

[4]   And this same tyme that I sawe this bodyly syght, oure Lorde
schewyd me a gastelye sight of his hamly lovynge. I sawe that he es to us
alle thynge that is goode and comfortabylle to oure helpe. He es oure
clethynge, for loove wappes us and wyndes us, halses us and alle
beteches [us],[f] hynges aboute us for tendyr loove, that he maye nevere
leve us. And so in this syght Y sawe sothelye that he ys alle thynge that
ys goode, as to myne understandynge.

And in this he schewyd me a lytille thynge, the qwantyte of a
haselle nutte, lyggande in the palme of my hande, and to my

---

[e] flesche] P; fleschly A.   [f] us] A *bis*.

undyrstandynge that, it was as rownde as any balle. I lokede theropon and thought, 'Whate maye this be?' And I was aunswerde generaly thus, 'It is alle that ys made.' I merveylede howe that it myght laste, for me thought it myght falle sodaynlye to nought for litille. And I was aunswerde in myne undyrstandynge, 'It lastes and ever schalle, for God loves it; and so hath alle thynge the beynge thorowe the love of God.'

In this lytille thynge I sawe thre partyes. The fyrste is that God made it, the seconde ys that he loves it, the thyrde ys that God kepes it. Botte whate is that to me? Sothelye the makere, the lovere, the kepere. For to I am substancyallye aned to hym, I may nevere have love, reste, ne varray blysse; that is to saye that I be so festenede to hym that thare be ryght nought that is made betwyxe my God and me. And wha schalle do this dede? Sothlye hymselfe, be his mercye and his grace, for he has made me thereto and blysfullye restoryd.

In this God brought owre Ladye to myne undyrstandynge. I sawe hir gastelye in bodilye lyekenes, a sympille maydene and a meeke, yonge of age, in the stature that scho was when scho conceyvede. Also God schewyd me in parte the wisdom and the trowthe of hir saule, whareyn I undyrstode reverente beholdynge, that sche behelde hyre God that ys hir makere, mervelande with grete reverence that he wolde be borne of hir that was a sympille creature of his makynge. For this was hir mervelynge, that he that was hir makere walde be borne of hir that was [made]^g. And this wysdome of trowthe and knawande the gretnes of hir makere and the lytelleheede of hirselfe that ys made, made hir for to saye mekelye to the angelle Gabrielle, 'Loo me here, Goddys handemaydene.'[7]

In this sight I sawe sothfastlye that scho ys mare than alle that God made benethe hir in worthynes and in fulheede. For abovene hir ys nothynge that is made botte the blyssede manhede of Criste. This lytille thynge that es made that es benethe oure Ladye Saynt Marye, God schewyd it unto me als litille as it hadde beene a hasylle notte. Me thought it myght hafe fallene for litille.

In this blyssede revelacyon God schewyd me thre noughtes, of whilke noughttes this is the fyrste that was schewyd me: of this nedes ilke man and woman to hafe knawynge that desyres to lyeve contemplatyfelye, that hym lyke to nought alle thynge that es made for to hafe the love of God that es unmade. For this es the cause why thaye

^{g} made] P; a sympille creature of his makynge A.

that er occupyede wylfullye in erthelye besynes and evermare sekes
warldlye wele er nought here of his in herte and in sawlle; for thaye love
and seekes here ryste in this thynge that is so lytille whare no reste ys
yn, and knawes nought God that es alle myghtty, alle wyse, and alle
goode, for he is verraye reste. God wille be knawen, and hym lykes that
we reste us in hym. For alle that ar benethe hym suffyces nought to us.
And this is the cause why that na saule ys restede to it be noghthed of
alle that es made. When he is noughthid for love, to hafe hym that is
alle that is goode, than es he abylle to resayve gostlye reste.

[5]   And in that tyme that oure Lorde schewyd this that I have nowe
saydene in gastelye syght, I saye the bodylye syght lastande of the
plentyvouse bledynge of the hede,[8] and als longe as Y sawe that syght Y
sayde oftyntymes, '*Benedicite Dominus*'. In this fyrste schewynge of
oure Lorde I sawe sex thynges in myne undyrstandynge. The furste is
the takyns of his blysfulle passion and the plentevous schedynge of his
precyous blode. The seconde is the maydene, that sche ys his
dereworthy modere. The thyrde is the blysfulle godhede that ever was
and es and ever schalle be: alle myghty, alle wysdome, and alle love.
The ferthe is alle thynge that he has made; it is mykille and fayre and
large and goode. Botte the cause why it schewed so lytille to my syght
was for I sawe itte in the presence of hym that es makere. For to a sawle
that sees the makere of alle thynge, alle that es made semy[s][b] fulle
litylle. The fyfte es that he has made alle thynge that ys made for love,
and thorowe the same love it is kepydde, and ever schalle be withowtyn
ende, as it is before sayde. The sexte es that God is alle thynge that ys
goode, and the goodenes that [alle][i] thynge has is he.
     And alle thynge oure Lorde schewyd me in the fyrst syght, and
gafe me space and tyme to behalde it. And the bodyly syght styntyd,
and the gastely syght dwellyd in myne undyrstandynge; and I abade
with reverente drede, joyande in that I sawe and desyrande as Y durste
for to see mare, yif it ware his wille, or the same langer tyme.

[6]   Alle that I sawe of myselfe, I meene in the persone of alle myne
evyn-Cristene, for I am lernede in the gastelye schewynge of oure Lorde
that he meenys so. And therfore I praye yowe alle for Goddys sake, and
cownsayles yowe for yowre awne profyt, that ye leve the behaldynge of

---

[b] semys] P; semyd A.   [i] alle] of alle A.

the wrechid worlde[s]^j synfulle creature that it was schewyd unto, and
that ye myghtlye, wyselye, lovandlye, and mekelye behalde God, that
of his curtays love and of his endles goodnes walde schewe generalye
this visyon in comforthe of us alle. And ye that hyerys and sees this
vision and this techynge that is of Jhesu Cryste to edificacyon of youre
saule, it is Goddys wille and my desyrere that ye take it with als grete
joye and lykynge as Jhesu hadde schewyd it yowe as he dyd to me.

For the schewynge I am not goode but yif Y love God the better,
and so may and so schulde ylke man do that sees it and heres it with
goode wille and trewe menynge. And so ys my desyre that it schulde be
to every ilke manne the same profytte that I desyrede to myselfe, and
therto was styrryd of God in the fyrste tyme when I sawe itte. For yt
[is]^k comon and generale as we ar alle ane, and I am sekere I sawe it for
the profytte of many oder. For sothly it was nought schewyd unto me
for that God loves me bettere thane the leste sawlle that is in grace.^{9} For
I am sekere thare ys fulle many that nevere hadde schewynge ne syght
botte of the comon techynge of haly kyrke that loves God better than I.
For yyf I loke syngulerlye to myselfe I am ryght nought. Botte in
generalle, I am in anehede of charyte with alle myne evyn-Cristende.
For in this anehede of charyte standes the lyfe of alle mankynde that
schalle be safe. For God is alle that ys goode, and God has made alle
that ys made, and God loves alle that he has made.

And yyf anye man or woman departe his love fra any of his
evyn-Crysten, he loves ryght nought, for he loves nought alle.^{10} And so
that tyme he ys nought safe, for he es nought in pees; and he that
generaly looves his evyn-Crystyn, he loves alle that es. For in
mankynde that schalle be saffe is comprehende alle, that ys, alle that ys
made and the makere of alle. For in manne ys God, and so in man ys
alle. And he that thus generalye loves alle his evyn-Crystene, he loves
alle; and he that loves thus, he is safe. And thus wille I love, and thus I
love, and thus I am safe. For Y mene in the person of myne
evyn-Crystene. And the more I love of this lovynge whiles I am here,
the mare I am lyke to the blysse [that I]^l schalle have in hevene
withowten ende, that is God that of his endeles love wolde become
owre brothere and suffer for us. And I am sekere that he that behaldes it
thus, he schalle be trewly taught and myghttelye comforthtede if hym
nede comforthe.

^{i} worldes] worlde A. ^{k} is] A om. ^{l} that I] A bis.

Botte God forbede that ye schulde saye or take it so that I am a
techere, for I meene nought soo, no I mente nevere so.[11] For I am a
woman, leued, febille, and freylle. Botte I wate wele this that I saye. I
hafe it of the schewynge of hym tha[t]*ᵐ* es soverayne techare. Botte
sothelye charyte styrres me to telle yowe it, for I wolde God ware
knawen and myn evyn-Crystene spede, as I wolde be myselfe, to the
mare hatynge of synne and lovynge of God.

Botte for I am a woman, schulde I therfore leve that I schulde
nought telle yowe the goodenes of God, syne that I sawe in that same
tyme that is his wille that it be knawen? And that schalle ye welle see in
the same matere that folowes aftyr, if itte be welle and trewlye takyn.
Thane schalle ye sone forgette me that am a wrecche, and dose so that I
lette yowe nought, and behalde Jhesu that ys techare of alle. I speke of
thame that schalle be safe, for in this tyme God schewyd me non
othere. Bot in alle thynge I lyeve as haly kyrke techis, for in alle thynge,
this blyssede schewynge of oure Lorde I behelde it as ane in God syght,
and I undyrstode never nathynge thereyn that stonez me ne lettes me of
the trewe techynge of halye kyrke.

[7]   Alle this blyssede techynge of oure Lorde God was schewyd to me
in thre partyes, that is be bodylye syght, and be worde formede in myne
undyrstandynge, and be gastelye syght. Botte the gastelye syght I maye
nought ne can nought schewe it unto yowe als oponlye and als fullye as
I wolde.[12] Botte I truste in oure Lorde God allemyghtty that he schalle,
of his goodnes and for youre love, make yowe to take it mare gastelye
and mare swetly than I can or maye telle it yowe, and so motte it be, for
we are alle one in loove. And in alle this I was mekylle styrrede in
charyte to myne evyn-Crystene, that thaye myght alle see and knawe
the same that I sawe, for I walde that it ware comforthe to thame alle as
it es to me. For this syght was schewyd in generalle and nathynge in
specyalle. Of alle that I sawe, this was the maste comforthe to me: that
oure Lorde es so hamlye and so curtayse, and this maste fillyd me with
lykynge and syekernes in saule. Than sayde I to the folke that were
with me, 'Itt es todaye domesdaye with me', and this I sayde for I
wenede to hafe dyed. For that daye that man or woman dyes ys he
demyd as he schalle be withowtyn eende. This I sayde for Y walde
thaye lovyd God mare, and sette the lesse pryse be the vanite of the

ᵐ that] thas A.

worlde, for to make thame to hafe mynde that this lyfe es schorte, as thaye myght se in ensampille be me; for in alle this tyme I wenede to hafe dyed.

[8]   And aftyr this I sawe with bodely syght the face of the crucifixe that hange before me, in whilke I behelde contynuely a party of his passyon: despite, spittynge in sowlynge of his bodye, and buffetynge in his blysfulle face; and manye langoures and paynes ma than I can telle, and ofte chaungynge of coloure, and alle his blyssede face atyme closede in dry blode. This I sawe bodylye and hevelye and derkelye; and I desyred mare bodelye lyght to hafe sene more clerelye. And I was aunswerde in my resone that yyf God walde schewe me mare he schulde, botte me nedyd na lyght botte hym.

And aftyr this I sawe God in a poynte, that es in myne undyrstandynge, by whilke syght I sawe that he es in alle thynge. I behelde with vysemente, wittande and knawande in that syght that he dose alle that es done. I merveylede in this syght with a softe drede and thought, 'Whate es synne?' For I sawe trulye that God dothe alle thynge, be itt nevere so litille; nor nathynge es done be happe ne be eventure, botte the endeles forluke of the wysdome of God. Wharefore me behovede nedes grawnte that alle thynge that es done es wele done, and I was sekyr that God dose na synne. Therfore it semed to me that synne is nought, for in alle thys, synne was nought schewyd me. And Y walde no lengyr mervelle of this, botte behalde oure Lorde, whate he wolde schewe me. And in anothyr tyme God schewyd me whate syne es, nakydlye be the selfe, as Y schalle telle aftyrwarde.

And aftyr this I sawe behaldande the bodye plentevouslye bledande, hate and freschlye and lyfelye, ryght as I sawe before in the heede. And this was [schewyd]^n me in the semes of scowrgynge, and this ranne so plentevouslye to my syght that me thought yyf itt hadde bene so in kynde for that tyme, itt schulde hafe made the bedde alle on blode and hafe passede on abowte. God has made waterse plentevouse in erthe to oure servyce and to owre bodylye eese, for tendyr love that he has to us; botte yit lykes hym bettyr that we take fullye his blessede blode to wasche us with of synne, for thare ys no lykoure that es made that hym lykes so welle to gyffe us, for it is so plentevouse and of oure kynde.

---

^{n} schewyd] A *bis.*

And aftyr this, [or][o] God schewyd me any wo[r]des,[p] he suffyrde me to behalde langere and alle that I hadde seene and alle that was thereyn. And than was withowtyn voyce and withowte openynge of lyppes formede in my sawlle this worde, 'Herewith ys the feende overcomyn.' This worde sayde oure Lorde me[n]ande[q] his passyon, as he schewyd me before. In this oure Lorde brought unto my mynde and schewyd me a perte of the fendys malyce and fully his unmyght, and for that he schewyd me that the passyon of hym is overcomynge of the fende. God schewyd me that he hase nowe the same malyce that he had before the incarnacyon, and als sare he travayles and als contynuelye he sees that alle chosene saules eschapes hym worschipfullye, and that es alle his sorowe. For alle that God suffers hym to do turnes us to joye and hym to payne and to schame, and he has als mekylle sorowe when God gyffes hym leve to wyrke as when he werkys nought. And that es for he maye nevere do als ille as he wolde, for his myght es alle lokene in Goddys hande. Also I sawe oure Lorde scorne his malyce and nought hym, and he wille that we do the same.

For this syght I lugh myghttelye, and that made tham to laugh that were abowte me, and thare laughynge was lykynge to me. I thought Y wolde myne evyn-Cristene hadde sene as I sawe. Than schulde thaye alle hafe laughyn with me. Botte I sawe nought Cryste laugh. Neverthelesse, hym lykes that we laugh in comfortynge of us, and er joyande in God, for the feende ys overcomyn. And aftyr this I felle into a saddehete and sayde, 'I see thre thynges: game, scorne, and arneste. I see game, that the feende ys overcomen; and I see scorne, that God scornes hym and he schalle be scornede; and I see arneste, that he es overcomen be the passion of oure Lorde Jhesu Cryste and be his dede, that was done ful erneste and with sadde travayle.' Aftyr this oure Lorde sayde, 'I thanke the of thy servyce and of thy travayle, and namly in thi yough.'

[9] God schewyd me thre degrees of blysse that ylke saule schalle hafe in hevene that wilfullye hase servyd God in any degree heere in erthe. The fyrste is the wyrschipfulle thankkynge of owre Lorde God that he schalle resayfe when he es delyverede fro payne. This thanke is so hyghe and so wyrschipfulle that hym thynke it fylles hym, thowgh thare ware no mare blys. For me thought that alle the payne and

[o] or] S; houre A; or that P. [p] wordes] P; woundes A.
[q] menande] menyng PS; mevande A.

travayle that myght be suffyrde of alle lyffande men myght nought hafe
deservede the thanke that a man schalle hafe that wylfullye has
servydde God. For the seconde, that alle the blyssede creatures that er
in hevene schalle see that worschipfulle thankynge of oure Lorde God,
and he makys his servyce to alle that er in heven knawen. And for the
thyrde, that als new ande als lykande as it es resayvede that tyme, ryght
so schalle itt laste withowten ende: I sawe that goodelye and swetlye
was this sayde and schewyd to me, that the age of everylk man schalle
be knawen in heven and rewardyd for his wilfulle servyce and for his
tyme, and namelye the age of thame that wilfullye and frelye offers
thare yought unto God es passande rewardede and wondyrlye thankkyd.

And aftyr this oure Lorde schewyd me a soverayne gastelye
lykynge in my sawlle. In this lykynge I was fulfillyd of everlastande
sekernesse, myghtlye festnede withowtyn any drede. This felynge was
so gladde to me and so goodly that I was in peez, in ese, and in ryste, so
that there was nothynge in erthe that schulde hafe grevyd me. This
lastyd botte a while, and I was turnede and lefte to myselfe in hevynes
and werynesse of myselfe and yrkesumnesse of my lyfe, that unnethes I
cowthe hafe pacyence to lyeve. Thare was none ese ne na comforthe to
my felynge botte hope, faythe, and charyte, and this Y hadde in
trowthe botte fulle lytille in felynge.

And anone aftyr, God gafe me agayne the comforth and the reste
in saule, likynge and syekyrnesse so blysfulle and so myghtty that no
drede, no sorowe, no payne bodylye no gastelye that myght be sufferde
schulde have dissesede me. And than the payne schewyd agayne to my
felynge, and than the joye and than the lykynge, and than the tane and
nowe the tothere, dyverse tymes, I suppose abowte twentye sythes.
And in the tyme of joye I myght hafe sayde with Paule: 'Nathynge
schalle departe me fro the charyte of Cryste'; and in the payne Y myght
hafe sayde with Saynte Petyr: 'Lorde, save me, I perysche.'[13]

This vision was schewyd me to lere me atte my undyrstandynge
that it es nedefulle to ylke man to feele on this wyse: sumtyme to be in
comforthe and sumtyme to fayle and be lefte to hymselfe. God wille
that we knowe that he kepes us everelyke syekyr in wele and in woo,
and als mykille loves us in woo as in weele.[14] And sumtyme, for the
profytte of his saule, a man es lefte to hymselfe and to whethere synne
es nought the cause. For in this tyme I synnede nought wherefore I
schulde be lefte to myselfe, ne also I deservede nought to hafe this
blysfulle felynge. Botte frelye God gyffez wele when hym lykes, and

suffers [us]' in wa sumtyme, and bothe es of love. For it is Godys wille that we halde us in comforthe with alle oure myght, for blys es lastande withowtyn ende and payn es passande and schalle be brought to nought. Therefore it es nought Goddys wille that we folowe the felynges of payne in sorowynge and in mournynge for thaim, botte sodaynlye passe on and halde us in endelesse lykynge, that es God allemyghtty, oure lovere and kepare.

[10]   Aftyr this Cryste schewyd me a partye of his passyone nere his dyinge. I sawe that swete faace as yt ware drye and bludyelesse with pale dyinge, sithen mare dede, pale, langourande, and than turnede more dede to the blewe, and sithene mare blewe, as the flesche turnede mare deepe dede. For alle the paynes that Cryste sufferde in his bodye schewyd to me in the blyssede faace als farfurthe as I sawe it, and namelye in the lyppes. Thare I sawe this foure colourse, thaye that I sawe beforehande, freschlye and ruddy, lyflye and lykande to my syght.

   This was a hevy chaunge to see, this deepe dyinge, and also the nese c[l]aungede⁵ and dryed to my sight. This lange pynynge semede to me as he hadde bene a seven nyght dede, allewaye sufferande payne. And me thought the dryinge of Crystes flesche was the maste payne of his passion, and the laste. And in this dryhede was brought to my mynde this worde that Cryste sayde, 'I thryste.'¹⁵ For I sawe in Criste a doubille thyrste, ane bodylye, ane othere gastelye. This worde was schewyd to me for the bodylye thirste, and for the gastelye thyrste was schewyd to me als I schalle saye eftyrwarde. And I undyrstode of bodelye thyrste that the bodye hadde of faylynge of moystere, for the blessede flesche and banes ware lefte allane withowtyn blode and moystere. The blyssyd bodye dryede alle ane lange tyme, with wryngynge of the nayles and paysynge of the hede and weyght of the bodye, with blawynge of wynde fra withoutyn that dryed mare and pyned hym with calde mare than myn herte can thynke, and alle othere paynes. Swilke paynes I sawe that alle es to litelle that Y can telle or saye, for itt maye nought be tolde. Botte ylke saule aftere the sayinge of Saynte Pawle schulde feele in hym that in Criste Jhesu.¹⁶ This schewynge of Criste paynes fillyd me fulle of paynes, for I wate weele he suffrede nought botte anez, botte as he walde schewe yt me and fylle me with mynde as I hadde desyrede before.

' us] P; A *om.*   ⁵ claungede] clange s; chaungede A.

My modere that stode emangys othere and behelde me lyftyd uppe hir hande before me face to lokke myn eyen, for sche wenyd I had bene dede or els I hadde dyede. And this encresyd mekille my sorowe, for noughtwithstandynge alle my paynes, I wolde nought hafe been lettyd for loove that I hadde in hym. And to whethere, in alle this tyme of Crystes presence, I felyd no payne botte for Cristes paynes, than thought me I knewe ful lytylle whate payne it was that I askyd. For me thought that my paynes passede any bodylye dede. I thought, 'Es any payne in helle lyke this payne?' And I was aunswerde in my resone that dyspayre ys mare, for that es gastelye payne. Bot bodilye payne es nane mare than this: howe myght my payne be more than to see hym that es alle my lyfe, alle my blys, and alle mye joye [suffyr]? [Here]*ᵗ* felyd I sothfastlye that Y lovede Criste so mekille aboven myselfe that me thought it hadde beene a grete eese to me to hafe dyede bodylye.

Hereyn I sawe in partye the compassyon of oure Ladye Saynte Marye, for Criste and scho ware so anede in loove that the gretnesse of hir loove was the cause of the mykillehede of hir payne. For so mykille as scho lovyd hym mare than alle othere, her payne passed alle othere, and so alle his disciples and alle his trewe lovers suffyrde paynes mare than thare awne bodelye dying. For I am sekyr be myn awne felynge that the leste of thame luffed hym mare than thaye dyd thamselfe. Here I sawe a grete anynge betwyx Criste and us; for when he was in payne, we ware in payne, and alle creatures that myght suffyr payne soffyrde with hym. And thaye that knewe hym nought, this was thare payne, that alle creatures, sonne and the mone, withdrewe thare servyce,¹⁷ and so ware thaye alle lefte in sorowe for the tyme. And thus thaye that lovyd hym sufferde payne for luffe, and thay that luffyd hym nought sufferde payne for faylynge of comforthe of alle creatures.

In this tyme I walde hafe lokyd besyde the crosse botte I durste nought, for I wyste wele whilys I lukyd uppon the crosse I was sekyr and safe. Therfore I walde nought assente to putte my sawle in perille, for besyde the crosse was na syekernesse, botte uglynesse of feendes. Than hadde I a profyr in my resone, as yyf it hadde beene frendelye i-sayde to me, 'Luke uppe to heven to his Fadere.' Than sawe I wele, with the faythe that Y felyd, that thare ware nathynge betwyx the crosse and heven that myght hafe desesyd me, and othere me behovyd loke uppe or els aunswere. I answerde and sayde, 'Naye, I may nought,

---

ᵗ suffyr Here] P; suffyrde hir A.

for thowe erte myne heven.' This I sayde for I walde nought; for I
hadde levyr hafe bene in that payne to domysdaye than hafe comen to
hevene otherewyse than be hym. For I wyste wele he that bought me so
sare schulde unbynde me when he walde.

[11] Thus chese I Jhesu for my heven wham I saw onlye in payne at
that tyme. Me lykede non othere hevene than Jhesu whilke schalle be
my blysse when I am thare. And this has ever beene a comforthe to me,
that I chesyd Jhesu to my hevene in alle tyme of passyon and of sorowe.
And that has beene a lernynge to me, that I schulde evermare do so, and
chese anly hym to my heven, in wele and in wa. And thus sawe I my
Lorde Jhesu langoure lange tyme, for the anynge of the godhede for
love gafe strenght to the manhede to suffyr mare than alle men myght. I
mene nought anly mare payne anly than alle men myght suffyr, bot
a[lso]*u* that he suffyrde mare payne than alle men that ever was fra the
fyrste begynnynge to the laste daye. No tonge maye telle, ne herte fully
thynke,[18] the paynes that oure savyoure sufferde for us, haffande
rewarde to the worthynes of the hyest worschipfulle kynge and to the
schamefulle, dyspyttous and paynfulle dede. For he that was hieste and
worthyest was fullyest noghthede and witterlyest dyspyside. Botte the
love that made hym to suffere alle this, itt passes als fare alle his payns
as heven es aboven erthe. For the paynes was a dede done in a tyme be
the wyrkynge of love, botte luffe was withowtyn begynnynge, and es
and evere schalle be withowtyn any ende. And sodaynlye, me
behaldande in the same crosse, he chaunchede into blysfulle chere: the
chawngynge of his chere chaungyd myne, and I was alle gladde and
mery as yt was possybille. Than brought oure Lorde merelye to my
mynde, 'Whate es any poynte of thy payne or of thy grefe?' And I was
fulle merye.

[12] Than sayde oure Lorde, askande, 'Arte thou wele payde that I
suffyrde for the?'
     'Ya, goode Lorde', quod I. 'Gramercy, goode Lorde, blissyd mut
thowe be.'
     'Yyf thowe be payede', quod oure Lorde, 'I am payede. It es a joye
and a blysse and ane endlesse lykynge to me that ever Y suffyrde
passyon for the, for yyf I myght suffyr mare, I walde suffyr.'

---

u also] P; anly A.

In this felynge myne undyrstandynge was lyftyd uppe into heven, and
thare I sawe thre hevens; of the whilke syght I was gretlye merveylede,
and thought, 'I sawe thre hevens, and alle of the blessyd manhede of
Cryste; and nane is mare, nane is lesse, nane is hiare, nane is lawere,
botte evene like in blysse.'

For the fyrste heven schewed Criste me his Fadere, bot in na
bodelye lyknesse, botte in his properte and in his lykynge. The
wyrkynge of the Fadere it is this: that he gyffes mede tille his sone Jhesu
Criste. This gyfte and this mede is so blysfulle to Jhesu that [his]^v
Fadere myght haffe gyffene na mede that myght hafe likede hym
bettere. For the firste heven, that is blissynge of the Fadere, schewed to
me as a heven, and itt was fulle blysfulle. For he is fulle blyssede with
alle the dedes that he has done abowghte oure salvacyon, wharefore we
ere nought anely his thurgh byingge, botte also be the curtayse gyfte of
his Fadere. We ere his blysse, we er his mede, we er his wyrschippe, we
er his crowne.

This that I saye is soo grete blysse to Jhesu that he settys atte
nought his travayle, and his harde passion, and cruelle and schamefulle
dede. And in this wordes 'Yyf I myght suffyr mare, I walde suffyr mare',
I sawe sothly that yif he myght dye als ofte als fore everilke man anes
that schalle be safe, as he dyed anes for alle, love schulde never late hym
hafe reste to he hadde done it. And when he hadde done it, he walde
sette it atte nought for luff, for alle thynge hym botte litylle in regarde
of his love. And that schewed he me wele sobarly, sayande this worde
'Yyffe I myght suffere mare'. He sayde nought 'Yif it ware nedfulle to
suffyr mare' botte 'Yif I myght suffyr mare'. For thowgh it be nought
nedefulle and he myght suffyr mare, mare he walde. This dede and this
werke abowte oure salvacyon was als wele as he myght ordayne it, it
was done als wyrschipfullye as Cryste myght do it. And in this I sawe a
fulle blysse in Cryste, botte this blysse schulde nought hafe bene done
fulle yyf it myght any bettere hafe bene done than it was done.

And in this thre wordes 'It is a joye, a blysse, and ane endeles
likynge to me' ware schewed to me thre hevens, as thus: for the joye, I
undyrstode the plesaunce of the Fadere; for the blysse, the wirschippe
of the Sone; and for the endeles lykynge, the Haly Gaste. The Fadere is
plesed, the Sone ys worschippyd, the Haly Gaste lykes. Jhesu wille that
we take heede to this blysse that is in the blyssedfulle Trinite of oure

salvacion, and that we lyke als mekylle with his grace whyles we er
here. And this was schewyd me in this worde 'Erte thow wele payed?'
Be the tothere worde that Cryste sayde – 'Yyf thou be payed, I am payd'
– he schewed me the undyrstandynge, as yyf he had sayde: 'It is joye
and lykynge enough to me, and I aske nought els for my travayle botte
that I myght paye the.' Plentyvoslye and fully was this schewyd to me.
Thynke also wyselye of the gretnesse of this worde 'That ever I suffred
passion for the', for in that worde was a hye knawynge of luffe and of
lykynge that he hadde in oure salvacion.

[13] Fulle merelye and gladlye oure Lorde lokyd into his syde and
behelde and sayde this worde 'Loo, how I lovyd the', as yf [he]*ʷ* hadde
sayde, 'My childe, yyf thow kan nought loke in my godhede, see heere
howe I lette opyn my syde, and my herte be clovene in twa, and lette
oute blude and watere alle that was thareyn.¹⁹ And this lykes me, and
so wille I that it do the.' This schewed oure Lorde me to make us gladde
and mery.

     And with the same chere and myrthe he loked downe on the ryght
syde and brought to my mynde whare oure Ladye stode in the tyme of
his passion, and sayde, 'Wille thowe see hir?' And I aunswerde and
sayde, 'Ya, goode Lorde, gramercy, yyf it be thy wille.' Ofte tymes I
prayed it, and wened to haffe sene here in bodely lykenes, botte I sawe
hir nought soo. And Jhesu in that worde schewed me a gastelye syght
of hire. Ryght as I hadde before sene hire litille and sympille, ryght so
he schewed here than, hye and nobille and gloriouse and plesaunte to
hym aboven alle creatures. And so he wille that it be knawyn that alle
tha that lykes in hym schulde lyke in hire, and in the lykynge that he
hase in hire, and scho in hym. And in that worde that Jhesu sayde –
'Wille thou see hire?' – me thought I hadde the maste lykynge that he
myght hafe gyffen me, with the gastelye schewynge that he gafe me of
hire. For oure Lorde schewed me nothynge in specyalle botte oure Lady
Saynte Marye, and here he schewyd me in thre tymes. The fyrste was as
sche consayved, the seconde was as scho were in hire sorowes undere
the crosse, and the thryd as scho is nowe: in lykynge, wirschippe and joye.

     And eftyr this oure Lorde schewyd hym to me mare gloryfyed as
to my syght than I sawe hym before, and in this was I lerede that ilke
saule contemplatyfe to whilke es gyffen to luke and seke God schalle se

ʷ he] A *bis*.

hire and passe unto God by contemplacion. And eftyr this techynge, hamelye, curtayse and blysfulle and verray lyfe, ofte tymes oure Lorde Jhesu sayde to me, 'I it am that is hiaste. I it am that thou luffes. I it am that thowe lykes. I it am that thowe serves. I it am that thou langes. I it am that thowe desyres. I it am that thowe menes. I it am that is alle.[20] I it am that haly kyrke preches the and teches the. I it am that schewed me are to the.' Thies wordes I declare nought botte for ilke man, eftyr the grace that God gyffes hym in undyrstandynge and lovynge, resayfe tham in oure Lordes menynge.

And eftyr, oure Lorde brought unto my mynde the langynge that I hadde to hym before. And I sawe that nathynge letted me bot syn, and so I behelde generallye in us alle, and me thought, 'Yyf syn hadde nought bene, we schulde alle hafe bene clene and lyke to oure Lorde, as he made us.' And thus in my folye, before this tyme, ofte I wondrede why, be the grete forseande wysdome of God, syn was nought lettede; for than thought me that alle schulde hafe bene wele.

This styrrynge was mekylle to forsayke, and mournynge and sorowe I made therfore withoutyn resone and dyscrecion, of fulle grete pryde. Neverthelesse, Jhesu in this vision enfourmede me of alle that me neded. I saye nought that me nedes na mare techynge, for oure Lorde, with the schewynge of this, hase lefte me to haly kyrke; and I am hungery and thyrstye[21] and nedy and synfulle and freele, and wilfully submyttes me to the techynge of haly kyrke, with alle myne even-Crysten, into the ende of my lyfe.

He aunswerde be this worde and sayde, 'Synne is behovelye.' In this worde 'Synne' oure Lorde brought to my mynde generallye alle that is nought goode: the schamefulle dyspyte and the utter noghtynge that he bare for us in this lyfe and in his dyinge, and alle the paynes and passyons of alle his creatures, gastelye and bodelye. For we ere alle in party noghted, and we schulde be noghted folowande oure maister Jhesu to we be fulle purgede, that is to say to we be fully noghted of oure awne dedely flesche, and of alle oure inwarde affeccion[s][x] whilke ere nought goode.

And the behaldynge of this, with alle the paynes that ever ware or ever schalle be, a[lle][y] this was schewed me in a toch and redely passed overe into comfort, for oure goode Lorde God walde noght that the saule ware afferdede of this uglye syght. Botte I sawe noght synne, fore

---

[x] affeccions] P; affeccion A.   [y] alle] and A; and alle PS.

I lefe it has na manere of substaunce, na partye of beynge, na it myght
nought be knawen bot be the paynes that it is cause of. And this payne,
it is sumthynge, as to my syght, for a tyme; for it purges us and makes
us to knawe oureselfe and aske mercye. For the passion of oure Lorde is
comforth to us agaynes alle this, and so is his blyssyd wille to alle that
schalle be saffe. He comfortes redely and swetlye be his wordes, and
says, 'Botte alle schalle be wele, and alle maner of thynge schalle be wele.'

Thyes wordes ware schewed wele tenderlye, schewande na
ma[ne]re^z of blame to me, na to nane that schalle be safe. Than were it
a grete unkyndenesse of me to blame or wondyr of God for my synnes,
syn he blames not me for synne. Thus I sawe howe Cryste has
compassyon of us for the cause of synne. And ryght as I was before
with the passyon of Cryste fulfilled with payne and compassion, lyke in
this I was in party fyllyd with compassion of alle myn even-Cristene;
and than sawe I that ylke kynde compassyone that man hase of his
even-Cristene with charyte, that it is Criste in hym.

[14]   Bot in this ye schalle studye: behaldande generallye, drerelye, and
mournande, sayande thus to oure Lorde in my menynge with fulle grete
drede, 'A, goode Lorde, howe myght alle be wele for the grete harme
that is comon by synne to thy creatures?' And I desired as I durste to
hafe sum mare open declarynge wharewith I myght be hesyd in this.
And to this oure blyssede Lorde aunswerde fulle mekelye and with fulle
lovelye chere, and schewed me that Adames synne was the maste
harme that ever was done or ever schalle to the warldes ende. And also
he schewed me that this is opynly knawy[n]^a in alle haly kyrke in erthe.

Forthermare he lered me that I schulde behalde the gloriouse
asethe, for this aseth-makynge is mare plesande to the blissede
Godhede and mare wyrschipfulle to mannes salvacion withowtene
comparyson than ever was the synne of Adam harmfulle. Thanne
menes oure Lorde blyssede thus in this techynge, that we schulde take
hede to this: 'For sen I hafe made wele the maste harme, it is my wille
that thowe knawe therby that I schalle make wele alle that is the lesse.'

He gaffe me undyrstandynge of twa partyes. The ta party is oure
saviour and oure salvacion. This blyssed party is opyn and clere and
fayre and lyght and plentious, for alle mankynde that is of goode wille
or that schalle be es comprehendyd in this partye. Hereto ere we

---

^{z} manere] P; mare A. ^{a} knawyn] P; knawynge A.

byddyn of God and drawen and consayled and lered inwardlye be the
Haly Gaste and outwarde by haly kyrke by the same grace. In this wille
oure Lorde that we be occupyed, enjoyande in hym, for he enjoyes in
us. And the mare plentyvouslye that we take of this with reverence and
mekenesse, the mare we deserve thanke of hym and the mare spede to
oureselfe. And thus maye we saye, enjoyande, oure parte is oure Lorde.

The tother parte is spared fra us and hidde, that is to saye, alle
that is besyde oure salvacion. For this is oure Lordys prive consayles
and it langes to the ryalle lordeschyp of God for to have his prive
consayles in pees, and it langes to his servauntys for obedyence and
reverence nought to wille witte his councelle. Oure Lorde has pite and
compassyon of us for that sum creatures makes tham so besy theryn;
and I am sekyr yyf we wyste howe mekille we schulde plese hym and
ese oureselfe for to lefe it, we walde. The sayntes in heven wille
nathynge witte bot that oure Lorde wille schewe thame, and also there
charyte and ther desyre is rewlyd eftyr the wille of oure Lorde. And
thus awe we to wille ne to be lyke to hym, and than schalle we nathynge
wille ne desyre botte the wille of oure Lorde, as he does, for we er alle
ane in Goddys menynge. And here was I lered that we schalle anely
enjoye in oure blissid saviour Jhesu and trist in hym for alle thynge.

[15]   And thus oure goode Lorde answerde to alle the questyons and
doutes that I myght make, sayande fulle comfortabelye on this wyse: 'I
wille make alle thynge wele, I schalle make alle thynge wele, I maye
make alle thynge wele, and I can make alle thynge wele; and thowe
schalle se thyselfe that alle thynge schalle be wele.' There he says he
'maye', I undyrstande for the Fadere; and there he says he 'can', I
undyrstande for the Sone; and ther he says 'I wille', I understande for
the Hali Gaste; and there he says 'I schalle', I undirstande for the unyte
of the blyssede Trinyte, thre persones in a trewthe; and there he says:
'Thowe schalle se thyselfe', I undyrstande the anynge of alle mankynde
that schalle be sayfe into the blysfulle Trinyte.

And in this fyve wordes God wille be closed in ryste and in pees,
and thus has the gastely thyrst of Cryste ane ende. For this is the gastely
thyrste, the luff langynge, and that lastes and ever schalle to wee see
that syght atte domesdaye. For we that schalle be safe, and schalle be
Crystes joye and his blysse, ere yit here and schalle be unto the daye.
Therefore this is the thyrste, the falynge of his blysse, that he has us
nought in hym als haelye as he schalle thanne haffe. Alle this was

schewed me in the schewynge of compassion, for that schalle sese atte domesdaye. Thus he hath rewthe and compassion of us, and he has langynge to hafe us, botte his wysdome and his love suffers nought the ende to come to the beste tyme.

And in thies same fyve wordes beforesayde: 'I may make alle thynge wele', I undyrstande a myghtty comforthe of alle the werkys of oure Lorde that ere for to come. For ryght as the blissyd Trinyte made alle thynge of nought, ryght soo the same blyssed Trinyte schalle make wele alle that es nought wele. It is Goddys wille that we hafe grete rewarde to alle the dedys that he has done, for he wille that we knawe thereby alle that he schalle do; and that schewyd he me in this worde that he sayde: 'And thou schalle see thyselfe that alle manere of thynge schalle be wele.' This I undyrstande in twa manerse: ane, I am wele payed that I wate it noght; anothere, I am gladde and mery for I schalle witte itt. It is Goddys wille that we witte that alle schalle be wele in generalle; botte it is nought Goddys wille that we schulde witte it nowe, botte as it langes to us for the tyme, and that is the techynge of haly kyrke.

[16] God schewyd me fulle grete plesaunce that he has in alle men and women that myghttelye and mekelye and wyrschipfullye takes the prechynge and the techynge of haly kyrke, for he is haly kyrke. For he is the grownde, he is the substaunce, he is the techynge, he is the techare, he is the ende, he is the myddes wharefore ilke trewe sawlle travaylles. And he is knawen and schalle be knawen to ylke saule to whame the Haly Gaste declares it. And I am sekyr that alle tho that sekes thus schalle spede, for thay seke God. Alle this that I hafe nowe sayde, and mare that I schalle saye eftyr, es comforthynge agayne synne. For fyrst, when I sawe that God does alle that es done, I sawe nought synne, and than sawe I that alle is wele. Bot when God schewyd me synne, than sayde he, 'Alle schalle be wele.'

And when God allemyghttye hadde schewed me plentyouslye and fully of his goodnesse, I desyred of a certayne person that I lovyd howe it schulde be with hire. And in this desyre I lettyd myselfe, for I was noght taught in this tyme. And than was I answerde in my reson, als it ware be a frendfulle man, 'Take it generally, and behalde the curtayssy of thy Lorde God as he schewes it to the, for it is mare worschippe to God to behalde hym in alle than in any specyalle thynge.' I assentyd, and therwith I lered that it is mare wyrschippe to

God to knawe alle thynge in generalle than to lyke in any thynge in specialle. And yyf I schulde do wysely eftyr this techynge, I schulde nought be glad for nathynge in specyalle, na desesed for na manere of thynge, for alle schalle be wele. God brought to my mynde that I schulde synne, and for lykynge that I hadde in behaldynge of hym I entendid nought redely to that schewynge. And oure Lorde fulle curtayslye abayde to I walde entende; and than oure Lorde brought to mynde with my synnes the synne of alle myne even-Cristen, alle in generalle and nathynge in specialle.

[17] Iff alle oure Lorde schewyd me that I schulde synne, be me allayn I understode alle. In this I consayved a softe drede, and to this oure Lorde answerde me thus, 'I kepe the fulle sekerly.' This worde was sayde to me with mare love and sekernes of gastely kepynge than I can or maye telle. For as it was before schewed to me that I schulde synne, ryght so was the comforth schewed to me: sekernesse of kepynge for alle myne even-Cristen.

What may make me mare to luff myne even-Cristen than to see in God that he loves alle that schalle be safe, as it ware alle a saulle? And in ilke saule that schalle be sayfe is a goodely wille that never assentyd to synne, na never schalle. For as ther is a bestely wille in the nethere party that maye wille na goode, so is thare a goodely wille in the over partye that maye wille nane eville, botte ever goode, na mare than the persones of the blissed Trinyte. And this schewyd oure Lorde me in the holehed of luffe that we stande in his sight, ya, that he luffez us nowe als wele whiles we ere here as he schalle do when we ere thare before his blissed face.

Also God schewed me that syn is na schame, bot wirschippe to man. For in this sight myn understandynge was lyfted up into heven, and than com verrayly to my mynde David, Peter and Paule, Thomas of Inde and the Maudelayn[22] – howe thaye er knawen in the kyrke of erth with thare synnes to thayre wirschippe. And it is to tham no schame that thay hafe synned – na mare it is in the blysse of heven – for thare the takenynge of synne is turned into wirschippe. Right so oure Lorde God schewed me tham in ensampille of alle othere that schalle cum thedyr.

Syn is the scharpyste scourge that any chosen saule maye be bette with, whilke scourge it alle forbettes man and woman, and alle forbrekes tham and noghtez hymselfe in thare awne syght sa fare forth that hym thynke that he is noght worthy bot as it ware to synke into helle. Botte when contricion takes hym be the towchynge of the Haly Gaste, than turnes he bitternesse into hope of Goddys mercye. And than begynnes his woundys to hile and the sawlle to qwykkyn, turnyd in to the lyfe of haly kyrke. The Haly Gaste leddes hym to confessyon, wilfully to schewe his synnes, nakedlye and trewly with grete sorowe and grete schame that he hase swa defowled the fayre ymage of God. Than he takes pennaunce for ylke a synne, enjewnyd be his domesman, that is growndyd in haly kyrke be the techynge of the Haly Gaste. Be this medycyn behoves everilke synfulle sawlle be heled, and namlye of synnes that ere dedely in the selfe. Though he be heled, his woundes er sene before God, nowht as woundes bot as wyrschippes. And so on contrarye wyse, as it es punysched here with sorowe and with pennaunce, it schalle be rewarded in heven be the curtayse love of oure Lorde God allemyghttye, that wille that nane that comes thare lese his travayle. That mede that we salle resayfe thare salle nought be litelle, bot it schalle be hy, gloriouse, and wirschipfulle, and so schalle alle schame turne into wyrschippe and into mare joye. And I am sekere be myn awne felynge, the mare that ilke kynde saule sees this in the kynde and curta[ys]e^b love of God, the lathere es hym for to synne.

[18] Bot yyf thowe be styrred to saye or to thynke, sen this is sothe, than ware it goode for to synne for to hafe the mare mede, beware of this styrrynge and dispice it, for it is of the enmy. For whate saule that wilfully takys this styrrynge, he maye never be safe to he be amendyd as of dedely synne. For yif it ware layde before me, alle the payne that is in helle and in purgatorye and in erth, dede and othere and synne, I had lever chese alle that payne than synne. For synne is so vyle and so mykille for to hate that it maye be likened to na payne, whilke payne es nought syn, for alle thynge is goode botte synne, and nathynge is wikkyd botte synne. Synne es nowthere deed no lykynge, botte when a saule cheses wilfully synne that is payne as fore his God, atte the ende he hase ryght nought. That payne thynke me the herdeste helle, for he hase nought his God. In alle paynes a saule may hafe God botte in synne.

And als myghtty and als witty as God is for to safe man, als willy he is. For Criste hymselfe is grownde of alle the lawe of Crysten men, and he has tawht us to do goode agaynes eville. Here may we see that

---

^{b} curtayse] P; curtasye A.

he es hymselfe this charite, and does to us as he teches us to do; for he wille that we be lyke to hym in anehede of endeles luffe to oureselfe and to oure even-Cristen. Na mare than his love es broken to us for oure synne, na mare wille he that oure love be broken to oureselfe ne to oure even-Cristen, botte nakedlye hate synne and endeleslye love the saule as God loves it. For this worde that God sayde es ane endelesse comforth, that kepes us fulle sekerlye.

[19] Aftyr this oure Lorde schewed me fo[r]^c prayers. I sawe ii condicyons in tham that prayes, aftyr that I hafe felyd in myselfe. Ane es, thaye wille nought praye for nathynge that may be, botte that thynge that es Goddes wille and his wirschippe. Anothere is that thay sette tham myghttelye and contynuely to beseke that thynge that es his wille and his wirschippe. And that es as I hafe undyrstandide be the techynge of haly kyrke. For in this oure Lorde lered me the same, to hafe of Goddes gyfte faith, hope, and charyte, and kepe us therein to oure lyves ende. And in this we say 'Pater noster', 'Ave', and crede, with devocion, as God wille gyffe it. And thus we praye fore alle oure even-Cristen and for alle manere of men, that Godes wille es, for we walde that alle maner of men and women ware in the same vertu and grace that we awe to desyre to oureselfe. Botte yitt in alle this ofttymes oure triste is nowht fulle, for we ere nought sekare that God almyghtty hyeres us, as us thynke for oure unworthynesse and fore we fele ryght nought. Fore we ere als barayne and als drye oftymes eftyr oure prayers as we ware before, and thus in oure felynge oure foly es cause of oure waykenesse, for thus hafe I felede in myselfe.

And alle this brought oure Lorde sodaynlye to my mynde, and myghttely and lyfely, and comfortande me agaynes this maner of waykenesse in prayers, and sayde, 'I am grownde of thy besekynge. First it is my wille that thou hafe it, and syne I make the to will it, and syne I make the to beseke it. And yif thou beseke, howe schulde it than be that thou schulde nought hafe thy besekynge?' And thus in the fyrste reson, with the thre that folous eftere, oure Lorde schewed a myghtty comforth. And the fyrst, thare he says 'And thowe beseke', thare he schewes fulle grete plesaunce and endelese mede that he wille gyffe us for oure besekynge. And in the fourte reson thare he sais 'Howe schulde it than be that thou schulde noght hafe thy besekynge?', thare he schewes a sobere undertakynge, for we tryste nought als myghtelye als we schulde do.

Thus wille oure Lorde that we bath praye and triste, for the cause of the resones beforsayde is to make us myghty agaynes waiknesse in oure prayers. For it is Goddis wille that we pray, and therto he styrres us in thies wordes beforsayde. For he wille that we be sekere to hafe oure prayere, for prayer pleses God. Prayer pleses man with hymselfe, and makes hym sobure and meke that beforehand was in strife and travayle. Praiere anes the saule to God, for thowgh the saule be ever lyke God in kynde and in substaunce, it is oft unlike in condicion thurgh syn of mannes party. Than makes prayer the saule like unto God, when the sawlle wille as God wille, and than es it lyke to God in condicyon as it es in kynde. And thus he teches us to pray and myghttely tryste that we schalle hafe that we praye fore, for alle thynge that es done schulde be done thowgh we never prayed it. Botte the luff of God es so mykille that he haldes us parcyners of his goode deede. And therfore he styrres us to praye that hym lykes to do, for whate prayere or goode wille that we hafe of his gyfte, he wille rewarde us and gife us endelese mede. And this was schewed me in this worde: 'And thou beseke it'.

In this worde God schewed me so grete plesaunce and so grete lykynge, as yif he ware mekille behaldene to us for ilke goode dede that we do, alle yif it es he that does it. And for that, we beseke besily to do that thynge that hym lykes, as yif he sayde: 'Whate myght thowe plese me mare than to bisike bisily, wisely, and wilfullye to do that thynge that I wille do?' And thus makes prayere accorde betwix God and mannes saule, for whate tyme that mannes saule es hamelye with God, hym nedes nought to praye, botte behalde reverentlye whate he says. For in alle this tyme that this was schewed me, I was noght stirred to praye, botte to hafe allewaye this welle in my mynde for comforth, that when we see God we hafe that we desyre, and than nedes us nought to praye. Botte when we se nought God, than nedes us to pray for faylynge and habelynge of oureselfe to Jhesu. For when a saule es tempted, trubled, and lefte to itselfe be unreste, than es it tyme to pray and to make hymselfe symple and boxsom to God. Bot he be boxom, na maner of prayer makes God souple to hym, for he is ever ylyke in love. Botte in the tyme that man is in synne, he is so unmyghttye, so unwyse, and so unluffande that he can nought love God ne hymselfe.

The maste myschefe that he hase es blyndnesse, for he sees

nought alle this. Than the hale luffe of God allemyghty that ever is ane
gyffes hym sight to hymselfe, and than wenes he that God ware wrathe
with hym for his synne. And than is he stirred to contricion, and be
confessyon and othere goode dedys to slake the wrathe of God, unto
the tyme he fynde a reste in saule and softnesse in conscience. And than
hym thynke that God hase forgyffen his synnes, and it es soth. And
than is God, in the sight of saule, turnede into the behaldynge of the
saule, as yif it had bene in payne or in prison, sayande thus: 'I am
gladde that thou erte comen to reste, for I hafe ever loved the and nowe
loves the, and thou me.' And thus with prayers, as I hafe before sayde,
and with othere goode werkys that ere custumab[yll]e*d* be the techynge
of haly kyrke, is the saule aned to God.

[20] Before this tyme I hadde ofte grete langynge, and desyred of
Goddys gyfte to be delyvered of this warlde and of this lyfe, for I
schulde be with my God in blysse whare I hope sikerlye thurgh his
mercye to be withowten ende. For ofte tymes I behelde the waa that is
here and the weele and the blyssede beynge thare; and yyf thare hadde
bene na payn in erthe bot the absence of oure Lorde God, me thought
sumtyme it ware mare than I myght bere. And this made me to mourne
and beselye lange.

Than God sayde to me, for pacience and for sufferaunce, thus:
'Sudanly thowe schalle be takene fra alle thy payne, fra alle thy disese,
and fra alle thy waa; and thowe schalle comen up aboven, and thowe
schalle hafe me to thy mede, and thowe schalle be fulfyllede of joye and
blysse, and thowe schalle never hafe na maner of payne, na maner of
sekenes, na maner of myslykynge, na wantynge of wille, botte ever joye
and blysse withouten ende. Whate schulde it than greve the to suffyr
awhile, sen it is my wille and my wirschippe?'

Also in this reson 'Sudanly thou schalle be taken', I sawe how
God rewardys man of the pacience that he has in abydynge of Goddes
wille in his tyme, and that men lengthes his pacyence owere the tyme of
his lyffynge for unknawynge of his tyme of passynge. This is a grete
profytte, for yif a man knewe his tyme, he schulde noght hafe pacience
owere that tyme. Also God wille that whiles the saule es in the bodye,
that it sem[e]*e* to itselfe that it es ever atte the poynte to be taken. For
alle this lyfe in this langoure that we hafe here is bot a poynte, and

when we ere takene sodaynly oute of payne into blysse, it schalle be nought. And therfore sayde oure Lorde: 'Whate schulde it than greve the to suffere awhile, sen it is my wille and my wyrschippe?' It is Goddys wille that we take his behestys and his confortynges als largelye and als myghtelye as we maye take thame; and also he wille that we take oure abydynge and oure desese als lyghtelye as we may take tham, and sette tham atte nought. For the lyghtlyere we take tham, the lesse price we sette be tham for luff, the lesse payne salle we hafe in the felynge of tham, and the mare thanke we schalle hafe for tham.

In this blyssed revelacion I was trewly taught that whate man or woman wilfully cheses God in his lyfe, he may be sekere that he is chosene. Kepe this treulye, for sothly it is Godys wille that we be als sekere in tryste of the blys in heven whiles we ere here as we schulde be in sekernesse when we ere thare. And ever the mare likynge and the joye that we take in this sekernesse with reverence and mekenes, the bettere likes hym. For I am sekyr, yif thare hadde nane ben bot I that schulde be safe, God wolde hafe done alle that he hase done for me. And so schulde ilke saule thynke in knawynge of his lovere, forgettande yif he myght alle creatures, and thynkkande that God hase done for hym alle that he hase done. And thys thynke me schulde styrre a saule for to luff and lyke hym, and nought drede bot hym, for it is his wille that we witte that alle the myght of oure enmye is loken in oure frendes hande. And therfore a saule that wate sekerly this schalle nought drede botte hym that he loves, and alle othere dredes sette tham emange passyons and bodelye sekenesse and ymagynacions.

And therfore yif a man be in so mekylle payne, in so mekylle waa, and in so mekylle deseses, that hym thynke that he can thynke ryght nought bot that that he es in or that he feles, als sone as he maye, passe lyghtlye owere and sette it atte nought. And why? For God wille be knawen. For yyff we knewe hym and luffed hym, we schulde hafe pacience and be in grete reste, and it schulde be lykynge to us, alle that he does. And this schewed oure Lorde me in thies wordes that he sayde: 'Whate schulde it than greve the to suffyr awhile, sen it is my wille and my wirschippe?' And here was ane ende of alle that oure Lorde schewed me that daye.

[21]   And efter this sone I felle to myselfe and into my bodelye seknes, understandande that I schulde life, and as a wrech that hevyed and mourned for the bodely paynes that I feled, and thought grete

irksumnes that I schulde langere lyffe. And I was als barane and drye as
yif I hadde never had comforth before bot litille, for fallynge to my
paynes and faylynge of gastelye felynge.

Than com a religiouse person to me and asked me howe I farde,
and I sayde that I ha[dd]e^f raved that daye. And he lugh lowde and
enterlye. And I sayde, 'The crosse that stode atte my bedde feete, it bled
faste.' And with this worde the person that I spake to wex alle sadde
and mervelande. And onane I was sare aschamed for my reklessenes,
and I thought thus: 'This man takys it sadlye, the leste worde that I
myght saye, that says na mare therto.' And when I sawe that he toke it
so sadelye and with so grete reverence, I wex ryght gretly aschamed
and walde haffe bene schryfen. Bot I couth telle it na preste, for I
thoght: 'Howe schulde a preste leve me? I leved nought oure Lorde
God.' This I leved sothfastlye for the tyme that I sawe hym, and so was
than my wille and my menynge ever for to do withowten ende. Bot as a
fule I lette it passe fro my mynde. Loo, I, wrich! This was a grete synne
and a grete unkyndnes that I, for folye of felynge of a litille bodelye
payne, so unwyselye lefte for the tyme the comforth of alle this blissede
schewynge of oure Lorde God. Here maye ye see whate I am of myselfe;
botte herein walde nought oure curtayse Lorde leve me.

And I laye stille tille nyght, tristande in his mercye, and than I
beganne to slepe. And in my slepe, atte the begynnynge, me thought the
fende sette hym in my throte and walde hafe strangelede me, botte he
myght nought.^{23} Than I woke oute of my slepe, and unnethes hadde I
my lyfe. The persones that ware with me behelde me and wette my
temples, and my herte began to comforth. And onane a lytelle smoke
come in atte the dore with a grete hete and a fowle stynke. I sayde,
'*Benedicite Dominus!* Is alle on fyre that is here?' And I wened it hadde
bene a bodely fyre that schulde hafe brenned us to dede. I asked tham
that ware with me yyf thaye felyd any stynke. Thay sayde naye, thay
felyd nane. I sayde, 'Blissede be God!', for than wiste I wele it was the
fende was comen to tempest me. And onane I tuke tha that oure Lorde
hadde schewed me on the same daye with alle the fayth of hali kyrke,
for I holde it as bathe ane, and fled therto as to my comforth. And
alsone alle vanysched awaye, and I was brought to gret reste and pees,
withoutene seknes of bodye or drede of conscyence.

---

^{f} hadde] P; hafe A.

[22] Bot than lefte I stylle wakande, and than owre Lorde openedde my gastely eyen and schewyd me my saule in myddys of my herte. I sawe my saule swa large as it ware a kyngdome, and be the condicions that I sawe therin, me thought, it was a wirschipfulle cite. In myddys of this cite sittes oure Lorde Jhesu, verraye God and verray man, a fayre persone and of large stature, wyrschipfulle, hiest lorde. And I sawe hym cledde solemplye in wyrschippes. He sittes in the saule even ryght in pees and reste, and he rewles and yemez heven and erth and alle that is. The manhede with the Godhede sittis in reste, and the Godhede rewles and yemes withowtyn any instrumente or besynes – and my saule blisfullye occupyed with the Godhede, that is sufferayn myght, sufferayne wisdome, sufferayne goodnesse. The place that Jhesu takes in oure saule he schalle never remove it withowtyn ende, for in us is his haymelyeste hame and maste lykynge to hym to dwelle in.

This was a delectabille syght and a restefulle, for it is so in trowth withowten ende; and the behaldynge of this whiles we ere here es fulle plesande to God, and fulle grete spede to us. And the saule that thus behaldys, it makys it lyke to hym that is behaldene, and anes in reste and in pees. And this was a singulere joye and a blis to me that I sawe hym sitte, for the behaldynge of this sittynge schewed to me sikernes of his endelesse dwellynge. And I knewe sothfastly that it was he that schewed me alle before.

And when I hadde behalden this with fulle avisement, than schewed oure Lorde me wordys fulle mekelye, withowtyn voyce and withowten openynge of lyppes, as he hadde done before, and sayde fulle soberlye, 'Witte it welle, it was na ravynge that thowe sawe today. Botte take it, and leve it, and kepe the therto, and thou schalle nought be overcomen.' This laste wordes ware sayde to me for lernynge of fulle trewe sikernes, that it is our Lorde Jhesu that schewed me alle. For ryght as in the fyrste worde that oure Lorde schewed me,[24] menande his blissyd passion – 'Herewith is the fende overcomen' – ryght so he sayde in the laste worde, with fulle trewe sikernesse, 'Thow schalle nought be overcomen.'

And this lernynge and this trewe comforthe, it es generalle to alle myne even-Cristen, as I haffe before sayde, and so is Goddys wille. And this worde, 'Thowe schalle nought be overcomen', was sayde fulle scharpely and fulle myghtely, for sekernes and comforth agayne alle tribulacions that maye com. He sayde nought: 'Thou salle not be tempestyd; thowe schalle not be travayled; thou schalle not be deseced.' Bot he sayde: 'Thou schalle nought be overcomen.' God wille that we take hede of his worde, and that we be ever myghtty in sekernesse, in wele, and in waa. For he luffes us and likes us and so wille he that we luff hym and lyke hym and myghtely triste in hym, and alle schalle be wele. And sone eftyr alle was close, and I sawe na mare.

[23]   After this the fende com agayne with his heete and with his stynke and made me fulle besye. The stynke was so vile and so paynfulle, and the bodely heete also dredfulle and travaylous; and also I harde a bodely jangelynge and a speche, as it hadde bene of two bodyes, and bathe to my thynkynge jangled at anes, as yif thay had haldene a parliamente with grete besynes. And alle was softe mutterynge, and I understode nought whate thay sayde, botte alle this was to stirre me to dispayre, as me thought. And I triste besely in God and comforthede my sawlle with bodely speche, as I schulde hafe done to anothere person than myselfe that hadde so bene travaylede. Me thought this besynes myght nought be lykned to na bodely besenes. My bodelye eyghen I sette on the same crosse that I hadde sene comforth in before that tyme, my tunge I occupyed with speche of Cristes passion and rehersynge of the faith of hali kyrke, and my herte I festende on God, with alle the triste and alle the myght that was in me. And I thought to myselfe, menande, 'Thowe hase nowe grete besynes; walde thou nowe fra this tyme evermare be so besy to kepe the fro synne, this ware a soferayne and a goode occupacion.' For I trowe sothlye, ware I saffe fra synne, I ware fulle saife fra alle the fendes of helle and enmyse of my saule. And thus thay occupied me alle the nyght, and on the morn tille it was aboute pryme dayes. And than onane thay ware alle gane and passed, and there lefte nathynge bot stynke, and that lasted stille a while. And I scorned thame, and thus was I delyvered of tham be the vertu of Cristes passion. For tharewith is the fende overcomen, as Criste sayde before to me.

    A, wriched synne! Whate ert thou? Thowe er nought. For I sawe that God is alle thynge: I sawe nought the. And when I sawe that God hase made alle thynge, I sawe the nought; and when I sawe that God is in alle thynge, I sawe the nought; and when I sawe that God does alle thynge that is done, lesse and mare, I sawe the nought. And when I sawe oure Lorde Jhesu sitt in oure saule so wyrschipfully, and luff and lyke and rewle and yeme alle that he has made, I sawe nought the. And thus I am sekyr that thou erte nought; and alle tha that luffez the, and

lykes the, and folowes the, and wilfully endes in the, I am sekyr thay
schalle be brought to nought with the, and endleslye confownded. God
schelde us alle fra the. Amen par charyte.

And whate wrecchednesse is I wille saye, as I am lernede be the
schewynge of God. Wrecchydnesse es alle thynge that is nought goode:
the gastelye blyndehede that we falle into in the fyrste synne, and alle
that folowes of that wrecchydnesse, passions and paynes, gastelye or
bodely; and alle that es in erth or in othere place whilke es nought
goode. And than may be asked of this: whate er we? And I answere to
this: yif alle ware departed fra us that is nought goode, we schulde be
goode. When wrechidnesse is departed fra us, God and the saule is alle
ane, and God and man alle ane.

Whate is alle in erthe that twynnes us? I answere and saye: in that
that it serves us it is goode, and in that that it schalle perisch it [is]ᵍ
wricchednes, and in that that a man settys his herte theropon othere
wyse than thus it is synne. And for that tyme that man or woman loves
synne, yif any be swilke, he is in payne that passes alle paynes. And
when he loves nought synne, botte hates it and luffez God, alle is wele.
And he that trewlye doez thus, thowgh he syn sumtyme by frelty or
unkunnynge in his wille, he falles nought, for he wille myghtely ryse
agayne and behalde God, wham he loves in alle his wille. God has
made tham to be loved of hym or hire that has bene a synnere, bot ever
he loves, and ever he langes to hafe oure luffe. And when we myghttelye
and wisely luffe Jhesu, wee er in pees.

Alle the blissede techynge of oure Lorde God was schewed to me
be thre partyes as I hafe sayde before, that es to saye, be the bodely
sight, and be worde formed in myn undyrstandynge, and by gastelye
syght. For the bodely sight, I haffe sayde as I sawe, als trewlye as I can.
And for the wordes fourmed, I hafe sayde tham ryght as oure Lorde
schewed me thame. And for the gastely sight, I hafe sayde somdele, bot
I maye never fully telle it. And therfore of this gastely sight I am stirred
to say more, as God wille gyfe me grace.

[24] God schewed me twa manerṣ of sekenes that we hafe, of whilke
he wille that we be amended. The tone es inpacyence, for we bere our
travaylle and oure payne hevely. The tothere is dispayre of doutefulle
drede, as I schalle saye efterwarde. And thiese twa er it that moste

ᵍ is] A *om.*

travayles us and tempestes us, as by that oure Lorde schewed me, and maste lefe to hym that thiese be amendede. I speke of swylke men and women that for Goddes love hates synne and dysposes tham to do Goddes wille. Than ere thiese twa prive synnes, and maste besye aboute us. Therefore it is Goddys wille that thay be knawen, and than schalle we refuse tham as we do othere synnes.

And thus fulle mekelye oure Lorde schewed me the pacience that he hadde in his harde passyon, and also the joye and the lykynge that he hafes of that passion for love. And this he schewed me in ensampille, that we schulde gladlye and esely bere oure paynes, for that es grete plesynge to hym and endelesse profitte to us. And cause why we ere travayled with tham is for unknawenge of luffe. Thowgh the persones in the blissede Trinyte be alle even in properte, luffe was moste schewed to me, that it is moste nere to us alle, and of this knawynge er we moste blynde. For many men and women leves that God is allemyghty and may do alle, and that he is alle wisdome and can do alle. Botte that he is alle love and wille do alle – thar thay stynte. And this unknawynge it is that most lettis Goddes luffers, for when thay begyn to hate synne, and to amende tham by the ordynnaunce of holye kyrke, yit there dwelles a drede that styrres tham to behaldynge of thamselfe and of ther synnes before done. And this drede thay take for a mekenesse, bot this is a fowlle blyndehede and a waykenesse; and we can it nought dispyse, for yif we knewe it we schulde sodaynly dispice it, as we do ane othere synne that we knawe, for it comes of the enmy, and it is agayne the trewthe.

For of alle the propertees of the blissed Trinite, it is Goddes wille that we hafe moste sekernesse in lykynge and luffe. For luffe makes myght and wisdome fulle meke to us; for ryght as be the curtasye of God he forgettys oure synne for tyme we repente us, right so wille he that we foregette oure synne, and alle oure hevynesse, and alle oure dowtefulle dredes.

[25] Fore I saw foure maner of dredes. One is drede of afray that comes to a man sodanly be frelty. This drede is good, for it helpes to purge a man, as does bodely seknes or swylke odere payne that is nought synne; for alle swylke paynes helpes man yif thay be paciently taken. The secunde is drede of payne, wharby a man is styrred and wakned fro slepe of syn. For man that is harde in slepe of syn, he is nought able for the tyme to resayfe the soft comforth of the Hali Gaste,

to he hafe getyn this drede of payne of bodely dede and of the fyre of purgatory. And this drede styrres hym to seke comforth and mercy of God. And thus this drede helpys hym as ane antre, and ables hym to hafe contricion be the blysfulle techynge[25] of the Hali Gaste. The thyrde is a doutfulle drede; for thowgh it be litille in the selfe, and it ware knawen, it is a spice of dispayre. For I am sekyr that alle doutefulle dredes God hates, and he wille that we hafe tham departed fro us with trewe knawynge of lyfe.[26] The fourthe is reverente drede, for thare is na drede that pleses hym in us bot reverente drede, and that is fulle swete and softe for mekillehede of luffe. And yit is this reverente drede and luffe nought bathe ane, bot thay er twa in properte and in wyrkynge, and nowthere of tham may be hadde withowtyn othere.

Therfore, I am sekyre, he that luffez, he dredes, thowgh he fele bot litille. Alle dredes othere than reverente dredes that er proferde to us, thowgh thay com undere the coloure of halynes, thay ere not so trewe. And hereby may thaye be knawen and discerned, whilke is whilke. For this reverente drede, the mare it is hadde, the mare it softes and comfortes and pleses and restes; and the false drede, it travayles and tempestes and trubles. Than is this the remedye: to knawe tham bath and refuse [th]e[h] fals, righte as we walde do a wikkyd spiritte that schewed hym in liknes of a goode angelle. For ryght as ane ille spyrit, thowgh he com undere the coloure and the liknes of a goode angelle, his daliaunce and his wirkynge thowgh he schewe never so fayre, fyrst he travayles and tempes[tes][i] and trubles the person that he spekes with, and lettes hym and lefez hym alle in unreste; and the mare that he comonez with hym, the mare he travayles hym, and the farthere is he fra pees. Therfore it is Goddes wille and oure spede that we knawe tham thus ysundure; for God wille ever that we be sekere in luffe, and peessabille and ristefulle as he is to us. And ryght so of the same condicion as he is to us, so wille he that we be to oureselfe, and to oure even-Cristen. Amen.

Explicit Juliane de Norwych

[h] the] ye A.   [i] tempestes] tempes A.

17 *Revelations of Divine Love*
(longer version)

(Chapters 51 and 60)

The rubric to the last chapter of Julian's longer version declares 'the good Lord shewid this booke shuld be otherwise performid than at the first writing' (ch. 86), while the chapter itself suggests that Julian regards even this longer text as still uncompleted ('This booke is begunne be Gods gift and his grace, but it is not yet performid, as to my syte . . . '). The same chapter reveals that the teaching it contains ('Love was his mening . . . ') was not vouchsafed until fifteen years after the shewings (i.e. in 1388), while Julian's receiving of 'techyng inwardly' on her vision of the Lord and Servant[1] did not occur 'for xx yeres after the tyme of the shewing, save iii monethis' (i.e. not before March 1393). Such references underline how Julian's longer text is the outcome of her many years of meditation on her shewings. The focus shifts: visionary shewing leads on even more to contemplative insight, in an intricately structured text. The narrative of what was seen, itself revised and augmented, is now framed within a commentary of Julian's extended meditations on those revelations. The author's relation to her audience and her material is comparably altered: the text now addresses and identifies with all 'even-Cristen', its serene assurance reflected in an eloquent style.

Julian's transformation of her shorter into her longer text, involving numerous interpolated passages of varying lengths, is too diverse a process to be summarized. No shewing is left without revision and added meditation – the original vision sometimes supplemented with graphic details – and in the first shewing Julian's added passages stressing devotion to the Trinity and her sense of God's courtesy in showing himself 'homely' to us, his servants, introduce what will prove key themes throughout. After the fourteenth shewing Julian interpolates a lengthy sequence of meditative chapters (44–63) which respond to questions raised by her preceding visions, a sequence in which chapter 51 (on the Lord and Servant) and chapter 60 (on Jesus our Mother) distil some of Julian's most characteristic concerns and methods. Afterwards the narrative of the fifteenth and sixteenth shewings briefly resumes (chs. 64–9), to be followed by further added contemplations until the end of the book (chs. 70–86).

The long-delayed understanding of the vision of the Lord and Servant (absent from the shorter text) answers deeply to Julian's deep anxiety at the seeming divergence between orthodox teaching on the 'blame of our synne' and her sense that 'I ne se the shewyn to us no manner of blame' (ch. 50). Recording her process of coming to discern the levels of allegory involves Julian in describing her contemplative method, in a kind of spiritual diary of culminative insight won over years of meditation. Precisely distinguished modes of contemplative understanding are applied to details of colour, gesture and scene, so as to draw out the hidden, layered meanings of this mysterious parable of humanity and deity.

Devotional allusion to Jesus as mother[2] – probably originating in various biblical texts – may be found in Anselm and in William of St Thierry, in St Mechtild of Hackeborn, among thirteenth-century Franciscans, in the *Ancrene Wisse* and *The Chastising of God's Children* (see below, p. 259). Traditional devotional themes already included the motifs of the sacrament as the mother's suckling, and of God as the loving mother hiding in play from her child, or wisely letting the child learn from chastening experiences. Julian's visionary originality is to apply with theological precision her notion of Jesus as mother – and with it the complementary balance of male and female natures – to the relationships within the Trinity. In a series of chapters (57–63) Julian pursues the motherhood theme in contemplating her revelations: witness her cross-references to the earlier shewings and locutions within these later meditations.

Base manuscript: BL MS Sloane 2499 (s), fols. 33r–37r, 43r–44r. Also cited: Bibliothèque Nationale, Paris, fonds anglais 40 (P).

The answere to the doute afor by a mervelous example of a lord and a servant; and God will be abidyn, for it was nere xx yeres after ere she fully understode this example; and how it is understod that Crist syttith on the ryth hand of the Fader – li chapter.

And than our curtes Lord answerd in shewing full mystily a wondirful example of a lord that hath a servant, and gave me syte to my understondyng of botyrn; which syte was shewid double in the lord, and the syte was shewid dowble in the servant: than on partie was shewid gostly in bodily lyknes, and the other partie was shewid more gostly without bodyly lyknes. For the first thus: I saw ii persons in bodyly likenes, that is to sey, a lord and a servant; and therewith God gave me gostly understondyng. The lord sittith solemnly in rest and in peace, the servant standyth by, aforn his lord reverently, redy to don his lords will. The lord lookyth upon his servant ful lovely and swetely, and mekely he sendyth hym to a certain place to don his will. The servant, not only he goeth, but suddenly he stirtith and rynnith in grete haste for love to don his lords will. And anon he fallith in a slade and takith ful grete sore. And than he gronith and monith and waylith and writhith, but he ne may rysen ne helpyn hymself be no manner wey. And of all this the most myscheif that I saw him in was faylyng of comforte; for he cowde not turne his face to loke upon his lovyng lord, which was to hym ful nere, in whom is ful comfort; but as a man that was febil and onwise for the tyme, he entended to his felyng, and induryd in wo, in which wo he suffrid vii grete peynes. The first was the sore brosyng th[at]ᵃ he toke in hys fallyng, which was to hym felable peyne. The ii was the hevynes of his body. The iii was febilnes folowyng of these two. The iiii, that he was blinded in his reason and stonyed in his mend so ferforth that almost he had forgotten his owne luf. The v was that he myte not rysen. The vi was most mervelous to me, and that was that he lay alone. I lokid al aboute and beheld, and fer ne nere, hey ne low, I saw to him no helpe. The vii was that the place which he lay on was a lang, herd, and grevous.

I merveled how this servant myte mekely suffren there al this wo. And I beheld with avisement to wetyn if I cowth perceyve in hym any defaute, or if the lord shuld assigne in hym any blame, and sothly ther was none seen; for only his good will and his grete desire was cause of his fallyng. And he was as onlothful and as good inwardly as whan he stode afor his lord redy to don his wille. And ryth thus continualy his lovand lord ful tenderly beholdyth him; and now with a double cher; on outward, ful mekely and myldely, with grete ruth and pety, and this was of the first; another inward, more gostly, and this was shewid with a ledyng of my understondyng into the lord, which I saw hym heyly enjoyen, for the worshipful resting and nobleth that he will and shall bryng his servant to be his plentevous grace, and this was of that other shewyng; and now my understondyng led agen into the first, both kepand in mynd.

Than seith this curtes lord in his menyng: 'Lo, lo, my lovid servant!³ What harme and disese he hath takeyn in my service for my love, ya, and for his good will! Is it not skyl that I award hym his afray

ᵃ that] P; the S.

and his drede, his hurt and his mai[m]e*ᵇ* and al his wo? And not only this, but fallith it not to me to gevyn a geft that be better to hym and more worshipfull than his own hole shuld have ben? And ell me thynkyth I dede hym no grace.' And in this an inward gostly shewing of the lords menyng descendid into my soule, in which I saw that it behovith neds to ben, stondyng his grete and his own worship, that his dereworthy servant which he lovid so mech shuld ben verily and blisfully rewardid without end, aboven that he shuld a ben if he had not fallen. Ya, and so ferforth that his fallyng and his wo that he hath taken therby shall be turnyd into hey and overpassing worship and endles bliss.

And at this poynte the shewing of the example vanishid, and our good Lord led forth myn understondyng in syte and in shewing of the revelation to the end. But notwithstondyng al this forthledyng, the mervelyng of the example cam never from me; for methowth it was goven me for an answere to my desir, and yet cowth I not taken therin ful understondyng to myn ese at that tyme. For in the servant that was shewid for Adam,⁴ as I shal seyn, I saw many dyvers properties that myten be no manner way ben aret to single Adam. And thus in that tyme I stode mekyl in onknowyng, for the full understondyng of this mervelous example was not goven me in that tyme; in which mystye example iii propertes of the revelation be yet mekyl hidde, and notwithstondyng this I saw and understode that every shewing is full of privities, and therfore me behovith now to tellen iii propertes in which I am sumdele esyd. The frest is the begynnyng of techyng that I understod therein in the same tyme; the ii is the inward lernyng that I have understodyn therein sithen; the iii al the hole revelation from the begynnyng to the end, that is to sey, of this boke, which our Lord God of his goodnes bryngyth oftentymes frely to the syte of myn understondyng. And these iii arn so onyd, as to my understondyng, that I cannot, ner may, depart them. And be these iii as on I have techyng wherby I owe to leyvyn and trostyn in our Lord God, that of the same godenes that he shewed it, and for the same end, ryth so of the same goodnes and for the same end he shal declaryn it to us whan it is his wille.

For xx yeres after the tyme of the shewing, save iii monethis, I had techyng inwardly, as I shal seyen: 'It longyth to the to taken hede to all the propertes and condition that weryn shewid in the example, thow

---

ᵇ maime] P; maine S.

thou thynke that they ben mysty and indifferent to thy syte.' I assend wilfully with grete desire, [seeing]^c inwardly with avisement al the poynts and propertes that wer shewid in the same tyme, as ferforth as my witt and understondyng wold servyn; begynning myn beholdyng at the lord and at the servant, and the manner of sytting of the lord, and the place that he sate on, and tho color of his clothyng and the manner of shapp, and his cher withouten, and his nobleth and his godeness within; at the manner of stondyng of the servant and the place wher and how, at his manner of clothyng, the color and the shappe, at his outward havyng and at his inward goodnes and his onlothfulhede.

The lord that sate solemnly in rest and in peace, I understond that he is God. The servant that stode aforn the lord, I understode that it was shewid for Adam, that is to seyen: on man was shewid that tyme, and his fallyng, to maken that ther[by]^d understonden how God beholdith a[l]^e man and his fallyng. For in the syte of God al man is on man and on man is all man. This man was hurte in hys myte and made ful febil; and he was stonyed in his understondyng, for he turnyd from the beholdyng of his lord. But his will was kept hole in God sygte; for his will I saw our Lord commenden and approven, but hymselfe was lettid and blindhed of the knowing of this will, and this is to him grete sorow and grevous disese; for neither he seith clerly his lovyng lord, which is to him ful meke and mylde, ne he seith trewly what himself is in the sygte of his lovyng lord. And wel I wote, when these ii are wysely and treuly seyn, we shall gettyn rest and peas her in parte, and the fulhede of the bliss of hevyn, be his plentivous grace. And this was a begynnyng of techyng which I saw in the same tyme, wherby I myte com to k[n]owyng^f in what manner he beholdyth us in our synne. And than I saw that only paynys blamith and punishith, and our curtis Lord comfortith and sorowith, and ever he is to the soule in glad cher, lovand and longand to brynen us to bliss.

The place that our Lord sat on was symple, on the erth barren and desert, alone in wildernes. His clothyng was wide and syde, and ful semely as fallyth to a lord. The color of his cloth was blew as asure, most sad and fair. His cher was merciful, the color of his face was faire browne with ful s[e]mely^g featours; his eyen were blak, most faire and semely, shewand ful of lovely pety; and within him an hey ward, longe and brode, all full of endles hevyns. And the lovely lokeing that he

^{c} seeing] P; and S. ^{d} therby] P; ther S. ^{e} al] P; a S. ^{f} knowyng] P; kowyng S.
^{g} semely] P; somely S.

loked upon his servant continuly, and namely in his fallyng, methowte it myte molten our herts for love and bresten hem on to for joy. The fair lokyng shewid of a semely medlur which was mervelous to beholden: that on was ruth and pety, that other was joye and bliss. The joy and bliss passith as fer reuth and pite as hevyn is aboven erth. The pite was erthly and the blis was hevenly. The ruth in the pite of [the]*ᵇ* Fadir was of the falling of Adam, which is his most lovid creatur: the joy and the bliss was of his dereworthy Son, which is evyn with the Fadir. The merciful beholdyng of his lofly cher fulfilled al erth and descendid downe with Adam into helle, with which continuant pite Adam was kept from endles deth. And this mercy and pite dwellyth with mankind into the tyme we com up into hevyn. But man is blindid in this life, and therfore we may not sen our Fader, God, as he is. And what tyme that he of his goodnes will shewin hym to man, he shewith him homley as man; notwithstonding I ne saw sothly, we owen to knowen and levyn that the Fader is not man.

But his sitting on the erth barreyn and desert is this to menyn: he made mans soule to ben his owen cyte and his dwellyng place, which is most plesyng to hym of al his werks. And what tyme that man was fallen into sorow and peyne he was not al semly to servyn of that noble office; and therfore our kind Fader wold adyten him no other place but sitten upon the erth abeydand mankynd, which is medlid with erth,ˢ till what time be his grace his derworthy Son had bowte ageyn his cyte into the noble fayrhede with his herd travel. The blewhede of the clothing betokinith his stedfastnes. The brownhede of his fair face with the semely blakhede of the eyen was most accordyng to shew his holy sobirnes. The larghede of his clothyng, which were fair, flamand abowten, betokenith that he hath beclesid in hym a[ll]ⁱ hevyns and al joy and blis. And this was shewid in a touch wher I sey: 'Myn understondyng was led into the lord', in which I saw him heyly enjoyen for the worshipful restoring that he wil and shal bring his servant to be his plenteous grace.

And yet I mervellyd, beholdyng the lord and the servant afornseid. I saw the lord sitten solemnly, and the servant stondand reverently aforn his lord, in which servant is double understondyng: on withouten, another within. Outward, he was clad simply, as a labourer which wer disposid to travel, and he stode ful nere the lord, not even

ᵇ the] P; S *om.*   ⁱ all] P; a S.

fornempts hym, but in partie asyd, that on the lift. His clothyng was a
white kirtle, sengil, old and al defacid, died with swete of his body,
streyte fittyng to hym and short, as it were an handful benethe the knee,
bar, semand as it shuld sone be weryd up, redy to be raggid and rent.
And in this I mervelid gretly, thynkand: 'This is now an onsemely
clothyng for the servant that is so heyly lovid to stondyn afor so
worship lord.' And inward, in him was shewid a ground of love, which
love he had to the lord was even like to the love that the lord had to
hym. The wisdam of the servant saw inwardly that ther was on thing to
don which shuld be to the worshipp of the lord. And the servant for
love, haveing no reward to hymselfe ne to nothing that might fallen on
him, hastely he stirt and ran at the sendyng of his lord to don that thing
which was his will and his worship. For it semyd be his outward
clothyng as he had ben a continuant labourer of leng tyme; and be the
inward syte that I had, both in the lord and in the servant, it semyd that
he was anew, tha[t]^j is to sey, new begynnyng to travellyn, which
servant was never sent out aforn.

　　Ther was a tresor in the erth^6 which the lord lovid. I mervelid and
thowte what it myte ben. And I was answered in myn understondyng:
'It is a mete which is lovesome and plesant to the lord.' For I saw the
lord sitten as a man, and I saw neither mete ner drynke wherwith to
servyn hym. This was on mervel; another mervel was that this solemn
lord had no servant but on, and hym he sent owte. I beheld, thynkyng
what manner labour it myte ben that the servant shud don. And than I
understode that he shuld don the gretest labor and herdest travel that is
– he shuld ben a gardiner; delvyn and dykyn, swinkin and swetyn, and
turne the earth upsodowne, and sekyn the depnes, and wattir the plants
in tyme. And in this he shuld continu his travel and make swete flods to
rennen, and noble and plenteous fruits to springen, which he shuld
bryng aforn the lord and servyn hym therwith to his lykyng. And he
shuld never turne agen till he had dygte this mete al redye as he knew
that it lekyd the lord, and than he shuld take this mete, with the drinke
in the mete, and beryn it ful worshipfully aforn the lord. And in al this
tyme the lord shuld sytten on the same place abydand his servant
whome he sent out.

　　And yet I merveylid from whens the servant came; for I saw in the
lord that he hath wythyn hymselfe endles lif and al manner of goodnes,

^{j} that] P; tha S.

save that tresor that was in the erth – and that was groun[dy]d^k in the lord in mervelous depenes of endles love – but it was not all to the worship till this servant had dygte thus nobly it, and browte it aforn him, in hymself present. And without the lord was nothing but wildernes. And I understod not all what this example ment, and therfore I merveylid whens the servant cam. In the servant is comprehendid the second person in the Trinite; and in the servant is comprehendid Adam, that is to sey, al man. And therfore whan I say 'the Son', it menyth the Godhede which is even with the Fadir, and whan I sey 'the servant', it menyth Christs manhood which is rythful Adam.^{7} Be the nerehede of the servant is understode the Son, and be the stondyng on the left syde is understod Adam. The lord is the Fadir, God. The servant is the Son, Christ Jesus. The Holy Gost is even love which is in them both.

Whan Adam fell, God Son fell; for the rythfull onyng which was made in hevyn, God Son myte not fro Adam, for by Adam I understond all man. Adam fell fro lif to deth, into the slade of this wretchid world, and after that into hell. Gods son fell with Adam into the slade of the mayden wombe, which was the fairest dawter of Adam, and therfor to excuse Adam from blame in hevyn and in erth; and mytyly he fetchid him out of hell. Be the wisdam and goodnes that was in the servant is understode Godds Son. Be the por clothyng as a laborer standand nere the left syde is unde[r]stode^l the manhood and Adam, with al the mischef and febilnes tha[t]^m folowith. For in al this our good Lord shewid his owne Son and Adam but one man. The vertu and the goodnes that we have is of Jesus Criste, the febilnes and the blindnes that we have is of Adam; which ii wer shewid in the servant. And thus hath our good Lo[r]d^n Jesus taken upon him al our blame; and therfore our Fadir may, ne will, no more blame assigne to us than to his owen Son, derworthy Criste. Thus was he the servant aforne his comeing into [the]^o erth, stondand redy aforne the Fader in purpos till what tyme he would send hym to don that worshipfull dede be which mankynde was browte ageyn into hevyn; that is to seyn, notwithstondyng that he is God, evyn with the Fadir as anempts the Godhede, but in his forseeing purpose that he wold be man to saven man in fulfilling of his Faders will, so he stode afore his Fader as a servant, wilfully takyng upon hym al our charge. And than he stirt full redily at the Faders will,

^{k} groundyd] P; grounld S. ^{l} understode] P; vndestode S. ^{m} that] P; tha S.
^{n} Lord] P; Lod S. ^{o} the] P; S *om.*

and anon he fell full low in the maydens womb, haveing no reward to himselfe ne to his herd peyns. The whi[t]^p kirtle is the flesh; the syngulhede is that there was ryte no[ght]^q atwix the Godhod and manhede; the steytehede is povertye; the eld is of Adams waring; the defaceing of swete, of Adams travel; the shorthede shewith the servant labour.

And thus I saw the Son stonding, sayeing in his menyng: 'Lo, my der Fader, I stond befor the in Adams kirtle, al redy to sterten and to rennen. I wold ben in the erth to don thy worship whan it is thy will to send me. How long shal I desiren?' Ful sothfastly wist the Son whan it was the Fader will, and how long he shal desiren; that is to sey, anempt the Godhede, for he is the wisdam of the Fader. Wherfor this mening was shewid in understondyng of the manhode of Criste; for all mankynd that shal be savid be the swete incarnation and blisful passion of Criste, al is the manhood of Criste. For he is the hede and we be his members; to which members the day and the tyme is onknown whan every passand wo and sorow shal have an end, and the everlestyng joy and bliss sha[ll]^r be fulfyled; which day and time for to se al the company of hevyn longyth. And al that shall ben under hevyn that shal come thider, ther wey is be longyng and desire; which desir and longing was shewid in the servant stondyng aforen the lord, or ell thus, in the Sons stondyng aforn the Fadir in Adams kirtle. For the langor and desire of al mankynd that shal be savid aperid in Jesus. For Jesus is al that shal be savid and al that shal be savid is Jesus; and al of the charite of God, with obediens, mekeness and patience, and vertues that longyn to us.[8]

Also in this mervelous example I have techyng with me, as it were the begynnyng of an ABC, wherby I may have sum understondyng of our Lo[r]dis^s menyng; for the privities of the revelation ben hidd therin, notwithstondyng that al the shewing arn ful of privityes. The syttyng of the Fadir betokynyth his Godhede, that is to sey, for shewyng of rest and peas; for in the Godhede may be no travel. And that he shewid hymselfe as lord betokynith to our manhode. The stondyng of the servant betokynyth travel; on syde and on the left betokynyth that he was not al worthy to stonden ever ryth aforn the lord. His stertyng was the Godhede, and the rennyng was the manhede; for the Godhede sterte from the Fadir into the maydens wombe, falling into the taking

---

^{p} whit] P; which S. ^{q} noght] P; now S. ^{r} shall] P; sha S. ^{s} Lordis] P; Lodis S.

of our kynde; and in this falling he toke gret sore. The sore that he toke
was our flesh in which he had also swithe felyng of dedly peynis. Be that
he stod dredfully aforn the lord, and not even ryth, betokynith that his
clothyng was not honest to stond in eve[n]^t ryth aforn the lord: ne that
myte not, ne shuld not, ben his office whil he was a laborer; ne also he
myte not sitten in rest and peace with the lord till he had woon his
peace rythfully with his herd travel; and be the left syde, that the Fadir
left his owne Son wilfully in the manhode to suffre all mannys paynys
without sparing of him. Be that his kirtle was in poynte to be raggid
and rent is understonden the sweppys and the scorgis, the thornys and
the naylys, the drawyng and the draggyng, his tender flesh rendyng; as I
saw in sum partie, the flesh was rent from the hedepanne, falland in
pe[cy]s^u into the tyme the bledyng failyd; and than it began to dryand
agen, clyngand to the bone. And be the wallowyng and wrythyng,
gronyng and monyng, is understonden that he myte never rysen al
mytyly from the tyme that he was fallen into the maydens wombe till
his body was slaine and ded, he yeldyng the soule in the Fadirs hands
with al mankynd for whom he was sent.

And at this poynte he began first to shewen his myte; for he went
into helle, and whan he was there he reysid up the grit rote out of the
depe depenes which rythfully was knit to hym in hey hevyn. The body
was in the grave till Estern morow, and from that tyme he lay never
more; for then was rythfully endid the walowyng and the wrythyng,
the groning and the monyng. And our foule dedly flesh that Gods Son
toke on hym – which was Adams old kirtle, steyte, bare and short –
than be our savior was made fair now, white and bryte and of endles
cleness, wyde and syde, fairer and richer than was than the clothyng
which I saw on the Fadir. For that clothyng was blew, and Christs
clothyng is now of a fair, semely medlur which is so mervelous that I
can it not discrien – for it is al of very worshipps.

Now sittith not the lord on erth in wilderness, but he sittith in his
noblest sete, which he made in hevyn most to his lekyng. Now stondith
not the Son aforn the Fadir as a servant aforn the lord dredfully,
unornely clad, in party nakid, but he stondith aforn the Fadir ever
rythe, rechely clad in blissfull largess, with a corone upon his hede of
pretious richess. For it was shewid that we be his corone, which corone
is the Fadirs joye, tho Sonys worshippe, the Holy Gost lekyng, and

^{t} even] P; eve S. ^{u} pecys] P; pets S.

endless mervelous bliss to all that be in hevyn. Now stondith not the
Son aforn the Fadir on the left syde as a laborer, but he sittith on his
Fadirs ryte hond in endles rest and peace. But it is not ment that the Son
syttith on the ryte hond, syde be syde, as on man sittith be another in
this lif, for ther is no such syttyng, as to my syte, in the Trinite; but he
sittith on his Fadirs ryte hand, that is to sey, in the heyest noblyth of the
Fadirs joyes. Now is the spouse, Gods Son, in peace with his lowid
wife, which is the fair mayden of endles joye. Now sittith the Son, very
God and man, in his cety in rest and peace, which his Fadir hath adyte
to him of his endles purpose; and the Fadir in the Son, and tho Holy
Gost in the Fadir and in the Son. . . .

*How we be bowte ageyn and forthspred be mercy and grace of
our swete, kynde and ever lovyng moder Jesus, and of the
propertes of moderhede; but Jesus is our very moder, not
fedyng us with mylke but with himselfe, opening his syde onto
us and chalengyng al our love – lx chapter.*

But now behovyth to sey a litil mor of this forthspredyng,[9] as I
understond in the menyng of our Lord: how that we be bowte agen be
the moderhede of mercy and grace into our kyndly stede wher that we
were made be the moderhede of kynd love; which kynd love it never
levyth us. Our kynd moder, our gracious moder, for he wold al holy
become our moder in althyng, he toke the ground of his werke full low
and ful myldely in the maydens womb. And that he shewid in the first,[10]
where he browte that meke mayde aforn the eye of myn understondyng
in the simple statur as she was whan she conceivid; that is to sey, our
hey God is sovereyn wisdom of all, in this low place he raysid him and
dyte him ful redy in our pore flesh, himselfe to don the service and the
office of moderhede in allthyng. The moders service is nerest, redyest,
and sekirest, for it is most of trueth. This office ne myte, ne couthe, ne
never non don to the full [but][v] he alone. We wetyn that all our moders
beryng is us to peyne and to deyeng; and what is that but our very
moder Jesus, he, al love, beryth us to joye and to endles lyving – blissid
mot he be! Thus he susteynith us within himselfe in love, and traveled
into the full tyme that he wold suffre the sharpist throwes and the
grevousest peynes that ever were or ever shall be, and dyed at the last.

v but] P; s om.

And when he had don, and so born us to bliss, yet myte not al this makyn aseth to his mervelous love; and that shewid he in these hey overpassing wordes of love: 'If I myte suffre more, I wold suffre more.'[11] He myte no more dyen, but he wold not stynten of werkyng. Wherfore than him behovyth to fedyn us, for the dereworthy love of moderhede hath made him dettor to us. The moder may geven hir child soken her mylke, but our pretious moder Jesus, he may fedyn us with himselfe; and doith full curtesly and full tenderly with the blissid sacrament, that is pretious fode of very lif. And with al the swete sacraments he susteynith us ful mercifully and graciously. And so ment he in this blissid word wher that he seid 'I it am that holy church prechith the and techith the.'[12] That is to sey: 'All the helth and lif of sacraments, al the vertue and grace of my word, all the godness that is ordeynid in holy church for the, I it am.' The moder may leyn the child tenderly to hir brest, but our tender moder Jesus, he may homley leden us into his blissid brest be his swete open syde, and shewyn therin party of the Godhede and the joyes of hevyn, with gostly sekirnes of endless bliss; and that he shewid in the [x],[w] gevyng the same understondyng in this swete word wher he seith 'Lo, how I lovid the', beholdand into his syde, enjoyand.[13] This fair lovely word 'moder', it is so swete and so kynd of the self that it may ne verily be seid of none but of him, and to hir that is very moder of hym and of all. To the properte of moderhede longyth kinde love, wisdam and knowing, and it is good; for thow it be so that our bodily forthbrynging be but litil, low and simple in regard of our gostly forthbringing, yet it is he that doth it in the creatures be whom that it is done. The kynde, loveand moder that wote and knowith the nede of hir child, she kepith it ful tenderly, as the kind and condition of moderhede will.[14] And as it wexith in age, she chongith her werking, but not hir love. And whan it is waxen of more age, she suffrid that it be bristinid in brekyng downe of vices, to makyn the child to receivyn vertues and graces. This werkyng, with al that be fair and good, our Lord doith it in hem be whom it is done. Thus he is our moder in kynde be the werkyng of grace in the lower parte, for love of the heyer parte. And he will that we know it; for he will have al our love festynyd to him. And in this I saw that all our dett that we owen, be Gods biddyng, be faderhede and

moderhede, for Gods faderhede and moderhede is fulfillid in trew
lovyng of God;[15] which blissid love Christ werkyth in us. And this
was shewid in all, and namly in the hey plentivous words wher he
seith: 'I it am that thou lovest.'[16]

MARGERY KEMPE
(*c*.1373 – *c*.1440)

18 *The Book of Margery Kempe*

(Chapters 17, 18 with cuts, 35, 36)

Margery Kempe, daughter of John Brunham – who was member of parliament, justice of the peace, and five times mayor of King's Lynn – was married aged twenty to John Kempe, who proved a less successful man than her father. After a vision of Christ during a breakdown following her first childbirth, and after early failures as a businesswoman, Margery Kempe saw further visions and felt herself summoned to a spiritual life. Around the age of forty, when she had borne fourteen children, she persuaded her husband to join her in a mutual vow of chastity and then embarked on an eventful life of pilgrimage in England, Europe and the Holy Land, seeking counsel from both great and humble religious figures of her day (including, at Norwich, the saintly Richard of Caister and Dame Julian). Her devotion characteristically expressed itself in loud weeping and crying out, which repeatedly divided priests, congregations and fellow-pilgrims into friends or detractors, and she was sometimes suspected of heresy despite the evident orthodoxy of her devotion. Margery Kempe could neither read nor write, but towards the end of her life she dictated (twice over, for the first version proved illegible) her recollections of her visions and experience.[1] Conversation – from intimate confabulations with God, or with the spiritually minded, to sharp exchanges with her critics – is what structures Margery's recollections and hence her *Book*, which nevertheless shows the imprint of the mystical literature that she has heard read. From such books Margery retains something of the symbolism and figurative language of the spiritual life which she then uses on her own terms, as in her vividly direct understanding of the nuptial imagery of her marriage to the Godhead, her apprehension of the Holy Ghost, or the white flurry of angels that she knows encompass her about.

The books mentioned in chapter 17 below – Hilton's work, Rolle's *Incendium*, the *Stimulus Amoris* and the *Revelations* of St Bridget of Sweden –

give some indication of how what Margery heard read nourished her experience of contemplation. In chapter 58 she specifies the same four works, among unnamed others, when recalling how a young priest 'red to hir many a good boke of hy contemplacyon', in addition to the 'Bybyl wyth doctowrys þer-upon'. In chapter 62 both an English version of the *Stimulus* ('Þe Prykke of Lofe') and Rolle's *Incendium* are cited in defence of Margery's crying, as are a 'boke' on the life of Mary of Oignies and a 'tretys' concerning Elizabeth of Hungary.² In St Bridget's life and writing were influential models for Margery, and from Bridget's *Liber Celestis* Margery could recall Christ's words:

'I haue chosen þe and taken þe to mi spouse, for it pleses me and likes me to do so, and for I will shewe to þe mi preuai secretis. For þou arte mine be a manere of [r]ight, foralsmikill as þou assigned thi will into mi handes at þe time of diinge of þi husband, eftir whose bereinge þou had grete þoght and made praiere how þou might be pore for me: and þou had in will and desire to forsake all þinge for me. And þan when þou had bi right made þe þus mine, it langed to me to puruai and ordeine for þe; wharefore I take þe to me as mi spouse vnto mi awen propir delite, eftir it is acordinge and seminge þat God haue his delite with a chaste saule. As þou knawes, it langes to a spouse to be honestli and semingli araied and to be redi when þe husband will make þe weddinge. . . .'³

In chapter 20, after Margery sees a vision during mass, God tells her 'My dowtyr, Bryde, say me neuyr in þis wyse', and furthermore both endorses St Bridget's book and declares it will be validated by Margery's experience ('rygth as I spak to Seynt Bryde ryte so I speke to þe, dowtyr, & I telle þe trewly it is trewe euery word þat is wretyn in Brides boke, & be þe it xal be knowyn for very trewth').

How much Margery's amanuensis may have contributed remains an open question, but *The Book of Margery Kempe* is a unique testimony, resisting generic classification, and through recollected experience validating the pains and raptures of a woman in the world who feels herself called by God to contemplation.

Sole manuscript: BL MS Add. 61823, fols. 19r–20r, 21r–21v, 42r–44v.

(17) On a day long befor this tyme,⁴ whyl thys creatur⁵ was beryng chylder and sche was newly delyveryd of a chyld, owyr Lord Cryst Jhesu seyd to hir sche schuld no mor chyldren beryn, and therfor he bad hyr gon to Norwych.

And sche seyd, 'A, der Lord, how schal I gon? I am bothe feynt and feble.'

'Drede the not, I schal make the strong inow. I byd the gon to the vykary of Seynt Stefenys,[6] and sey that I gret hym wel and that he is an hey chossyn sowle of myn. And telle hym he plesyth me mech wyth hys prechyng, and schew hym thy prevytes and myn cownselys swech as I schewe the.'

Than sche toke hyr wey to-Norwych-ward and cam into hys cherch on a Thursday a lytyl befor noon. And the vykary went up and down wyth another prest whech was hys gostly fadyr, that levyd whan this boke was mad. And this creatur was clad in blak clothyng that tyme. Sche salutyd the vykary, preyng hym that sche mygth speke wyth hym an owyr or ellys tweyn owyrs at aftyrnone whan he had etyn, in the lofe of God. He, lyftyng up hys handys and blyssyng hym, seyd, 'Benedicite! What cowd a woman ocupyn an owyr er tweyn owyrs in the lofe of owyr Lord? I schal nevyr ete mete tyl I wete what ye kan sey of owyr Lord God the tyme of on owyr.'

Than he sett hym down in the chirche. Sche, syttyng a lytyl besyde, schewyd hym all the wordys whech God had revelyd to hyr in hyr sowle. Sythen sche schewyd hym al hyr maner of levyng fro hyr chyldhod, as ny as it wolde come to hir mende – how unkynd sche had ben ageyn owyr Lord Jhesu Crist; how prowde and veyne sche had ben in hir aport; how obstynat ageyns the lawes of God, and how envyows ageyn hir evyn-Cristen; sythen, whan it plesyd owyr Lord Crist Jhesu, how sche was chastysed wyth many tribulacyons and horrybyl temptacyons; and aftyrward how sche was fed and comfortyd wyth holy medytacyons and specyal in the mende of owyr Lordys passyon. And, whyl sche dalyed in the passyon of owyr Lord Jhesu Crist, sche herd so hedows a melodye that sche mygth not ber it. Than this creatur fel down as yf sche had lost hir bodyly strength and lay stylle a gret whyle, desyryng to put it away, and sche mygth not. Than knew sche wel be hir feyth that ther was gret joye in hevyn, wher the lest poynt of blys wythowtyn any comparyson passeth al the joye that evyr myt be thowt er felt in this lyfe. Sche was gretly strengthyd in hir feyth and mor bold to tellyn the vykary her felyngys whech sche had be revelacyons bothen of qwyk and of ded and of hys owyn self.

Sche teld hym how sumtyme the Fadyr of Hevyn dalyd to hir sowle as pleynly and as veryly as o frend spekyth to another be bodyly spech; sumtyme the Secunde Persone in Trinyte; sumtyme alle thre Personys in Trinyte and o substawns in Godhede dalyid to hir sowle and informyd hir in hir feyth and in hys lofe – how sche schuld lofe hym, worshepyn hym, and dredyn hym – so excellently that sche herd nevyr boke, neythyr Hyltons boke, ne [B]ridis*a* boke, ne *Stimulus Amoris*, ne *Incendium Amoris*,[7] ne non other that evyr sche herd redyn, that spak so hyly of lofe of God but that sche felt as hyly in werkyng in hir sowle, yf sche cowd or ellys mygth a schewyd as sche felt. Sumtyme owyr Lady spak to hir mend. [Sumty]me*b* Seynt Petyr, sumtyme Seynt Powyl, sumtym Seynt Kateryn,[8] er what seynt in hevyn sche had devocyon to, aperyd to hir sowle and tawt hir how sche schuld lovyn owyr Lord and how sche schuld plesyn hym. Her dalyawns was so swet, so holy and so devowt that this creatur myt not oftyntymes beryn it, but fel down and wrestyd wyth hir body, and mad wondyrful cher and contenawns, wyth boystows sobbyngys and gret plente of terys, sumtyme seyng 'Jhesu, mercy,' sumtyme 'I dey.'[9] And therfor mech pepyl slawndryd hir, not levyng it was the werke of God, but that sum evyl spyrit vexid hir in hir body, er ellys that sche had sum bodyly sekenesse.

Notwythstondyng the rumowr and grutchyng of the pepyl ayen hir, this holy man, vykary of Seynt Stefenys Chyrch of Norwych, whom God hath exaltyd and thorw mervelyows werkys schewyd and prevyd for holy, evyr held wyth hir and supportyd hir ayen hir enmys into hys powyr aftyr the tyme that sche be the byddyng of God had schewyd hym hir maner of governawns and levyng, for he trustly belevyd that sche was wel lernyd in the lawe of God and indued wyth grace of the Holy Gost, to whom it longyth to enspyr wher he wyl. And, thow hys voys be herd, it is not wyst of the werld fro when it comyth er whedyr it goth. Thys holy vykary aftyr this tyme was confessowr to this creatur alwey whan sche cam to Norwych and howsyld hir wyth hys owyn handys. And, whan sche was on a tyme moneschyd to aper befor certeyn offycerys of the Byschop to answer to certeyn artyculys whech schuld be put ageyn hir be the steryng of envyows pepyl, the good vykary, preferryng the lofe of God befor any schame of the world, went wyth hir to her hir examynacyon and delyveryd hir fro the malys of hyr enmys. And than was it revelyd to this creatur that the good vykary schuld levyn sevyn yer aftyr[10] and than he sculd passyn hens wyth gret grace, and he dede as sche had . . . of . . . [MS damaged].*c*

(18) . . . And than sche was bodyn be owyr Lord for to gon to an

<hr/>

a Bridis] pridis; brigytts *in margin.*   *b* Sumtyme] Sumty *destroyed in MS.*
c had . . . of] *MS eaten away here.*

ankres in the same cyte whych hyte Dame Jelyan. And so sche dede and schewyd hir the grace that God put in hir sowle of compunccyon, contricyon, swetnesse and devocyon, compassyon wyth holy meditacyon and hy contemplacyon, and ful many holy spechys and dalyawns that owyr Lord spak to hir sowle, and many wondirful revelacyons whech sche schewyd to the ankres to wetyn yf ther wer any deceyte in hem, for the ankres was expert in swech thyngys and good cownsel cowd yevyn. The ankres, heryng the mervelyows goodnes of owyr Lord, hyly thankyd God wyth al hir hert for hys visitacyon, cownselyng this creatur to be obedyent to the wyl of owyr Lord God and fulfyllyn wyth al hir mygthys whatevyr he put in hir sowle yf it wer not ageyn the worshep of God and profyte of hir evyn-Cristen. For, yf it wer, than it wer nowt the mevyng of a good spyryte but rathar of an evyl spirit.

'The Holy Gost mevyth nevyr a thing ageyn charite, and, yf he dede, he wer contraryows to hys owyn self, for he is al charite. Also he mevyth a sowle to al chastnesse, for chast levars be clepyd the temple of the Holy Gost,[11] and the Holy Gost makyth a sowle stabyl and stedfast in the rygth feyth and the rygth beleve. And a dubbyl man in sowle is evyr unstabyl and unstedfast in al hys weys.[12] He that is evyrmor dowtyng is lyke to the flood of the see, the whech is mevyd and born abowte wyth the wynd, and that man is not lyche to receyven the yyftys of God.[13]

'What creatur that hath these tokenys, he m[uste][d] stedfastlych belevyn that the Holy Gost dwellyth in hys sowle. And mech mor, whan God visyteth a creatur wyth terys of contrisyon, devosyon, er compassyon, he may and owyth to levyn that the Holy Gost is in hys sowle. Seynt Powyl seyth that the Holy Gost askyth for us wyth mornynggys and wepyngys unspekable:[14] that is to seyn, he makyth us to askyn and preyn wyth mornynggys and wepyngys so plentyvowsly that the terys may not be nowmeryd. Ther may non evyl spyrit yevyn thes tokenys, for Jerom seyth that terys turmentyn mor the Devylle than don the peynes of helle.[15] God and the Devyl ben evyrmor contraryows, and thei schal nevyr dwellyn togedyr in on place, and the Devyl hath no powyr in a mannys sowle.

'Holy wryt seyth that the sowle of a rytful man is the sete of God,[16] and so I trust, syster, that ye ben. I prey God grawnt yow perseverawns. Settyth al yowr trust in God, and feryth not the langage of the world. For the mor despyte, schame and repref that ye have in

---

[d] muste] uste *destroyed*.

the world, the mor is yowr meryte in the sygth of God.[17] Pacyens is
necessary unto yow, for in that schal ye kepyn yowr sowle.'[18]

Mych was the holy dalyawns that the ankres and this creatur
haddyn be comownyng in the lofe of owyr Lord Jhesu Crist many days
that thei were togedyr. . . .

(35) As this creatur was in the Postelys Cherch at Rome[19] on Seynt
Laterynes Day,[20] the Fadyr of Hevyn seyd to hir, 'Dowtyr, I am wel
plesyd wyth the, in-as-meche as thu belevyst in alle the sacramentys of
holy chirche and in al feyth that longith therto, and specialy for that
thu belevyst in manhode of my sone and for the gret compassyon that
thu hast of hys bittyr passyon.' Also the Fadyr seyd to this creatur,
'Dowtyr, I wil han the weddyd to my Godhede, for I schal schewyn the
my prevyteys and my cownselys, for thu schalt wonyn wyth me
wythowtyn ende.'

Than the creatur kept sylens in hir sowle and answeryd not
therto, for sche was ful sor aferd of the Godhed; and sche cowde no
skylle of the dalyawns of the Godhede, for al hir lofe and al hir
affeccyon was set in the manhode of Crist, and therof cowde sche good
skylle, and sche wolde for nothyng a partyd therfro. Sche was so meche
affectyd to the manhode of Crist that whan sche sey women in Rome
beryn children in her armys, yyf sche myth wetyn that thei wer ony men
children, sche schuld than cryin, roryn and wepyn as thei sche had seyn
Crist in hys childhode. And, yf sche myth an had hir wille, oftyntymes
sche wolde a takyn the childeryn owt of the moderys armys and a
kyssed hem in the stede of Criste. And, yyf sche sey a semly man, sche
had gret peyn to lokyn on hym les than sche myth a seyn hym that was
bothe God and man. And therfor sche cryed many tymes and oftyn
whan sche met a semly man, and wept and sobbyd ful sor in the
manhod of Crist as sche went in the stretys at Rome, that thei that seyn
hir wondryd ful mych on hir, for thei knew not the cawse.

And therfor it was no wondyr yyf sche wer stille and answeryd
not the Fadyr of Hevyn whan he teld hir that sche schuld be weddyd to
hys Godhed. Than seyd the Secunde Persone, Crist Jhesu, whoys
manhode sche lovyd so meche, to hir, 'What seyst thu, Margery,
dowtyr, to my Fadyr of thes wordys that he spekyth to the? Art thu wel
plesyd that it be so?' And than sche wold not answeryn the Secunde
Persone but wept wondir sor, desiryng to have stille hymselfe and in no
wyse to be departyd fro hym. Than the Secunde Persone in Trinite

answeryd to hys Fadyr for hir and seyde, 'Fadyr, have hir excused, for sche is yet but yong and not fully lernyd how sche schulde answeryn.'

And than the Fadyr toke hir be the hand[21] in hir sowle befor the Sone and the Holy Gost, and the Modyr of Jhesu, and alle the xii apostelys, and Seynt Kateryn and Seynt Margarete and many other seyntys and holy virgynes, wyth gret multitude of awngelys, seying to hir sowle, 'I take the, Margery, for my weddyd wyfe, for fayrar, for fowelar, for richar, for powerar, so that thu be buxom and bonyr to do what I byd the do. For, dowtyr, ther was nevyr childe so buxom to the modyr as I schal be to the, bothe in wel and in wo, to help the and comfort the. And therto I make the suyrte.' And than the Modyr of God and alle the seyntys that wer ther present in hir sowle[22] preyde that thei myth have mech joy togedyr.

And than the creatur wyth hy devocyon, wyth gret plente of terys, thankyd God of this gostly comfort, heldyng hirself in hir owyn felyng ryth unworthy to any swech grace as sche felt, for sche felt many gret comfortys, bothe gostly comfortys and bodily comfortys. Sumtyme sche felt swet smellys wyth hir nose; it wer swettar, hir thowt, than evyr was ony swet erdly thyng that sche smellyd beforn, ne sche myth nevyr tellyn how swet it wern, for hir thowt sche myth a levyd therby yyf they wolde a lestyd. Sumtyme sche herd wyth hir bodily erys sweche sowndys and melodiis that sche myth not wel heryn what a man seyd to hir in that tyme les he spoke the lowder. Thes sowndys and melodiis had sche herd ny-hand every day the terme of xxv yere whan this boke was wretyn, and specialy whan sche was in devowt prayer, also many tymes whil sche was at Rome and in Inglond bothe.

Sche sey wyth hir bodily eyne many white thyngys flying al abowte hir on every syde as thykke in a maner as motys in the sunne; it weryn ryth sotyl and comfortabyl, and the brygtare that the sunne schyned, the bettyr sche myth se hem. Sche sey hem many dyvers tymes and in many dyvers placys, bothe in chirche and in hir chawmbre, at hir mete and in hir praerys, in felde and in towne, bothyn goyng and syttyng. And many tymes sche was aferde what thei myth be, for sche sey hem as wel on nytys in dyrkenes as on day-lygth. Than, whan sche was aferde of hem, owir Lord seyd onto hir, 'Be this tokyn, dowtyr, beleve it is God that spekyth in the, for wherso God is hevyn is, and wher that God is ther be many awngelys, and God is in the and thu art in hym. And therfor be not aferde, dowtyr, for thes betokyn that thu hast many awngelys abowte the, to kepyn the bothe day and nygth that

no devyl schal han power ovyr the, ne non evyl man to der the.'[23] Than
fro that tyme forwarde sche usyd to seyn whan sche saw hem comyn,
'*Benedictus qui venit in nomine Domini.*'[24]

Also owr Lord yaf hir another tokne, the whech enduryd
abowtyn xvi yer and it encresyd evyr mor and mor, and that was a
flawme of fyer[25] wondir hoot and delectabyl and ryth comfortabyl,
nowt wastyng but evyr incresyng, of lowe, for, thow the wedyr wer
nevyr so colde, sche felt the hete brennyng in hir brest and at hir hert, as
verily as a man schuld felyn the material fyer yyf he put hys hand or hys
fynger therin. Whan sche felt[26] fyrst the fyer of love brennyng in her
brest, sche was aferd therof, and than owr Lord answeryd to hir mend
and seyde, 'Dowtyr, be not aferd, for this hete is the hete of the Holy
Gost, the whech schal bren awey alle thi synnes, for the fyer of lofe
qwenchith alle synnes. And thu schalt undirstondyn be this tokyn the
Holy Gost is in the, and thu wost wel wher-that-evyr the Holy Gost is
ther is the Fadir, and wher the Fadyr is ther is the Sone, and so thu hast
fully in thi sowle al the Holy Trinite. Therfor thow hast gret cawse to
lovyn me ryth wel, and yet thu schalt han grettar cawse than evyr thu
haddyst to lovyn me, for thu schalt heryn that thu nevyr herdist, and
thu schalt se that thu nevyr sey, and thu schalt felyn that thu nevyr feltist.

'For, dowtyr, thu art as sekyr of the lofe of God as God is God.
Thy sowle is mor sekyr of the lofe of God than of thin owyn body, for
thi sowle schal partyn fro thy body, but God schal nevyr partyn fro thi
sowle, for thei ben onyd togedyr wythowtyn ende. Therfor, dowtyr,
thu hast as gret cawse to be mery as any lady in this werld. And yyf thu
knew, dowtyr, how meche thu plesyst me whan thu suffyrst me wilfully
to spekyn in the, thu schuldist nevyr do otherwyse, for this is an holy
lyfe and the tyme is ryth wel spent. For, dowtyr, this lyfe plesyth me
mor than weryng of the haburion or of the hayr, or fastyng of bred and
watyr. For yyf thu seydest every day a thowsand Pater Noster, thu
schuldist not plesyn me so wel as thu dost whan thu art in silens and
sufferyst me to speke in thy sowle.'

(36) 'Fastyng, dowtyr, is good for yong begynnars and discrete
penawns, namly that her gostly fadyr yevyth hem er injoyneth hem for
to do. And for to byddyn many bedys it is good to hem that can no
bettyr do, and yet it is not parfyte. But it is a good wey to-
perfeccyon-ward. For I telle the, dowtyr, thei that arn gret fastarys and
gret doers of penawnce, thei wold that it schuld ben holdyn the best

lyfe; also thei that yevyn hem to sey many devocyons, thei wold han
that the best lyfe; and thei that yevyn mech almes, thei wold that that
wer holdyn the best lyfe. And I have oftyn-tymes, dowtyr, teld the that
thynkyng, wepyng, and hy contemplacyon is the best lyfe in erthe. And
thu schalt have mor meryte in hevyn for o yer of thynkyng in thi mende
than for an hundryd yer of preyng wyth thi mowth; and yet thu wylt
not levyn me, for thu wilt byddyn many bedys whedyr I wil or not. And
yet, dowtyr, I wyl not be displesyd wyth the, whedir thu thynke, sey, or
speke, for I am alwey plesyd wyth the. And yyf I wer in erde as bodily as
I was er I deyd on the cros, I schuld not ben aschamyd of the, as many
other men ben, for I schuld take the be the hand amongs the pepil and
make the gret cher, that thei schuldyn wel knowyn that I lovyd the ryth
wel.

'For it is convenyent the wyf to be homly wyth hir husbond. Be he
nevyr so gret a lorde and sche so powr a woman whan he weddyth hir,
yet thei must ly togedir and rest togedir in joy and pes. Ryght so mot it
be twyx the and me, for I take non hed what thu hast be but what thu
woldist be. And oftyn-tymes have I telde the that I have clene foryove
the alle thy synnes. Therfore most I nedys be homly wyth the and lyn in
thi bed wyth the. Dowtyr, thow desyrest gretly to se me, and thu mayst
boldly, whan thu art in thi bed, take me to the as for thi weddyd
husbond, as thy derworthy derlyng, and as for thy swete sone, for I wyl
be lovyd as a sone schuld be lovyd wyth the modyr, and wil that thu
love me, dowtyr, as a good wife owyth to love hir husbonde. And
therfor thu mayst boldly take me in the armys of thi sowle and kyssen
my mowth, myn hed and my fete as swetly as thow wylt. And, as
oftyn-tymes as thu thynkyst on me er woldyst don any good dede to
me, thu schalt have the same mede in hevyn as yyf thu dedist it to myn
owyn precyows body whech is in hevyn. For I aske no mor of the but
thin hert for to lovyn me that lovyth the, for my lofe is evyr redy to the.'
Than sche yaf thankyng and preysing to owr Lord Jhesu Crist for the
hy grace and mercy that he schewyd unto hir, unworthy wrech.

Thys creatur had divers tokenys in hir bodily heryng. On was a
maner of sownde as it had ben a peyr of belwys blowyng in hir ere.
Sche, beyng abasshed therof, was warnyd in hir sowle no fer to have,
for it was the sownd of the Holy Gost. And than owr Lord turnyd that
sownde into the voys of a dowe, and sithyn he turnyd it into the voys of
a lityl bryd whech is callyd a reedbrest, that song ful merily oftyn-tymes
in hir ryght ere. And than schuld sche evyrmor han gret grace aftyr that

sche herd swech a tokyn. And sche had been used to swech tokenys abowt xxv yer at the writyng of this boke. Than seyd owr Lord Jhesu Crist to hys creatur, 'Be thes tokenys mayst thu wel wetyn that I love the, for thu art to me a very modir and to al the world, for that gret charite that is in the; and yet I am cawse of that charite myself, and thu schalt have gret mede therfor in hevyn.'

ANONYMOUS ENGLISH TRANSLATORS

19 *The Mirrour of Simple Soules*

(English translator's commentary; chapters 1, 3, 4, 8, 9, 13; selections)

Le mirouer des simples ames was condemned and burned as heretical; its author Marguerite Porete was later burned as a heretic at Paris in 1310. The translator's prologue to the anonymous, late fourteenth-century English version describes it as his second attempt, because in his first 'I am enfourmed that some wordis therof have be mystake', and he interpolates into his very literal rendering a series of glosses written in a lively English and signalled by his initials: 'M.', the first letter of his first name, at the beginning, and 'N.', the first letter of his surname, at the end of each gloss.[1] Evidently unaware of the French text's affiliations with the heretical 'Movement of the Free Spirit', M. N. is always concerned to set aside misleading and literal understandings, drawing out reservations and exceptions which he sees as implicit in the text, and so pursuing a benign and spiritually fruitful interpretation for his English audience, even when confronted – in the exchanges between Lady Love, Reason and the soul – with some of the original's more startling assertions. These include: the soul may take leave of virtues; scripture, knowledge, intellect alike become unnecessary; the soul desires neither masses, sermons nor prayers, and gives to nature all that nature asks; the soul's name is 'Oblivion'; the soul has enough faith without works; all that men say of God is lying and deceptive; a soul in the true freedom of pure love does nothing against that which her inward peace requires; the soul on earth can have a constant perception and experience of the divine nature; the free soul does not pray.

Some of the passages glossed by M. N. – as in the first gloss below – are made more difficult by corruptions in the French text, as the English translator's prologue warns ('The Frensche booke þat I schal write aftir is yuel writen and in summe places for defaute of wordis and silables þe reson is aweie,' ed. Doiron, p. 249). He nonetheless prays to be able to assist 'goostli

237

louers, þat ben disposed and clepid to þis hiȝe eleccion of þe fredom of soule'
(p. 247). Dry and unsavoury are the 'spekinges and writynges of þese hiȝe
goostli felynges of þe loue of God to hem þat haue not taasted þe swetnesse
þerof', and the translator warns that 'loue in þis boke leieþ to soules þe
touches of his diuine werkis priueli hid vndir derk speche' (p. 248). But when
touched with grace ('bi whiche sche haþ taasted sumwhat of þe swetnesse of
þis diuine fruycion, and bigynneþ to wade and draweþ þe drauȝtes to-hir-ward'),
the soul is glad 'to heere and to rede of al þing þat perteyneþ to þese hiȝe
felinges of þe werkinges of diuine loue' in increasing her love and devotion:
'Þus sche entriþ and walkiþ in þe wey of illuminacion, þat sche myȝte be cauȝt
into þe goostli influences of þe diuine werk of God, þere to be drenchid in þe
hiȝe floode, and vnyed to God bi rauyschinge of loue bi whiche sche is al oon,
oon spirite wiþ hir spouse' (p. 248).

Base manuscript: St John's College, Cambridge, MS 71, fols. 4r–5r, 7r–8v, 10r–12v, 13r–13v,
15r–15v, 28v–29r, 32r–32v, 53r–54v, 62r–62v, 78r. No variants.

(1)   ... 'Sotheli,' seith this soule that this boke lete write, 'this I seie for
me: so fare I. I heere speke of a kyng of greet myght that for curtesie and
greet largesse is a noble Alisaundre. But so fer is he fro me and I fro him,'
seith this soule, 'that I kan not take comfort of mysilf. And to clepe me he
yave me this boke,[2] the whiche presenteth summe usages of the love of
himsilf. But notforthanne I dwelle not in fredom of pees, though I have
his ymage; but I am in a straunge lond fer fro the pees,[3] where that these
noble lovyers of this lord dwelle that ben al endid and pure, and bi the
yiftes of this lord maad fre, with whom thei dwelle. Heere I schal seie
you hou "not we lordis fre of al, but love of him for us." '[4]
    M. Yee auditoures of this boke, taketh kepe of these wordis that
seith: 'not we lordis fre of al'. For whiles we ben in this world we may
not be fre of al. This is to seie, to be departid contynuelli from alle
spottes of synne. But whanne a soule is drawe into hirsilf from al
outward thing, so that love werkith in the soule – bi whiche the soule is
for a tyme departid fro al synne and is unyed to God bi unyoun –
thanne is the soule fre. As for that tyme of unyoun, ful litel tyme it is.
And whanne sche cometh doun therfro, thanne is sche thralle, fallynge
or fadinge. To this acordeth hooli writ, where that it seith: *Septies in
die cadit iustus.*[5] But this fallinge of the rightwise is more merit than
synne, bicause of the goode wille that stondith unbroken, and is unyed
to God. A creature may be enhabited bi grace in fredom forevere; but
to stonde contynuelli in fredom withoute synne, it may not, for the
unstabilte of the sensualite that is alwei flittinge. And therfore it is

arettid the fallynge to the sensualite, and not to the hooli soules that
parfiitli have sett her wille in God, bi whiche love maketh hem fre for
the noblei of his werk. Therfore it may wel be seid: 'not we lordis fre of
al, but love of him for us'. N. . . . (fols. 4r–5r).

(3) . . . 'I assente, Lady Love,' seith this soule. . . . 'Therfore I seie:
Vertues, I take leeve of you for evermore. . . . O, I was thanne youre
servaunt, but now I am delivered out of youre thraldom.' . . .

M. Touchynge these wordis that this soule seith: sche taketh
leeve of vertues, Love declareth. But yitt I am stired heere to seie more
to the matere as thus: first whanne a soule yiveth hir to perfeccion sche
laboreth bisili day and nyght to gete vertues bi counsel of reson, and
stryveth with vices at every thought, at every word and dede that sche
perceyveth cometh of hem, and bisili enserchith vices, hem to distrie.
Thus the vertues ben mastresses, and every vertu maketh hir to werre
with hir contrarie, the whiche ben vices. Many scharpe peynes and
bittirnesse of conscience felith the soule in this werre. And these paynes
and passions ben not oonli in excercise of the spirite, bi puttinge awei
vices in getynge of vertues, but thei ben also of bodili excercise bi
comaundementis of vertues and bi counseil of reson: to faste and wake,
and to do penaunce in many sundri wises, and forsake alle her owen
plesaunces and alle lustes and likynges; and in the bigynnynge of al
this, it is oftentymes ful scharp and hard. But this sche dide al bi
comaundementis of vertues that weren first ladies and mastressis of
this soule. And sche was soget to hem al the while that sche felte this
peyne and werre withynne hirsilf. But so longe oon may bite on the
bitter bark of the note, that at the laste he schal come to the swete
kernel. Right so, goostli to undirstande, it fareth bi these soules that
ben ycome to pesiblete. Thei have so longe stryven with vices and
wrought bi vertues, that thei be come to the note kernel, that is to seie,
to the love of God whiche is swetnesse. And whanne the soule hath
depeli taasted this love, so that this love of God werkith and hath his
usages in the soule, thanne the soule is wondir light and gladsom, and
that is no mervaile, for the swete taastes of love dryven out from the
soule alle peynes and bittirnesse and alle doutes and dredes. Thanne is
sche mastresse and lady over the vertues, for sche hath hem alle
withynne hirsilf, redy at hir comaundement, withouten bittirnesse or
peynfulnesse to felinge of the soule. And thanne this soule taketh leeve
of vertues, as of thraldom and payneful travel of hem that sche hadde

bifore, and now sche is lady and soverayn, and thei ben sogettis. Whanne the soule wroughte bi comaundementis of vertues, thanne the vertues weren ladies and sche soget. And now that the vertues werken bi comaundementis of this soule, thei ben sogettis to this soule, and this soule is lady over vertues. And thus it is mened, that this soule taketh leeve of vertues. N.[6]

'This soule,' seith Love, 'ne recketh of schame, ne of worschip, ne of povert, ne richesse, ne of eese, ne of disese, ne of love, ne of hate, ne of helle, ne of paradise.'

'O Love, for God,' seith Reson, 'what is this to seie that ye have seid?'

'What is this to seie?' seith Love. 'Woot thei (and noon othir) to whom God hath yove the undirstandinge. For no scripture techith it, ne mannes witt may not comprehende it, ne travel of creature, ne desert, may not areche it. But it is a yifte yoven of the right highe, in whom this creature is lost bi plente of knowynge, and bicome nought in hir undirstondinge.'

M.   O, these wordis semen ful straunge to the rederis, that seith the soule is lost in the right highe bi plente of knowinge, and bicome nought in hir undirstandinge. And not oonli these wordis, but also many mo othir wordis that ben writen bifore and aftir, semen fable or errour, or hard to undirstande. But for the love of God, ye reders, demeth not to soone, for I am siker that whoso redith over this booke bi good avisement twies or thries and be disposid to tho same felynges, thei schulen undirstonde it wel ynowgh. And though thei be not disposid to tho felynges, yitt hem schal thenke that it is al wel yseid. But whoso taketh the nakid wordis of scriptures and leveth the sentence, he may lightli erre. N. . . . (fols. 7r–8v).

'Of these soules,' seith Love, 'we wole take oon for alle, for to speke the more redili. This soule ne desireth dispite, ne povert, ne tribulacion, ne diseese, ne masses, ne sermons, ne fastynge, ne orisons, and she yiveth to nature al that he askith, withoute grucchynge of conscience.'

M.   This is to seie, that this soule is unyed to God, and whiles sche stondith in that unyon, sche ne hath wille, ne werk, ne no desire; sche thenkith on nothing that is binethe that. Also anothir undirstandinge ther is, and is this. First, whanne creatures yiven hem to perfeccion, thei sette al her desire and al her entencions in these poyntes aforeseid, and al her labour bi fervour of love, in whiche thei werke and lede. Thei desire for Goddis sake dispite, povert, tribulacioun, disese, massis and sermons, fastynges and orisons, and binemeth nature al his askinge, in refusynge al thing that is lusti and plesaunt to the fleisch, for bi this wey and bi scharp contricion, soules moste go, er than thei come to these divine usages. And whanne thei have taasted of the swete drawtes of hevenli fluences, it savoureth hem so wel, that thei attenden fulli therto. And thanne love of hir curtesie werkith in these soules and makith hem stynte of that formeste laboure, not of the deede to leeve the werk undo for evermore, but of that maner of labour in doynge of it, as thus: Whanne love werkith in the soule and heeldith in hir the sparklis of his brighte beemes, sche undirstandith wel thanne bi cleerte of that light and bi swetnesse of the licour that sche hath dronken, that the werk of love is more worth and drawith more to the unyon in God than doith hir owen werk. Therfore sche takith it as for the mooste worthi and settith bi that principalli, so that al her attendaunce and al hir besinesse that was bifore in the othir outward werkis is now sett to folewe this. But yit also sche doith the tothir, as bi usage of good custom, as Love seith in this booke, that bi usage of good custom this soule doith these outward werkis. But sche doith it withoute desire and withoute that maner of usage that sche hadde bifore, in laborynge bi forayn willes. But fulli sche attendith in al that sche may to the usages of love, the whiche ben alle divine and upward. So whatevere this creature doith, it is so unyed to love, that it is love that doith it, and thus sche suffrith love to werke in hir. Therfore this that Love seith, that these soules ne desiren masses, ne sermons, fastinges ne orisons, it schulde not be so ytake that thei schulde leeve it undoon. He were to blynde that wolde take it in that wise; but alle suche wordis in this booke moste be take goostli and divineli. For these soules nowten so hemsilf bi verrey mekenesse, that thei make hemsilf as noon, for synne is nothing, and thei holde hemsilf but synne. Therfore in her owen biholdynge thei don nought, but God doith in hem his werkis. Also these soules have no propre wille ne desire, thei have al yplauntid it in God, so that thei may nothing wille ne desire, but God willith in hem and maketh hem to do his wille. Thus thei don nothing as in her owen sight and doom, but God doith al thing that good is. And sche yiveth to nature al his askinge, withouten undirnymynge of conscience.

Now God forbeede that eny be so fleischli to thenke that it schulde mene to yive to nature eny lust that drawith to fleischli synne, for God knowith wel it is not so ymened. For synne moste be had in conscience, wil a man or nyl he so, in the tyme or aftir. This may every creature wel wite that hath eny witt and discrecion. For this I seie of trouthe, that these soules that ben suche as this booke deviseth, thei ben so mortified from suche wrecchidnesse, and so enlumyned with grace, and so araied with love of God, that it quenchith al fleischli synne in hem, and driveth myghtili doun alle bodili and goostli temptacions. Thus love, that is God the Hooli Goost, werkith graciousli in these soules, in whom he holdeth his scole, and araieth hem so with feir floures of his highe noblesse, that ther may no spottes ne dragges in hem abide. N. . . . (fols. 10r–11v).

'A, Love,' seith Reson, 'nameth this soule bi hir right name.' . . . And Love nameth hir bi thus many names: 'The right mervelous. And the unknowen. . . . Foryetel is hir name.'

   M.   Foryetel is hir name, for it is hir maner myche to comprehende and soone to foryete. Sche comprehendith myche whanne sche biholdeth God, hou worthi and gloriouse he is, and hou myghtful he is in alle his greete werkis. Sche seeth wel thanne, that God bi his highe myght, he is al in al. Ferthirmore sche seeth hou good and mercyable, benigne and meke he is in al thing. And in this biholdinge, ful often love cometh to hir with his ravyschinge dartes, and woundeth hir so sweteli, that sche foryetith al that sche afore sawe and wiste. Also sche comprehendith myche, what tyme sche is unyed to God. Thanne in a moment of tyme sche foryetith hirsilf, and al othir thing that was afore thought. Thus sche comprehendith myche and soone foryeteth. N. . . . 'A, Love,' seith Reson, 'ye have named this soule bi many names, so that the actyves may have sum knowinge. . . . Now I preie you for the contemplatives . . . that alwei desiren to encrese in divine knowinge.' 'Thei ben yvel constreyned, Reson,' seith Love, 'to that that thou seist.' M.   As who seith, the verrei contemplatives schulde have no desire, but plaunte it al in divine wil of God, and knytte her willes al hoole in him to his wil, and have no propre wil ne desire, but willen parfiitli the divine wil of God, for as bi right, the contemplatyves schulde passe the state of scolers, as maistres of divinite ben passid scoles. N. . . . (fols. 11v–12v).

'The secunde poynt [seith Love] is that this soule saveth hir bi feith withouten werk.' . . .
   M.   Holi writ seith: *Unde sapiens, Iustus ex fide vivit.*[7] This is to

seie, the rightwis man liveth of feith, and so doon these soules. But this – that thei saven hem bi feith withouten werk, and that thei kan no more werke – it is not mened that thei stynten of alle goode werkis for evermore, and nevere don no werke, but sitten in slouthe and ydelnesse of soule and body; for who that takith it so, thei mysundirstanden it. But it is thus: God is enabited in hem, and werkith in hem, and these soules suffren him werke his divine werkis in hem. What this werk is and hou it is, Love schewith it in this booke; and whatevere the bodies of these soules don of foreyn deedis, the soules that ben thus highe sett, taken not so greet reward to these werkes that thei saven hem therbi, but oonli trusten to the goodnesse of God, and so thei saven hem bi feith, and leven not ne tristen not to her owen werkis, but al in Goddis goodnesse. N. . . . [8] (fol. 13r–13v).

'Sotheli, whatevere men seie, thei ne I kan not seie sumthing of youre goodnesse, but the more that I heere speke of you, the more I am abaisched. Thanne is this greet vilanye, that men don me, to wite, that men schal seie me sumthing of the goodnesse of you. But thei ben deceyved that leeven it, for I am in certeyn, that men may not seie. And if God wole, I schal no more be deceyved. I wole no more heere gabbe of youre divine goodnesse.'

M. This is an usage in loves daliaunce, bi whiche these soules have thanne so cleer sight in divine biholdinges that it semeth hem al that thei or othire seien it is but gabbynges as in regarde of the highe goodnesse and greet noblesse that is in God, the whiche may not be knowe for multitude of greetnesse but of himsilf. And therfore thei thenken that thei ne othire kunne not ne mowe not seie but al is gabbinge, for as myche as thei may not areche to a poynt of the fulhede of soothfastnesse. N. . . . (fol. 15r–15v).

(4) . . . 'O ladi Love,' seith Reson, 'seie us what it is to meene, this that ye seie: that thanne is this soule in hir right fredom of pure clene love whanne sche doith nothing that is ayens the askinge of the pees of hir inward beynge?'

'I schal seie you,' seith Love. 'It is that sche do nothing for nought that may falle that be ayens the parfite pees of hir spirite. Thus don,' seith Love, 'the verrei innocentes, and the beynge the whiche we speke of is verrei innocence. . . . Biholde the child that is a verrei pure innocent. Doith he enything or leeveth he to do, for high or for lowe, but if it plese him?'

'I graunte wel, Love,' seith Reson, 'I am wiis of my demaunde.'

M. This ensample that Love maketh of the innocentis, that thei don nothing, ne leveth to do, for highe ne for lowe, but if it plese hem, it is to meene that these creatures schulde not do for oon ne for othir that myghte unreste the quiete of her spiritis. For these spirituel soules that ben lovyers of God, to whom Love spekith in the persoone of oon for alle to be undirstonde, thei ben so meved and updrawen bi the werk of the Hooli Goost that thei may not suffre that enything towche hem but the pure touchinges of love or thing the whiche ledith therto. Ne the spirite of hem may not endure that the bodi obeie bi deliberacion to do enything of outward werkis that myghte lette this divine love, ne the usages that ben meenes and leden to this pure love. So thei stonden for to attende and waite to folewe the Lordis werk, that is soverayne maister, for if thei don the contrarie, sotheli, it wole unreste hem. And therfore Love biddith hem that thei do nothing that myghte breke the pees and reste of her spirites. N. . . . (fols. 28v–29r).

'O my loved,' seith this soule, 'hou dwelle I in my witte whanne I thenke on the yiftes of youre bounte, the whiche ye have yove me? Ye have yoven to my soule the vision of the Fadir and of the Sone and of the Hooli Goost that my soule schal se withouten ende. Thanne sithen that I schal se so highe thing as is the Trinite, thanne schal not be bynome me the knowinge of aungels and of soules, and sithen that so greet thinges is yoven me in yifte, it schal not be withhalden from me the vision of litel. This is to undirstonde of alle tho thinges that ben lasse than God. . . . Sothli, Lord, I am so abaisched of that that I knowe, that I kan not but abaische me. I have noon othir usage, ne noon othir usage may have, so me on cometh this knowinge in continence.'

M. Taketh kepe of these wordis that the soule seith, that sche hath noon othir usage ne noon othir may have. That is to seie, as for the tyme of that usage, for right so every usage stondeth for the tyme of his werk, not that a soule is contynuelli beynge in hem, for that may not be, but every usage is had oon aftir anothir, as love werkith and as disposicions comen and goon, but these usages ben enabited in the soule and used in custom. Therfore is it seid in suche termes as 'alwei', 'thus'. In this wise many suche othir wordis in this booke moste be take. N. . . . [9] (fol. 32r–32v).

(8) . . . 'O, where redresse ye you, right swete lady soule, seie us,' seith Reson, 'ye that don nothing of laboure in this synagoge but bi love and feith that ben above these othire yiftes.'

'No, sootheli,' seith this soule, 'I am of that yquitte. Othir weies I me dresse, that is so fer from that doynge that it may not be leid in comparison ne put in speche. In God is this chois, but it hath not of tyme, where that ne may the myn his atteyne.'[10]

M. Lo, the free soule seith that sche adressith hir othir weies than thei of labour ne doith, that is so fer from that doynge that it may not be put in speche. In God is this chois but it hath not of tyme. This is in the tyme of ravyschinge and unyon in God; it hath not of tyme, for it lasteth but litel while in eny creature heere in this world, for the corrupcion of the fleisch lettith it that the soule may not there longe abide. So thanne there ne may heris his atteyne, for her sensualite wole not suffre it. Also at him heris may not his atteyne, for al the wit and undirstandinge that sche hath or myghte have sche may not areche to the knowinge of his myght, nor of his wisdom, nor of his goodnesse. Thus heris may not his areche in no wise.

Right thus alle suche wordis moste be declared withinne hemsilf that reden this boke. For these derke wordis and highe maters derkli spoken in this writynge, it is don for to make the soules of the rederis that ben disposid to goostli felinges to circuie and enserche bi sotilte of wit to come to these divine undirstandinges, bi the whiche thei may be the more able to receyve and folewe these hevenli usages of Goddes werk. In diverse places of this booke the free soule repreveth in manere hem that ben goostli, that stonden alwei in laboures and in suche maner doynge outforth, and wolen no ferthir seche inforth, for this: that thei schulden stynte sumtyme and folwe these restful usages of pure love. Thus seith the prophete in hooli writte: 'Stynte ye sumtyme and beholdeth God';[11] as who seith, restith sumtyme of youre owne werkis of outforth laboures and biholdeth God hou good he is, and suffreth him werke in you and thanne he wole sowe his divine seedis in you. Also this soule that sitteth ful highe in seete of pees, sche seith sche preieth not. This is not to be undirstande that this soule preieth nevere, but in sundri usages that sche hath sche preieth nevere as thus: these soules of this disposicion ben drawen othirwhile to beholde Goddis privei werkis, his jugementis and his highe providences. Thanne with verrei love thei printen so her willes in Goddis wille bi meke obedience that thei kan not preie in this tyme for hemsilf ne for noon othir. It

plesith hem best that it be as God wole have it don, though thei myghte
bi her preiere have it eny othirwise, thei offren al into his divine
ordenaunce and wille. Also in othire usages that ben al inforth, thei
preien not neithir, but al it prieeth afore God. But yit thei preien among
bi the rule and ordynaunce of hooli chirche and unyen alwei her wille
to his wille in alle thinges that hem hath made and bought. But thei don
never werk with bodi ne not may do in tyme of such divine usages.
Therfore it moste be take as for the tyme alwei of the usages. Thus this
booke moste be take as for usages, for suche usages and suche touches,
suche mevynges and suche biholdinges these soules have, as it is writen
in this booke, and many mo, forsothe, as ye wel may conceyve. And
now I schal stynte of my wordis but if it be the more neede. I have
answerid to tho poyntes that have be mystake aftir my lewid
kunnynge. Anothir schulde have don it myche bettir. I preie you alle
that reden this booke, haveth me excused, for I that am lewid and
unkunnynge may not do but lewidli. Amende ye my defautes and if eny
word I have seid that sowneth to eny goodnesse to profite of soules, to
God oonli be the worschip, fro whom al goodnesse cometh. *Non nobis
Domine, non nobis, sed nomini tuo da gloriam.* N.... [12] (fols. 53r–54v).

(9)   ... 'Thei that loven the deite felen litel of the humanite, as for the
tyme of that usage. Never was a soule knytte, ne ooned, ne divineli
fulfillid, that bodili thinges feelith. Wherof schulde the inwardnesse of
these soules feele? For God ne him meveth, ne nought sche this ne hir
meveth. Now undirstondith bi noblesse of undirstandinge the glose of
these wordis.'
     M. The menynge of these wordis that this soule seith – that her
inwardnesse ne felith, ne sche hirsilf ne meveth – it is yment for the
tyme of ravychinge in unyon. Ther ben thre maners of goostli unyons
that devout soules felen in sondri disposicions, but I mene of the
highest that is best and that is the unyon that thorwgh ravyschinge of
love the soule is knyt and unyed to God so that God and the soule is
oon spirit. For Seynt Poul seith, it is not two spiritis, God and the soule,
that is thus unyed to him, but it is al oon spirit in tyme of this unyon.[13]
Wherof thanne, in the tyme of this unyon, schulde hir inwardnesse fele
or sche hirsilf meve? O, sche may not do it, for sche is al molten in God
for the tyme. A, this blessid oonnesse lasteth but litel while in ony
creature that is heere in this deedli liif, for the sensualite of mankynde
may not suffre it. But it may ofte be had bi the goodnesse of God that is

werker of this werk in soules there he foucheth-saaf. To him be offrid al glorie and preisynges to everlastynge laude. Lo, ye that studien this booke, thus ye moste withynne youresilf glose suche derke wordis, and if ye may not come soone to the undirstondinge therof, offrith it mekeli up to God, and bi custom of ofte redynge theron ye schulen come therto. A fewe wordis mo I seie in this booke to brynge you in the weie, not withstondinge that I was in purpos afore to have glosed no more. God graunte us alwei to do his plesynge and bringe us to him whanne it is his wille. N. . . . (fol. 62r–62v).

(13) . . . 'For no more than God may synne that may not wille it, no more may I synne if my wille wole it not, such fredom hath the summe of me of his pure bounte bi love y-yoven me.'

M. The summe of this soule is the knowinge that sche hath of the goodnesse of God, and this goodnesse of God that is the Hooli Goost werkith in hir that yave hir fre wille. N. . . . (fol. 78r).

20 A Ladder of Foure Ronges by the which Men Mowe Wele Clyme to Heven

(English translator's interpolations; extracts)

A late fourteenth-century translation of the *Scala Claustralium* on contemplative prayer (attributed to Guigo II, ninth Prior of the Grande Chartreuse and probably written *c.* 1150), the English *Ladder* derives from a revised version of the Latin treatise, rearranged so as to be less didactic and schematic, more suitable for devotional reading. The Latin text refers to 'scala claustralium qua de terra in coelum sublevantur' (p. 84), (a ladder for monks by which they are lifted from earth to heaven). The English translator – referring instead to 'the ladder of cloysterers, and of othere Goddis lovers' – apparently envisages an audience 'consisting primarily of clerics, both within and outside the cloister, but also including the very pious among the laity'.[1] The source is artfully reshaped into a work accessible to a wider audience, which the manuscripts attest included nuns and pious laywomen: the *Ladder* is extant in three fifteenth-century devotional miscellanies: Bodleian Library MS Douce 322; BL MS Harley 1706; and CUL MS Ff. 6. 33, which was made by William Darker, a member of the Carthusian house at Sheen, perhaps for the Brigittine nuns at Syon (it also contains an English translation of the Brigittine rule).[2] Each of the ladder's 'rungs' is carefully explained:

> Lesson is a besy lokyng vpon holy writte with intencion of the wille and in the witte. Meditacion is a studious inserchyng with the mynde to knowe that ere was hydde thurwe wischyng of propir skylle. Prayer is a devoute desiryng of the hert for to gete that that is good & to fordoo that is eville. Contemplacion is a risyng of hert into God that tastith sumdele of heuenly swettnesse & savourith. Lesson sekyth, meditacion fyndith, orison askith, contemplacion felith. (MS Ff. 6. 33, fol. 116r)

The Middle English *Ladder* includes five lengthy interpolations: the identification of the 'ladder of cloysterers' with Jacob's ladder (fols. 115v–116r); discussion of the three degrees of grace (fols. 118r–122v), and of the capacity of the simple-minded in spiritual matters (fols. 127r–128r); comparison of God with an innkeeper (fols. 132r–132v), and of the contemplative with Jacob wrestling with the angel (fols. 133v–134v).

Base manuscript: CUL MS ff. 6. 33, fols. 115r–116r, 120v–121v, 127r–128r, 132r–134v. No variants.

[a]   As I was occupied on a day in bodyly traveyle and thought on gostly werkys that were nedefulle to Goddis servauntys, foure gostly werkes comme soon to my mynde, that is to sey: lesson, meditacion, orison, and contemplacion. This is the ladder of cloysterers, and of othere Goddis lovers, by the which they clymbe from eerth into hevyn. This is a longe laddir and a mervelous thoughe it have but foure stavis, for the oon ende stondith on the grounde and the other ende thrillyth the clowdys and shewith to the clymber hevenly pryvetees. This is the ladder that Jacob sawe, as Genesis tellith, that stode upon the erthe and rawght into hevyn, by the whiche he sawe angellis of hevyn goyng upward and downward, and God lenyng to the ladder. By goyng up and downe of these angellis is undirstonde that the angellis of hevyn gladyn us with many gostly comfortis and bere up oure prayers to oure Lorde in hevyn there he sittyth on hye, and brynge from hym to us desires of oure hertys, as it may be provid by Danyel. By the lenyng of God to this laddir is undirstond that he is evere redye to help alle tho that by thes iv staves of this ladder wylle clymbe wisely, ne thar hym drede no snaperyng ther suche a laddyr wolle trewly helpe hym. . . . (fols. 115r–116r).

[b]   God he is as felawe in half getyng in werkes of God, and doothe with us as a felawe that wille wynnyng have. He yevith his grace, and we oure werkes, as merchauntys to sette wynnyng that fallith to them. And wondirly he chalengyth the lovyng and the worship to have for his part of man, but we as fals wretchis benemme hym frawdabylly. And we wene that we wynne alle, and we lese alle, for we doo injury and fraude, we yevyn oure love to the feend and oure worshipe to the worlde and to the flessh, and so oure love ys withdrawe from oure gracious partenere. . . . And we defraude hym of his parte that he bought with so grete price, that is with the blode of the undefyled Lambe, Crist Jhesu. We depart oureself from the blisse of oure Lorde willfully, lyke as the hownde dyd that bare a chese by a watyr syde, and as he lokyd in the watyr he sawe a shadwe of the chese, and he openyd his mouth to take it, and it fel from hym. And so he loste that he hadde, and that he desirid to have hadde. . . . (fols. 120v–121v).

[c]   Grete myght risith than of mekenes that is worthy to conceyve and wynne that thurwe witte of man may not be lernyd, ne with bodily

ere herde, ne wyth tunge tolde. This witte hath God holdyn oonly to his
chosun, that alle resonable creatures knowe and undirstonde that ther
is a maistyr techyng and redyng in hevyn, that techith sothfast wysdom
and lore to his chosyn scolers, and thurwe his grace lyghtenyth hem
withyn, and makith hem to knowe and fele that no worldly witte may
wynne to. Thoue mayst se if thoue wilte beholde a symple olde pore
woman that is pore of witte, that neyther sothly can sey the Pater
Noster ne the Crede, such likyng wille have in so litel a while, so in sely
moornyng the hert al tomeltyth, that withoute terys and moornyngys
may she not praye. Who, wenyst thou, techith hir thus to praye? Not
witte of this worlde, but grace from above. Howe a pore sely man that
so dul of witt is, that lyveth by his swynke, thoughe he shulde lese his
hedde he cowde not bryng to an eende a reson, to this lore and to this
wysedom as perfightly may wynne therto as the wisest in a londe,
whatsoevere he be; and he doo that in hym is, whatsoevere he be.
Sothly he may wele be callid a maistyr overe alle other that this name
beryth, that unwytty so kan teche wysdom withoute wittys to fele and
undirstonde that thurwe no witte of this worlde men may reche to, so
that man doo that therto fallyth, and bowe the ere of his herte to lysten
that lore. . .. (fols. 127r–128r).

[d]   So doth God Almyghty to his loveris in contemplacion as a
taverner – that good wyne hathe to selle – dooth to good drynkeris that
wolle drynke wele of his wyne and largely spende. Wele he knowith
what they be, there he seeth hem in the strete. Pryvely he wendyth and
rowndith hem in the eere and seyth to them that he hath a clarete, and
that alle fyne for ther owyn mouth. He tollyth hem to howse and
yevyth hem a taast. Sone whanne they have tastyd therof and that they
thynke the drynke good and gretly to ther plesauns, than they drynke
dayly and nyghtly, and the more they drynke, the more the[y] may.
Suche lykyng they have of that drynke that of none other wyne they
thynke, but oonly for to drynke their fylle and to have of this drynke
alle their wylle. And so they spende that they have, and syth they
spende or lene to wedde surcotte or hode and alle that they may, for to
drynke with lykyng whiles that them it good thynkith. Thus it faryth
sumtyme by Goddis loveris that from the tyme that they hadde tastyd
of this pyment, that is of the swettnesse of God, such lykyng thei
founde theryn that as drunkyn men they did spende that they hadde
and yafe themself to fastyng and to wakyng and to other penauns

doyng. And whan they hadde no more to spende they leyde their weddys, as apostelys, martyrys, and maydenys younge of yeris dyd in their tyme. Summe yafe their bodyes to brenne in fyre, summe lete her hedys of to be smytte, summe yafe her pappys corvyn from ther breestys, summe yaf ther skyn drawn from the flessh, and somme their bodyes wyth wylde horsys to be drawe. And alle that they dyd they sette it at nought for the desyre of that lastyng wele that they desired fully to have in the lyfe that is withouten eende. But this likyng is here yeven but for to taste, but alle tho that desyre fully to have it, them behovith to folowe Crist fote by fote, and evyn lyke steryn hym wyth their lovys, as these drynkeris the tavernarys doon. Therfor whan God eny gostly lykyng to thy sowle sendyth, thynke that God spekyth to the, and rownyth in thyn eere, and sayth: 'Have nowe this litelle, and taste howe swete I am. But yf thou wylt fully fele that thou ofte hast tastyd, renne aftyr me and folowe the savoure of myn oyntementys. Heve up thyn hert to me there I am syttyng on the ryght half of my Fadyr, and ther shalt thou se me, not as in a myrroure, but thou shalt se me face to face. And than thou shalt fully have at thy wylle that joye that thoue hast tastyd evere wythouten ende. And that joye or lykyng noon shalle the reve or take fro.'

But ho so wylle in contemplacion of this lykyng taste and clyme to the steyre that stondithe so high, hym behovyth to be Jacob here in this lyfe; that is, hym behovyth to doo that this name spellyth, that is holde undir fote alle worldly welth. Alle folye and synnes trede undyr fote, for the more that a man undyr his fote castyth, it helpyth hym the more on hyghe to clymbe or to reche. And than shalle his name to Israel be turnyd, that ys in Englysshe: 'God he shalle se'; thurwe whiche syght he shalle be fulfyllyd of that lykyng that alle othir passythe wythoute comparison. Of this Jacob in the Boke of Genesis it tellith: the angel wyth Jacob wrestyllyd, and longe stroglyde wyth maystry hym to have. But Jacob as the myghty stalworthely wythstode, and the maistry wan. Whan the angel sawe that he myght no more, he towchid the hyppe of Jacob, and the synewis dryed, and evere aftyr that tyme he haltyd on the oon foote; and aftir that the foote was hym benome, fro Jacob to Israel his name was turnyde.

By this Jacob is undirstonde man that in contemplacion is lyfte on hygh. Than he stroglyth with the angelle and stryvith whan he traveylith wyth alle his myght God for to knowe. But than at the laste is the angelle overecomme and undyrcaste, whan man thurwe a depe

thought in a love-longynge to knowe what God is and to fele in
contemplacion, and that he desirethe, conceyvith and felyth in his
sowle of this swettnesse, and so is overtakyn on the lykyng of hym that
alle the wele of this worlde he settyth it at noughte. But what is it to
meen that whann the angelle sawe that he was overecome he towchyd
Jacob upon the hyppe and the synewis dryed? For myghtful God that
alle may, whan he to his loverys sendith his grace that they thurwe his
grace sothly may knowe that alle flesshly desyres and other unthewys
that be senewys are undirstonde, he them fordothe and makyth hem
drye as they dedde were. And they that byfore upon two fete yede and
that wolde have lykyng in God and in the world bothe, aftyr that they
in contemplacion swetnes have founde, that oon foote in ther love is
hool and in the tother they halte, for worldly love qwenchyth in them,
and wexeth alle drye. The love of God is hool and sownde, and evere
lyke stronge more and more. Whoso on this fote stallworthly stondyth
may no woo of this worlde hyme overecaste. By a fote in holy wrytte is
love undirstond. . . . (fols. 132r–134v).

The Doctrine of the Hert

(Chapter 7; with cuts)

This Middle English 'tretice made to religious wommen' is translated from *De doctrina cordis* (attributed to Gerard of Liège or Hugh of St Cher,[1] and probably written in the first half of the thirteenth century). The last chapter analyses seven tokens of 'extatik love', which recall the signs of 'the loveris maladye Of Hereos' (*Knight's Tale*, I, 1373–4). In his preface the English translator (calling himself 'oon of thoo whiche oure Lord hath clepid to his seruise in religioun') says he has 'compilid this tretice . . . to edificacioun of symple soules', also remarking: 'Hertly redyng is a gracious meene to goostly felyng: in this wise þerfor shuld this tretice be rad or herd.'[2]

Base manuscript: Trinity College, Cambridge, MS B. 14. 15 (T), fols. 70r–75v. Also cited: Fitzwilliam Museum, Cambridge, MS McClean 132 (M).

. . . Take hede, sister, to the wordis of Seynt Austyn. He seith that he was led into a gostli unusid affeccion, into a merveyllous swetnes, he not what, and he was anon throwe doun into his corruptible bodi fro that blessid swetnesse. This unusid gostli affeccion may wel be lykned to extatik love. Extatik love is such a thyng that it alieneth the soule fer fro here meynde unto the love of that thyng the which it lovyth. This extatik love otherwhile is take for good love, as Seynt Dionyse seith,[3] that clepith extatik love such love the which brynggith a lover al hool into the use and profite of that thyng that is lovyd. With such love our Lord lovyd us, yevyng hymself al hool into our use and profite.

Extatik love also is take in another wise. It is take otherwhile for alienacion of the meynde bi love, as ben al suche fleshly loves that wexyn mad for love, the which is cause of overpassyng desir of the herte and of affliccion of thoughttes set upon fleshly love. Al such love is reprovable and it shuld be a grete confusion to any creature so to be alened for such wreched love. Nevertheles, for to prove gostli extatik love bi the condicion of fleshly extatik love, thou shalt undirstonde that ther ben many tokenes to knowe whan extatik fleshli love worchith in amourous fleshly creatures. Among al seven ther ben, the which I shal declare to the, that apperyn most in such amourous loveris.

The first tokene is of such amourous fleshly loveres that thei coveyte moche, and speke litel, and also speken here wordis unperfitly. Right so gostly, al spiritual loveres speken many sentences of love and can not be undirstonde unnethe of any but of such that ben gostly loveres as thei ben. Cristes spouse in the Boke of Love rehersith many such unperfyte and defectif spechis. Among al this is on: *Dilectus meus mihi et ego illi.*[4] That is, 'My love to me and I to hym.' But these wordis were more openli declared, it semyth right unperfite, for she tellith not what here love is to here, ne what she is to here love. But like as Aaron spak for Moises, so most gostli reson speke for our affeccion and fulfille the unperfite wordes of a lovyng soule, and sey thus: 'My love to me is able.' Or thus: 'Like as my love to me is mede and reward of al my laboures, of al my sorowes and of al my fatigacions, right so I am the rest of his labour, sorow and fatigacion, whiche he suffered for to raunsom me. And therfor, like as he suffered deseses and tribulacions for to have me, so shal I gladli suffre deseses and tribulacions for to have hym.' Or thus: 'My love to me lyved and for me died, so shal I lyve to hym and for hym shal I dygh.' Lo, sister, thus thou maist know hou many declaracions a lovyng soule nedith for to have in expounyng of here defectif and unperfit wordis, and yit mony mo than here ben expounyd. Nevertheles, it nedith nevere a dele to be expouned to a lovyng soule, for the shortist sentence of love is opyn inow to hem.

The secunde tokene of an extatik lover is drynesse of al the bodili lemys, and whi that is I shal telle the: because the hert is sore applied with alle the bodily myghttes to that thyng that it lovyth. Right so, to our gostly purpose, a lovyng soule, for the grete passyng love that she hath to God, is in maner dried up fro the humoris of fleshly lust. Of this I feynde a figure in holy writ, where I rede thus: that our Lord departed the Rede See bi the blast of a grete brennyng wynd.[5] Bi this rede see is undirstonde fleshly lust. It may wel be called a see, for what that ever it pretendith of eny maner fantastik swetnesse, it endith in bitternysse. It is also called red for it restith in the vissious levyng of the flesh. Bi this grete weynd and brennyng is undirstonde a fervent love in God that drieth up in maner alle carnel affeccions in a clene lovyng soule. With such a gret brennyng wynd, the holy apostles on Wytsonday were brent bi love and dried up fro carnal affeccions. Thus than, bi that weynd thou shalt undirstonde the Holi Gost. Suche that ben so dried up in maner fro fleshly lustes ben to the fende right ferful.

The thrid tokyn of an extatik love is holownesse of the eighen. Alle extatik loveres han holow eighn, for the eighen folowyn the spirit, drawyng togedres into o place where thei supposyn that love is most fervent. Right so the inward eighen of a lovyng soule, undirstondyng and affeccion, ben sonke depe into the hert, for al that such a soule sekith is withinforth, al that it lovyth is inward and not outward. Also, the gostly eighen of such a lovyng soule is sonke in, for to see that nothyng be in the consiens that shuld displese here lover. Thei ben also sonkyn for to espye the prevy goyng and comyng of her lover. Our Lord comyth whan he t[ou]chith[a] the soule with love and devocion that she felt never afore. He goth whan he withdrawith devocion, bicause a soule shuld knowe here infirmite, thenckyng that such devocion comyth onli of God and not of here self. Also, he withdrawith such special devocion, that whan it comyth ayen it myght be kept more deyntosly. Many ther ben that han such special devocion and swetnes of love. But ofte tymes thei puttyn it away from hem by ydil occupacions, idil wordes, and other scurilite, the which besemyth hem not, and ofte tymes receyvyn outward solace unmoderatly. And also thei seyn her servyse of God withoute hertli attencion and shewen to moche tendirnes to here carnal frendes. Alle these thyngges puttyn away specialli gostli swetnes.

The fourthe tokne of an extatik lover is drighnes of his eighen and lackyng of teris, but yif it come of sum special thought or remembraunce of his love, in-so-muche that nouther deth of frendes ne lostis of temporal goodes mowe in no wyse make such extatik loveres for to wepe, but it be onli from special meynde of the love that it lovyth. Right so farith a lovyng soule: she is not sori for no maner of thyng, ne can noght wepe, but yif it be for that thyng that she lovyth. Lo, sister, yif thou love God tendirly, thou makist non inly sorowe for nothyng, but it be for that thyng that longgith to love of our Lord Jhesu, for thogh al thyngges were lost fro the, thi principal lover Jhesu is saf to the.

To thyngges ther ben that makith loveres for to wepe. On is songges of love; another is the feere that thei have lest thei lese here lover. As for the first, a lover that is fer fro his love synggith songges of love in meynde of his lover. So, sister, most thou do; in as moche as thi love is fir fro the thou moste in this leif syngge songges of love. Songges of love I calle the songges of holi chirche. Suche songges thou moste syngge devoutli in meynde of thi love, meltyng in swetnesse of devocion. Such a lover was Seynt Austyn whan he seyde thus in his Confession: 'I wept plentuously in ympnys and songges, swetly sounnyng in the voyce of holi chirche.'[6] Thus do, sustyr, in meynde of thy lover. Sum ther ben that synggy[n][b] in holi chirche as a belle rynggith in the weynd, more for praysyng of here fair voyces than for eny special love to God. What don thei but fillyn the eeris of the peple with noyse? And wel may such synggyng be called noyse, for al that sounnyth not in the eeris of our Lord bi devocion is but noise. Good sister, fille not onli the eeris of othir, but specialli with devocion the eeris of hym that biddith the thus: *Sonet vox tua in auribus meis*.[7] 'Syng,' so seith our Lord in the Boke of Love, 'that thi voyce mow devoutly sounne in myn eris.' Wote wel, synggyng sterith the peple to devocion, but yit thou shuldist have such devocion in songgis of holi chirche that it soun rathir in Goddes eere than in mannes eere. Therfore whan thou shalt syngge, syngge as Seynt Poule seith: *Psallas spiritu [et psallas][c] mente*.[8] 'Syngge in thi spirite and syng in thi soule.' Thou synggist wel in thi spirit, that is in thi gostli strengthe, whan thou synggist with devout melody of thi bodily voyce. Thou synggist wel in thi soule, whan thou synggist savorly in gostly undirstondyng of thi soule. The secunde thyng that makith a lover to wepe is feere that he hath for to lese his lover. So wept David and Jonathas whan thei shulde departe asundir, but yiit David wept moche more, for he lovyd more. Right so, drede of separacion, the which is a maner of deth, makith a devout lover for to wepe.

The fifte token of an extatik lover is an unordinat pous. Every amorous lover hath outher to sclak a pous or to swift a pous, after diverse apprehencions that he hath of his lover. A sclak pous he hath whan he is in doute of here whom he lovyth. He hath also a swift pous whan he hopith for to have here whom he lovyth. Thus it farith in a lovyng soule. The pous of a lovyng soule is affeccion, the which is swift whan a soule hopith to have hym that she lovyth. Such apprehencion of love had David whan he seide: *Cor meum et caro mea exultaverunt in Deum vivum*.[9] 'Myn hert,' he seide, 'and my flesh han gret joye in God.' By the hert thou shalt undirstonde thought, and bi the flesh affeccion.

---

[b] synggyn] M; synggyng T.   [c] et psallas] p. e. TM.

His thought and his affeccion joyed so moche in God for love that it skipped out gostly from itself into God. Also the pous of gostly affeccion in an extatik lover goth sclakly whan a soule considerith here synnes and the perel of gostly deth, perseyvyng hou other more myghtier, more strengger in vertu, han falle in synne. Forther, sumtyme the affeccion of the soule went sweftly for love; than it goth sclakly for drede of fallyng.

The sixte tokne of an extatik lover is whan al his thoughttes and al his meynde is turned depli into the hert, so ferforth that ther may no noyse adawe such a lover fro his depe thought, but only whan she herith any word mevyd of here love. For it is the condicion of an amorous fleshly lover, speke to hym of what thyng thou list, but yif it be of his love he not what thou menest. And speke to hym the leste word that thou canst of his love, anon he wot what thou menyst. Whi is this, trowist thou? Treuly, for al his thout and entent is inwardly sette upon here. In the same wyse a lovyng soule that lovyth our Lord cannot undirstonde seculer wordes, wordly tales and wordly tydyngges, for it longgith not ne towchith not to here lover. But yif any thyng be mevyd to here of Crist Jhesu, here lover, or of such thyng that longgith or touchith to hym, she undirstondith it quykly, for here meynde is ful set upon hym, and of hym she list to here and of non other. Alle the questions and demaundes that suche on schal make, schal be of love, as Salamon seith in voice of gostly loveres in the Boke of Love, thus: *Numquid quem diligit anima mea vidistis?*[10] 'Sey ye not hym,' she seith, 'whom my soule lovyth?' It is the manere of gostly loveres for to here evere and axe tidyngges of here love, Jhesu. Sori than mow thei be that han a dul wit to undirstondyng of gostly thynggis and a pliaunt wit for to undirstonde wordly thyngges and wordly tithyngges. It is a verri tokne that such on wantith love. Therfore, sister, be not lightly wakid out of thi lovely sclep bi no wordly tales, but only whan thou herist any word or question of thi love, Jhesu.

The seventhe tokene of an extatik lover is that whan the hert of such an amorous fleshli lover is so teyd and fastned to here that he lovyth, that is whan that ever he seith any thyng that is like to his love in here absence, he is anon from hymself in a manere of wodnes. In the same wise a lovyng soule, whan that ever she tastith, be it never so litell, of the excellent goodnesse and swetnesse of God in this lif, anon she is from here self and she bygynnyth for to speke she not what, as Seynt Petir dide whan he was with our Lord in the mounte of Thabor and sey hym transfigured into a clernesse of gret shynyng light. Anon he was from hymself for joye and seyde he nyst what, whan he seide thus: *Domine bonum est nos hic esse, faciamus hic tria taburnacula, tibi unum, Moysi unum et Heliae unum*.[11] 'Lord,' he seide, 'it is best to abyde here; lete us make here thre dwellyng places: on to the, another to Moyses, and the thrid to Helye'. Treuly he wist not what he seyde whan he seyde so.

For, as dottouris seyn,[12] he herd hou our Lord seyde afore that he shold suffre deth in Jerusalem, and yit he seyde that it were best to abyde there. By this thou maist undirstonde that Petir was from hymself. For he was gostly drunke of the swetnesse of Cristes precense, and therfor he axed there for to abyde. He had foryete that tyme what Crist seyde afore, hou he scholde suffre passion in Jerusalem. Of o thyng take hede: he desired no duellyng place for hymsel[f] but for other. In tokyn that al such, the which ben so gostly dronke, ben more liberal and large to other in hert than to hemself, he seyde not 'to me on', but 'to the on, to Moyses oon, and to Hely oon'. He reservyd nothyng to hymself and that was a gret charite, the which sekith rathir the ese of othir than of itself. Also he wist not what he seyde for o thyng, for he was so dronke in love that he wende the joye which he sigh had be the same joye that shal be had in hefne, and that was not so, but a liknesse therof. For the prophete seith: 'Non eigh may see in erthe that excellent joye in blisse, the which our Lord hath ordeyned for hem that loven hym.'[13] That joye that lovyng soules schul have schal be to hem an opyn, clere knowyng of parfit love and of the goodnesse of God, and siker possession of everlastyng blisse – to the which blisse and joye that never schal have ende bryng us he that bought us on the rode tre! Amen.

Here endith a tretice made to religious wommen which is clepid the Doctrine of the Hert.

22 *The Chastising of God's Children*

(Chapters 1 and 4; extracts)

The Chastising was popular throughout the fifteenth century, and is thought
to have been composed in the 1380s or 1390s. The author's prologue presents
him as writing for a woman religious to whom he acts as spiritual adviser. The
title is the author's, referring to his theme – the profit to the soul of spiritual
and physical afflictions – on which he has skilfully anthologized, edited and
woven together teaching compiled from a range of texts. Chapter 1 includes
borrowings from the *Ancrene Riwle* and from Suso's *Horologium Sapientiae*;
chapter 4 draws on a Latin version of Ruusbroec's *The Spiritual Espousals*.[1]

Base manuscript: Bodleian Library MS Bodley 505 (B), fols. 5v–6v, 12r–13v. Also cited:
Trinity College, Cambridge, MS B. 14. 19. (T).

(1) . . . Whanne oure Lord suffrith us to be tempted in oure
bigynnynge, he pleieth with us as the modir with hir child, whiche
sumtyme fleeth awei and hideth hir, and suffreth the child to wepe and
crie and besili to seke hir with sobbynge and wepynge. But thanne
cometh the modir sodeinli with mery chier and laughhynge, biclippynge
hir child and kissynge, and wipeth awei the teeris.[2] Thus farith[3] oure
Lord with us, as for a tyme he withdraweth his grace and his comfort
from us, in so moche that in his absence we bien al cold and drie,
swetnesse have we noon ne savour in devocion, slough we bien to preie
or to travaile, [the wrecchid soule sodeynli chaunged][a] and made ful
hevy and ful of sorwe and care. Thanne is the bodi sluggi and the hert
ful hard, and al oure spirites so dulle that the lif of oure bodi is to us
noyous. Al that we heere or see, though it be goode, yit for the tyme it
saverith nat; and sooth for to seie, weri be we thanne of goodenesse,
and lik to falle in vices, and fieble to withstonde temptaciouns. Suche
hevynesse we fynde in the absence of oure fadir, and yit oure fadir
lovith us never the lasse, but hidith him for a tyme, and pleieth with us

[a] the wrecchid . . . chaunged] T; B *om.*

259

for grete love. This absence and forsakynge for a tyme the profete
undirstode wele whanne he seide: 'Lord, forsake me nat at al tymes.'[4]
Therfore upon these wordis seith Seint Gregori: 'He knewe wele that
he shuld be forsake but for a while, that asked nat to be forsake at al
tymes.'[5]

The presence of oure Lorde I clepe his gracious wirchynge in us,
and I clepe his absence the withdrawynge [of][b] his comfortis fro us. But
now sum man that redith this paraventure wil seie: 'This is a queynt
pleie – what is this pley, that thus hevy we bien in the absence of oure
love?' The pley of love[6] is joye and sorwe, the whiche two comen sundri
tymes oon aftir another, bi the presence and absence of him that is oure
love. This is a propirte of love, that whanne we han him presente that
we love, we knowe nat hou moche that we love, but whanne he is awei,
thanne we perceyven bi his absence what matier we han to love to hym.
The joie of his presence causith sorwe in his absence, nat so that he is
cause of sorwe, but for his presence is to us so joieful that with his
absence nedis we must be sorwful. I have rehersid heere shortli what
matier of sorwe we han in his absence, for ye shul have it more opinli aftir.

But seeth now what joie cometh and matier of joie bi his blissed
presence. Anon at his comyng the soule wexith light and joieful, the
conscience is clier and myche in reste, the spirites that weren dulle and
deed bien quyk and redi to travaile, and al thing that was hard and
sharp and impossible to semynge, anon thei wex softe and swete, and
al maner excercises, in fastynge and in wakynge and alle goode werkis,
suche excercises bien turned into mirth. For grete desire and love, the
soule is fulfilled with charite, and al maner clennesse; she is fed with
such goostli swetnesse that for grete likynge in suche goostli fedynge al
outwarde thinges bien almost foryeten. . . .

(4) . . . Whanne the sunne in tyme of yeere bigynneth to drawe
donward, than he reigneth in a place that we clepen 'Virgyn', and the
cause whi it is clepid Virgyn is for that tyme of yeer is nat fructuous, no
more thanne a mayde that berith no fruyt of children. In this tyme of
the yeere, the hete of the wedir is lessid, hard fruyt, corn and wyne bien
gadred hom, and thanne is sum seede sowen to profite of man. Al the
werkynge of the sunne as for that yeere is than fulfilled. In the same
maner, whanne oure glorious sunne, Crist Jesu, bigynneth to come

[b] of] T; B om.

doun, and to hide the inward shyneng of his sunne beame, and whanne he forsakith us and leveth us aloone, thanne is ther litel fervour of love; thanne fynde we us silf poore and al forsake, as outlawis; that was bifore likyng and hoote is thanne ful cold and [e]lenge,*c* and al that was so plentevouse is come to nede and povert. Thanne of oure owne wrecchidnesse we wondren, and seien: where is al the fervent love and thankyng to God, where is al this likynge and worshippes to God, and where is the soules comfort, gladnesse and savour? What may al this be, whidir is al this become, whi faileth al this now, hou is it that al this stronge love and al these noble yiftis bien al awey and deede? Thus we faren as men unwise, that thenken oure travaile lost; and sumtyme in sum men and wymmen the bodili kynde is fiebled bi a sodein hevynesse in her bigynnynge, and thei witen nat whi, and that is sumtyme for a strif that is betwixt the spirit and the flesshe. Sume bi slouth and folie wilfulli leven her travaile; sum fallen in doute whether thei shullen traveile or nought; summe, whanne thei shulden slepe, thanne hem lust to wake and preie; summe, whan thei shuld wake and preie, thanne hem lust to slepe. But many bi grace kepen her journey, and thanne fallith to hem whiche wolen abide and travele that sumtyme oure Lord for grete love preveth hem soorer than other. For thanne of his suffraunce thei leesen outward benefettis and likynges, that is to seie friendis and kynesmen, and lightli bien forsake of al other knowlechynge: thei that diden hem chier bifore haven hem now in scorn; truthe fynde thei nowher noon, but wronges, detraccions and unkyndenesses. Thei han also grete infirmitees both in body and in soule. Summe fallen in perplexites for a thinge that nought is to charge or litel, and there thei coude counseile other in that and other doutes, thei stande thanne hemself desolate and in grete doute. Summe bien so hard preved with goostli temptacions, whiche passen al disease, that what for drede and doute al comfort is lost, save oonli hope and mercy; of whiche goostli temptacions and tribulacions ye shullen see more opinli aftirward. A, goode God, what grace is in thi presence, hou precious is thi love, whan al love and grace faileth in thin absence!. . . .

c elenge] T; clenge B.

23 The Treatise of Perfection of the Sons of God

(Chapters 2, 10, 11; selections)

This early fifteenth-century literal translation of Willem Jordaens' Latin version of Ruusbroec's *Vanden blinckenden Steen* survives in one devotional miscellany, BL MS Add. 37790. Not for beginners in contemplation, Ruusbroec's terse, abstruse original was for the 'hidden sons of God', whose reward shall be mystical union with Him.

Sole manuscript: BL MS Add. 37790, fols. 117v, 124r–125r.

(2) . . . Wherfore us behoves to grownde oure lyfe upon a profounde depenesse; and so we maye in everlastynge love drowne, and alle of oure selfe into inserchable depnesse be drown[d]e,*ᵃ* in the whiche love we schalle be alterate into ane incomprehensible heyght. And also with that love whiche is wantynge maner we schalle grope, and it schalle lede us and brynge us agayne into the gate of the incomprehensible depnesse of charite, in the whiche we schalle flowe frome oureselfe, and flow[e]*ᵇ* agayne in unknawyn swetnesses thorowe the spirit of the goodnes of God, in the whiche we schalle be made liqued and stable everlastyngly be the joye of God. So that I schewe than that in eche of thees symylitudes is exercyse to be contemplatyfe. . . .

(10) . . . For sothly, yyf we hafe faythe, hope and charite, than withowt dowte we hafe takyn God, for he with his grace dwellys in us, and sendys us furthe as trewe servantys to kepe his commawndmentis. And he callys us ayayne inwarde as his secrete frendes, yif alonely we folowe his counseyles; and be that he schewes us that we are his sonnys, yif onely we knowe oure lyfe contrary to the worlde. Bot forsothe, yif that we wille taste God overe alle thynge, or fele in us everelastynge lyfe, it is necessary, as I consayve, that above resoun of oure consayte we intende God, abydynge ther ydle, that is to saye frome alle ymagynacioun and

---

ᵃ drownde] drowne.   *ᵇ* flowe] flowys.

feynynge of alle erthly symylitudys, lyftynge up be love oure mynde
into the manyfeste barnesse, where sothly in love alle thyngis we
overpasse, dyynge be alle consyderacioun into a manere of ryghtwysnesse
and derknesse. Thoo we do and wyrk in the everlastynge worde, the
whiche is the ymage of the fathere; and in that ydlenesse of oure spyrrit
we take that unconsavable clerenes, the whiche takyn, we flowe overe,
that is to saye, we passe mesure of resoun in consayvynge the clere
syrkle of the sonne, yet overe the substaunce. And that trewe clerenesse
is nought ellys bot a byholdynge and a inspeccioun of ane unknawen
ende. For that that we are we beholde, and that we beholde we are. And
why? For sothly oure lyfe, mynde and alle othere thynge that we hafe
allonely are lyfte up and knyt to the verrey trewthe, whiche is God.
Wherfore in that allonly beholdynge we be one lyfe and one spirrytte
with God; and this I calle contemplatyfe lyfe, for where that we drawe
nere God in love, ther we exercyse the best parte, and where as above
alle thynge ascendynge supersubstancyally we serche, ther holye we
possesse God. And unto this contemplacioun evermore drawes the
exercyse of the unknawen manere, that is to saye, lyfe drawynge to
nought. Bot we forsothe hase drawyn ourselfe into a derknesse and
into an unsershable wantynge manere, thayre evermore schynes that
simple beynge of the clerenesse of God, in the whiche we be growndyd,
that is to saye, the whiche of ourselfe drawys us into the moste hyghe
beynge and felaschip of his love, unto the whiche felaschippe of love
exercyse, that es to saye bysenes, is the drawere in, and the folowere of
trewe love wantynge manere. For love may nought be ydle, bot thorow
thryst and smellynge it is aboutwarde to serche unsers[h]able^{c} ryches,
lyffynge in his grownde, that is to saye in the grownde of love.

(11) This forsayde sothlye is the impacient hungre, besylye goynge, as
a floode swyftly rynnynge. It maye not be lefte ne yit takyn; to wante it
is intollerable, to folowe it impossible. It may not be schewed open ne
yit hid in silence. It excedys alle resoun and witt, and it is abofe alle
creatures, and therfore it may on no wyse be touched. Neverthelesse,
beholdynge oureselfe we feele the spirit of God dryfe us and put us into
that inpacient taryynge; bot beholdynge above oureselfe we persayve
the spirit of God of oureselfe drawynge us, and turnyng us to nought in
hymselfe, that is, in Cryste, with a superessencialle love, unto whome

---

^{c} unsershable] unsersable.

we be everychone lo[w]ere[d] and alle thynge we possesse largere. This
hafynge is meke savoure of the unsaable depnesse of alle goodnesse and
of everelastynge lyfe, in the whyche taste we are made wyde, owtetake
that resoun passes into the moste depe unmevable everlastynge
rystfulnesse of dyvynyte. Of the whiche the verre trewthe allonlye
teches experience; for whore, howe or whate it is, nowther resoun ne
exercyse may serche or knowe. And therfore oure folowynge exercyse
abydys unstabille and not knowynge manere; for that infynyte
goodnesse, the whiche we taste and possesse, we may not consayfe ne
yit undyrstonde, nor oure exercyse unto it any tyme comme. Wherfore
in oureselfe we are pore,[1] bot in God more hid is oure discrecioun, for
betwyx us and God we may fele that ther is no discrecioun.
Neverthelesse oure resoun abydes, beholdynge with opun eyghe into
the hye dyrkenesse, and into ryghtwysnesse withoute ende. In the
whiche derknesse is hid unto us the hie clerenesse, for his infynytenesse,
commynge abofe, dymmys oure resoun, goynge abofe us, in symplenesse
itselfe infourmynge abofe his consayvynge. . . .

[d] lowere] lovere.

RICHARD METHLEY
(1451/2–1527/8)

24 *To Hew Heremyte: A Pystyl of Solytary Lyfe Nowadayes*

Three groups of texts by the Carthusian Richard Methley survive. Trinity College, Cambridge, MS o. 2. 56 (1160) contains a series of autobiographical spiritual treatises in Latin from the first period of Methley's monastic life and recording received graces: *Scola Amoris Languidi* (written August 1484); *Dormitorium Dilecti Dilecti* (1485); and *Refectorium Salutis*, a kind of mystical diary recording a sequence of ecstatic experiences and spiritual presentiments day by day over several months in 1487. The London Public Record Office Collection SP 1/239 contains the second half (chs. 14–27) of *Experimentum Veritatis*, which apparently dealt as a whole with the discretion of spirits and stirrings, and Methley's English *Pystyl to Hew Heremyte*. Pembroke College, Cambridge, MS 221 contains Methley's glossed translations into Latin of *The Cloud of Unknowing* and *The Mirrour of Simple Soules*, the latter completed on 9 December 1491. The extant texts also allude to some now lost works, including a *Defensio Solitarie sive Contemplative Vita*.

The *Refectorium* records that Methley entered Mount Grace Charterhouse aged twenty-five, and here he apparently spent all his Carthusian life, recorded at his death as vicar. He was perhaps born at Methley, near Leeds, but a note in Pembroke MS 221 indicates that his real name was Furth. Although a competent Latinist, Methley's autobiographical writings say nothing about his education, but he was evidently well-read in English spiritual writings of the previous century: in the *Refectorium* he distinguishes his position from that of Rolle;[1] he is aware of the problematic aspects of *The Mirrour*; and in translating and commenting on *The Cloud*, he suggests a developing spiritual maturity. Methley's self-description in his *Refectorium* may point to early engagement with enthusiastic sensory devotion, but his writings overall – as in

Experimentum Veritatis – reveal him as a careful spiritual director of others, steeped in the English mystical tradition at the close of the Middle Ages (although complaining in his *Cloud* translation that books on contemplation are only understood with great difficulty 'in modern times'). In his *Pystyl of Solytary Lyfe Nowadayes* Methley responds with discreet wisdom to a hermit's request for guidance.

Sole manuscript: Public Record Office, London, SP 1/239, fols. 266r–267v.

> To *Hew Heremyte. Here begynneth a pystyl of solytary lyfe nowadayes.*

(1)   God almyghty, al wytty, al lovely, in whome is al goodnes, the wel of mercy and grace; the gloryous Trynyte, one God and persones thre (that is for to say, the Fader and the Sonne and the Holy Gost): he blys us with his gracyous goodnes and bryng us unto his blys in hevyn! Dere broder in Christ Jesu, thy desyre is good and holy that thou wold be infourmed after thy state that is an hermyt: how thou shuldest pleas God to his worship and profight to thy selfe. God – for his mykyl mercy, mekenes and grace – gyfe us bothe grace: me to say wel, and the to do therafter to his worship and our mede. Amen.

(2)   *Eripe me de inimicis meis Domine; ad te confugi; doce me facere voluntatem tuam, quia Deus meus es tu.*[2] That is to say in Englisshe thus: 'Lord, delyver me fro myn enemys; to the I have fled; tech me for to do thy wyl, for thou art my God.' These wordys ar pert[e]ynyng[a] to al Christen pepyl that askys to be delyverd fro ther enemyse bodely and goostly, the which do fle f[ro][b] the love of the world. But specyally they perteyne to the that hast fled to God in the wyldernes fro mannys felyship, that thou may the better lerne to do his wil; for he is thy God, and thou art to love hym specyally. Therfor how thou shalt aske hym to be delyverd fro thyn enemys, I shal by his grace tel the.

(3)   Thou hast pryncypally thre enemys: the world, thy flesshe, and the evil spyryt. Thou mayst fle fro the world to God. But thy flesshe and thy enemye wyl go with the into the wyldernes. Thou hast mervel why I say 'into the wyldernes', whan thou dwellyst in a fayer chapel of our Lady – blessyd, worshipped and thanked mut she be! Aske no more felyshyp for to talke withal but her, I pray the; and then I sey that thou

---

[a] perteynyng] pertyynyng.   [b] fro] for.

dwellyst wel in the wyldernes. And sythen yt ys so that thou hast fled fro al women, yf thou may not fle fro thyn owne flesshe, have no woman in thy mynde so ofte as her, and then wel I wot thou shalt overcome thy thre enemys by thes thre vertues, that ys to say: agaynst thyn enemy, gostly obedyence; agayn thy flesshe, clene chastyte; agaynst the world, that thou turne not to yt agayn, bot kep poverte with a good wyl. And then may thou wel say to God almyghty: 'Lord, delyver me fro myn enemyes, for I have fled to the; teche me to do thy wyl, for thou art my God.' *Eripe me de inimicis meis Domine; ad te confugi; doce me facere voluntatem tuam quia Deus meus es tu.*

(4)   But how shalt thou kepe wel obedyence, chastyte and poverty? Be obedyent to God almyghty after hys lawe, and as thou promysed before the byshop whan thou toke the to an heremyte lyfe; and also now be obedyent to thy curete, that ys thy gostly fader after God and hath charge of thy soule. Remember the then every mornyng and evenyng what thou art bounden to, and thanke God that hath called the therto, and aske hym mercy of al that thou hast not wel kept, and say to hym thus: *Eripe me de inimicis meis Domine; ad te confugi; doce me facere voluntatem tuam quia Deus meus es tu.* And aske hym grace for to do bettyr in tyme for to come.

(5)   Also clene chastyte must thou nedys kepe. I know none other in the but thou doste kepe yt. But yet I shal tel as I trow wyl do the good, by Goddys grace, and thou kepe clene chastyte by Goddys grace in body and in soule trewly to pleas God and our Lady withal, ther ys no vertue that so sone shal bryng the to the trew felyng of the love of God in erthe. But how shalt thou kepe yt by grace perfightly? Fle al womens felyshyp, and also the thought of them put out of thy mynde as sone as yt cometh, and ryse up in thy thought, in thy hert and in thy worde to God in hevyn, and say thus: Jesu, Jesu, Jesu! *Eripe me de inimicis meis Domine; ad te confugi; doce me facere voluntatem tuam quia Deus meus es tu.*

(6)   And I let the wyt ther is no maner of way that is leful to the to have the lust of thy flesshe. And thynke on wel that I say 'no maner of way': nowther lyttyl, nor mekyl, nowther one way, nowther other. And therfor a remedy I shal nowe tel the, and I pray the kepe yt wele. Thy thought may not be clene alway. But yf yt be in hevyn with God

and our Lady, or with some other good saynt or aungel, and thy thought be there with love, drede and reverence and mekenes – than dwellys thou ther as Saynt Paule sayth: *Nostra conversacio in celis est.*[3] 'Our lyvyng ys in hevyn.' And I pray the love wel our blessyd Lady and let her be thy leman swete, and say to her thus: *Tota pulchra es amica mea et macula non est in te.*[4] 'Al fayer thou art, O leman myne, and ther ys not one spot in the.' And to her pray and by her sende thy prayers to God and say thus: *Eripe me de inimicis meis Domine; ad te confugi; doce me, etc.*

(7)   Agaynst ryches of the world ys wylful poverte a good remedy. And yt ys callyd wilful poverte for yt must be with a good wyl, and yt wold be ful of a good wyl, yf thou kepe it perfightly. But how shalt thou come to this good wel? By the love of God, for scripture saith thus: *Si dederit homo omnem substanciam domus sue pro dileccione quasi [nihil]*[c] *despiciet eam.*[5] 'If a man shuld have gyven al the ryches of his howse for the love of God, as yt were noght he shal despyse yt.' And I say, and thou feld onys in thy hert the love of God, thou woldest despyse al the world, not despysyng the creatures of God, but thynkyng – in comparyson of the love of God – al the world ys but vanyte.[6] And therfor whan thou art temptyd to have goodys of the world: at the first begynnyng of thy thought, tary no longer but say to God thus in Englisshe or in Latyn as thou hast most devocyon: *Eripe me de inimicis meis Domine, etc.* And I shal teche the to understand wel this verse: *O Domine,* 'O Lord'; *eripe,* 'delyver thou'; *me,* 'me'; *de inimicis meis,* 'of myn enemys'; *confugi,* 'I have fled al togedyr'; *ad te,* 'to the'; *Doce me,* 'Teche me'; *facere voluntatem tuam,* 'to do thy wyl'; *quia Deus meus es tu,* 'for why thou art my God'.

(8)   Other thre thynges ther is nedeful for the to kepe wel: one ys thy syght; another thy sel; the third ys thy sylens, that ys to say, hold thy tonge wel. Thy syght must be nedys kepyd wel fro vanytes, and than thynke to come to hevyns blys, for the prophete Jeremy saith thus: *Oculus meus depredatus est animam meam.*[7] 'Myne eye hath deprayd my soul.' That ys for to say: Myn eye hath refte my soule a pray – as thevys do, the which lye in the weys syde to rob men, and wayten ther pray when ony come by. So whan thou shuldest thynke on goodnes –

---

[c] *nihil] non.*

that is for to say, on God and hevynly or helthful thynges for thy soule –
thyn eye wil ravysshe thy mynde here and there, but yf thou kepe yt
wel. And then as ofte as thou synnest therby, so ofte robbys thou thy
soule as a robber in the way. And as great as the synne ys, so great a
vertue takist thou fro thy soule, and so great a stroke gyves thou thy
soule. And wete thou wel that ther ys no synne lytel, but in comparyson
of a gretter: yt ys no lytel thyng to offend God almyghty. And have no
dowte: thou shalt have great stryfe with thyselfe, or thou canst
overcome thy sight. But aske God mercy, helthe and grace, and say to
hym thus: *Eripe me de inimicis meis, etc.*

(9)   Thy selle ys the second thyng that I sayd, and what cal I thy selle,
trowest thou, but the place or the chapel of owr blessyd Lady where
thou dwellyst? And wote thou wel, thou hast great cause to kepe yt wel,
for thou thar not rynne here and there to seke thy lyvyng. God hath
provyded for the, and therfor kepe thy selle, and yt wyl kepe the fro
synne. Be no home-rynner for to see mervels, no gangrel fro towne to
towne, no land-leper wavyng in the wynde lyke a laverooke. But kepe
thy sel, and yt wyl kepe the. But now thou sayst, peradventure: thou
mayst not kepe yt, for thou art sent for to gentils in the contre, whome
thou dare not displeas. I answer and say thus: Tel them that thou hast
forsakyn the world, and therfor – but in the tyme of very great nede, as
in the tyme of dethe or suche other great nede – thou mayst not let thy
devocion. And when thou shalt help them, loke thou do yt trewly for
the love of God, and take nothyng but for thy cost. And when thou
syttest by thy one in the wyldernes and art yrke or wery, say this to our
Lady as Saynt Godryke[8] sayd (that holy hermyte): *Sancta Maria, virgo
mater Jesu Christi Nazareni, protege et adiuva tuum Hugonem, suscipe
et adduce cito tecum in tuum regnum vel in Dei regnum.* (He said
adiuva tuum Godricum, but thou may [say][d] *tuum Hugonem,* for thy
name ys Hewe). This is thus to say in Englyshe: Saynt Mary, mayden
and moder of Jesu Christ of Nazareth, holde and help thy Hewe, take
and lede soave with the into thy kyngdom (or say: 'into the kyngdom of
God' – bothe ys good). And I councel the: love wel Saynt Hew,[9] of our
order of the chartyr[10] monkes. But now thou sayst, I trowe, thou must
come forthe to here messe that ys ful wel semyng but yf thou had masses
song withyn thy chapel. But when thou hast hard masse, then fle home,

---

[d] say] MS *om.*

but if thou have a ful good cause, as thou sayst in this verse: *Ad te confugi*; To the, Lord, I have fled holy bothe body and soule, as thou [art my]*ᵉ* al. For, and thou fle with thy body and not with thy hert fro the world, then art thou a fals ypocryte, as scripture sayth: *Simulatores [et]ᶠ callidi provocant iram Dei.*[11] That is thus in Englisshe: 'Fals wyly dyssemblers provoke the yre of God.' Therfor in thy nede agaynst suche temptacyons say this verse: *Eripe me de inimicis meis, etc.*

(10)   The third thyng ys thy sylence. And wete thou wele: yt wyl do the great good, and then thynk thus in thy hert, makyng no vowe but yf thou lyst: 'Good Lord, by thy grace, I thynke this day to kepe wel my tong to thy worshyp and my wele.' And specyally on fastyng dayes I councel the kepe thy sylence and speke with no creature, and thou mayst eschew yt. I have knowen some holy persones that wold so kepe ther sylence, as on Fryday, on Wedynsday, or great sayntes evyns. And the prophet Davyd sayth thus: *Obmutui et humiliatus sum et silui a bonis.*[12] 'I have hold my tonge and I have bene mekyd, and I have kepyd me styl fro good speche.' Note wel what he sayth. Fro good thynges or fro good speche I have kept me styl. And why? For fere that among good speche happon some yl. For wote thou wel: thou canst not speke mekyl good speche but some wyl be voyd or yl. And on the day of dome every man must gyf a counte of every ydel worde that he spekyth. And therfor eschew speche. And when thou felyst the temptyd to speke, say this verse: *Eripe me Domine, etc.*

(11)   Now thou mayst aske me how thou shalt be occupied day and nyght. I say: with thy dewty that thou art bounden to. And then with more that thou puttest to yt by grace and thy devocyon. Fyve thynges ther be accordyng for the, that ys to say: good prayer; medytacyon, that is callyd holy thynkyng; redyng of holy Englisshe bokes; contemplacyon, that thou mayst come to by grace and great devocyon, that ys for to say, to forget al maner of thynges but God and for great love of hym be rapt into contemplacyon; and good dedys with thy hand. And I pray the do thyn owne chores thyselfe, and thou may; and when thou art temptyd to have worke men where no myster ys, say the sayd verse: *Eripe me, etc.*

ᵉ art my] *space in MS; conjectural reading.*   *ᶠ et]* MS om.

(12) What I say nowe I pray the gyf good hede. Scripture sayth thus: *Non enim habet amaritudinem conversacio ill[ius]ᵍ nec tedium convictus illius: sed leticiam et gaudium.*¹³ Understonde yt thus: 'The conversacyon' – that ys to say, the holy lyvyng of a good man with God – 'hath no bytternes in hert nor yrksomenes to lyfe with God, but gladnes and joy.' So if thou wilt lyfe alwey in joy, kepe thy thought alwey on God with love and drede and other vertues. And in the mornyng and evenyng use long prayers or other spiritual exercyses, as ys medytacyon (as I sayd before) and other lyke; and betwene morne and evyn many prayers or spiritual exercyses, but shortly and ofte, and werke betwyxt them, and in the tyme of thy werke let not thy mynd go fro God. And in the be[gyn]nyngʰ thou shalt fele some penaunce or payne, but ever after thou shalt lyfe lyke a throstelcok or a nyghtynggale for joy! And thanke God, and pray for me, and as ofte as thou haste myster say the seid verse: *Eripe me, etc.*

Deo gracias, Amen, quoth Ricardus Methley de Monte Gracie ordinis carthusiensis fratri Hugoni devoto heremite.

ᵍ *illius] illorum.*   ʰ begynnyng] benyng.

NOTES

Introductory essay

1 Page references in the Introductory essay are to texts in this book.

2 Cf. G. Constable, 'Twelfth-Century Spirituality and the Late Middle Ages', *Medieval and Renaissance Studies*, 5 (1971), 27–60, and N. Watson, 'The Methods and Objectives of Thirteenth-Century Anchoritic Devotion', in Glasscoe, *MMTE* (1987), 132–53. See J. Ayto and A. Barratt (eds.), *Aelred of Rievaulx's De Institutione Inclusarum*, EETS, o.s. 287 (Oxford, 1984) for two Middle English translations of Aelred's *De Institutione* (c. 1160–2). The later version, of the mid fifteenth century, translates the whole work, while the earlier, late fourteenth-century version, translates Aelred's latter sections on the anchoress's inner life. On the popularity in the fourteenth and fifteenth centuries of the thirteenth-century *Mirror* of St Edmund of Abingdon, see H. P. Forshaw (ed.), *Edmund of Abingdon, Speculum Religiosorum and Speculum Ecclesie*, Auctores Britannici Medii Aevi III (London, 1973), p. 16. For the French version, see A. D. Wilshere (ed.), *Mirour de Seinte Eglyse*, Anglo-Norman Text Society (London, 1982); for the English version, see C. Horstman (ed.), *Yorkshire Writers* (London, 1895), I, pp. 219–61. John Whiterig ('The Monk of Farne'), a Benedictine monk of Durham, was a fourteenth-century English mystic whose meditations were written in Latin: see W. A. Pantin, 'The Monk-Solitary of Farne: A Fourteenth-Century English Mystic', *English Historical Review*, 59 (1944), 162–86, and H. Farmer, '*Meditaciones Cuiusdam Monachi Apud Farneland Quondam Solitarii*', *Studia Anselmiana*, 41 (1957), 141–245.

3 On the works of Ruusbroec and Suso in England, see p. 288, n. 1, and the Guide to further reading, pp. 297–8.

4 On transmission and readership, see the Guide to further reading, pp. 298–9.

5 The *Defensorium contra Oblectratores eiusdem Ricardi quod composuit Thomas Basseth sancte memorie* is edited in M. G. Sargent, 'Contemporary Criticism of Richard Rolle', *Kartäusermystik und -mystiker*, AC, 55.1 (1981), 160–205, and Allen, *Writings*, 529–37.

6 On possible awareness of each other's work in Hilton and the *Cloud*-author, see J. P. H. Clark and R. Dorward (eds.), *Walter Hilton: 'The Scale of Perfection'* (Mahwah, 1991), Introduction, pp. 24–7.

7 By 'anoþer mans werk' the early fifteenth-century copy of *The Cloud* in University College, Oxford, MS 14 has the marginal note *hyltons*, probably in an early sixteenth-century hand, as noted in P. Hodgson (ed.), *The Cloud of Unknowing and Related Treatises* (Salzburg, 1982), p. 170.

8 M. G. Sargent (ed.), *Nicholas Love's 'Mirror of the Blessed Life of Jesus Christ'* (New York, 1992), p. 10. At the close of his discussion of the active and contemplative lives, Love refers his reader to the 'tretees þat þe worþi clerk & holi lyuere Maister Walter Hilton þe Chanon of Thurgarton wrote in english' for 'vertuese exercise þat longeþ to contemplatif lyuyng, & specialy to a recluse, & also of medelet life, þat is to sey sumtyme actife & sumtyme contemplatif, as it longeþ to diuerse persones þat in worldly astate hauen grace of gostly loue' (p. 124).

9 Cf. W. A. Pantin, 'Instructions for a Devout and Literate Layman', in *Medieval Learning and Literature: Essays Presented to R. W. Hunt*, ed. J. J. G. Alexander and M. T. Gibson (Oxford, 1976), 398–422.

10 BL MS Harley 6579: the passage on charity is written on a slip of vellum sewn to the outer edge of fol. 48, so as to form part of ch. 70.

11 For other 'forestalled questions', all at chapter openings, see *Cloud*, chs. 8, 28, 34, 41, 42.

12 'De illis secularibus loquor qui absque preceptore doctoreque ydoneo homine uel libro proprium motum animi sequentes viam vite spiritualis aggredi non formidant, quorum plures hoc capiuntur errore vanitatis, et pauci euadunt. Si enim nulla ars eciam minima perfecte adquiri poterit ab aliquo nisi aliquo docente et instruente, quanto difficilius ergo ars arcium, videlicet perfectus Dei cultus in vita spirituali apprehendi poterit absque preceptore homine' (*Walter Hilton's Latin Writings*, ed. Clark and Taylor [Salzburg, 1987], i, 137–8).

13 Ed. M. S. Westra (The Hague, 1950), 68. The *Talking* is a late fourteenth-century reworking of two early thirteenth-century pieces from the 'Wooing Group' of lyrical meditations, the *Ureisun of God Almihti* and *ÞeWohunge of ure Lauerd*.

14 Cf. 'Right as deth doth to þe body: so doth loue to þe soule', *The Tree and XII Frutes of the Hooly Goost*, Fitzwilliam Museum, Cambridge, MS McClean 132, fol. 125r; ed. J. J. Vaissier (Groningen, 1960), 46.

15 Lambeth Palace Library MS 472 – containing texts of *The Scale of Perfection*, Books I and II, *Mixed Life*, *Eight Chapters on Perfection*, the psalm commentaries *Qui Habitat* and *Bonum Est*, and the commentary on the *Benedictus* – collects together most of the works either by Hilton or associated with him (except *Of Angels' Song*), and is the base manuscript for *Mixed Life*, *Eight Chapters* and *Qui Habitat* in the present book. It belonged to one John Killum, grocer of London (d. 1416), and a contemporary inscription indicates that it was a 'common profit' book, i.e. to be circulated amongst acquaintances and bequeathed to others who would continue the circulation: 'And so be it delyuerid and committid fro persoone to persoone, man or womman, as longe as þe booke enduriþ' (fol. 260r). On 'common profit' books, see J. Griffiths and D. Pearsall (eds.), *Book Production and Publishing in Britain 1375–1475* (Cambridge, 1989), pp. 312–13, 319–20.

16 In *Fourteenth-Century English Poetry* (Oxford, 1983), Elizabeth Salter comments: 'The finest work of Hilton, of the author of the *Cloud of Unknowing*, and of Dame Julian of Norwich was done in highly specialized contexts for named or unnamed disciples of special vocation, and in close contact with other specialist literature of the contemplative life. The best religious prose of the

century was written for a spiritual elite' (p. 43). In an introductory essay –
'Contemplative Literature and Bourgeois Piety in Late Medieval England' – in
M. G. Sargent (ed.), *Nicholas Love's 'Mirror of the Blessed Life of Jesus Christ'*
(New York, 1992), pp. lviii–lxxii, it is also observed that 'the most influential
late fourteenth-century contemplative and devotional writings became so
precisely because they were appropriated by an early fifteenth-century audience
of literate, well-to-do London burghers . . . . Within perhaps two decades of
their author's death, therefore, Walter Hilton's *Scale of Perfection* and *Of
Mixed Life* were being copied for, and presumably read by, devout, prosperous
London businessmen . . .' (pp. lix, lxii).

17 'My dere brother and sister, I se weel that many wolde ben in religioun but they
mowe nowt for poverte or for awe or for drede of her kyn or for bond of
maryage. Therfore I make here a book of relygyoun of the herte, that is of the
Abbey of the Holy Goost, that all tho that mow nout been in bodylyche
relygyon mow been in gostly', N. F. Blake (ed.), *Middle English Religious Prose*
(London, 1972), p. 89.

18 'Al-so I reproue not gret ȝernynges and louely longyngis þat sum men han to
God þat ȝeuen hem onli to tente to him in contemplacioun and to no þynge
elles, for þat is gode, but my menynge is for to telle hou a man may with werkis
of actif lyfe haue contemplacioun of ihesu crist' (ed. H. Kane [Salzburg, 1983],
ch. 16). On the Vernon manuscript compiler as also drawn towards the idea of
the mixed life, see S. S. Hussey, 'Implication of Choice and Arrangement of
Texts in Part 4', in D. Pearsall (ed.), *Studies in the Vernon Manuscript*
(Cambridge, 1990), 61–74.

19 'Nam in conceptibus tuis es multum singularis et altus, ymaginando, inuestigando
et extendendo cor tuum in meditacione tua aliter et ad alia quam via[m]
ueritatis quam nobis experti tradiderunt. Multum es curiosus in proferendo
que sentis et quasi mirabilis, vix ab aliquo intelligibilis. Non totaliter reprobo,
sed timeo. . . . ' (ed. Clark and Turner [Salzburg, 1987], ii, 225).

20 Cf. *The Chastising of God's Children*, ed. J. Bazire and E. Colledge (Oxford,
1957), ch. 10: 'Sum of these men bi a grete singularite desiren of God sum
special gifte above other [either of worchynge myraclis or visions, either
revelacions or sum other specialte]; . . . a ful litel thing may comforte suche
men, for thei knowen nat what hem lackith' (p. 135; material in square brackets
added to Ruusbroec). Cf. also the tracts *Vt inclusi non querant signa et
mirabilia* (in Christ's College, Cambridge MS DD. 1. 11), and *Confirmacio
ordinis Carthusiensis* (in Trinity College, Cambridge, MS O. 8. 26) which
insists 'Multi enim fuerunt sancti et sunt qui non fecerunt miracula neque
faciunt, nec canonizati sunt' (fol. 86v).

21 Cf. *Scale*, I, 11; II, 29.

22 *Qui Habitat*, ed. B. Wallner (Lund, 1954), 22; *De Lectione*, ed. Clark and
Turner (Salzburg, 1987), ii, 228; *Scale*, II, 26 . Cf. J. P. H. Clark, 'Walter Hilton
and Liberty of Spirit', *DownR*, 96 (1978), 61–78.

23 Bodleian Library MS Douce 114; CUL MS Hh. 1. 11. See the Guide to further
reading, p. 296. MS Douce 114, from the Charterhouse of Beauvale in
Nottinghamshire, contains Middle English versions of three lives of *béguines*

from the Low Countries: Jacques de Vitry's life of Mary of Oignies; Philip of
Clairvaux's life of Elizabeth of Spalbeck; and Thomas of Cantimpré's life of
Christina Mirabilis.
24 Cf. P. S. Jolliffe, 'Two Middle English Tracts on the Contemplative Life', *MS*,
37 (1975), 85–121.
25 The following items in this book are edited from manuscripts with Carthusian
connections: 8, 13, 16, 18, 19, 20, 22, 23, 24. See also pp. 278–9, n. 1. On the
Carthusians, see the Guide to further reading, p. 298, and on various later
selections and adaptations of mystic texts, see pp. 298–9.
26 It includes Misyn's Englishings of Rolle's *Emendatio Vitae* and *Incendium
Amoris*; extracts from Rolle's *Form of Living* arranged as a piece *De triplici
genere amoris spiritualis*; extracts from *Form of Living* (as *Tractatus de
diligendo Deo*), and *Ego Dormio*; the only extant copies of the shorter version
of Julian's *Revelations* and *The Treatise of Perfection of the Sons of God*; *The
Mirrour of Simple Soules*; an extract from the English version of Suso's
Horologium Sapientiae; a brief piece from an English version of the *Revelations*
of St Bridget of Sweden, together with some other brief pieces.

The Fire of Love

1 'Admirabar magis quam enuncio quando siquidem sentiui cor meum primitus
incalescere, et uere non imaginarie, quasi sensibile igne estuare. Eram equidem
attonitus quemadmodum eruperat ardor in animo, et de insolito solacio;
propter inexperienciam huius abundancie, sepius pectus meum si forte esset
feruor ex aliqua exteriori causa palpitaui. Cumque cognouissem quod ex
interiori solummodo efferbuisset, et non esset a carne illud incendium amoris,
et concupiscencia, in qua continui, quod donum esset Conditoris, letabundus
liquefactus sum in affectum amplioris dileccionis' (Emmanuel College,
Cambridge, MS 35, fol. 63r; ed. M. Deanesly [Manchester, 1915], p. 145).
2 'Feruorem autem uoco, quando mens amore eterno ueracitur incenditur, et cor
eodem modo amore ardere non estimatiue sed realiter sentitur. Cor enim in
igne conuersum sensum prebet incendii amoris. Canorem uoco quando iam in
animo, abundante ardore, suscipitur suauitas laudis eterne, ac cogitatus in
canticum conuertitur, et mens in mellifluum melos immoratur. Hec duo non in
ocio percipiuntur, sed in summa deuocione, ex quibus tercium, scilicet,
dulcedo inestimabilis adest. Feruor enim et canor mirabilem in anima causant
dulcorem; et eciam ob nimiam dulcedinem illa causari possunt' (fol. 75r; p. 185).
3 'Dum enim in eadem capella sederem, et in nocte ante cenam psalmos prout
potui decantarem, quasi tinnitum psallencium uel pocius canencium supra me
ascultaui. Cumque celestibus eciam orando toto desiderio intenderem, nescio
quomodo mox in me concentum canorum sensi, et delectabilissi nam armoniam
celicus excepi, mecum manentem in mente. Nam cogitacio mea continuo in
carmen canorum commutabatur, et quasi odas habui meditando, et eciam
oracionibus ipsis et psalmodia eundem sonum edidi. Deinceps usque ad
canendum que prius dixeram, pre affluencia suauitatis interne prorupi, occulte
quidem, quia tantummodo coram Conditore meo' (fol. 18r; pp. 189–90).

4 Cf. the thirteenth-century Anglo-Latin poems of divine love: John of Hoveden's
   Philomena, ed. C. Blume (Leipzig, 1930), and John Pecham's *Philomela*, in
   Opera Omnia Sancti Bonaventurae, ed. A. Peltier, 15 vols. (Paris, 1864–71), xii,
   162–66.

5 Cf. 'Swet Jhesu, þy body is lyke a boke written al with rede ynke; so is þy body
   al written with rede woundes. Now, swete Jhesu, graunt me to rede upon þy
   boke, and somwhate to undrestond þe swetnes of þat writynge, and to have
   likynge in studious abydynge of þat redynge' (*Meditations on the Passion*, Text
   II, in H. E. Allen (ed.), *English Writings of Richard Rolle* (Oxford, 1931), p. 36).
   For the meditations on the Passion attributed to Rolle, see also S. J.
   Ogilvie-Thomson (ed.), *Richard Rolle: Prose and Verse*, EETS, o.s. 293
   (Oxford, 1988).

6 That part of Rolle's commentary on the Canticles treating Canticles 1: 3
   (*Oleum effusum nomen tuum*; 'Thy name is as ointment poured forth')
   circulated separately as the tract *Encomium Nominis Jesu*, and was also
   rendered into English versions that enthusiastically expound devotion to the
   Holy Name, as in this extract from a text in BL MS Harley 1022:
   'A, þat wondurful name! A, þat delytabul name! Þis is þo name þat es
   aboue al names, name alþer-heghest, with-outen qwilk na man hopes hele. Þis
   name es swete & Ioyful, gyfand sothfast comforth vnto mans hert. Sothle þo
   name of Ihesu es in my mynde Ioyus sang, in myn ere heuenly sounde, in my
   mouth hunyful swetnes. . . . I can noght pray, I can noght haue mynde, bot
   sownand þo name of Ihesu. . . . Qwar-so I be, qwar-so I sit, qwat-so I do, þo
   mynd of þo name of Ihesu departes noght fra my mynde. I haue set it as a
   takenyng opon my hert, als takenyng apon myn arme. . . . ' (fol. 62; ed.
   Horstman, i, 186–7).

7 'Istum ergo librum offero intuendum, non philosophis, non mundi sapientibus,
   non magnis theologicis infinitis quescionibus implicatis, sed rudibus et
   indoctis, magis Deum diligere quam multa scire conantibus. Non enim
   disputando sed agendo scietur, et amando. Arbitror autem ea que hic
   continentur ab istis questionariis et in omni sciencia summis, sed in amore
   Christi inferioribus, non posse intellegi. Unde nec eis scribere decreui, nisi
   postpositis et oblitis cunctis que ad mundum pertinent, solis Conditoris
   desideriis inardescant mancipari' (fol. 63v; p. 147).

The Mendynge of Lyfe

1 On the English versions of *Emendatio Vitae* (of which the present extract serves
   as a brief example), see M. G. Amassian, 'The Rolle Material in Bradfer-Lawrence
   MS 10 and its Relationships to other Rolle Manuscripts', *Manuscripta*, 23
   (1979), 67–78.

2 Cf. this summary of the twelve chapters in Bodleian Library MS Douce 322:
   'ffurst that a man turne hym to god by good werk*es* and loue hym. Howe that a
   man shuld dispyse the world. Howe that a man shuld lyve in wylfull*e* pouerte.
   Howe that a man shuld ordeyne and dispose hys lyvyng. Of tribulacions and
   disceytes of the fende. Of pacyence ayenst tribulaciouns and temptacions. Of
   prayer in temptacioun or in tribulacioun. Of meditacions. Of redyng. Of

purete and clennesse. Of the loue of god. Of contemplacioun' (fol. 78r).

3 On Rachel, see pp. 90, 118–19.
4 Psalms 88: 16 (89: 15).
5 I Corinthians 13: 12.
6 Psalms 138 (139): 12.
7 II Corinthians 3: 18.
8 Luke 24: 45.
9 Revelation 4: 1.
10 Psalms 17: 12 (18: 11); Psalms 98 (99): 7.
11 Cf. Psalms 33: 9 (34: 8); 118 (119): 103.
12 Canticles 8: 1.

Ego Dormio

1 Canticles 5: 2.
2 Pseudo-Dionysius the Areopagite first enumerated the nine orders of angels. Cf. Colossians 1: 16; Ephesians 1: 21.
3 The first nine lines derive from a Latin meditation *Respice in Faciem Christi*, attributed in the Middle Ages to Augustine, and used by Rolle in *Incendium Amoris*, ch. 27. (The whole lyric is redolent of the *Incendium*). The three lines 'Nayled . . . blody syde' derive from another Latin meditation, *Candet Nudatum Pectus*. For vernacular versions, see Carleton Brown (ed.), *Religious Lyrics of the XIVth Century* (Oxford, 1924), 1–2, 241–3.
4 The opening recalls *Incendium*, chs. 42 and 34; cf. also *Dulcis Jesu Memoria*, 74–6, in F. J. E. Raby (ed.), *The Oxford Book of Medieval Latin Verse* (Oxford, 1959), 350 ('mi Iesu, quando venies? / quando me laetum facies? / me de te quando saties?').
5 Rolle's meaning here is now obscure. H. E. Allen (*English Writings*, 150), taking the line to refer to a knight's stall with his arms above, translates: 'My heart paints the banner [with some badge of Jesus] by which we know our place.' S. J. Ogilvie-Thomson (*Richard Rolle*, 206), taking *pall* as the cloth covering the chalice, and hence the Eucharist, translates: 'My heart imagines/depicts the Eucharistic sacrifice/ support which is the cause of our salvation.'

The Commandment

1 Cf. Rolle's account of the three degrees of love in *Emendatio Vitae* (ch. 11): 'Þi loue is insuperable whan no thing þat is contrarye to Goddes wille may ouercome it. . . . On þis manere shal þi loue be insuperable: þat no thing may bringe it doun to doo sinne, but þou art springinge up thoruh vertues. . . . Whan þi soule is on him euere thinkinge, no time him foryetinge, but undepartably cleueth to Jhesu Crist, þi loue is called inseparable & euerelastinge. What loue may þer be more þan þis? Yit is þer þe þridde degree, þat is called singuler. . . . A soule þat is set in þis degree loueth Crist for himself. Jhesu she thristeth; Jhesu she coueyteth; him oonly she desireth; in him she brenneth, and in him she brennyngely resteth. No thing is so sweete to hire, no thing savoury, but if it be menged with Jhesu, whos mynde is as a melodye of musike, in a feste of wyne' (CUL MS Ff. 5. 30, fols. 158v–159r). See also *Form of Living*, ch. 8.

2 Proverbs 8: 17.
3 Cf. Job 21: 13.

The Form of Living

1 Psalms 58: 10 (59: 9).
2 Variously attributed to Jerome; for 'Bernard', cf. William of St Thierry, *Epistola ad Fratres de Monte Dei* (PL, 184.328).
3 Joshua 1: 7.
4 Revelation 1: 9ff.
5 Cf. Cassian's *Collationes*, 14.11 (PL, 49.1025); II Corinthians 11: 14.
6 Cf. Hugo Argentinensis, *Compendium theologicae veritatis*, ii, 66.
7 Ecclesiastes 5: 2; Ecclesiasticus 34: 7.
8 Lamentations 1: 15.
9 With the next four paragraphs on sins 'of the hert', 'of the mowthe', 'of dede' and 'of omission', cf. *Comp. theol. ver.*, iii, 30, 31, 32, 33, and see Ogilvie-Thomson, *Richard Rolle*, 196–8.
10 The remainder of the chapter has links with *Emendatio Vitae*, ch. 4.
11 Ecclesiasticus 7: 40.
12 Canticles 2: 5.
13 I Corinthians 15: 41.
14 Cf. St Bernard, *Sermo in Cantica* (PL,183.847): 'Jesus mel in ore, in aure melos, in corde jubilus'.
15 Romans 13: 10.
16 For much of this paragraph, cf. Pomerius, *De Vita Contemplativa* (PL , 59.463), cited in *Comp. theol. ver.*, v, 23.
17 Cf. I Corinthians 13: 2–3.
18 Cf. Matthew 7: 15.
19 Cf. Isaiah 66: 2.
20 Cf. Canticles 8: 6.
21 Cf. Psalms 75: 3 (76: 2).
22 Ecclesiastes 9: 1–2.
23 Cf. St Augustine, Sermon LXX (PL, 38.444).
24 Hosea 2: 14.
25 Cf. variant ending in some copies: 'and kepe þe from alle yuel & bringe þe to þi spouse þat þou hast take þe to, þe whiche is euer lyvynge wiþouten ende' (Gonville and Caius College, Cambridge, MS 669/644, fol. 209).

The Cloud of Unknowing

1 He writes that God will stir others 'to ʒeue us oure needful þinges þat longen to þis liif, as mete & clothes wiþ alle þeese oþer, ʒif he se þat [we] wil not leue þe werke of his loue for besines aboute hem' (ch. 23). In ch. 10, after the phrase 'in þee, & in alle oþer þat han in a trewe wile forsaken þe woreld', BL MS Harley 674, and other MSS, have a cancelled addition: '& arte oblischid vnto any degree in deuoute leuyng in Holi Chirche, what-so it be, priue or aperte, & þer-to þat wil be rewlid not after þeire owne wille & þeire owne witte, bot after

þe wille & þe counsel of þeire souereins, what-so þei be, religious or seculeres' (fol. 35v). In *Discrecion of Stirings* he warns against abnormal ascetic discipline and 'singulere abites of diuerse & deuisid broþerhedes' (ed. Hodgson, *Deonise Hid Diuinite*, p. 70). No vows of obedience or regular observance of the divine office are ever mentioned. It remains an open question whether author or recipient were Carthusians. In his Latin translation of *The Cloud* Richard Methley was persuaded, commenting (Pembroke College, Cambridge MS 221, fol. 4v) on the author's reference (ch. 1) to the 'singular' form of life: 'scilicet, heremitarum anachoritarum, vel precipue cartusiensium, unde videtur quod cuidam carthusiensi hic liber compositus fuit, quia . . . non solent moderni de approbata religione exire ad heremum vt antiquitus sed ad Cartusienses' [that is hermits, anchorites and especially Carthusians. Hence we may conclude that this book was written for a Carthusian, since it is not customary now as it was once to leave an approved religious order for a hermitage, but only for Carthusians].

2 On sources of *The Cloud*, see the Guide to further reading, pp. 291–2.

3 Cf. I Corinthians 13: 12.

4 Cf. I Corinthians 15: 52.

5 Cf. I Corinthians 15: 47, 49; Colossians 3: 9.

The Book of Privy Counselling

1 In *The Cloud* reference to scripture and authorities had been judged unnecessary for the recipient, with tart comments on the temptations of an over-quoted style: 'For somtyme men þouȝt it meeknes to sey nouȝt of þeire owne hedes, bot ȝif þei afermid it by Scripture & doctours wordes; & now it is turnid into corioustee & schewyng of kunnyng. To þee it nediþ not, & þerfore I do it nouȝt' (ch. 70).

2 Cf. I Corinthians 13: 12.

3 Matthew 9: 21; Mark 5: 28.

4 Proverbs 3: 9, 10.

5 Cf. Exodus 3: 14.

6 Proverbs 3: 13–14, 21–6.

7 Romans 13: 10.

8 Matthew 22: 40.

9 Love as the 'foot' of the soul is a traditional notion; cf. *A Ladder of Foure Ronges*, p. 252.

10 Proverbs 4: 22.

11 Proverbs 3: 25.

12 Proverbs 3: 26.

13 Psalms 67: 28 (Vulgate).

14 Cf. *Liber de Praecepto et Dispensatione*, ch. 6 (PL, 182.868).

15 I.e. *The Epistle of Prayer*, *The Cloud of Unknowing* and *Hid Diuinite*. No Middle English version is extant of the *Benjamin Major*, in which Richard of St Victor uses the Exodus account of the building of the Ark of the Covenant to structure his teaching on contemplation.

16 Cf. Colossians 2: 2–3.

280   *to pages 93–118*

17 Matthew 16: 24.
18 John 10: 9; 10: 1.
19 John 15: 5.
20 John 16: 7.
21 A commonplace; the title 'doctor' was sometimes applied to the early Fathers, sometimes to schoolmen (e.g. to Aquinas in *The Epistle of Prayer*).
22 I Corinthians 8: 1.

Mystical Prayer

1 See p. 77 above, and cf. '& ȝif we wil ententifly preie for getyng of goodes, lat us crie, ouþer wiþ worde or wiþ þouȝt or wiþ desire, nouȝt elles, ne no mo wordes, bot þis worde GOD' (*Cloud*, ch. 39).

Epistle on the Mixed Life

1 Cf. A. B. Emden, *A Biographical Register of the University of Cambridge to A. D. 1500* (Cambridge, 1963), s.v. Hilton, Walter de.
2 On Hilton's defence of orthodoxy, it may be noted that in 1388 the Prior of Thurgarton was authorized to arrest, examine and imprison heretics.
3 For Gregory on the 'mixed life', see C. Butler, *Western Mysticism* (London, 1926), 176-86.
4 Cf. *Scale*, I, 5: 'Þe secund partie of contemplacioun lies principaly in affeccioun withouten vnderstondyng of gostly thynges, and þis is comunly of symple & vnlettred men whilk gyuen hem holly to deuocioun' (CUL MS Add. 6686, p. 281).
5 *Mixed Life* survives in a longer and shorter version, and is here edited from a manuscript of the longer. The shorter version lacks two passages at the opening and close (beginning at 'Grace and goodnesse' and ending at 'overpressid of himself', pp. 111, 130). Both versions contain the allusions to a wealthy married recipient known personally to the author. The longer version – variously addressed in manuscripts to 'Brothir and sustir' or 'Bretherne and systerne' – is hence usually regarded as an adaptation for a wider audience of a text originally addressed 'Dere brothir in Crist'. The manuscripts show such diversity over the text's division into chapters as to suggest that no extant scheme is authorial. Chapter divisions in the base text have therefore been omitted.
6 I Corinthians 11: 9.
7 I Corinthians 15: 46.
8 Canticles 2: 4.
9 Cf. Luke 10: 38–42.
10 Cf. Gregory, *Homiliarium in Ezechielem Libri*, 2.2.11 (PL, 76.954).
11 Luke 6: 12.
12 Cf. Romans 12: 4–5, and Gregory, *Moralium Libri*, 19.25.45 (PL, 76.126).
13 Genesis 29.
14 For Gregory on Leah and Rachel, cf. *Hom. in Ezech.* 2.2.10 (PL, 76.954); *Mor.* 6.37.61 (PL, 75.764).
15 Genesis 29: 17.

16 Leviticus 6: 12.

17 Deuteronomy 4: 24; Hebrews 12: 29; cf. *Scale*, ii, 33.

18 Luke 12: 49.

19 Cf. *Epist. Joannis ad Parthos*, 4.6 (*PL*, 35.2008), and *Cloud*, ch. 75 ('Seint Austyne ... seiþ þat "al þe liif of a good Cristen man is not elles bot holy desire"').

20 II Corinthians 5: 6-9.

21 Colossians 2: 9.

22 Ecclesiastes 3: 1.

23 Cf. Hilton's definition of the highest degree of contemplation in *Scale*, i, 9: 'And also þoȝ a man whilk is actif haue þe ȝyft of it by a special grace, neuerþeles þe full vse of it as I hope may no man haue bot he be solitarie and in lyfe contemplatif' (CUL MS Add. 6686, p. 284).

24 Proverbs 25: 27.

25 Ecclesiasticus 3: 22.

26 *Mor.* 22.19.45 (*PL* 76.240); *Hom. in Ezech.* 2.3.3 (*PL* 76.959).

Of Angels' Song

1 On mankind's fallen sensuality that will 'wrechidly & wantounly weltre, as a swine in þe myre, in þe welþes of þis woreld & þe foule flessche', see *Cloud*, ch. 66.

Eight Chapters on Perfection

1 Selection of chapters in the five partial manuscripts extant can offer pointers to what contemporary readers especially valued: BL MS Add. 60577 has ch. 8 (fols. 146v–150r); BL Harley 6615 has ch. 2 (fols. 100v–103v); CUL MS hh. 1. 12 has chs. 1, 5, 8 (fols. 96r–99r); Lambeth Palace Library MS 541 has part of ch. 5, and ch. 8 (fols. 147r–150v). St John's College, Oxford, MS 94 includes both ch. 2 and chs. 3, 5, 8 (fols. 141v–144v), and also has a variant concluding address: 'Therfore taketh þis trety to herte, & beeth war for ȝowre self, and for alle þoo þat been under ȝowre gouernayle, and þat þai been in good gouernayle. *Qui fecit celum et terram, det nobis vitam sempiternam.* Amen'. The *Disce Mori* compilation also includes ch. 8: see A. Hudson, 'A Chapter from Walter Hilton and Two Middle English Compilations', *Neophilologus*, 52 (1968), 416–21.

2 On Lluis de Font, see A. B. Emden, *A Biographical Register of the University of Cambridge to A. D. 1500* (Cambridge, 1963), 236. Hilton's knowledge of de Font's work suggests his continuing contact with Cambridge circles later in his career.

3 *Dicta Catonis*, iii, 2 ('Mind not ill tongues, if you live straight of soul'), in J. W. Duff and A. M. Duff (eds.), *Minor Latin Poets*, Loeb Classical Library (London, 1984), 610.

4 II Corinthians 1: 7.

5 II Corinthians 3: 17.

6 Galatians 5: 18.

7 II Peter 2: 19.

8 I Corinthians 6: 17.

9 Six extant manuscripts containing ch. 8 read 'men and wommen', and four read 'men' (including Lambeth Palace Library MS 472, base text for this edition). One manuscript (Bibliothèque Nationale, Paris, fonds anglais 41) has as a colophon the material used as an incipit in some manuscripts (as in Lambeth 472), but reads: 'Here eenden þese eiȝte chapitris necessarie for men & wommen þat ȝeuen hem to perfeccioun . . . ' and describes the work as having been translated into the English tongue 'for þe comown profyȝt' (fol. 156r). Concluding its anthology of chapters St John's College, Oxford, MS 94 has: 'Koueth not mekul to plese to be loued, for it is a gret distraccion to þe herte, & turbacion to þe mynde, and þou schalt vnderstonde ho þat couetuth to be loued of wemen, he schal not lacken of temptacion, and he schal haf mater of schrewed occupacions, and continual occasions of turbacions & peynful, and he schal not wanten of suspicius obseruans. *Gregorius in Moralia: Suspicio non est sine tribulacione et angustia*' (fol. 144v).

The Scale of Perfection, Book I

1 In *Scale*, II, 17, on the distance between reforming in faith and in feeling, Hilton writes: 'Fro þe lowest to þe heiȝest may not a soule sodeynly stirte, no more þan a man þat wil clymbe vpon an hiȝe laddre & settiþ his fot vpon þe lowest stele, may at þe neȝst flien vp to þe heiȝest, bot hym behouiþ gon by processe on aftir anoþer til he may come to þe ouerest' (BL MS 6579, fol. 79r).

2 Sixty-two manuscripts are known to survive (including Wynkyn de Worde's edition of 1494); six contain extracts only. Cf. S. S. Hussey, 'Editing the Middle English Mystics', *AC*, 35.2 (1982), 167, and 'The Text of *The Scale of Perfection*, Book II', *NM*, 65 (1964), 75-92.

3 Joel 2: 32.

4 I John 1: 8.

5 John 14: 2

6 Canticles 5: 1.

7 Luke 10: 42

8 Deuteronomy 11: 24.

The Scale of Perfection, Book II

1 I John 1: 5.

2 Psalms 35: 10 (36: 9).

3 Deuteronomy 4: 24; Hebrews 12: 29.

4 II Corinthians 4: 18.

5 John 17: 3.

6 Psalms 28 (29): 4.

7 Hebrews 4: 12.

8 Revelation 8: 1.

9 Romans 8: 16.

10 II Corinthians 1: 12.

11 Cf. Psalm 63: 7.

12 Hosea 2: 14.

13 Isaiah 24: 16.
14 Revelation 2: 17.
15 Canticles 5: 2.
16 Luke 9: 32.
17 Job 34: 29.
18 Canticles 3: 1.
19 Canticles 2: 17.
20 Canticles 1: 2.
21 Hebrews 10: 38; Romans 1: 17.
22 John 3: 8.

Qui Habitat

1 No explicit attribution in any extant manuscript is known, although in a
now-lost volume at Syon (MS M 26) *Qui Habitat* was apparently ascribed to
Hilton, along with the commentary on Psalm 91 (*Bonum Est*), which is not now
attributed to him (cf. Mary Bateson (ed.), *Catalogue of the Library of Syon
Monastery, Isleworth* [Cambridge, 1898], 227, 96–115). For parallels with
other Hilton works, see J. P. H. Clark, 'Walter Hilton and the Psalm
Commentary *Qui Habitat*', *DownR*, 100 (1982), 235–62, who points out (p.
248) that *Qui Habitat* seems to refer itself to those who are not necessarily
living in the cloister.
2 Matthew 5: 8.

The Prickynge of Love

1 Manuscripts with attributions to Hilton are: CUL MS HH. 1. 12; Durham
University Library, Cosin V. III; Somerset Record Office, Heneage MS 3084;
Stonor Park (now University of Pennsylvania English MS 8).
2 In ch. 26 the original's long description of spiritual joys that follow 'inebriation'
becomes in English simply 'what he schal gyve thee aftir this drunkenesse, bi
asaie thou maist wite, if he wole'. In ch. 27 the translator introduces some
original passages in an attempt to distinguish between the two classes of
spiritual sweetness which his source describes, adding sundry cautions and
comfortings, and invoking – as throughout his work – the name of Christ.

Revelations of Divine Love (shorter version)

1 Linking Julian's carefully orthodox remarks on 'payntyngys of crucyfexes' (in
the first paragraph of the shorter version) with the sensitivity of this matter in
view of Lollard antagonism to images, Nicholas Watson has argued – 'The
Composition of Julian of Norwich's *Revelation of Love*', *Speculum*, 68 (1993),
637–83 – that the Amherst version dates from no earlier than 1382, and
probably several years later (rather than from the 1370s, as widely assumed),
and that Julian's longer version consequently dates from near the end of her life
(rather than from the 1390s, to which Julian dates her further understanding of
the vision of the Lord and Servant).
2 Editorial division into chapters corresponds to divisions signalled by large

initial capitals in the manuscript.

3 On Mary as type figure of contemplatives, see p. 153.

4 For the martyrdom of St Cecilia – who survived miraculously for three days despite three terrible blows to her neck from her executioners – see Chaucer's *Second Nun's Tale.*

5 The longer version interpolates here a brief passage beginning 'And in the same sheweing sodenly the Trinite fullfilled the herte most of ioy', and ending 'And this was shewed in the first and in all; for where Iesus appereith the blissid Trinite is understond, as to my sight' (ch. 4).

6 'Bless you, Lord.'

7 Luke 1: 38.

8 An extended interpolation here in the longer version enlarges on the bleeding, and continues: 'And of all the sight it was most comfort to me that our God and lord, that is so reverent and dredefull, is so homley and curtes . . . . It is the most worshippe that a solemne king or a grete lord may doe a pore servant if he will be homely with him' (ch. 7).

9 Cf II Corinthians 12: 5.

10 Cf. I John 4: 8, 20.

11 Cf. I Corinthians 14: 34; I Timothy 2: 12.

12 Cf. II Corinthians 12: 4.

13 Cf. Romans 8: 35; Matthew 8: 25, 14: 30.

14 Cf. Isaiah 54: 7.

15 Cf. John 19: 28.

16 Cf. Philippians 2: 5; Acts 17: 28; I Corinthians 6: 17.

17 Cf. Matthew 24: 29; Mark 13: 24.

18 Cf. I Corinthians 2: 9.

19 Cf. John 19: 34.

20 Cf. Colossians 2: 9.

21 Cf. Matthew 5: 6.

22 Cf. II Samuel 11; Matthew 26: 69–75; Acts 7: 58; John 20: 25–8; Luke 7: 37.

23 Cf. II Corinthians 12: 7.

24 I.e. in the 5th shewing.

25 The LV manuscripts read 'touching' (ch. 74).

26 The LV manuscripts read 'love' (ch. 74).

Revelations of Divine Love (longer version)

1 For the servant in chapter 51, cf. the 'Servant Songs' of Isaiah 52: 13; 53: 4–7, 10–11.

2 On Jesus our Mother, see the Guide to further reading, p. 294.

3 Cf. Isaiah 42: 1.

4 Cf. I Corinthians 15: 21–2.

5 Cf. Genesis 2: 7.

6 Cf. Matthew 13: 44.

7 Cf. I Corinthians 15: 45–9.

8 Cf. Philippians 2: 1–11.

9 Chapter 59 has ended on three 'manner of beholdyng of moderhede in God', third of which is 'moderhede of werkyng, and therin is a forthspreadyng, be the

same grace, of length and bredth and of heyth and of depenes withouten end, and al his own luf'. Chapter 61 comments on Jesus' allowing us to fall: 'For it nedith us to fallen, and it nedith us to sen it. . . . And be the assay of this failyng we shall have an hey mervelous knoweing of love in God without end'.

10 I.e. the first revelation (sv, ch. 4; LV, ch. 4).
11 I.e. the ninth revelation (sv, ch. 12; LV, ch. 22).
12 I.e. the twelfth revelation (sv, ch.13; LV, ch. 26).
13 I.e. the tenth revelation (sv, ch. 13; LV, ch. 24).
14 Cf. Isaiah 66: 9, 12–13.
15 Cf. Matthew 12: 50.
16 I.e. the twelfth revelation (sv, ch. 13; LV, ch. 26).

The Book of Margery Kempe

1   In a chapter (II, 5) which probably records events in 1433 Margery describes herself as about sixty (and she is known to have been still alive in 1439). Her visions therefore began in the 1390s. Book I of her *Book* was completed in 1436; Book II was begun in 1438. The unique manuscript (BL Add. MS 61823) was owned by the Carthusians of Mount Grace, where it was annotated (see below, pp. 288–9, n. 1). Cf. S. B. Meech and H. E. Allen (eds.), *The Book of Margery Kempe*, EETS, o.s. 212 (London, 1940).
2   On Mary of Oignies and Elizabeth of Hungary, see the Guide to further reading, pp. 296.
3   R. Ellis (ed.), *The 'Liber Celestis' of St Bridget of Sweden*, Vol. I, EETS, o.s. 291 (Oxford, 1987), p. 8.
4   In ch. 16 Margery had described her interview with Archbishop Arundel in his garden at Lambeth Palace.
5   Throughout the *Book* Margery is referred to in the third person.
6   Later named (ch. 43) as Richard of Caister, sometimes credited with composing the popular Middle English devotional lyric 'Jesu, Lorde, that madest me'. After his death Margery seems to regard him as a saint (ch. 60).
7   Presumably a version of the *Revelations* of St Bridget of Sweden, perhaps Hilton's *Scale of Perfection*, the pseudo-Bonaventuran *Stimulus Amoris*, and Rolle's *Incendium Amoris* ('of R. hampall' as the manuscript annotator records).
8   I.e. St Catharine of Alexandria.
9   The manuscript annotator comments in the margin 'feruent loue'.
10 Richard of Caister died on 29 March 1420, which would date the present episodes to *c.* 1413.
11 I Corinthians 6: 19.
12 James 1: 8.
13 James 1: 6–7.
14 Romans 8: 26.
15 Popularly attributed to St Jerome, although no precise equivalent occurs in his writings.
16 Cf. II Corinthians 6: 16; Revelation 21: 3; Ezekiel 37: 27-8.
17 Luke 6: 22–3.
18 Luke 21: 19.

19 The Church of the Santi Apostoli in Rome.

20 Probably 9 November 1414, the feast of the dedication of St John Lateran.

21 The manuscript annotator adds 'gostle' in the margin, with a caret before 'in'.

22 'in hir sowle': crossed through in red by the annotator.

23 Cf. Psalms 90 (91): 11.

24 'Blessed is he that comes in the name of the Lord.'

25 'ignis divini amoris' (fire of divine love) notes the commentator.

26 'so s. R. hampall' is noted in the margin. Cf. p. 15, above.

The Mirrour of Simple Soules

1 Only one manuscript of the French text survives (Chantilly, Musée Condé F xiv 26), although there are five extant medieval translations: two Latin (one by Richard Methley: see p. 265), two Italian, and one English. The three surviving manuscripts of the English version (BL Add. 37790; Bodley 505; St John's College, Cambridge, 71) all have Carthusian connections. See M. Doiron (ed.), 'Margaret Porete: *The Mirror of Simple Souls*, A Middle English Translation', *Archivio Italiano per la Storia della Pietà*, 5 (1968), 241–355.

2 The Chantilly MS reads: 'et pour moy souvenir de lui il me donna ce livre' (Doiron, 251).

3 The Chantilly MS reads: 'et loing du palais' (Doiron, 251).

4 The French of the Chantilly MS is corrupt: 'And so we shall say how our Lord is in no way set free from Love, but Love is free of him, for us. . .'; the Italian version in MS Riccardiana 1468 may be more faithful to the original: 'And we shall tell you in what way they are wholly free, and yet not we, but Love will tell you of herself for us. . .' (Doiron's translations, p. 246). In his Latin version of *The Mirror* (in which he worked from M. N.'s text) Richard Methley comments: '*Here I shall tell you how*: that is, these noble lovers of God are wholly consumed, purified, liberated, and in this way. *We are not lords*: this regards our own frailty, prone to sin, and it therefore says *We are not lords, free of all*, that is, free of all sins and obstacles to the virtues, for a soul will never constantly be so, but in this life only for very brief intervals. In the text there follows *But Love, from God, for us. From God*: that is to say that Love is of the gift of God, and when we have Love, truly and sensibly, at that time we cannot sin by deliberation, not even venially while that rapturous union lasts. And this is the liberty which Love by grace causes us to have, and this is an antecedent grace, and so it makes us free, to that extent and for that time' (translated from Pembroke College, Cambridge, MS 221, fol. 50r, in E. Colledge and R. Guarnieri, 'The Glosses by "M. N." and Richard Methley to *The Mirror of Simple Souls*', *Archivio Italiano per la Storia della Pietà*, 5 (1968), 357–82, at p. 374).

5 Proverbs 24: 16.

6 Methley comments: 'When she says to the Virtues, "I say farewell to you", as friends are accustomed to say as they leave one another, it is to be understood so. It is as if I were to say to you that once I was wholly exercised in my heart in order to win you for God, but now, by grace and habit, exercised as it were naturally, I have won you to readiness for deeds, and so my heart is no longer

concerned to win you. And so constantly I give thanks to God and I rejoice in him that now without labour I have brought you to this point' (fol. 53r; Colledge and Guarnieri, 380).

7 Cf. Habakkuk 2: 4; Romans 1: 17; Galatians 3: 11.

8 Methley comments: 'She saves herself, that is, she considers herself to be saved in whom the Holy Spirit so dwells that whether she sits in purest contemplation or occupies herself in works, she is more worked upon by him than that she herself works' (fol. 55r; Colledge and Guarnieri, 380).

9 Colledge and Guarnieri note: 'M. N. takes this whole passage, once again, as referring only to the Soul's moments of rapture, and although he does not attempt to define *usage* (wisely, we may think, since it is one of the most ambiguous and suspect terms used in the *Miroir*), he implies that it means the Soul's cognitive response to these extraordinary graces' (378). They note that in this context Methley translates *usage* as *visitacio* and that he comments: '"Visitation", properly speaking, is divine fruition, but because of its great frequency it is called "visitation"; and in the time in which these perceptions continue, this Soul can experience nothing else' (fol. 66r; p. 378).

10 Cf. French text: 'mais je l'ay pour le myen de luy atteindre; le mien est, que je soie en mon nient plantee' (Doiron, 304).

11 Psalms 45: 11 (46: 10).

12 Psalms 113: 9 (115: 1).

13 I Corinthians 6: 17.

A Ladder of Foure Ronges

1 George R. Keiser, '"Noght how long man lifs; bot how wele"': The Laity and the Ladder of Perfection', in Michael G. Sargent (ed.), *De Cella in Seculum: Religious and Secular Life and Devotion in Late Medieval England* (Cambridge, 1989), 145–59.

2 On the MSS, see A. I. Doyle, 'Books connected with the Vere Family and Barking Abbey', *Transactions of the Essex Archaeological Society*, n.s. 25.2 (1958), 229–30.

The Doctrine of the Hert

1 See A. Wilmart, 'Gérard de Liège: Un traité inédit de l'amour de Dieu,' *Revue d'ascétique et de mystique*, 12 (1931), 349–430; G. Hendrix, 'Hugh of St. Cher O.P., Author of Two Texts attributed to the Thirteenth-Century Cistercian, Gerard of Liège', *Studie cistercienses*, 21 (1950), 1, 343–56; 'Les *Postillae* de Hugues de Saint-Cher et la traité *De doctrina cordis*', *Recherches de théologie ancienne et médiévale*, 47 (1980), 114–30.

2 Fitzwilliam Museum, Cambridge, MS McClean 132, fol. 1v.

3 I.e. the *amor ecstaticus* analysed by Pseudo-Dionysius in his *De divinis nominibus*.

4 Canticles 2: 16.

5 Cf. Exodus 14: 21.

6 St Augustine, *Confessions*, 9. 6.

7 Canticles 2: 14.

8 I Corinthians 14: 15.
9 Psalms 83: 3 (84: 2).
10 Canticles 3: 3.
11 Cf. Matthew 17: 4.
12 *De doctrina cordis* indicates that the doctor is St John Chrysostom.
13 Cf. Isaiah 64: 4; I Corinthians 2: 9.

The Chastising of God's Children

1 The *Chastising* is organized in twenty-seven short chapters, each ending with
   the exhortation *Vigilate et orate* (Matthew 26. 41). In chapters 2–4 and 7–12
   there are substantial borrowings from *Die Geestelike Brulocht (The Spiritual
   Espousals)* – via Gerard Groote's Latin version *De Ornatu Spiritualis
   Desponsationis* – together with borrowings elsewhere from Cassian, Isidore,
   Gregory, *Stimulus Amoris*, *De Remediis contra Temptationes* by William Flete
   (the English associate of St Catherine of Siena), and Alphonse of Pecha's
   Epistola Solitarii ad Reges (written to prove the divine origin of the Revelations
   of St Bridget of Sweden). Moderate, cautious, mindful of his audience: the
   Chastising author addresses such topics of contemporary concern to contemplatives as recognition of heresy, avoidance of excesses and 'enthusiasm',
   discerning of spirits, and the place of private devotions. In so doing he edits out
   Ruusbroec's more advanced material, and also carefully edits what he borrows
   from the *Epistola Solitarii*.
2 Cf. J. R. R. Tolkien (ed.), *Ancrene Wisse*, EETS, o.s. 249 (London, 1962),
   118–19 ('He pleieð wið us as þe moder wið hire ȝunge deorling . . . ').
3 From here to the end of this extract from chapter 1 (except 'Suche hevynesse . . .
   at al tymes') is borrowed from Suso's *Horologium Sapientiae*, 1, viii. See J.
   Bazire and E. Colledge (eds), *The Chastising of God's Children and the
   Treatise of Perfection of the Sons of God* (Oxford, 1957), 263–5.
4 Psalms 118 (119): 8.
5 Cf. *Moralia*, Job 24: 13 (*PL* 76.168B).
6 The notion of the 'play of love' (*ludus amoris*) probably derives via Suso from
   Stimulus Amoris. The Middle English version of Suso's *Horologium* refers to
   'þe pleye of loue þe whiche I am wonte to vse in an amarose sowle' (*Anglia*, 10
   [1888], 335).

The Treatise of Perfection of the Sons of God

1 'we are pore': a long passage, containing one of Ruusbroec's most vivid
   'sea-figures', has here been omitted by the English translator, perhaps because
   it might be misinterpreted as preaching the doctrine of emanation. See J. Bazire
   and E. Colledge (eds.), *The Chastising of God's Children and the Treatise of
   Perfection of the Sons of God* (Oxford, 1957), 330–2.

To Hew Heremyte: A Pystyl of Solytary Lyfe Nowadayes

1 On Rolle, Methley comments in his *Refectorium*: 'vita mea consistit in amore,
   languore, dulcore, fervore, canore; rarius tamen in sensibili fervore, quia

dilectus michi promisit, quod frequencius in languore, sicut et ille almus Ricardus, dictus "de Hampol", frequencius in calore, de quo non legi quod tam frequens fuerit in languore' [my life consists of love, languor, sweetness, heat, song; but not often of sensible heat, since the beloved promised me more frequent experience of languor – just as that bountiful Richard, known as 'of Hampole', more often experienced heat, of whom I have never read that he was so much in languor]. This may be set against some of the Mount Grace annotations to the *Book of Margery Kempe* manuscript: where Margery marvels 'how hir hert mygth lestyn that it was not consumyd wyth ardowr of lofe' (ch. 13), a marginal note reads 'R. Medlay. v. was wont so to say'; where Margery 'beheld . . . in hir sowle' (ch. 73) the parting of Christ from his mother on Maundy Thursday (and fell down, crying and roaring), a note beside 'beheld' comments 'father M. was wont so to doo'; and where Margery's cryings become so frequent that they 'madyn hir ryth weyke' (ch. 28), a note to 'weyke' reads 'so fa RM & f Norton & of Wakenes of the passyon' (BL MS Add. 61823, fols. 15r, 85r, 33v). The latter reference is to John Norton (d. 1522), sixth prior of Mount Grace: where Margery 'wrestyd hir body' from one side to another (ch. 44), the annotator comments 'so dyd prior Nort in hys excesse' (fol. 51v). On Norton, see the article by J. Hogg in the *Dictionnaire de Spiritualité*, 11 (1982), 446–8.

2 Psalms 142 (143): 9–10.
3 Philippians 3: 20.
4 Canticles 4: 7.
5 Canticles 8: 7.
6 Ecclesiastes 1: 2.
7 Lamentations 3: 51.
8 St Godric (d. 1170) became a hermit at Finchale, near Durham.
9 St Hugh (*c.* 1140–1200), Prior of Witham Charterhouse; from 1186 Bishop of Lincoln.
10 I.e. Carthusian.
11 Job 36: 13.
12 Psalms 38: 3 (39: 2).
13 Wisdom 8: 16.

GUIDE TO FURTHER READING

General

For full bibliography, see V. M. Lagorio and R. Bradley (eds.), *The 14th-Century English Mystics: A Comprehensive Annotated Bibliography* (New York, 1981). For manuscript information, see P. S. Jolliffe, *A Check-List of Middle English Prose Writings of Spiritual Guidance* (Toronto, 1974).

There is much useful information in the anthologies by C. Kirchberger (ed.), *The Coasts of the Country* (London, 1952) and E. Colledge (ed.), *The Mediaeval Mystics of England* (London, 1962), and also in two collections of essays: C. Davis (ed.), *English Spiritual Writers* (London, 1961), and J. Walsh (ed.), *Pre-Reformation English Spirituality* (London, 1965). Informative introductory essays on the mystics are included in A. S. G. Edwards (ed.), *Middle English Prose: A Critical Guide to Major Authors and Genres* (New Brunswick, 1984), and in P. Szarmach (ed.), *An Introduction to the Medieval Mystics of Europe* (New York, 1984). Further studies have been published in *The Medieval Mystical Tradition in England (MMTE)*, 5 vols. (Exeter, 1980, 1982; Woodbridge, 1984, 1987, 1992), edited by M. Glasscoe, and in *Mystics Quarterly* and *Studia Mystica*.

Booklength studies of the mystics include D. Knowles, *The English Mystical Tradition* (London, 1961); P. Hodgson, *Three 14th-Century English Mystics* (London, 1967); W. Riehle, *The Middle English Mystics* (London, 1981); and M. Glasscoe, *English Medieval Mystics: Games of Faith* (London, 1993).

Valuable information on women mystics is to be found in K. M. Wilson (ed.), *Medieval Women Writers* (Athens, Ga., 1984); E. A. Petroff (ed.), *Medieval Women's Visionary Literature* (New York, 1986); A. Barratt (ed.), *Women's Writing in Middle English* (London, 1992); and F. Beer, *Women and Mystical Experience in the Middle Ages* (Woodbridge, 1992). See also C. M. Meale (ed.), *Women and Literature in Britain, 1150–1500* (Cambridge, 1993), and U. Wiethaus (ed.), *Maps of Flesh and Light: The Religious Experience of Medieval Women Mystics* (Syracuse, 1993).

Richard Rolle

On Richard Rolle's career and for data on manuscripts, H. E. Allen, *Writings Ascribed to Richard Rolle, Hermit of Hampole, and Materials for his Biography*, MLA Monograph Series, 3 (New York, 1927) is still a valuable resource. The *Officium* is translated in Allen, 55–71, and in F. M. Comper, *The Life of Richard Rolle, Together with an Edition of his English Lyrics* (London, 1928). N. Watson,

Richard Rolle and the Invention of Authority (Cambridge, 1991) provides an up-to-date evaluation of Rolle's life and work.

Editions of Rolle's Latin works: M. Deanesly (ed.), *Incendium Amoris* (Manchester, 1915), and C. Wolters (trans.), *The Fire of Love* (Harmondsworth, 1972); E. J. F. Arnould (ed.), *Melos Amoris* (Oxford, 1957). Misyn's English versions of the *Fire of Love* and *Mending of Life* are edited by R. Harvey, EETS, o.s. 106 (London, 1896).

Editions of Rolle's English works: H. E. Allen (ed.), *English Writings of Richard Rolle* (Oxford, 1931); S. J. Ogilvie-Thomson (ed.), *Richard Rolle: Prose and Verse*, EETS, o.s. 293 (Oxford, 1988); R. S. Allen (ed.), *Richard Rolle: The English Writings* (Mahwah, N.J., 1988).

Latin translations of *The Form of Living* and *Ego Dormio* survive in Gonville and Caius College, Cambridge, MS 140/80, fols. 108–118v. Cf. M. G. Amassian and D. Lynch, *MS*, 43 (1981), 218–49.

On Rolle as mystic: M. Jennings, 'Richard Rolle and the Three Degrees of Love', *DownR*, 93 (1975), 193–200; V. Gillespie, 'Mystic's Foot: Rolle and Affectivity', in Glasscoe, *MMTE* (1982), 199–203; J. P. H. Clark, 'Richard Rolle: A Theological Re-assessment', *DownR*, 101 (1983), 108–39; R. Allen, 'Singular Lufe: Richard Rolle and the Grammar of Spiritual Ascent', in Glasscoe, *MMTE* (1984), 28–54.

On aspects of Rolle the writer: J. Alford, 'Biblical *Imitatio* in the Writings of Richard Rolle', *ELH*, 40 (1973), 1–23; J. P. H. Clark, 'Richard Rolle as Biblical Commentator', *DownR*, 104 (1986), 165–213; L. Smedick, 'Parallelism and Pointing in Rolle's Rhythmical Style', *MS*, 41 (1979), 404–67; R. Copeland, 'Richard Rolle and the Rhetorical Theory of the Levels of Style', in Glasscoe, *MMTE* (1984), 55–80.

The Anonymous Author of *The Cloud of Unknowing*

Editions of the *Cloud*-author: P. Hodgson (ed.), '*The Cloud of Unknowing*' and *Related Treatises* (Salzburg, 1982) is a revised edition of her two classic editions, '*The Cloud of Unknowing*' and '*The Book of Privy Counselling*', EETS, o.s. 218 (London, 1944), and '*Deonise Hid Diuinite*' and *Other Treatises on Contemplative Prayer Related to '*The Cloud of Unknowing*', EETS, o.s. 231 (London, 1955). Two independent translations of the *Cloud* into Latin are extant: Richard Methley's *Caligo Ignorancie* in Pembroke College, Cambridge, MS 221; and *Nubes Ignorandi* in MS Bodley 856. See J. Clark (ed.), *The Latin Versions of '*The Cloud of Unknowing*', 2 vols. (Salzburg, 1989).

On the *Cloud*-author's sources, see: J. P. H. Clark, 'Sources and Theology in *The Cloud of Unknowing*', *DownR*, 98 (1980), 83–109; A. J. Minnis, 'The Sources of *The Cloud of Unknowing*: A Reconsideration', in Glasscoe, *MMTE* (1982), 63–75; and J. Walsh (ed.), *The Cloud of Unknowing* (Ramsey, N.J., 1981), 'Introduction' (where it is argued that *Viae Sion Lugent* by the Carthusian Hugh of Balma is a source for the *Cloud*-author). On other important aspects, see: J. A. Burrow, 'Fantasy and Language in *The Cloud of Unknowing*', *EC*, 27 (1977), 283–98; and A. J. Minnis, 'Affection and Imagination in *The Cloud of Unknowing* and Hilton's *Scale of Perfection*', *Traditio*, 39 (1983), 323–66. Cf. also R. A. Lees,

The Negative Language of the Dionysian School of Mystical Theology (Salzburg, 1983).

On Hilton's possible authorship of *The Cloud*, see H. Gardner, 'Walter Hilton and the Authorship of *The Cloud of Unknowing*', *RES*, 9 (1933), 129–47; P. Hodgson, 'Walter Hilton and *The Cloud of Unknowing*: A Problem of Authorship Reconsidered', *MLR*, 50 (1955), 395–406; L. C. Gatto, 'The Walter Hilton and *Cloud of Unknowing* Controversy Reconsidered', *Studies in Medieval Culture*, 5 (1975), 181–9; W. Riehle, 'The Problem of Walter Hilton's Possible Authorship of *The Cloud of Unknowing* and its Related Tracts', *NM*, 78 (1977), 31–45; J. P. H. Clark, 'The Lightsome Darkness – Aspects of Walter Hilton's Theological Background', *DownR*, 95 (1977), 95–109. See also: J. P. H. Clark, '*The Cloud of Unknowing*, Walter Hilton, and St John of the Cross: A Comparison', *DownR*, 96 (1978), 281-98, and 'Some Monastic Elements in Walter Hilton and in the *Cloud* Corpus', *Kartäusermystik und -mystiker*, AC, 108:1 (1983), 237–57.

Walter Hilton

On Hilton's career, see J. Russell-Smith, 'Walter Hilton and a Tract in Defence of the Veneration of Images', *Dominican Studies*, 7 (1954), 180–214; J. P. H. Clark, 'Walter Hilton in Defence of the Veneration of Images and of the Religious Life', *DownR*, 103 (1985), 1–25.

Texts of Hilton: for a lightly modernized text from Lambeth Palace MS 472 of *Mixed Life, Eight Chapters, Qui Habitat, Bonum Est*, and *Benedictus*, see D. Jones (ed.), *Minor Works of Walter Hilton* (London, 1929). On the authenticity of some minor works attributed to Hilton, see J. P. H. Clark, 'The Problem of Walter Hilton's Authorship: *Bonum Est, Benedictus*, and *Of Angels' Song*', *DownR*, 101 (1983), 15-29.

Epistle on the Mixed Life: S. J. Ogilvie-Thomson (ed.), *Walter Hilton's 'Mixed Life' Edited from Lambeth Palace MS 472*, Elizabethan and Renaissance Studies 92:15 (Salzburg, 1986); also edited from the Vernon and Thornton manuscripts in Horstman, *Yorkshire Writers*, 1, 264–92. For Hilton's teaching on 'mixed life', see J. Russell-Smith, 'Walter Hilton', reprinted from *The Month* (1959) in J. Walsh (ed.), *Pre-Reformation English Spirituality* (London, 1965), 182–97; W. H. Beale, 'Walter Hilton and the Concept of Medled Lyf', *American Benedictine Review*, 26 (1975), 381–94; J. P. H. Clark, 'Action and Contemplation in Walter Hilton', *DownR*, 97 (1979), 258–74; and J. Hughes, *Pastors and Visionaries: Religion and Secular Life in Late Medieval Yorkshire* (Woodbridge, 1988). See also H. M. Carey, 'Devout Literate Laypeople and the Pursuit of the Mixed Life in Late Medieval England', *Journal of Religious History*, 14 (1987), 361–81.

Of Angels' Song: edited from BL MS Add 27592 by T. Takamiya, in *Studies in English Literature*, English Number 1977 (Tokyo, 1977), and reprinted in *Two Minor Works of Walter Hilton* (Tokyo, 1980), with F. Kuriyagawa's edition of *Eight Chapters on Perfection* (see below); edited from the Thornton manuscript and CUL MS Dd. 5. 55 in Horstman, *Yorkshire Writers*, 1, 175-82.

Eight Chapters on Perfection: edited from Bibliothèque Nationale, Paris, fonds anglais 41, by F. Kuriyagawa, in *Studies in the Humanities and Social*

Relations, 9 (Tokyo, 1967), and from Inner Temple MS Petyt 524 in *Studies in English Literature*, English Number 1971 (Tokyo, 1971); reprinted with T. Takamiya's edition of *Angels' Song* in *Two Minor Works of Walter Hilton* (Tokyo, 1980). Chapter 8 is edited from BL MS Add 60577 by T. Takamiya in *Poetica*, 12 (Tokyo, 1981 [for 1979]), 142–9.

The Scale of Perfection: edited by E. Underhill, and lightly modernized, from BL MS Harley 6579 (London, 1923). See also H. Gardner, 'The Text of *The Scale of Perfection*', *MAE*, 5 (1936), 11–30; S. S. Hussey, 'The Text of *The Scale of Perfection*, Book II', *NM*, 65 (1964), 75–92; and M. G. Sargent, 'Walter Hilton's *Scale of Perfection*: The London Manuscript Group Reconsidered', *MAE*, 52 (1983), 189–216.

Both books of *The Scale of Perfection* were translated into Latin (the *Liber de Nobilitate Anime*) by the Carmelite Thomas Fishlake, possibly by 1400. The Latin can offer a valuable check on the English text, and Fishlake amplifies the Christocentric emphasis in Book II. Twelve manuscripts have Book I in Latin, and thirteen have Book II, with York Cathedral Chapter Library MS XVI K 5 offering the best text of the whole. See further S. S. Hussey, 'Latin and English in *The Scale of Perfection*', *MS*, 35 (1973), 456–76; and J. P. H. Clark, 'English and Latin in *The Scale of Perfection*: Theological Considerations', *Spiritualität Heute und Gestern*, *AC*, 35:1 (1982), 167–212.

For Hilton's four Latin epistles, see J. P. H. Clark and C. Taylor (eds.), *Walter Hilton's Latin Writings*, 2 vols. (Salzburg, 1987), which also contains the short piece *Firmissime crede*, the *Pystille Made To A Cristene Frende* (a Middle English version of *Epistola ad Quemdem Seculo . . .*), and a Middle English commentary on a lost letter by Hilton which was apparently addressed to a Gilbertine nun (BL MS Harley 2406, fols. 58r–60v). For a modern translation of *Epistola de Lectione*, sometimes called *Epistola ad Solitarium*, see J. Russell-Smith, 'Letter to a Hermit', *The Way*, 6 (1966), 230–41.

For a full text of *Qui Habitat* (from the Vernon MS, Bodleian Library, MS Eng. Poet. a. 1), see B. Wallner (ed.), *An Exposition of 'Qui Habitat' and 'Bonum Est' in English*, Lund Studies in English, 23 (Lund, 1954). For attribution to Hilton, see J. P. H. Clark, 'Walter Hilton and the Psalm Commentary *Qui Habitat*', *DownR*, 100 (1982), 235–62.

On Hilton's possible authorship of *The Prickynge of Love*, see J. P. H. Clark, 'Walter Hilton and the *Stimulus Amoris*', *DownR*, 102 (1984), 79-118. For full text, see H. Kane (ed.), *The Prickynge of Love*, 2 vols. (Salzburg, 1983), and for a modernized version, with helpful introduction, see C. Kirchberger (ed.), *The Goad of Love* (London, 1952).

For a substantial introduction to Hilton's work, see J. P. H. Clark and R. Dorward (eds. and trans.), *The Scale of Perfection* (Mahwah, N.J., 1991). See also: H. Gardner, 'Walter Hilton and the Mystical Tradition in England', *E&S*, 22 (1937), 103–27; G. Sitwell, 'Contemplation in *The Scale of Perfection*', *DownR*, 67 (1949), 276–90, 68 (1950), 21–34, 271–89; D. Knowles, *The English Mystical Tradition* (London, 1961), ch. 6; A. C. Hughes, *Walter Hilton's Direction to Contemplatives* (Rome, 1962); J. E. Milosh, *'The Scale of Perfection' and the English Mystical Tradition* (Madison, 1966); S. S. Hussey, 'Walter Hilton:

Traditionalist?' in Glasscoe, *MMTE* (1980), 1–16; D. G. Kennedy, *The Incarnational Element in Hilton's Spirituality* (Salzburg, 1982); M. G. Sargent, 'The Organization of *The Scale of Perfection*', in Glasscoe, *MMTE* (1982), 231–61. On style, see J. I. Mueller, *The Native Tongue and the Word: Developments in English Prose Style 1380–1580* (Chicago, 1984), ch. 2.

For a series of studies on aspects of Hilton by J. P. H. Clark (in addition to those already mentioned) see: 'Walter Hilton and Liberty of Spirit', *DownR*, 96 (1978), 61–78; 'Image and Likeness in Walter Hilton', *DownR*, 97 (1979), 204–20; 'Intention in Walter Hilton', *DownR*, 97 (1979), 69–80; 'Augustine, Anselm and Walter Hilton', in Glasscoe, *MMTE* (1982), 102–26; 'The Trinitarian Theology of Walter Hilton's *Scale of Perfection*, Book Two', in H. Phillips (ed.), *Langland, the Mystics and the Medieval Religious Tradition: Essays in Honour of S. S. Hussey* (Cambridge, 1990), 125–40.

Julian of Norwich

Editions of Julian of Norwich: E. Colledge and J. Walsh (eds.), *A Book of Showings to the Anchoress Julian of Norwich*, 2 vols. (Toronto, 1978) presents both the shorter version and the longer (from Bibliothèque Nationale, Paris, fonds anglais 40). For the shorter text, see: F. Beer (ed.), *Julian of Norwich's 'Revelations of Divine Love'* (Heidelberg, 1978). For the longer version from BL MS Sloane 2499, see: M. Glasscoe (ed.), *Julian of Norwich: A Revelation of Love* (Exeter, 1976).

On the two versions, see B. A. Windeatt, 'Julian of Norwich and her Audience', *RES*, n.s. 28 (1977), 1–17; M. Glasscoe, 'Visions and Revisions: A Further Look at the Manuscripts of Julian of Norwich', *SB*, 42 (1989), 103–20; B. A. Windeatt, 'Privytes to us: Knowing and Re-vision in Julian of Norwich', in T. Takamiya and R. Beadle (eds.), *Chaucer to Shakespeare* (Cambridge, 1992), 87–98; N. Watson, 'The Composition of Julian of Norwich's *Revelation of Love*', *Speculum*, 68 (1993), 637–83.

For biographical data, Norwich in Julian's day, and her intellectual formation, see Colledge and Walsh, *Showings*, 33–59. On Julian as possibly a widow and mother, see Sister Benedicta Ward SLG, 'Julian the Solitary', in K. Leech and Sr Benedicta SLG, *Julian Reconsidered* (Oxford, 1988), 11–29, and 'Lady Julian and Her Audience: Mine Even-Christian', in G. Rowell (ed.), *The English Religious Tradition and the Genius of Anglicanism* (Oxford, 1992), 47–63. Cf. also N. P. Tanner, *The Church in Late Medieval Norwich 1370–1532* (Toronto, 1984).

On Jesus our Mother: A. Cabassut, 'Une dévotion médiévale peu connu: la dévotion a Jésus nôtre mère', *Revue d'ascétique et de mystique*, 25 (1949), 234–45; R. M. Bradley, 'Patristic Background of the Motherhood Similitude in Julian of Norwich', *Christian Scholar's Review*, 8 (1978), 1–13; C. W. Bynum, *Jesus as Mother: Studies in the Spirituality of the High Middle Ages* (Berkeley, 1982); J. P. Heimmel, *'God is Our Mother': Julian of Norwich and the Medieval Image of Christian Feminine Divinity* (Salzburg, 1982); and Colledge and Walsh, *Showings*, I, 151–62.

On Julian's teachings: P. Molinari, *Julian of Norwich: The Teaching of a 14th-Century Mystic* (London, 1958); J. P. H. Clark, '*Fiducia* in Julian of

Norwich', *DownR*, 99 (1981), 97–108, 214–29, 'Predestination in Christ according to Julian of Norwich', and 'Nature, Grace and the Trinity in Julian of Norwich', *DownR*, 100 (1982), 79–91, 203–20, and 'Time and Eternity in Julian of Norwich', *DownR*, 109 (1991), 259–76; B. Pelphrey, *Love was his Meaning: The Theology and Mysticism of Julian of Norwich* (Salzburg, 1982), and *Christ our Mother* (London, 1989); and G. M. Jantzen, *Julian of Norwich* (London, 1987).

On reading Julian's work: B. A. Windeatt, 'The Art of Mystical Loving: Julian of Norwich', in Glasscoe, *MMTE* (1980), 55-71; M. Glasscoe, 'Means of Showing: An Approach to Reading Julian of Norwich', *Spätmittelalterliche geistliche Literatur in der Nationalsprache*, AC, 106:1 (1983), 155-77; V. Gillespie and M. Ross, 'The Apophatic Image: The Poetics of Effacement in Julian of Norwich', and N. Watson, 'The Trinitarian Hermeneutic in Julian of Norwich's *Revelation of Love*', in Glasscoe, *MMTE* (1992), 53-77, 79-100. Cf. also D. Despres, *Ghostly Sights: Visual Meditation in Late-Medieval Literature* (Norman, Okla., 1989).

Margery Kempe

Editions of Margery Kempe: S. B. Meech and H. E. Allen (eds.), *The Book of Margery Kempe*, EETS, o.s. 212 (London, 1940); B. A. Windeatt (ed.), *The Book of Margery Kempe* (Harmondsworth, 1985).

Booklength studies include: C. W. Atkinson, *Mystic and Pilgrim: The Book and the World of Margery Kempe* (Ithaca, 1983); J. C. Hirsh, *The Revelations of Margery Kempe: Paramystical Practices in Late Medieval England* (Leiden, 1989); and K. Lochrie, *Margery Kempe and Translations of the Flesh* (Philadelphia, 1991).

On further aspects, see: A. Goodman, 'The Piety of John Brunham's Daughter, of Lynn', in D. Baker (ed.), *Medieval Women* (Oxford, 1978), 347–58; S. Medcalf (ed.), *The Later Middle Ages* (London, 1981), ch. 3; S. Dickman, 'Margery Kempe and the Continental Tradition of the Pious Woman', in *MMTE* (1984), 150–68; S. Beckwith, 'A Very Material Mysticism: The Medieval Mysticism of Margery Kempe', in D. Aers (ed.), *Medieval Literature: Criticism, Ideology and History* (Brighton, 1986), 34–57; G. M. Gibson, *The Theater of Devotion: East Anglian Drama and Society in the Late Middle Ages* (Chicago, 1989), ch. 3; D. Aers, *Community, Gender, and Individual Identity: English Writing 1360-1430* (London, 1988), ch. 2; N. Partner, 'Reading *The Book of Margery Kempe*', *Exemplaria*, 3 (1991), 29–66; S. Beckwith, 'Problems of Authority in Late Medieval English Mysticism: Agency and Authority in *The Book of Margery Kempe*', *Exemplaria*, 4 (1992), 171–200; S. J. McEntire (ed.), *Margery Kempe: A Book of Essays* (New York, 1992); S. Beckwith, *Christ's Body* (London, 1993), ch. 4.

Reception in England of Continental women mystics' writing

For a text of what Margery Kempe calls 'Bridis boke', see: R. Ellis (ed.), *The 'Liber Celestis' of St Bridget of Sweden*, Vol. I, EETS, o.s. 291 (Oxford, 1987). See also: E. Colledge, '*Epistola Solitarii ad Reges*: Alphonse of Pecha as Organizer of Birgittine and Urbanist Propaganda', *MS*, 18 (1956), 19–49; R. Ellis, '*Flores ad Fabricandam . . . Coronam*: An Investigation into the Uses of the Revelations of St Bridget of

Sweden in Fifteenth-Century England', *MAE*, 51 (1982), 163–86; J. Hogg, 'The Brigittine Contribution to Late Medieval English Spirituality', *Spiritualität Heute und Gestern*, AC, 35:3 (1982), 153–74; F. R. Johnston, 'The English Cult of St Bridget of Sweden', *Analecta Bollandiana*, 103 (1985), 75–93; D. Pezzini, 'Brigittine Tracts of Spiritual Guidance in Fifteenth-Century England: a Study in Translation', in R. Ellis (ed.), *The Medieval Translator*, II (London, 1991), 175–207; G. Cleve, 'Margery Kempe: A Scandinavian Influence in Medieval England?' in Glasscoe, *MMTE* (1992), 163–78.

On allusions in *The Book of Margery Kempe* (chs. 62, 68) to the lives and writings of such women as Mary of Oignies and Elizabeth of Hungary, see R. Ellis, 'Margery Kempe's Scribe and the Miraculous Books', in H. Phillips (ed.), *Langland, the Mystics and the Medieval English Religious Tradition* (Cambridge, 1990), 161–75. A Middle English life of Mary of Oignies is extant in Bodleian Library MS Douce 114 (ed. C. Horstmann in *Anglia*, 8 (1885), 102–96), and this manuscript also contains a life of St Catherine of Siena, whose *Dialogo della divina providenza* was translated as *The Orcherd of Syon*. (See Sister Mary Denise RSM, '*The Orcherd of Syon*: An Introduction', *Traditio*, 114 (1958), 269–93; and P. Hodgson, '*The Orcherd of Syon* and the English Mystical Tradition', *PBA*, 50 (1964), 229–49.) In his edition of the *Lyf of Saint Katherin of Senis* (?1492; *STC* 24766) Wynkyn de Worde prints *The Revelacions of Saynt Elysabeth the kynges doughter of hungarye*, and another version of these revelations survives in CUL MS HH. I. II, fols. 122–7. (For extracts, see A. Barratt (ed.), *Women's Writing in Middle English* (London, 1992), 71–83.) It may be to this Elizabeth of Hungary that Margery Kempe refers, but see A. Barratt, 'The Revelations of St Elizabeth of Hungary: Problems of Attribution', *The Library*, 6th ser., 14 (1992), 1–11. In addition, there is evidence that the revelations of Elisabeth of Schönau were read in medieval England: see R. J. Dean, 'Manuscripts of St Elisabeth of Schönau in England', *MLR*, 32 (1937), 62–71, and cf. A. L. Clark, *Elisabeth of Schönau: A Twelfth-Century Visionary* (Philadelphia, 1992). There is also a range of evidence for knowledge in England of St Mechthild of Hackeborn, whose revelations recorded in the *Liber Specialis Gratiae* were translated into English: see T. A. Halligan (ed.), *The Booke of Gostlye Grace* (Toronto, 1979), Introduction, ch. 3 ('The Revelations in England'). See also U. Stargardt, 'The Beguines of Belgium, the Dominican Nuns of Germany, and Margery Kempe', in T. J. Heffernan (ed.), *The Popular Literature of Medieval England* (Knoxville, 1985), 277–313, and E. W. McDonnell, *The Beguines and Beghards in Medieval Culture* (New Brunswick, 1954).

The Mirrour of Simple Soules

On Marguerite Porete and her *Mirouer des simples ames anienties et qui seulement demourent en vouloir et desir d'Amour*, see P. Dronke, *Women Writers of the Middle Ages* (Cambridge, 1984), ch. 7; R. Guarnieri, 'Il Movimento del Libero Spirito: Testi e Documenti', *Archivio Italiano per la Storia della Pietà*, 4 (1965), 353–708; and P. Verdeyen, 'Le procès d'inquisition contre Marguerite Porete et Guiard de Cressonessart (1309–1310)', *Revue d'histoire ecclésiastique*, 81 (1986), 47–94. See also R. E. Lerner, *The Heresy of the Free Spirit in the Later Middle Ages*

(Berkeley, 1972). For the English text, see M. Doiron (ed.), 'Margaret Porete: *The Mirror of Simple Souls*, A Middle English Translation', *Archivio Italiano per la Storia della Pietà*, 5 (1968), 241–355; and also the appendix by E. Colledge and R. Guarnieri, 'The Glosses by M. N. and Richard Methley to *The Mirror of Simple Souls*', *ibid.*, 357–82. For the French text in parallel with a Latin version, see P. Verdeyen (ed.), *Margaretae Porete: Speculum Simplicium Animarum*, Corpus Christianorum Continuatio Medieualis, 69 (Turnhout, 1986).

A Ladder of Foure Ronges by the which Men Mowe Wele Clyme to Heven

For the full Middle English text of *A Ladder of Foure Ronges*, see P. Hodgson (ed.), *Deonise Hid Divinite*, EETS, o.s. 231 (1955), 100–17; on the interpolations in the English version, see P. Hodgson, '*A Ladder of Foure Ronges by the whiche Men Mowe Wele Clyme to Heven*. A Study of the Prose Style of a Middle English Translation', *MLR*, 44 (1949), 465–75. For the Latin text, with French translation: E. Colledge and J. Walsh (eds.), *Lettre sur la vie contemplative. Douze méditations*, Sources chrétiennes, 163 (Paris, 1970); English translation: E. Colledge and J. Walsh (eds.), *The Ladder of Monks and Twelve Meditations* (Garden City, 1978). Cf. G. R. Keiser, '"Noght how long man lifs; bot how wele": The Laity and the Ladder of Perfection', in M. G. Sargent (ed.), *De Cella in Seculum: Religious and Secular Life and Devotion in Late Medieval England* (Cambridge, 1989), 145–59.

English reception of the work of Ruusbroec and Suso

On Jan van Ruusbroec and mystical literature in medieval England, see J. Bazire and E. Colledge (eds.), *The Chastising of God's Children and the Treatise of Perfection of the Sons of God* (Oxford, 1957); G. B. Desoer, 'The Relationship of the Latin Versions of Ruysbroeck's "Die Geestelike Brulocht" to "The Chastising of God's Children"', *MS*, 21 (1959), 129–45; A. I. Doyle, 'A Text Attributed to Ruusbroec Circulating in England' in A. Ampe (ed.), *Dr L. Reypens Album* (Antwerp, 1964), 153–71; and M. G. Sargent, 'Ruusbroec in England: *The Chastising of God's Children* and Related Works', in J. de Grauwe (ed.), *Historia et Spiritualitas Cartusienses: Colloquii Quarti Internationalis Acta* (Ghent, 1983), 303–12. See also P. Mommaets and N. de Paepe (eds.), *Jan van Ruusbroec: The Sources, Content and Sequels of his Mysticism* (Louvain, 1984), and cf. J. Toussaert, *Le sentiment religieux en Flandre à la fin du Moyen Age* (Paris, 1963).

On reception of Suso's work in England, probably as early as the mid-1370s, see R. Lovatt, 'Henry Suso and the Medieval Mystical Tradition in England', in Glasscoe, *MMTE* (1982), 47–62. Suso's *Horologium Sapientiae* was selectively translated into English, omitting the more affective and personal passages, as *The Seven Poyntes of Trewe Wisdom* (ed. C. Horstman, from Bodleian Library MS Douce 114, in *Anglia*, 10 [1888], 323–89); the English preface claims that the translation was undertaken by a chaplain for his lady and declares its intention to omit material in the original that is applicable to the clergy.

For the *Treatise of Perfection*, with commentary referring to Jordaens' Latin and Ruusbroec's Dutch, see J. Bazire and E. Colledge (eds.), *The Chastising of God's Children and the Treatise of Perfection of the Sons of God* (Oxford, 1957). See also E. Colledge, '*The Treatise of Perfection of the Sons of God*: a Fifteenth-Century English Ruysbroek Translation', *ES*, 33 (1952), 49–66. A Latin text of *Calculus de Perfectione Filiorum Dei* is preserved in Heneage MS 3083 (Somerset Record Office, Taunton), a miscellany also containing *Emendatio Vitae*, a compilation mainly from *Incendium Amoris*, commentary on the first and second verses of the Canticles, and the Latin *Scale of Perfection*. Cf. M. G. Sargent, 'A New Manuscript of *The Chastising of God's Children* with an Ascription to Walter Hilton', *MAE*, 46 (1977), 49–65.

Richard Methley

Richard Methley's *To Hew Heremyte: A Pystyl of Solytary Lyfe Nowadayes* is edited with full commentary by J. Hogg in *AC*, 31 (1977), 91–119. There are also editions of *Refectorium Salutis*, by J. Hogg, in *Kartäusermystik und -mystiker, AC*, 55:1 (1981), 208–38; *Experimentum Veritatis*, by M. Sargent, and *Scola Amoris Languidi*, by J. Hogg, in *Kartäusermystik und -mystiker, AC*, 55:2 (1981), 121–37, 138–65; and *Dormitorium Dilecti Dilecti*, by J. Hogg, in *Kartäusermystik und -mystiker, AC*, 55:5 (1982), 79–103. On Methley's career, see D. Knowles, *The Religious Orders in England*, II (Cambridge, 1957), 224–6, and the article by J. Hogg in *Dictionnaire de Spiritualité*, 10 (1979), 1100–3.

Transmission and reception of the medieval English mystics

On aspects of reception and transmission, see: S. S. Hussey, 'Editing the Middle English Mystics', *Spiritualität Heute und Gestern, AC*, 35:3 (1983), 160–73; M. Aston, *Lollards and Reformers: Images and Literacy in Late Medieval Religion* (London, 1984), ch. 4 ('Devotional Literacy'); A. K. Warren, *Anchorites and their Patrons in Medieval England* (Berkeley, 1985); J. Hughes, *Pastors and Visionaries: Religion and Secular Life in Late Medieval Yorkshire* (Woodbridge, 1988); S. S. Hussey, 'The Audience for the Middle English Mystics', and A. M. Hutchinson, 'Devotional Reading in the Monastery and in the Late Medieval Household', in M. G. Sargent (ed.), *De Cella in Seculum: Religious and Secular Life and Devotion in Late Medieval England* (Cambridge, 1989), 109–22, 215–27; A. I. Doyle, 'Publication by Members of the Religious Orders', and V. Gillespie, 'Vernacular Books of Religion', in J. Griffiths and D. Pearsall (eds.), *Book Production and Publishing 1375–1475* (Cambridge, 1989), 109–23, 317–44.

On the role of the Carthusians in mystical literature in England, see: M. G. Sargent, 'The Transmission by the English Carthusians of Some Late Medieval Spiritual Writings', *Journal of Ecclesiastical History*, 27 (1976), 225–40; J. Hogg, 'Mount Grace Charterhouse and Late Medieval English Spirituality', *Collectanea Cartusiana 3, AC*, 82:3 (1980), 1–43; I. Doyle, 'Carthusian Participation in the Movement of Works of Richard Rolle between England and other parts of Europe in the 14th and 15th Centuries', *Kartäusermystik und -mystiker, AC*, 55:2 (1981), 109–20; and M. G. Sargent, *James Grenehalgh as Textual Critic*, 2 vols. (Salzburg, 1984).

On later selection, compilation and adaptation of mystical texts, see M. G.

Sargent, 'Minor Devotional Writings', in A. S. G. Edwards (ed.), *Middle English Prose: A Critical Guide to Major Authors and Genres* (New Brunswick, 1984), 147–75; and also V. Gillespie, 'The *Cibus Anime* Book 3: A Guide for Contemplatives?', *Spiritualität Heute und Gestern*, AC, 35:3 (1983), 90–119; '*Lukynge in haly bukes: Lectio* in some Late Medieval Spiritual Miscellanies', *Spätmittelalterliche geistliche Literatur in der Nationalsprache*, 2, AC, 106 (1984), 1–27; and 'Idols and Images: Pastoral Adaptations of *The Scale of Perfection*', in H. Phillips (ed.), *Langland, the Mystics and the Medieval English Religious Tradition* (Cambridge, 1990), 97–115.

On late medieval interest in the mystics, see especially C. A. J. Armstrong, 'The Piety of Cicely, Duchess of York: A Study in Late Medieval Culture', in D. Woodruff (ed.), *For Hilaire Belloc* (New York, 1942); reprinted in C. A. J. Armstrong, *England, France and Burgundy in the Fifteenth Century* (London, 1983); and G. R. Keiser, 'The Mystics and the Early English Printers: The Economics of Devotionalism', in Glasscoe, *MMTE* (1987), 9–26.

GLOSSARY

Entries correspond to the actual forms in the text. Grammatical analysis is only given where ambiguity may arise. For the head word, the most common spelling is used; variant spellings not easily referable to a head word are cited in their alphabetical place with a cross reference. Words are only glossed if their meaning departs from that of modern English, or if their form may not be readily recognizable. Except initially, *y* is treated alphabetically as *i*. Entries are ordered alphabetically according to their form in these texts.

abade, *awaited*
abet, *habit, dress*
abile, abyll, *able, fit*
able him to, *make himself capable of*
abouteward, *intent*
accidie, *sloth*
acknowe: be acknowe, *let be acknowledged*
acordabli, *harmoniously*
actueel, *active*
adawe, *arouse*
adyten, *assign*
affected, *inclined, disposed*
aferde, afferdede, *frightened*
afforce, *force, constrain, endeavour*
aforn, *before*
afray, *fright, sudden attack*
aftir, *according to*
agayne-say, *gainsay*
aghe, aght (*vb.*), *ought*
alde, *old*
algates, *always*
alieneth, *alienates, withdraws*
al if, *although*
alle-witty, *omniscient*
allyng (*pr. p.*), *making all*
alonely (*adj.*), *single;* (*adv.*), *exclusively*
als, *as*
alterate, *transported*
alther, *of all*
amonestand, *admonishing*
and, *if*
anedande, *breathing*

anehede, *unity*
an(e)ly, *only, peerless*
anempt(s), *as regards*
anez, *once*
anger, *affliction*
anguys, *anguish*
anynge, *union*
anker, *anchoress*
ankres, *anchoress*
antime, antymp, *anthem*
antre, *entrance*
a party, *in part*
apayed, *pleased, satisfied*
apert, *open*
aport, *bearing*
appayres, *injures*
ar, are, *before*
areche, *attain*
arely, *early*
arette (*vb.*), *attribute, ascribe*
arneste, *intense passion*
aseeth, *satisfaction*
assay, *attempt, testing, experience*
astoniing, *cause for consternation*
at (*conj.*), *that;* (*prep.*), *to;* tylle at, *until*
atent, *intent, purpose, attitude*
athomus, *twinkling of an eye*
atter, *venom*
aureole, *saint's crown or halo*
avaunten, *boast*
avere, *possession*
avise, *consider*

avisement, *deliberation*
ayayn, ayen, *again, back, against*
ayeenstonden, *withstand*
ayen(e)s, *against, in front of, in the presence of*

bak *(sb.)*, *bat*
bale, *evil*
bane, *bone*
banneth, *curses*
barne, *child*
barnhede, *childhood*
bath, *both*
beclesid, *enclosed*
bees, *is, remains*
beestly, *carnal, bestial*
beheste, *promise*
behovely, bihoofli, *necessary*
belde, *build*
belwys, *bellows*
bemene, *mean*
benedicite, *bless you! bless us!*
benyson, *blessing*
bete, *heal*
beteches, *guides*
bette, *beaten*
by *(vb.)*, *buy*
biclippynge, *embracing*
bydynges, *abidings*
byg *(vb.)*, *build*
bygyng, *establishing*
biheten, *promise*
bihoofful, *expedient*
binemeth, *take away*
birthen, *burden*
blaber, *gabble*
blabryng, *babbling*
blemysand, *darkening*
blenklyng, *turning away the eyes*
bleve, bileve, *remain*
blyn, *cease*
blyssede, *gladdened*
blissynge, *rejoicing*
blundryng, *blind motion*
bodiliched, *corporeality*
boistous, *undeveloped, unsubtle, loud, crude*
boistouste, *crude natural state*
bonyr, *obedient*
boond, *duty, obligation*
botyrn, *both*
botte, *without*

boxom, boxsom, *see* buxum
breide out, *were to analyse*
breste, *burst*
brether, *brethren*
brynandest, *most burning*
bristinid, *chastised*
brosyng, *bruising*
bunden, *bound*
bussching, *thrusting*
but, *unless*
buxum, *obedient*

caitives, *wretches*
cauteel, *stratagem*
cesably, *in a way liable to ceasing*
chalenge, *claim*
charge *(sb.)*, *responsibility*; *(vb.)*, *attach weight or importance to*
chaungabely, *alternately*
cheere, *expression*
cheitif, *wretch*
chese, *(vb.)*, *choose*
chesoun, *reason*
childly, *in childish terms*
circuie, *make the circuit, go round*
claungede, *clagged, clogged*
cled, cledde, *clothed*
clennes, *cleannes*
clepe, *call*
cleping, *calling*
clergial, *scholarly*
clergie, *scholarship*
clerte, *radiance*
cleth *(vb.)*, *clothe*
clethynge, *clothing*
cleve, *adhere*
clevynge, *persistent*
cloysterer, *monk, nun, friar*
clowtes, *clouts, rags*
cluppe, *embrace*
combred, *burdened*
comford, *comforted*
comoun *(vb.)*, *associate, commune*; *(adj.)*, *familiar*
comownynge, *fellowship, intercourse, conversing*
compleccioun, *temperament*
conand, *wise, learned*
conclude *(p.p.)*, *confounded*
confusion, *confutation*

conne, *know, understand, be able, know how to*

connyng, *power, skill, discretion, knowledge*

consayte, *notion, idea*

contenawns, *countenance*

continence, *moderation, continuity*

contynuaunce, *perseverance*

conversacioun, *company, society*

corious, *speculative, subtle, abstruse, fine*

coriouste, *inquisitiveness, subtlety, ingenuity, abstruseness*

costomable, *see* customable

cotidiane, *daily*

counseil, *judgement, spiritual direction, spiritual adviser*

covayte (*vb.*), *covet, desire*

covaytise (*sb.*) *covetousness, desire;* (*vb.*) *covet*

cover (*vb.*), *relieve*

coupuld, *coupled*

create, *created*

crokyng, *deflection*

cure, *spiritual charge*

curette, *curate*

curioseli, *elaborately*

curtayse, curtes, *courteous*

customable, *habitual*

daliaunce, *converse*

dalyed, *conversed*

deboner, *gentle, courteous*

debonerte, *gentleness*

ded(e), *death*

dedein (*vb.*), *disdain*

dedlye, *mortal*

defailing, *failing, want*

defoule, deful, *tread down, oppress, contaminate*

defouled, *desecrated*

deile, *grief*

deintee, *esteem*

deyntosly, *delightfully*

delyces, *delights*

delitabilite, *delightfulness*

delvyn, *dig*

deme (*vb.*), *judge*

departe (*vb.*), *part, separate, divide*

departyng, *distinction, division*

dere, *afflict, harm*

dereworthy, *beloved*

desayte, *deceit*

despite, *contempt, scorn*

dette, *debt*

dyght, *adorn, array, prepare;* dygte, *prepared*

dike, *ditch*

dykyn, *dig ditches*

dyng, *beat, smite*

dispit, *contempt, scorn*

dispitous, *cruel*

dole, *grief, pain, trouble*

dome, *judgement*

domesdaye, *day of judgement*

domesman, *judge*

donward, *downward*

doren, *dare*

dottoures, *teachers*

doughtely, *with his might*

dragges, *dregs*

drawght, *pulling, attraction, drink*

dreghe, *endure, bear*

dresse (*vb.*), *direct, dispose*

drewry, *sweetheart, treasure;* drewryse, *jewels*

dwere, *doubt, uncertainty*

effectuely, *effectively*

eft, *again*

eftyr, *according to*

eggen, *incite*

eggyng, *instigation*

egh, eygh, *eye*

eken, *increase*

ekand, *increasing*

eld, *age*

elenge, *very long, tedious*

ell, *else*

emangys, *among*

enabited, *resident*

enchesoun, *reason, cause*

enfors, *effort, exertion*

enjewnyd, *enjoined*

enjoyand, *rejoicing*

enoorned, *prepared, endowed*

enstorid, *stored up*

entende, *be attentive*

entendyd, *attended*

enterlye, *entirely, wholeheartedly*

entermete (*vb.*), *meddle, be involved*

entre, *entrance*

er, *err*

erdly, *earthly*

erytage, *inheritance*

erles, *foretaste*
erst, *first*
even-Cristen, *fellow Christians*
even ryth, *immediately in front of*
eventure, *chance*
evyn, *equal*
evyn forthe, *at eye level*
excesse, *ecstasy*
exercisen, *employ*

faa, *few*
fayn, *glad*
falles, *befalls*
falynge, *deficiency*
fandynge, *trial, temptation*
fantastic, *delusive*
fantome, *illusion*
farde, *fared*
fare, *go, fare*
fatigacions, *wearying exertions*
fautours, *tokens, supporting indications*
feerd, *afraid*
feerdnes, *fearsomeness*
feynynge, *dissimulation, reservation*
felable, *perceptible*
felichip, *fellowship*
felle (*vb.*), *put a stop to*
fenyng, *feigning*
ferforth, *far*
ferly, *wondrous*
fest (*adj.*), *fast, secured; (vb.), fasten.*
ficchid, *fixed*
files, *defile*
fylyng, *defilement*
flytand, *chiding, wrangling*
flytynge, *scolding*
fluence, *stream, flowing*
fo(o)nde, *endeavour*
forayn, *external, outward*
forbettes, *beats severely*
forbrekes, *crushes; weakens*
force: no force therof, *that does not matter;*
    haste no force, *attach no importance*
fordon, *destroy, render powerless*
fordone, *previously done*
forluke, *providence*
formeste, *first*
fornempts, *opposite*
forsobbid, *exhausted with sobbing*
forsonken, *plunged deeply*

forthi, *therefore, because*; forthi that, *because*;
    noght forthi, *nevertheless*
forthspredyng, *widening*
forwhi, *because*
foryetel, *forgetful*
foryeten, *forget*
foryeven, foryyven, *forgive*
foulden, *folded*
fournes, *furnace*
fra, *from*
frawerdnes, *perversity*
freele, *weak*
freelte, *frailty*
frenasie, *frenzy*
fructuous, *producing fruit*
fulheede, *fullness, abundance*
fulsomely, *abundantly*

ga, *go*; gase, *goes*
gamenly, *as in play*
gang, *go*; (*pr. p.*), gangand
gangars, *goers*
gangrels, *vagabonds*
gar (*vb.*), *make*
garnement, *garment*
gastly, *see* gostly
gate, *path*
geder, *gather*
gese, *gives*
gesture, *bearing*
gylder, *snare*
gyn, *given*
gyse, *fashion*
glose, *comment on, interpret*
gluttry, *gluttony*
gostly, *spiritual*
gramercy, *thanks*
granand, *groaning*
grave (*vb.*), *bury*
gre, *favour, degree*
grete, *weep*; gretyng, *weeping*
grounde, *foundation, apex (of the soul)*
groundli, *well-foundedly*
grucche, grotche, *grumble, complain*

habelynge, *enabling*
habett, *habit, dress*
haburion, *habergeon (worn as penitential*
    garment)
haelye, *wholly*

halde, *hold, keep*

hale, *whole*

haly *(adj.), holy; (adv.), wholly*

halyest, *most completely*

halynes, *holiness*

halowes, *saints*

halsinge, *embrace*

hamly, *intimate*; hamlyer, *more intimate*

happe, *chance, fortune*

hardely, *boldly*

hardynes, *courage*

hasylle, *hazel*

hate *(adj.), hot*

hateredyn, *hatred*

have, *behave*

havyng, *bearing, behaviour*

haylce, *greet, salute*

hayre, *hair-shirt*

he, hee, hegh, *high*

hedepanne, *skull*

hedows, *terrible*

heest, *highest*

heighed, *exalted*

heily, *supremely, profoundly*

heldande, *inclined*

hele *(sb.), health, cure, salvation*

hele, hile *(vb.), conceal;* hiled, *hidden*

helld *(vb.), pour, cast*

heler, *healer*

hend, *hand*

herbar *(vb.), harbour, shelter*

herd-sey, *hearsay, report*

hertli, *heartfelt*

hesyd, *assuaged*

hete *(vb.), promise*

hethen, *hence*

hethinge, *scoffing*

hevelye, *with difficulty*

hevyed, *grieved*

hew, *colour, complexion*

hile, *see* hele

hynder, *latter*

hyng, *hang*

hyte, *called*

hoge, *great, huge*

hole, *sound, healthy, perfect, recollected*

holehede, *health*

homely, hoomli, *intimate*

hope, *think, believe*

hopinglye, *in imagination*

hosbonde, *housekeeper*

hoteth, *promises*

howsyld, *administered Eucharist to*

huglye, *ugly*

humours, *vapours, 'humours'*

iche, ilch, *each*

ierarchi, *hierarchy*

if alle, *although*

ighen, *eyes*

il, *evil*

iliche, ilike, *alike*

incluse, *enclosed*

indifferent, *undetermined, indistinct*

indued, *endued*

inforth, *within*

inly, *inward, inwardly*

innermore, *further in*

insaable, *undescribable*

intil, *into, to*

irke *(vb.), be weary, bored; (adj.), weary*

irkyng, *growing weary*

jangle, *chatter*

janglers, *praters*

karols, *dances*

keep, *care, attention*

keyng, *king*

kele *(vb.), cool, grow cool*

kendeli, *natural*

kenned, *taught*

keping, *protection*

kesten, *cast*

kynd, kende, *nature*

kindly, *natural*

kynredyn, *kindred*

kirk, *church*

kirtel, *gown, short coat*

klennes, *purity*

knittyngly, *in union*

knowable, *that may know, intellectual*

knowlechand, *acknowledging*

kombraunce, *burden*

kon, kun, kunne, *see* conne

kunde, *known*

kunnyng, konnyng, *see* connyng

lache, *seize*

lackes, *blame*

lackyng, *disapproval*
langand, *longing*
langes, *longs*; me langes, *I long*
langour, *sorrow*
langourede, *languished*
languyst, *would languish*
lappe, *wrap, cover*; lap up, *include*
lappyd, *enveloped*
lare, *teaching*
largere, *in greater abundance*
largess, *fullness*
larghede, *ampleness*
lastand, *enduring*
lastyng it, *while it lasts*
late, *let, behave*
lathe (vb.), *feel disgust*
lathere, *more hateful*
latlyer, *less readily*
laude, *praise*
laverooke, *sky-lark*
law, *low*
layne, *conceal*
lee (sb.), *lie*
leef (adj.), *dear*; (sb.), *dear one*
leevyd, *believed*
lefte, *remained*
leful, *legitimate*
leiseer, *opportunity*
lekyng, *see* likyng
lemman, *sweetheart*
lende, *dwell*
lene to, *incline towards, rely on*
lent, *alighted*
lere, *teach*
lesyng, *lying, falsehood*
leste, *least*
lesten, *last*
let, lette, *hinder, desist*
lethe, *relieve*
lettynde, *hindering*
lettyng, *hindrance*
leufulli, *lawfully*
leve, *leave, leave off, remain, believe*
leve: haddist leve, *would as soon*
lever, *more pleasing*
lewed, leued, *ignorant, uneducated*
liberal, *generous*
lyevande, *living*
lygge (vb.), *lie*
lightned, *enlightened*

lighty, *shining*
liken (vb.), *please*
likyng (adj.), *pleasing, pleasant*; (sb.), *pleasure*
lykoure, *liquor*
liqued, *liquid, liquefied*
list, lyst, *pleases*
liste (sb.), *joy, inclination*
listely (adv.), *longingly, vigorously*
listy (adj.), *full of longing*
listines (sb.), *longing*
lither strengthe, *brute force*
lyvelye, *living*
logh, *laughed*
lokene, *secured*
lokynge, *supervision*
longe on, *dependent upon*
longith, *belongs*
looth: thenke looth, *be reluctant*
losith, *loosens*
lovely (adj.), *loving, of love, lovable*; (adv.),
    lovingly, in love, for love
lowe, *flame*
lowghand, *submitting*
lowid, *loved*
lowyng, *praising*
lufely, *lovingly*
lufreden, *love, good will*
lufsom, lovesome, *lovely*
lufyng, *beloved one*
lugh, *laughed*

maime (sb.), *bodily injury*
maistrye: litil maistrie, *easy*
malys, *malice*
malysoun, *curse*
manassand, *threatening*
mare, *more*
masid, *bewildered*
mast, *most*
mede, *reward*
medeled, *mixed*
medelynge, *mixing, blending*
medfulli, *profitably*
medlur, *mixture*
meyne, *household*
mekil: *see* mikel
meken, *humble*
melle, *mingle*
membres, *limbs*
mende, *mind, memory*

mene, meen, *intermediary*

menynge, *intention*

meritorie, *meritorious*

merke, *limit; (pl.), bounds*

meschief, *misfortune*

mete, *food*

mevyth, *moves*

myddes, *middle, means;* in myddes, *in the middle of*

mydelmost, *middlemost*

mikel, *much*

mykillehede, *greatness*

mynde, *thought*

myrke, *dark*

mirknes, *darkness*

missaiyng, *evil-speaking*

myscheves, *miseries, misfortunes*

myses, *discomfort*

myspay, *displease*

mister, *need*

misty, *obscure, mysterious*

mistily, *mystically, allegorically, darkly, mysteriously*

mochel, *much*

modeland, *wallowing*

moystere, *moisture*

mon, moun, *shall, will*

mond, *might, would*

moneschyd, *admonished*

motys, *motes*

mouthly, *in spoken words*

mowe *(vb.), may, be able*

mowe *(sb.), grimace*

muse ye not, *do not be shocked*

mut, *may*

nakyn, *strip naked*

namely, *especially*

neest, *nearest*

neighen, *approach*

neighhonde, *almost*

neyn, *nine*

ner, *nearer*

nerehande, *near*

nerehede, *closeness*

nese, *nose*

nevene, *name*

never-the-latter, *nevertheless*

ny-hand, *almost*

nobleth, *nobility*

Noe schyppe, *Noah's Ark*

no-gatis, *by no means*

noghten, *set at nought*

noghtynge, noughtnyng, *making nothing, annihilation*

noy, *annoyance, reluctance*

noious, *troublesome*

nokyns, *no kind of*

not, *does not know*

notforthanne, *nevertheless*

notforthi, *nevertheless*

nothere, nowthere, *nor*

notte, *nut*

nowmeryd, *numbered*

oblyst, *bound*

offerand, *offering*

oftsithe(s), *often*

oyses, *uses*

on, *one*

onane, *at once*

onyng *(sb.), union; (adj.), unitive*

onyth, *unites*

only, *alone*

onlynes, onlystede, *solitude*

onlothful, *reluctant*

open, *brazen*

or, *before*

ordayne, *prepare, dispose, direct*

ordand, *ordained, appointed*

ordinel, *regular*

ordiner, *ordainer, ruler*

orison, *prayer*

oure, owre *(adj.), over, too; (sb.), hour*

oute-take *(prep.), except; (vb.), exclude, except*

outforth, *outwardly*

outher, outhire, *either*

outrage, *excess;* outragely, *excessively*

overgoth, *rises above*

overhile, *cover over*

overmaistereth, *dominates*

overpassing *(sb.), transcendence; (adj.), surpassing*

overpressid, *overwhelmed*

overtravels, *overworks*

paraventure, *perhaps*

parcenel, parcyner, *partner, sharer*

partie-feelynge, *sympathy*

party(e): in party, *partly*
passande, *surpassingly*
passynge, *surpassing*
passioun, *suffering*
pay, *please, satisfy*
payng, *pleasure*
paysynge, *pressing down*
peesand, *appeasing*
peysible, *peaceable*
pere, *peer, equal*
perre, *jewellery*
person, *parson*
perte, *part*
pertineth, *belongs*
pesid, *calmed*
pike (*vb.*), *gather, steal*
pyment, *spiced wine*
pinchers, *fault-finders, carpers*
pyne, *torment*
pynyd, *tormented, suffered*
plastre, *plaster*
plat and pleyn, *exactly like*
pleyne, *complain*
plenarly, *fully*
plesaunce, *delight*
pliing, *pliant*
plowme, *plum*
pointe, *instant*; in poynte to, *in immediate peril of*; not a poynte, *not a whit*; the poynte and the prik, *the mark and the target*
polysyng, *polishing*
postel, *apostle*
potestates, *powers*
pouried, *purified*
pous, *pulse*
prees, *press*
prentis, *apprentice*
preve, *see* prive
pricke, prik, *target*
pryme dayes, *soon after sunrise*
principates, *principalities*
pryse, *value*
prive, *secret, private, personal*
privites, *secrets, mysteries*
proef, *proof, argument, experience*
profyr, *proposal*
profite (*vb.*), *advance, improve*
profiter, *benefactor, one who is making progress*
properte, *essential quality*

propred: is propred to, *is an attribute of*
prove, *test, try*; provid, *experienced*
prow, *profit*
purchase, purches, *acquire, gain*
pure, *poor*
purte, *purity*
pusonde, *poisoned*
put apon, *assail*
putteth to, *adds*

queemful, *pleasing, agreeable*
queeres, *choirs*
queynte, *curious, ingenious, unfamiliar*
questionaries, *scholastic questioners*
quik, *alive, ready*
quikken, *revive*
qwart, whart, *health, joy*
qwathes, *spasms*

rabill, *gabble*
radde, *afraid*
raggid, *go to rags*
ransakere, *investigator*
ransakyng, *close investigation*
rather, *more quickly*; rathest, *most quickly*
ravyn, *rapine*
ravysand, *ravishing*
rawght, *reached*
rebounde, *redound, overflow*
recche, recke, *care*
reccheleschipe, *carelessness*
rechelesnes, *carelessness, indifference*
recure, *recover*
refreynyng, *restraining*
reklees, *careless, negligent*
reliefe, *residue*
reparailed, *restored*
reprove (*sb.*), *disgrace*
reufully, *pitifully*
reve, *rob, take away*
rew, *have pity, rue, regret*
reward, *regard*
riftid, *belched forth*
ryghtynges, *rites*
rightwisly, *righteously*
ryste, *rest*
ritchesse, *riches*
rode, *rood, cross*
roon, *soft skin*
rose (*vb.*), *praise, boast*

rosynge, *boasting, vaunting*
roumynge, *clearing, decongesting*
rouners, *gossips*
rowndith, *whispers*
rude, *ignorant*
rudenes, *lack of education*
rusand, rusyng, *boasting*
ruth, *pity*

sa, *so*
saaf, safe, *saved*
sad, *steadfast, sober, dignified*
saddehete, *sadness*
sadly, *firmly*
sadnes, *constancy*
sampler, *model*
sandes, *gifts*
sare, *sore*
sari, *sorry*
satylde, *sank*
sautir, *psalter*
savely, *safely*
savorynge, *taste*
savorly, *with (spiritual) delight*
sawghes, *sayings*
sawyng, *sowing*
schadue, *shadow*
schenschipe, *disgrace*
schoter, *archer*
schryft-fader, *father-confessor*
sclak, *slack*
sclawnder *(vb.), slander*
seeth, *satisfaction*
seke, *ill*
sekenesse, *sickness*
seker, *see* siker
self, *same*
semely, *fitting, comely*
semes, *long incisions*
semes, *befits*
sensible, *endowed with the faculty of sensation, that can be felt*
sentence, *meaning, sense*
sere, *various, different*
servand, *servant*
sesse, *cease*
sethyn, *afterwards*
settel, *seat*
syb, *related, intimate*
side, *ample*

syhtyng, *sighing*
sikeli, *sickly*
siker, *safe, secure*
sikerli, *confidently*
sikernes, syekernes, *security*
symylitudes, *likenesses*
syngulerte, *singularity, independent judgement*
syngulhede, *being in one piece*
sith, *time*
sith, sithen *(adv.), afterwards; (conj.), since*
skilful, *reasonable*
skill, *reason, intelligence, mind;* kon skyle, *have knowledge*
skulker, *prowler, pilferer*
sla, *slay*
slade, *dell*
slake, *die down, appease*
slaw, *slow*
sleeng, *slaying*
sleygh, sleight, *wise*
sleight, sleght, *device, strategy, resourcefulness, trickery*
sleynge, *bringing to spiritual death*
slek, *abate*
slepyng sleight, *simulation of sleep*
sleuthe, *sloth*
slike, *of the kind mentioned*
sloken, *quench*
sluggi, *sluggish*
smert *(adj.), sharp, painful, cruel; (vb.), cause pain, smart*
snapir *(vb.), stumble*
soave, *safe*
sodeynte, *suddenness*
sogettis, *subjects*
sonar, *sooner*
soth, sothe *(adj.), true; (sb.), truth*
sothely, *truly*
sothfastnes, *truth*
sotil, *subtle, ingenious, intricate, refined, cunning*
sotylte, *ingenuity, refinement*
sowlynge, *defiling*
sowme, *sum*
sownes *(vb.), sounds*
sownyng *(sb.), sound*
sowre, *sour*
spared, *closed*
speciales, *favourites, intimates, dedicated ones*

sped, *furthered*
spede, *profit*
spedy, *efficacious*
speedful, *profitable, expedient*
speedly, *swiftly*
spered, *confined*
sperend, *shutting*
spice, *sort*
spicery, *spices*
spille, *destroy, ruin*
spirith, *breathes, blows*
spoyle, *strip*
sporne, *stumble*
stabel (*vb.*), *establish firmly*
stalworthly, *resolutely, vigorously, fervently*
standynge, *notwithstanding, being the case*
stavis, *rungs*
stedde (*vb.*), *place, fix*
stede, *place, position*
steytehede, *close fit*
steryng, *prompting, impulse, agitation*
sterne, *stars*
stertyng, *departure*
stie (*vb.*), *ascend*
stif, *strong, firm, bold*
stifly, *resolutely*
stiing up, *mounting up, ascent*
stinten, *cease*
stirtith, *goes quickly*
stoneth, *astounds*; stonyed, *astounded*
strande, *torrent*
straunge, *reserved*; makith straunge, *remains aloof*
straunged, *estranged*
streyne, *exert, restrain*
streit, *strict*
streyte fyttyng, *close fitting*
streitly, *single-mindedly*
strengh, *strength*
strenghfull, *strong*
strengthe (*vb.*), *fortify*
stryves, *quarrels*
substaunce, *essence, possessions*
sumdele, *somewhat*
superessencialle, *above the nature of created things*
supersubstancyally, *above that which is formed of matter*
suspect, *deserving suspicion*
sustan, susten, *sustain*

suyrte, *surety*
swa, *so*
sweppys, *blows*
swet (*sb.*), *sweat*
swette, *sweated*
swetyng, *darling*
swilk, *such*
swyng (*vb.*), *beat, scourge*
swink, *labour, toil*
swithe, *quickly*

tagild, *entangled*
takenynge, *betokening*
takyns, *tokens*
takked, *taken*
tale, *heed*
taried, *vexed*
taverner, *inn-keeper*
tempe, *tempt*
tempest (*sb.*), *perturbation*; (*vb.*), *assail*
tent (*sb.*), *care*
tentith, *attends*
thar, *is necessary, behoves*
tharbe, *thereby*
tharfra, *therefrom*
tharof, *thereof*
thartil, *thereto*
the, *thee*
their, there, *where*
thewes, *manners*
thiere, *these*
thynge hym, *seems to him*
thof, thow, *though*
thralle, *slave*
thrille, thyrl, *pierce*
thryst, *thirst*
thristand, *thirsting*
throstelcok, *male song-thrush*
til, tille, *to*; tille at, *until*
tyne, *lose*; tynt, *lost*
tyte, *quickly*; als tyte, *immediately*
tithing-tellers, *newsmongers*
to (*adv.*), *too*; (*conj.*), *until*
tollyth, *lures*
tome, *empty*
tomeltyth, *melts utterly*
touche, *mention briefly*
toure, *tower*
transfigure, *transform*
trasing, *enquiry*

travayle, travel *(sb.)*, *effort, toil, journey;* *(vb.)*, *labour, trouble, be anxious, suffer*
trayste, *trusted*
treisten, *trust*
treistily, *with faith*
triacle, *sovereign remedy, antidote*
trow, *believe*
trustly, *with faith*
tutilers, *whisperers, scandalmongers*
twynne *(vb.)*, *separate, depart*

umbethynk, *bethink, consider*
umbigo, *surround*
umbilappid, *enveloped*
umsett, *beset*
umwhile, *sometimes*
unavised, *without warning*
unbe *(vb.)*, *cease to be*
unbuxumnesse, *disobedience*
unceesabeli, *incessantly*
unconabyll, *unsuitable, improper*
unconsavable, *inconceivable*
uncouth, *unknowledgeable*
uncuthnes, *unfamiliarity*
undepartable, *indivisible*
undernymynge, *rebuke*
undertakynge, *rebuke*
unkunynge, *unlearned*
unlusti, *slothful*
unmesurable, *immoderate*
unmevable, *immovable*
unmyght, *impotence*
unnayte, *useless, vain, unprofitable*
unneth(es), *scarcely*
unordinat, *immediate*
unornely, *meanly, wretchedly*
unpartabli, *inseparably*
unpower, *weakness*
unpurchasid, *not acquired*
unsavory, *without savour*
unsee, *avoid seeing*
unskylful, *unreasonable*
unspecable, *unspeakable*
unthank, *no thanks*
unthewys, *bad habits*
untholmodnes, *impatience*
unwetyn, *not to be learnt*
unwhaynt, *unwise*
usages, *habitual working, devotional practices, experiences*

usce *(sb.)*, *use, practice*
use *(sb.)*, *indulgence*
usen *(vb.)*, *practise*
usur, *usury*
uttere, *entire, outward, external*

vagacion, *wandering*
vanys, *vanish*
velanye, *disgrace, ignominy*
verray, verra, *true*
verraily, verreile, *truly*
vertu, *power*
viile, *wretched*
vykary, *vicar*
vysemente, *deliberation*
voidid, *deprived of force*

wa, waa, *woe*
waker, *wakeful*
wakyns, *vigils*
wallowyng, *writhing*
wambe, *belly*
wanand, *lamenting, waning*
wante *(vb.)*, *lack*
wantoun, *untrained, unruly*
wappes, *wraps*
war *(adj.)*, *worse, wary*
ward, *citadel, prison*
wariyng, *cursing*
warnes, *caution*
wate, *know*
waxand, *growing*
wayke, *weak*
wedde, *pledge*, to wedde, *as a pledge*
wede, *garment*
weelwyllyng, weelwilnes, *goodwill*
weem, *stain, blemish*
weike, *weak*
wel, wele, *wealth, welfare, advantage*
welde, *govern, possess*
wene, *think, suppose*; wenande, *expecting*
wenynge, *supposing*
wer, *worse*
werdli, *see* wordli
werid, *damnable*
weryd up, *worn out*
werk, *ache*
wete, *know*
wetyng, *knowing*
wha, wham, whas, *who, whom, whose*

whart, *see* qwart

wha sa, *whosoever*

whatkyn, *what kind of*

whaynt, *wily*

wheme, *pleasing*

whilk, *which*

whore, *where*

wile, *vile*

wilful, *willing, voluntary*

wilfully, *willingly, voluntarily*

willed, *minded*

willy, *willing*

wyn(ne) to, til, *attain to*

wysses, *teaches*

wissynge, *guidance*

wiste, *knew*

wit(e) *(vb.), know*

wytes, *fades*

wittande, *knowing*; wittandly, *knowingly*

witte, wit, *mind, intelligence, understanding, intellect; (pl.) senses, intellectual faculties*

witterly, *truly*

witty, *wise*

wode, wood, *mad, enraged*

wodenes, woodnes, *madness*

wonder *(adj.) amazing; (adv.) amazingly*

won(en), *dwell*

wone *(p.p.), accustomed*

wonnyng-sted, *dwelling-place*

wonyng, *dwelling*

wordli, *worldly*

worschipe, *honour*

worth, *becomes*

wrestyd, *turned, twisted*

wreth *(sb.), wrath; (vb.), enanger*

wright, *carpenter*

writhe, *turn, be converted*

yede, yhede, *went*

yeldynge, *retribution*

yemes, *governs, protects*

yeven, *give*

yette, *poured, infused*

yheldand, *yielding*

yift, *gift*

yive, *see* yeven

yll, *evil*

ymang, *among*

ymyd, *amid*; ymyd gate, *half-way*

ympne, *hymn*

yotted, *poured out*

yought, *youth*

yoven, *given*

yyve, *see* yeven

DUE